EMERGING TRENDS IN TECHNOLOGY FOR EDUCATION IN
AN UNCERTAIN WORLD

PROCEEDINGS OF THE 6TH INTERNATIONAL CONFERENCE ON EDUCATION IN MUSLIM SOCIETY, (ICEMS 2020), JAKARTA, INDONESIA, 18–19 NOVEMBER 2020

# Emerging Trends in Technology for Education in an Uncertain World

*Edited by*

Dwi Nanto, Maila D.H. Rahiem & Tita Khalis Maryati
*UIN Syarif Hidayatullah Jakarta, Indonesia*

*Routledge is an imprint of the Taylor & Francis Group, an informa business*

Typeset by MPS Limited, Chennai, India

*Library of Congress Cataloging-in-Publication Data*

A catalog record has been requested for this book

First published 2021
by Routledge
2 Park Square, Milton Park, Abingdon, Oxon OX14 4RN
and by Routledge
605 Third Avenue, New York, NY 10158
e-mail: enquiries@taylorandfrancis.com
www.routledge.com – www.taylorandfrancis.com

ISBN: 978-1-032-11288-6 (Hbk)
ISBN: 978-1-032-11289-3 (Pbk)
ISBN: 978-1-003-21924-8 (ebk)
DOI: 10.1201/9781003219248

# Table of contents

## Social and humanities

## Information technology in language education

# Preface

Today's education must meet the needs of learners who are digital citizens and have made extensive use of technology. The advancements of computer technology, artificial intelligence, and robotics have accelerated teaching and learning. Furthermore, the COVID-19 pandemic placed humans in a state of Volatility, Uncertainty, Complexity, and Ambiguity (VOCA). Due to the pandemic, educators and learners shifted abruptly from face-to-face instruction to online instruction. The use of information and communication technologies (ICTs) has become a necessity. Educators and students have been pushed and pulled to become familiar with ICTs.

The world has experienced a dramatic acceleration in the use of ICTs in the years 2020 and 2021, included in Islamic educational institutions. As a result, Islamic schools and universities face significant challenges but also have high hopes for significant advancements in the learning practice, curriculum development, assessment, educational institution management, and educational personnel development through the use of ICTs.

This book discusses a variety of adaptation issues and efforts to integrate ICTs into the educational process. The contributors to this volume are practitioners, researchers, and educators from at least four countries: Indonesia, Australia, New Zealand, and Iran. They contextualize their perspectives, arguments, and empirical findings within the contexts of the countries from which they originate. This perspective's richness infuses this book with ideas for the future development of Islamic education and educational institutions.

To facilitate reading, this book is divided into four major sections: first, writings from invited speakers at the 6th International Conference on Education in Muslim Society. The invited speakers discussed research-based learning in STEM, the challenges and opportunities of twenty-first-century learning; technology-based higher education during and after COVID-19; and emerging trends in educational technology usages.

The second section contains a collection of humanities-related writings that discuss the use of educational technology in civic education subjects, the use of ICTs in primary schools, the assimilation of ICTs into indigenous communities, the use of ICTs for character education, and how the use of ICTs can increase students' motivation and achievement. The third section discusses the authors' use of various science and math-related themes, including the integration of Islam and science; science learning methods; and an overview of Indonesian students' high-order thinking. The final section discusses language, including mastery of speaking skills in EFL classes, strategies for improving critical reading comprehension skills, and students' perspectives on the affective factors that influence their English language learning participation.

It is critical to understand that this book does not simply present research findings; it also makes recommendations to governments, educational institutions, and other stakeholders on improving the quality of education through technology-based educational programs.

# Scientific Committee

## International Advisory Board

Prof. Mike Hardy, Conventry University, United Kingdom
Prof. Mohammad Abdallah, University of South Australia, Australia
Prof. Stephen Dobson, Victoria University of Wellington, New Zealand
Dr. Azmil Tayeb, University Sains Malaysia, Malaysia
Dr. Kevin W. Fogg, University of Nort Carolina at Chapel Hill, USA
Muhammad Zuhdi, M.Ed., Ph.D, UIN Syarif Hidayatullah Jakarta, Indonesia

## Chairman of Reviewers

Muhammad Zuhdi, M.Ed., Ph.D., UIN Syarif Hidayatullah Jakarta, Indonesia

## Reviewers

Prof. Aziz Safi Ismail, Lincoln University College, Malaysia
Prof. Cholis Sadijah, Universitas Negeri Malang, Indonesia
Prof. Dede Rosyada, MA, UIN Syarif Hidayatullah Jakarta, Indonesia
Prof. Stephen Dobson, Victoria University of Wellington, New Zealand
Prof. Zulkifli, UIN Syarif Hidayatullah Jakarta, Indonesia
Aodah Diamah M.Eng. Ph.D., Universitas Negeri Jakarta, Indonesia
Aries H. T. Susanto, Ph.D., UIN Syarif Hidayatullah Jakarta, Indonesia
Dr. Dalia Sukmawati M.Si, Universitas Negeri Jakarta, Indonesia
Dr. Desmadi Saharuddin, UIN Syarif Hidayatullah Jakarta, Indonesia
Dr. Fahriany, M.Pd, UIN Syarif Hidayatullah Jakarta, Indonesia
Dr. Fera Kurniadewi, Universitas Negeri Jakarta, Indonesia
Dr. Hani Susanti, Indonesian Institute of Sciences (LIPI), Indonesia
Dr. Harlita, Universitas Sebelas Maret (UNS), Indonesia
Dr. Ikhlasul Amal, Indonesian Institute of Sciences (LIPI), Indonesia
Dr. Isnaini Rosyida M.Si, Universitas Negeri Semarang, Indonesia
Dr. Iwan Sugihartono, Universitas Negeri Jakarta, Indonesia
Dr. Kadir, M.Pd, UIN Syarif Hidayatullah Jakarta, Indonesia
Dr. Kristina Wijayanti, Universitas Negeri Semarang, Indonesia
Dr. Lukita Ambarwati M.Si, Universitas Negeri Jakarta, Indonesia
Dr. Meiliasari, Universitas Negeri Jakarta, Indonesia
Dr. Priyanti, UIN Syarif Hidayatullah Jakarta, Indonesia
Dr. Ratna Sari Dewi, M.Pd, UIN Syarif Hidayatullah Jakarta, Indonesia
Dr. Rena Latifah, M.Psi, UIN Syarif Hidayatullah Jakarta, Indonesia
Dr. Rizhal Hendi Ristanto, Universitas Negeri Jakarta, Indonesia
Dr. Ruqiah G. Putri Panjaitan, Universitas Tanjungpura, Indonesia
Dr. Setia Budi, Universitas Negeri Jakarta, Indonesia
Dr. Sitti Ahmiatri, UIN Syarif Hidayatullah Jakarta, Indonesia
Dr. Sri Budiawanti, Universitas Sebelas Maret (UNS), Indonesia) Dr. Suharno, Universitas Sebelas Maret (UNS), Indonesia) Dr. Tian Abdul Aziz, Universitas Negeri Jakarta, Indonesia
Dr. Tita Khalis Maryati, S.Si, M.Kom, UIN Syarif Hidayatullah akarta, Indonesia
Dr. Yanti Herlanti, M.Pd, UIN Syarif Hidayatullah Jakarta, Indonesia
Dr. Zulfiani, M.Pd, UIN Syarif Hidayatullah Jakarta, Indonesia

## Organizing Committee

Dr. Tita Khalis Maryati, S.Si, M.Kom (General Chair)
Ahmad Dimyati, M.Pd.
Ahmad Irfan Mufid, S.Ag., M.A.
Cut Dhien Nourwahida, M.A.
Desi Nahartini, M.Ed.
Dila Fairusi, M.Pd.
Dina Rahma Fadila, M.Pd.
Dr. Erba Rozalina Y., M.Ag.
Dr. Gelar Dwirahayu, M.Pd.
Dr. Lia Kurniawati, M.Pd.
Dr. Maftuhah, M.A.
Dr. Raswan
Dr. Ratna Sari Dewi, M.Pd.
Dr. Sita Ratnaningsih, M.Pd.
Dr. Wati Susiawati, M.A.
Dr. Zaenul Slam, M.Pd.
Dwi Nanto, Ph.D.
Dzikri Rahmat Romadhon, M.Pd.
Eva Fadillah, M.Pd.
Fathiah Alatas, M.Si.
Fatkhul Arifin, M.Pd.
Finola Marta Putri, M.Pd.
Gusni Satriawati, M.Pd.
Ismalianing Eviyuliwati, S.Pd., M.Hum.
Iwan Permana Suwarna, M.Pd.
Khairunnisa, M.Si.
Khamida S. Nur Atiqoh, S.Pd., M.Pmat.
Kustiwan, Ph.D.
Lalah Alawiyah, M.A.
M. Anang Jatmiko, M.Pd.
M. Hafiz, M.Pd.
Mahmudah, M.Pd.
Marhamah Saleh, M.A.
Maya Defianty, Ph.D.
Nanda Saridewi, M.Si.
Ratna Faeruz, M.Pd.
Rizqy Nur Sholihat, M.Pd.
Tri Harjawati, M.Si.
Viviana Lisma Lestari, M.Pd.
Yazid Hady, M.Pd.
Yubaedi Siron, M.Pd.
Yudhi Munadi, M.Ag.
Zaharil Anasy, S.Ag., M.Hum.

# Acknowledgements

This work would not have been possible without the financial support of the Faculty of Education of UIN Syarif Hidayatullah Jakarta, Indonesia. The editors wish to express their gratitude to the Rector and Vice Rectors of UIN Syarif Hidayatullah Jakarta, as well as the Dean and Vice Deans of the Faculty of Education, UIN Syarif Hidayatullah Jakarta, for their contributions to the success of the 6th International Conference on Education in Muslim Society (ICEMS) and to the publication of the conference papers in an international reputable publication.

Additionally, the editors would like to thank all of the authors from Indonesia, Australia, New Zealand, and Iran for contributing their thoughts and research findings to this book.

The editors wish to express their heartfelt appreciation to everyone with whom they had the pleasure of working on this book project: the editorial support team, the chair and co-chairs, and the organizing committee of the 6th ICEMS.

*Information and education technology*

*Emerging Trends in Technology for Education in an Uncertain World – Nanto, Rahiem & Khalis Maryati (Eds)*
*© 2022 copyright the Author(s), ISBN 978-1-032-11288-6*

# Technology-based higher education institution toward the new normal

M. Ashari

*Rector/President, Institute Teknologi Sepuluh Nopember (ITS), Surabaya, Indonesia*

ABSTRACT:   This paper presents the use of technology and digitalization of education sector during the pandemic and the new normal after COVID-19. The education is one of the highest priority sectors that must not be interrupted by the pandemic. Digital technology relates to the internet connection has highly occupied in the last 6 months in Indonesia. The education has insisted immediately to use technology, especially online class meetings. Therefore, it is the critical time now for education, particularly in Indonesia to move forward involving digital technology. Not only to know and to use, but also capable of understanding and developing the technology-based innovation. Digitalization of university employs upgrading the infrastructure, developing ecosystem for digital education and research, digital services, and improving human resources. The organization structure of higher education also needs to change. Research center, innovation center, and triple helix collaboration are compulsory for higher education-based technology in the new normal era.

*Keywords*:   Covid-19, the new normal, digital technology, technology-based education.

## 1   INTRODUCTION

According to WHO reports, most of countries in the world are still suffering from the pandemic of Corona Virus Disease (Covid-19) during the end of 2020 [1]. The region of South East Asia gradually gets better, while the US, Europe and other places still fight against it. All sectors are disrupted by the pandemic. However, the education sector must not be interrupted under any circumstances.

Education sector has a very important contribution to the future of a nation. It is one of the highest priority sectors for countries all around the world. Nelson Mandela in his speech said that education is the most powerful weapon which you can use to change the world, in Madison Park High School, Boston, 23 June 1990 [2]. Closing schools may impact to 68-million students of 270-millions population in Indonesia. In fact, the enrollment rate for primary and secondary schools is 107.4% and 90.6%, according to BPS Statistics Indonesia in 2018/2019 [3]. Without any strategy, disruption to higher education that has 4700 institutions in Indonesia, will take an emergency to the nation's future.

## 2   THE CHANGE IN THE NEW NORMAL

The use of technology, especially online meeting has rapidly increased during the pandemic. This protects people from Covid-19 transmission due to away from each other. New normal of lifestyle begins. People are mandatory to wear mask, implementing social distancing, and hygienist. Work from home, teaching from home, and studying from home are popular words. Covid-19 may not stop soon, while the impact of the pandemic to the economics and society may be in longer term.

DOI 10.1201/9781003219248-1

Refer to BPS statistic Indonesia 2020, the economic growth was stable in 5.05% before the pandemic, but down to −5.32% during 2020/Q2 as shown in Figure 1 [3]. In this situation the management of universities shall evaluate the institution operation mode. When the Covid-19 impact is high to medium, resulting in slowdown economics, then university running mode shall be in "survival mode". The institution income will be shrunk due to fail of payment on student tuition fees, student dormitory, university business centers, etc. The university strategy shall be changed immediately, and new action plan should be prepared and executed immediately. The situation may occur in short-term, but it may lead to bankruptcy of the university. When the situation gets better, the new normal of economics improves to growth, the operation mode of universities can be turned back to "Fast Growing Mode". A new operation model may be needed to meet the change in the new normal.

One of the tasks of the higher education institution is to create innovative human resources. University graduated mostly work for industries. In the new normal, the industrial environment has changed. The workplace may change to flexible location, the work time changes to anytime, and work tasks change to digitalized ones, as shown in Figure 2. Thus, the talent competences, especially in the digital technology must be upgraded.

Figure 3 shows the digital competence according to the level of education. For primary school level, the digital technology is mainly for equipment support and analytical tools, useful for the

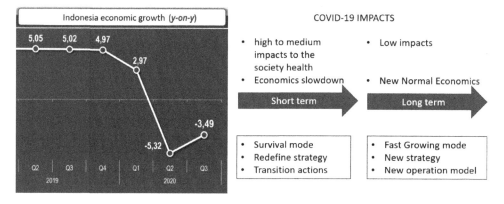

Figure 1.   Covid-19 impacts to the economics and the university operation mode.

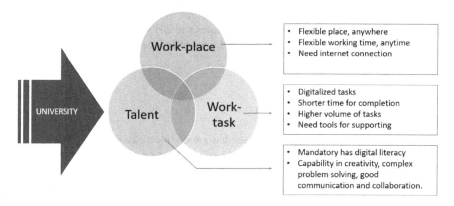

Figure 2.   The change of work-place, work-task, and talent in industrial world.

teacher. The students know that the school applies sophisticated equipment to support their learning. In secondary education level, students were helped to use the technology. Basic coding and implementation may introduce to students. Students in higher education level have to understand and able to develop the technology. Higher education is responsible to build competence human resources for professional, researcher, and entrepreneur. Higher education has built ecosystem for digital education, also for innovation.

## 3  LEARNING CASE FROM ITS AND DISCUSSION

ITS, stand for Institut Teknologi Sepuluh Nopember, is a leading public university in Surabaya, Indonesia [5]. Managing 20,000 students, 1000 faculty members, and 83 programs, ITS achieves the best 3 among 4700 higher education institutions in Indonesia, according to Times Higher Education WUR 2020. In Asia, ITS position is in 198th refer to QS Asia University Rank 2020. This institute of technology during the pandemic, has actively launched high-tech innovation products, such as intelligent robot for Covid-19 patients in hospital (RAISA robot), intelligent boat, and self-driving car as illustrated in Figure 4.

   RAISA robots have been used in 17 hospitals in Indonesia. It helps doctors and nurses to assist Covid-19 patients. RAISA brings medical equipment, food, clothes etc. to come into the isolated rooms of the patients. The robot also reduces the potency of Covid-19 transmission from the patient to the doctors. RAISA was developed within less than 2 months, collaboration between

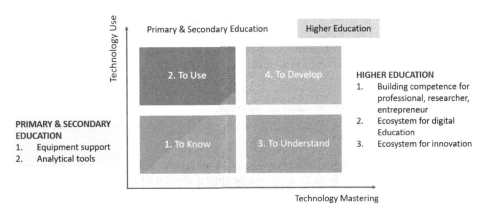

Figure 3.   Technology use and mastering for students.

Figure 4.   High-tech innovation products of ITS: robot assistance for hospital and autonomous vehicles.

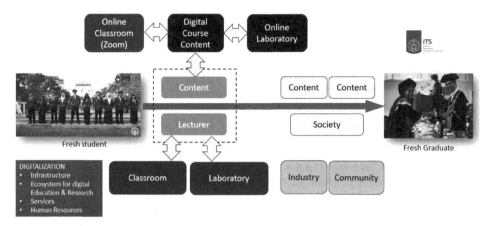

Figure 5.    Development of learning system for higher education institution.

ICT Robotics research center of ITS and Airlangga University hospital [6]. The i-Boat and i-Car shown in Figure 4, were launched by ITS in the Indonesia Independence Day 17th August 2020 [7]. The self-driving car is designed to be used inside the campus that has 180 hectares area, for student shuttle transportation [8]. Since the past 3 years, ITS has transformed the management and organization into a corporate-based university with wider autonomy. ITS has also implemented a digital transformation program for services, process, monitoring, and evaluation of education, research, and community services.

Facing the pandemic conditions, university must change the strategy, and operation modes. The university shall employ the technology in all aspects, including:

– upgrading the infrastructure
– developing ecosystem for digital education and research
– digital services
– improving the human resource

Developing ecosystem for digital education means the university shifts from the common operation method to new strategy, from conventional to digital content of courses. Figure 5 shows an example of development synchronous and asynchronous teaching systems. Traditional teaching requires physical classroom and laboratory, that the lecturer comes with his knowledge/experience. Digital education system includes on-line or long-distance teaching. The knowledge or experience of the professor is digitalized into video or other media in the cloud. Thus, students can access it anytime, while the schedule to meet or discuss with the professor can be arranged in other times. Other content may be provided by community or personal on the internet, instead of by the professor. The system builds a big data, combining with Artificial Intelligent can be used for further analytics and decision systems.

The organization structure of higher education institution needs also to change in order to build ecosystem for research and innovation. Traditional university mostly has a research center only. It produces a product in the Technology Readiness Level of 5, presenting laboratory prototype, not ready yet for mass product. The technology-based university may produce a break-through solution, from the concept to commercial ones. It connects among education, research and innovation. The triple helix, collaboration among the university, government, and industry results in proper products with in-time delivery to the market. Figure 6 depicts the triple helix collaboration. The university prepares the prototype from the centers of research and innovation. The government is responsible on the certification, standard, and regulation. Hence, the industry follows up the certified product to replica for massive volume to the market.

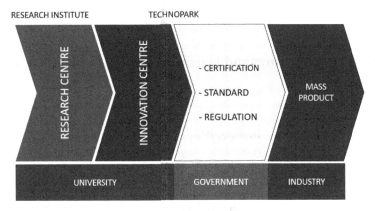

Figure 6.  Triple helix collaboration of research and innovation in university.

## 4  CONCLUSIONS

The pandemic of Covid-19 has changed almost all sectors including education. The transmission of Covid-19 occurs between human through droplet leading to new habits, such as wearing masker, social distancing, and avoiding crowd. This is an opposite way to the learning system that requires working together with no distance. The pandemic insists the education sectors to change the strategy and actions. Education sector must involve digital technology to develop innovative human resources. Digital technology adopted for universities includes:

– upgrading the infrastructure
– developing ecosystem for digital education and research
– digital services
– improving the human resource

By joining in the technology-based university, students have flexibility in time, place, and capable of develop their knowledge in-line with the change in industrial world.

## REFERENCES

[1] WHO Coronavirus Disease (COVID-19) Dashboard, accessed on 12 Sep 2020. https://covid19.who.int/
[2] Oxford essential quotation, Nelson Mandela, https://www.oxfordreference.com/view/10.1093/acref/9780191843730.001.0001/q-oro-ed5-00007046
[3] BPS Statistics Indonesia https://bps.go.id
[4] Deloitte, Future of Work accelerated: Learnings from the COVID-19 Pandemic, April 2020. https://www2.deloitte.com/content/dam/Deloitte/in/Documents/human-capital/in-consulting-accelerated-hc-consulting-noexp.pdf
[5] ITS, Institut Teknologi Sepuluh Nopember, Surabaya, Indonesia, https://www.its.ac.id/
[6] Wownews QS, Robot for medical assistance, Institut Teknologi Sepuluh Nopember, 8 June 2020, https://qswownews.com/two-medical-equipment-products-from-its-selected-as-the-national-flagship-products/
[7] Wownews QS, ITS launches intelligent boat, 9 Oct 2020, https://qswownews.com/its-launches-i-boat-an-autonomous-intelligent-boat/
[8] Wownews QS, i-Car the future Indonesia autonomous vehicle, Instutut Teknologi Sepuluh Nopember, 8 Sep 2020, https://qswownews.com/icar-its-the-future-of-indonesias-national-vehicle-2/

*Emerging Trends in Technology for Education in an Uncertain World – Nanto, Rahiem & Khalis Maryati (Eds)*
*© 2022 copyright the Author(s), ISBN 978-1-032-11288-6*

# Virtualization of education and learning: Identifying challenges and opportunities

H. Mottaqhi
*Al-Mustafa International University — Indonesia Branch*

ABSTRACT: Today, due to the different conditions the world is experiencing in the wake of the coronavirus pandemic, most universities and schools offer their education through cyberspace. Cyberspace is a vast realm that, despite its many applications, can also cause irreparable consequences. Most of the educational programs and researches conducted in this field focus on virtual education and neglect the critical issue of virtual education. It should be noted that the supply of religious teachings and educational models at all levels is necessary for the individual and social development of students and has to consider appropriate planning for its realization as in education. Based on descriptive method, this study tries to investigate the existing conditions and presents solutions to achieve objectives of education.

*Keywords*: Virtual Education, Conventional Method, E-Learning, Challenges, Opportunities

## 1  INTRODUCTION

Nowadays, due to the need of people to educate more than before, it seems that conventional methods are not accountable for this need. So online methods can be used in the event of economic and high quality (Redad et al. 2012). With the emergence of coronavirus pandemic, human life was affected in every way and education was practically no more than a virtualization of classrooms bringing learning home (Ray & Srivastava 2020). In recent years, the application of technology in education has increased rapidly and online courses have gained more popularity and credibility (Martin & Noonan 2010:1), and the idea that social media can be an effective tool for educational purposes has been taken into consideration (Tess 2013:60). The term "e-learning" was used in the mid-1990s, with developments in the world web and interest in asynchronous discussion (Garrison 2011:2).

Garrison (2011) believes that "in the information age and networking world, educators should reconsider their educational experiences, because value added in the knowledge-based future will be an environment for learning that encourages and develops the ability to think and learn independently and collaboratively, i.e., critical and self-centered, motivated and capable students can reflect, cooperate and maintain the motivation to continue learning all their life" (Garrison 2011).

The increasing expansion of educational methods and tremendous advances in information and communication technology and e-learning or virtual education with the pandemic period has entered a new phase. The educational system seems to be transitioning rapidly from the conventional period to the modern era. The hard approach of lecturer and university-centered in face-to-face education has replaced it simply and in a completely easy process without any obstacles and resistance toward the soft approach of student-centered. Students do not need to sit behind university and school desks for a long time and the speed of learning has become an important indicator in the complex and important process of learning and education. The element of time, along with e-learning, has found an undeniable and original nature. Careful and intelligent planning for the use of time is an important factor to accelerate the course of education.

DOI 10.1201/9781003219248-2

Educational institutions are facing the necessity of developing modern learning methods and are experiencing ups and downs. Although electronic and virtual education is one of the most important strategies for achieving social justice in the field of education, but it also faces challenges and disadvantages. Achieving this goal, while being easy, requires preparing in different fields for education and learning of students. Education and learning in the process of religious and Islamic education are the two main pillars in the process of growth and excellence of adolescents and young generation in educational institutions and learning centers.

Obviously, in order to virtual education, appropriate achievements have been achieved. But virtual education is an important issue that has been less addressed. This paper tries to investigate virtual education and its challenges. Furthermore, it makes serious effort to achieve strategies that are the result of experiences and study of scientific foundations in this field, to improve educational methods and pay attention to religious teaching and Islamic approach along with virtual education.

Establishing interactions between educators and students in online classes is one of the challenges that mutually strengthens academic learning and supports the community (Moorhead 2004:9). Some researchers have cited the lack of interaction as a disadvantage of the online classroom (Garry 1999). This interaction can be considered as the basis for an educational approach in cyberspace, and an interactive pattern in the educational and religious spheres can be considered in order to achieve the critical issue of education in a simultaneous way.

## 2 RESEARCH BACKGROUND

Considering that it is not long since online classes are held in Iran, there are few experiences of education, especially education through cyberspace. The following researches have addressed the disadvantages of virtual education, and the athers are the researches that consider virtual education:

Vatanparast et al. (2016) in a descriptive-analytical study conducted in the field of attitudes of Kerman nursing students toward virtual education showed that 85% of students had a positive attitude toward these classes and age of the subjects was reported to be a variable that was related to their satisfaction.

In a research on "Student's Satisfaction with the Quality of Educational Design of Virtual Education Courses", Radad et al. (2012) showed students' satisfaction scored 3.455 out of 5 and this meant their average and high satisfaction with the courses.

In a study entitled "Evaluation of the internal quality of the virtual curriculum of Ferdowsi University of Mashhad" which was done with a questionnaire and descriptive method, Rabiei et al. (2010) showed that the students are satisfied with the quality of the courses in terms of purpose, content, page design, materials. But on the contrary, they disappointed with elements such as learning and grouping activities.

Muilenburg and Berge (2005) examined students' barriers throughout online learning. The findings show that eight fundamental factors hinder online learning: administrative topics, social interaction, academic skills, technical skills, student motivation, time and support for studies, cost and internet access, and technical problems. They believe that variables such as gender, age, ethnicity, type of institution, self-assessment of online learning skills, effectiveness of online learning, enjoyment of online learning and biased behaviors in conventional classes are independent variables that affect these barriers.

Kiyan (2014) deals with the challenges of virtual education in a research titled "Challenges of Virtual Education: A Narrative of what is not Learned in Virtual University". The findings show that in virtual education, three main axes of education, creativity and power relationships are challenged, since there is no face-to-face communication element in virtual education; students are unable to model others. So there is little ground for education. Kiyan considers the solution to this problem to be more interactive in the learning environment using the capability of visual technologies.

Contrary to the mentioned researches which have mainly dealt with virtual education and neglected virtual education (parwaresh), Kiyan's study seeks to find out the impact of the expansion and necessity of turning to virtual education that the student is far from attending educational centers and not has a systemic communication with lecturers and counselors. This research is also to consider the duties of universities and lecturers toward the accurate and program-based accountability to the learning and educational needs of young people in achieving the educational goals of youth; namely how can the high goals of education be achieved among young people and adolescents while using media technologies? What is the responsibility of universities and lecturers in the field of education and learning using cyberspace? What are the strategies to strengthen educational processes in the field of virtual education?

## 3 CONCEPTUAL FRAMEWORK

This research does not intend to test the theory, but it does not mean that the mind is empty of theoretical foundations and the existing theories in this field have been cited as reference frameworks. Learning theories are among the theories that have been studied in this research.

The online learning method is attractive to many students because they can receive the course content at any time whenever they want. In fact, students expect a learning experience that is personal and immediate. On the other hand, in these courses, they can communicate more electronically with the lecturer and other students (Johnson 2013:13). Offline education has removed the limitations of learning for students, so it is one of the advantages of this method. Parker (1999) lists ten benefits of online learning as follows:

- We can use the day when we have the highest level of learning.
- We can learn content at your own pace.
- We can learn faster.
- We can have more contact with professors and other participants.
- There are more topics online.
- Participants can be present from all over the world.
- We can learn from leading experts.
- Learning online is cheaper, so it is more accessible.
- Internet links offer more resources.
- We can set up a virtual community (Muilenburg & Berge 2005).

Design of early learning systems based on a behavioral approach to learning. Behavioral approach was an approach that, in view of Skinner, observable behavior indicates the learner learns or does not learn. Some experts also believe that not all learning is observable and is more than a change in behavior.

As a result, cognitive learning theory has replaced behavioral theory. Cognitive psychologists claim that learning involves the use of memory, motivation, and thinking. This reflection plays an important role in the course of learning. They consider learning as an internal process and claim that its amount depends on the learner's processing capacity, the amount of effort spent during learning and the depth of processing and the structure of the learner's knowledge.

Recently, constructivist theory has emerged that the learner interprets information and the world according to his personality and personalizes knowledge for himself. Another theory is communication theory. Siemens argues that communication theory is achieved through integrating the principles of theories of chaos, networking, complexity, and theories of self-organization. Everything that is learned by the person in the past must be forgotten and the person must learn how to be adaptive with new information and evaluate it. Design of online learning contents can include principles from all three schools of thought that, according to Ertmer and Newby (1993), can shape the classification for learning. Behaviorist strategies are used to teach facts (what), use cognitive strategies to teach processes and principles (how) and build-up strategies for a higher level of thinking that promotes personal meaning and creates conceptual learning and deals with why (Anderson 2005:19–20).

Anderson (2005) presents a model that includes effective online learning components according to the above three approaches:

1. Preparing student: he should have an available map to understand the importance of using the online lesson and its usefulness, learn about the results of learning and check if they are ready for the lesson.
2. Student activity: all activities including text, listening to audio, video materials and viewing images, etc. should be included in the learning process;
3. Student interaction: There should be interaction between the student and others, and everyone should participate in a common cognition. This will help the student to personalize the information and create meaning of life (Anderson 2005:36).

The following model shows the above approaches:

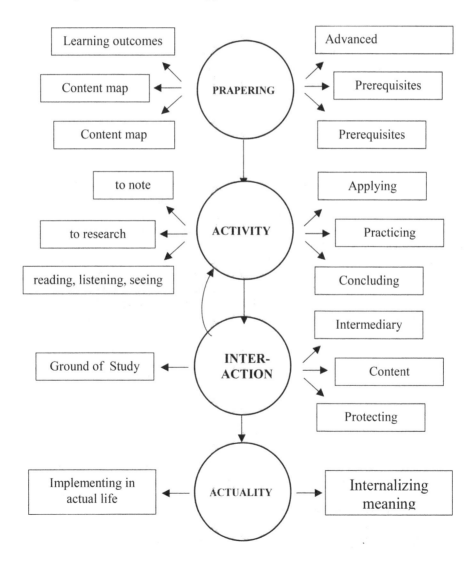

Cole (2000) believes that e-learning allows participants to save time and space, but educational content must be properly designed to enhance learning (Anderson 2008:16). It seems that according to the above model, the existence of more interaction between lecturers and students, the possibility of virtual education is simultaneously realistic.


## 4   RESEARCH METHODOLOGY

This study is based on descriptive research method that the researcher is looking at the subject and examining the status quo and studying its characteristics. The data collection tool in this study is library and utilization of personal and managerial experiences of the author.

This research is based on descriptive method that provide the researcher to observe how the subject is and examine the current situation and study its characteristics. The data collection tool in this research is a library and using the author's personal and managerial experiences.


## 5   FINDINGS

This article seeks to examine the aspects of the tasks of educational institutions and learning centers and provide logical solutions in carrying out the educational mission that, in the modern era of virtual education, has replaced face-to-face education. Among the requirements for the realization of virtual education can be summarized in the following cases:


### 5.1   *Preparing educational content in terms of age group and needs of students and learners*

The most important element in the fruiting of virtual education is educational content. The fact is that the use of electronic technologies in teaching and providing virtual learing in today's world has a history. But on the other hand, the rapid expansion of the use of virtual methods in education and at various levels of education in the pandemic period of Corona has faced many complexities for officials, principlas and managers in schools and universities. Necessity and speed in replacing face-to-face teaching with virtual learning cause aggregation of the ability of educational managers in providing learning units based on pre-designed programs so that do not leave an opportunity to pay deep and accurate attention to other matters such as teaching and educating students.

Developing and preparing educational contents for different levels of education of students in order to take advantage in virtual fields is one of the most important tasks of educational institutions so that the cycle and order in the education of young people is not disrupted. Although the preparation and compilation of educational contents in accordance with the conditions and complexities governing virtual education requires special attention and revision of methods, but the weakness of the necessary infrastructures and contents for the category of education is quite understandable. The most important result of compiling educational contents is to create unity of procedure in educational activities and to create the necessary grounds for the development of religious and moral standards among scholars.


### 5.2   *The necessity of establishing scientific and educational relationships between teachers and students*

The relationship between teacher-student is one of the most important elements in the management of the educational process. The spiritual and moral life of the student is tied to the efforts of teachers and lecturers. The kind teacher does his best to educate a good youth and deliver him to the society. It is common among the people of literature and culture in the Iranian society that human beings use two sources in the process of learning science and gaining experience: teacher and time. If one misses the opportunity to exploit the teacher and closes the ways of using the teacher's education easily and conveniently, he should wait for the lesson of the time. Learning from time a very difficult and life-hardtime. *"So take lesson, O you who have insight!"* (QS. 59:2).

It is necessary to learn from the days of every human life to learn and gain experience in numerous time periods, while the student sits on the table of the experiences of a teacher and benefits from the teacher's findings in the process of teaching. Managers of educational institutions should pay special attention and strengthen the communication between teachers and students, which is an important issue during the use of virtual methods of education. In the field of virtual education, teacher-student communication is one of the most vulnerable points in the education process, and logical organization of teacher-student communication using various models of virtual communication is an important issue to reduce disadvantages.

Of course, the acceptability of the teacher, scientific mastery of the subject, the capacity for technical teaching and effective discussion, divine ethics and tolerance of the teacher, the ability and the art of creating empathy and the sense of mutual understanding, sincerely solving all of the student's problems, and finally cultivate the motivation and developing the passion of study are the important factors in creating a teacher-student relationship. The teacher should try to realize these factors in the eyes of students to provide the grounds for constructive and effective communication. The systematic organization of the teacher-student relationship is doubly important for students entering university in the first semester. A new student have problems such as being alien to the university environment, being separated from the high school and family environment, not communicating mentally with the disciplines, lack of acquaintance with classmates and incompatibility with them. That teachers have an important and undeniable role in reducing or resolving such problems, and this role will be realized only within the framework of the teachers' humble and ethical relationship with students.

### 5.3 *The necessity of developing the education process from physical classes to virtual spaces*

The Corona pandemic has opened a new space for education policymakers. The post-Corona world is much more predictable than before. Corona led contemporary humans to think that one could not live in this world and was indifferent to the capacities that science and technology has created in the world. Technology, with all its disadvantages, has become the most effective means in order to devastate the effects of coronavirus pandemic. It can be claimed that the pandemic has opened another horizon to the future of the world. One of the most basic measures to be used is to investigate the mechanisms and infrastructures of content and technique to develop the learning process from physical class and school to virtual spaces and to provide a large part of the learning and its process using distance learning technology. Universities and schools should take great steps to formalize and develop virtual learning, and these steps should be combined into the field of education.

### 5.4 *Providing various educational programs for students and families in order to take advantage of their leisure time*

The Corona pandemic and the closure of schools and educational institutions have increased the survival time of young people at home or in their neighborhoods and naturally have a lot of leisure. High leisure time in the season of education is one of the most serious "pests" in the path of youth growth and excellence. Education planners in the corona are faced with the fact that the scale of educational impact that the "class" and the presence of scholars is greatly reduced and the opportunities for direct influence on scholars from planners are deprived. Transfer of educational and educational specials from face-to-face methods to virtual methods requires, along with the development of educational programs based on virtual model, quick action and in order to develop comprehensive educational programs based on new technologies.

The truth is that the "taste" of educating young people with face-to-face methods is very different from the taste of educating with the use of new technologies. The use of "art" by teachers and managers is necessary and undeniable to design education and learning programs. Applying artistic methods in conveying learning and education messages influences educational messages in the nature and institution of young audiences. The application of new methods in conveying scientific and educational messages and contents and establishing communication between teachers and students in virtual spaces requires the establishment or adherence of attractive methods such as attractive methods, skill and attractiveness of communication, and the formation of intertwined epistemic circles.

On the other hand, scientific management on the production of educational content and messages and observing the requirements of presence in virtual networks such as abbreviation in providing useful materials are prerequisites for success in providing programs. The truth is that the accelerated advancement of technology and the production of online applications and media deprives the check-and-balance opportunity from educational program managers.

All stakeholders must take the initiative to play a role in this field with complete accuracy and intelligence and manage the students' leisure time. Of course, it should be noted that these programs should always be considered and carefully along with face-to-face education programs, and the implementation of learning programs in virtual fields is guaranteed by the active participation of parents, especially in the management of students' leisure time.

## 5.5  *Promoting and developing the social culture*

Facilitating the promotion and development of the social culture of scholars is one of the most fundamental pillars of educational planning during the pandemic era of Corona. Today, the moral attributes of "self-sacrifice" and "altruism" have become very popular among human beings. Corona proved once again to human beings and human societies that no one can build a comprehensive life for himself without constructive social relations based on pure emotions. During the Corona outbreak, many people, inspired by revelatory and religious teachings, committed themselves to serving the victims of the Corona in various fields. An atmosphere of self-sacrifice and a sense of "altruism" overwhelmed human activities and social culture emerged among the general public. In this regard, one of the tasks of learning and education managers is to spread this culture among learners, scholars and students, to strengthen the spirit and macro-social culture so that move the cycle of communication between students and classmates. They are formed and moved during the corona pandemic period, as a result of cultivating collective behavior and shaping their social personality.

## 5.6  *Creating spiritual behavior circles in cyberspace*

One of the most important educational goals of universities in Islamic countries is to strengthen the religious foundations of students and their relationship with The Creator of the universe. In the Corona pandemic period, we do not see students and scholars participating in religious ceremonies conducted by universities. The closure of the physical activities of the universities has caused the process of religious education of the students who have been brought up in religious families to be interrupted, while at the same time, the process of their education using cyberspace is being implemented and developed. One of the tasks of education managers in universities is to create a relative balance between learning and education activities so that parents can witness the comprehensive growth of their children in universities.

Universities should provide tools and solutions that scholars can use to easily access religious services, religious and educational counseling. Serious efforts to use educational advisors and experts along with educational advisors should be on the main agenda of universities. Obviously, the use of specialized and efficient experts and the creation of virtual interactive environments between counselors and students provide the grounds for strengthening their religious foundations and teachings. Creating ethical circles among scholars with the focus on experts and experienced professors strengthens the spiritual dimensions of student life and provides the grounds for their spiritual conduct. The continuous communication of experts with groups, circles and communication channels in virtual fields has an effective role in the development of religious and spiritual culture of students and scholars.

# 6 SUGGESTIONS

Education is a serious issue that should be considered along with learning, because learning regardless of education, attention to religious and Islamic teachings and lack of a model for individual growth and excellence seems to be incomplete and defective. The following points is suggesting the use of technology to facilitate virtual education and make it possible to achieve education simultaneously:

## 6.1 *Compiling online programs in order to organize virtual courses of Quran memorizing and the laws of recitation*

Today, we are facing significant progress in the use of new technologies for the development of Quranic sciences in societies. The teaching of the Quran and its related sciences has always been in the context of the attentions of Islamic countries. Many digital quranic programs have been placed in the global network and have opened an unmatched opportunity for Quran students and scholars. The fact is that many digital programs that monitor the needs of the audience have been designed for specific environments and most of them have not been developed along with face-to-face learning and educational units in academic-scientific societies.

Practically, the Quran memorizing now is in the context of university curricula. So the development of specific programs in a way that is related to the formal and academic education process should be on the main agenda of universities. Obviously, learning and education managers should take full advantage of the capacities in virtual networks and avoid repetitive tasks. In this regard, identifying experienced managers and specialized professors in various fields of the Quran is necessary.

## 6.2 *Production of multimedia contents*

Multimedia films composed of text, audio, pictures, infographics, video and interactive contents are among the strongest and most influential media. Visual media in the minds of the audience embodies content that this visualization speeds up the transmission of concepts and messages. Transferring religious and educational teachings to students using multimedia films plays an important role in managing and meeting the educational needs of students during the pandemic period of Corona. What should be paid special attention to in this field is the production of new content inspired by comprehensive programs. The use of multimedia productions should be loaded out of the general approach and refered to the intellectual requirements of young scholars.

## 6.3 *Production of virtual contents and e-books*

The production of electronic content beside of an educational approach has been less considered by education managers in universities, and the rapid emergence and spread of the corona pandemic has created a deep crisis in the process of education and learning and practically deprived the opportunity to plan and build infrastructure for institutionalizing the process of learning and education. In the same situation, all the managers realized the development of educational programs and passing the educational units of students, and in a more precise sense, the universities only deal with "virtualized education" and presented the lessons based on the courses of the students in a virtual way.

In this process of virtualization of education, deep attention has not been paid to the process of educating ordinary scholars and it has been practically neglected or has little strength. One of the most important measures to institutionalize education in virtual spaces is the production of electronic content for educational programs. Obviously, the contents should have a suitable model with the intellectual and personality requirements of the scholars and make wide changes in both the content and the method, and at the same time follow the general policies of universities and educational centers.

### 6.4 *Empowerment and knowledge-enhancing courses*

During the Corona pandemic, it should be acknowledged that the academic and educational community of the world faced a sudden shift from face-to-face education to virtual education and e-learning. This transformation was accompanied by weakness in infrastructure. Practical and theoretical courses of scholars were disrupted. The graduation process of students was impaired and along with these problems, universities and educational institutions faced a reality such as lack of experience of lecturers and experts to provide virtual education. This defect also reveals in front of universities managers a range of students' dissatisfaction about the quality of the education and the materials.

All the defects mentioned above are precisely emerged in the process of learning and education. Accordingly, the students should design and implement empowerment and upgrading courses for two groups of lecturers and students in two areas of education and in the form of a comprehensive program so that lecturers can play a complete role in the process of education and on the other hand, students with a complete knowledge of virtual methods can take full advantage of the topics and content presented in virtual spaces.

### 6.5 *Providing weekly learning packages for limited Internet access*

The difference in the economic and social level of students is one of the realities in universities and educational institutions. The low economic level of some families has harmed their childrens during the pandemic period and forced them to work in line with the family's economy. On the other hand, the lack of access of such students to resources such as computers and high-speed Internet has caused all of them to face the same conditions. The universities faced the fact that creates a new atmosphere for learing and education managers. One of the most important measures that can somewhat eliminate the negative effects of these differences and lack of integration in the education process is to provide a variety of programs that can be considered and met the needs of students in any level.

Accordingly, preparing educational and educational packages along educational activities can meet the needs of students who do not have high economic levels so that they process of education is not disrapted.

### 6.6 *Shifting from teacher-centered approach to student-centered one*

Teacher and lecturer have a pivotal role in face-to-face learning. That is, teaching and learning activities are mainly led by the teacher. In this process, the teacher explains the topics and issues of the course, explains the cause of events and the relationship between concepts and ideas, and describes the processes in detail. This action of teacher, along with the tasks that are presented systemically based on the known needs of the in-person education process, creates enthusiasm in the students and thus increases the level of effectiveness in the audience. During the coronavirus outbreak and the popularity of virtual teaching methods, the course of education has also changed, and students and scholars play a central role in the education process and the teacher-centered gradually give away to student-centered. A student-centered in the process of education leads to the emergence of creativity, vitality and dynamism in students.

Educational programs should also reach a position where students are important agent in developing the foundations of religious education in student communities. Responsible participation along with the focus of students in the process of education and learning makes the programs dynamic and guarantees their implementation. In this method, the main subject of the topics is conveyed by the teacher and the lecturer, and other things are followed up and carried out under the supervision of the teacher through the activities and researches that the scholars themselves complete. Gradual passage from teacher-centered approach to student-centered one requires culturalization among teachers and students and creating the necessary infrastructures that universities and educational institutions should move in the line of comprehensive programs. In this approach, the scholar must change his position from a state of passivity in the process of learning science to an active state so that he believes in active role-playing.

## 7 CONCLUSION

E-learning has many benefits that can be referred to learning and educating at any time and place, collaborative learning, self-assessment and self-strategy (Radad et al. 2010). Apart from the numerous benefits of virtualization of education, its application in developing countries should also be noted. Despite their limited resources, these countries can improve their scientific skills in this way (Srivastava et al. 2013). In order to gain a competitive advantage, every organization must have human capital that is equipped with information and knowledge (Jafarifar et al. 2017).

Nowadays, due to the emerging application of technology in Islamic countries, very little attention has been paid to the important issue of virtual education. It should be noted that by using new technologies in the right direction, education and learning can be realized together, religious and Islamic teachings can be presented to students with a new approach through cyberspace and online classes. The solutions throughout this article can be used to address this important issue.

## REFERENCES

Garrison, D. R. (2011). E-learning in the 21st century: A framework for research and practice. Taylor & Francis.

Gray, S. (1999). Message. ListServ WWW Courseware Development. Retrieved October, 16, 2004.

Jafarifar, Zohreh, Khorasani, Abasalt, & Rezaeizadeh, Morteza. (2017). Syenasa'i va Rutbeh-bandi Mavani' Mudarresan dar Amuzesh va Behsazi Majazi Manabi' Ensani: Muthale'eh Mavridi Daneshgah Sayhid Beheshti. Education and Human Resource Development, 4 (12), 53–77.

Johnson, R. F. (2013). Student attitudes toward blended and online courses: A comparison of students in traditional classroom writing environments and students in blended writing environments.

Keane, Maryam. (2014). Chaleshhaye Amuzesh Majazi: Riwayate Ancheh dar Daneshgah Majazi Amukhteh Namisavad, 5 (3), 11–22.

Martin, F., & Noonan, D. (2010, July). Synchronous technologies for online teaching. In 2010 International Conference on Technology for Education (pp. 1–4). IEEE.

Muilenburg, L., & Berge, Z. L. (2005). Student barriers to online learning: A factor analytic study. Distance Education, 26, 29–48.

Muirhead, B. (2004). Encouraging interactivity in online classes. International Journal of Instructional Technology and Distance Learning.

Rabiei, M, Mohebbi Amin, S., & Rashid Haji Khajehloo, S. (2010). Arziyabi Kayfiyate Daruni Barnameh Darsi Davreh Amuzesh Majazi Daneshgah Firsausi Masyhad. Horizon Development of Medical Education, 4 (1), 29–36.

Radad, I., Jafari, S., & Ahmadi, E. (2012). Sanjesh Mizan Ridhayatmandi Daneshjuyan Daneshgah bainal Milali Imam Reza a.s. az Kayfiyat Tharrahi Amuzeshi Davrehhaye Amuzesh Majazi. Journal of Publishing, 3 (6), 61–73.

Ray, S., & Srivastava, S. (2020). Virtualization of science education: A lesson from the COVID-19 pandemic. Journal of Proteins and Proteomics, 1–4.

Srivastava, S., Özdemir, V., Ray, S., Panga, J. R., Noronha, S., Nair, B., et al. (2013). Online education: e-learning booster in developing world. Nature, 501, 316.

Tess, P. A. (2013). The role of social media in higher education classes (real and virtual) – A literature review. Computers in Human Behavior, 29 (5), A60–A68.

Vatanparast, M., Royani, Z., & Ghasemi, H. (2016). Barrese Negaresh Daneshjuyan Parastari Kerman Nisbat beh Amuzesh Majazi dari Sal 2009. Journal of Nursing Education, 5 (1), 53–61.

Zarghami, S., Attaran Naghibzadeh, M., & Mir Abdolhossein, B. (2006). Barresi Didgahaye Falsafi dar bareh Nisbat Fannavari Itthila'at va Ta'lim va Tarbiyat. Journal of Educational Innovations, (19).

*Emerging Trends in Technology for Education in an Uncertain World – Nanto, Rahiem & Khalis Maryati (Eds)*
© 2022 copyright the Author(s), ISBN 978-1-032-11288-6

# Research-based learning—STEM learning activities: Developing a secure CryptoKey by using rainbow antimagic coloring of graph to improve students combinatorial thinking skills

Dafik
*Department of Maths Edu. Postgrad., Universitas Jember, Jember, Indonesia*
*CGANT UNEJ, Universitas Jember, Jember, Indonesia*
*CEREBEL FKIP, Universitas Jember, Jember, Indonesia*

T.K. Maryati
*Universitas Islam Negeri (UIN) Syarif Hidayatullah Jakarta, Ciputat, Indonesia*

I.H. Agustin, R. Nisviasari, I.N. Maylisa & E.Y. Kurniawati
*CGANT UNEJ, Universitas Jember, Jember, Indonesia*

ABSTRACT: The combinatorial thinking skills are esensially important in now day era. The recent research regarded to improving the higher-order thinking skills is research-based learning (RBL) together with a STEM approach. Our research aims to describe a framework of RBL-STEM learning activities in developing a secure CryptoKey by using rainbow antimagic colorig of graph to improve the students combinatorial thinking skills. By rainbow antimagic coloring, we mean a bijection $f : V(G) \rightarrow \{1, 2, \ldots, |V(G)|\}$. The associated weight of an edge $uv \in E(G)$ under $f$ is $w_f(uv) = f(u) + f(v)$. The bijection $f$ is called an edge-antimagic vertex labeling if every edge has a distinct weight. Further $f$ is called a rainbow antimagic labeling of $G$ if all edge weights induce the rainbow colors and it should be guaranteed there exist a rainbow path for every $u$ to $v$, where $u, v \in V(G)$. The resulting rainbow antimagic coloring graph can potentially generates a secure CryptoKey.

## 1 INTRODUCTION

A thinking process is mindful effort made by an individual to solve his or her problems. The thinking process is closely related to decision-making in solving problems. The more often the individual carries out the thinking process, the better his ability to solve problems. This is because the mental processes that individuals have who always carry out the process of thinking are not just remembering and understanding the way out of the problems they have faced, but also developing efforts to solve problems they face so that one day it can be reused. A good thinking process is creative thinking skills that offer multiple variations of problem-solving. This will grow if students are trained to have combinatorial thinking skills. Combinatorial thinking skills are the ability to arrange combinations that might be used in solving problems, order, natural phenomenon, or social phenomenon. For example, in graph labeling of graphs, vertices or edges are assigned labels that meet certain properties. Suppose a path $P_5$, we assign labels with *{1,2,3,4,5}* such that the edge weights (sum of two adjacent vertices) are different. Students show not only one permutation of labeling being obtained but more than that, students must be able to identify, is there other labels that fulfills property? Then, is the labeling unique? Is that optimal? Can the answer be generalized? How to prove it for more general cases? This is the principle of combinatorial thinking skills.

According to Rezaie and Zahra (2011), there are four stages in the combinatorial thinking skills. These stages include (1) Identification of several problems, (2) Finding breakthrough solutions

DOI 10.1201/9781003219248-3

Table 1. The indicators and sub-indicator of the combinatorial thinking skills.

| Indicator | Sub-indicator |
| --- | --- |
| Identify some cases | a. Identify the properties/characteristics of the problem |
| | b. Solve the problem for some cases |
| Recognizing the pattern of all cases | a. Identify patterns of the solution |
| | b. Extend the pattern of the obtained solution |
| Generalize all cases | a. Apply mathematical symbolization |
| | b. Calculate the cardinality |
| | c. Develop the algorithms |
| Prove it mathematically | a. Perform a counting arguments |
| | b. Test the correctness of the algorithm |
| | c. Develop a bijection |
| | d. Apply inductive, deductive, or qualitative proof |
| Consider other combinatorial problems | a. Propose an open problem |
| | b. Identify new combinatorial problems |
| | c. Find potential applications |

to the problems, (3) Systematically describing the problem, (4) Turning the problem into other combinatorial problems. Meanwhile, Dafik et al. (2019) emphasized that there are five main indicators in combinatorial thinking skills, where each indicator has several different sub-indicators. The five main indicators are presented in Table 1.

The Combinatorial thinking skills cannot appear by students themselves, it takes a systematic effort elaborated by the lectures. Research related to combinatorial thinking skills can be seen in Hastuti et al. (2019), Maylisa et al. (2020), Ridlo et al. (2020a), and Septory et al. (2019). One model that can be used to encourage the realization of these skills is the Research-Based Learning (RBL) model. RBL is a learning model which involves contextual learning, authentic learning, problem-solving, cooperative learning, hands-on & minds-on learning, and an inquiry or discovery approach. The RBL implementation aims to encourage the development of higher-order thinking skills in students. Students are not only provided with information and science but it is also encouraged to attain higher-order thinking skills, collaborating or communicating. According to Arifin (2010), the Research-Based Learning model is divided into three stages, namely: *Exposure stage*, gathering information based on inquiry; *Experience stage*, namely identifying and formulating problems; *Capstone stage*, conveying plans or ideas in providing solutions, measurement or computational methods. Dafik (2016) strengthens the syntax of RBL by integrating the existence of a research group in higher education through (1) proposing problems based on problems in the research group, (2) finding breakthroughs in solving problems, (3) gathering information related to the obtained breakthroughs, (4) testing the effectiveness of the breakthrough, (5) generalizing through hypothesis testing or mathematical proof, (6) FGD involving research group members, (7) compiling project reports. Many findings related to the application of Research-Based Learning can be found (Dafik et al. 2019; Dini et al. 2019; Estuhono et al. 2019; Hidayatul et al. 2020; Monalisa et al. 2019; Nazula et al. 2019; Ridlo et al. 2019; Ridlo et al. 2020a, 2020b; Rohim et al. 2019; Sota & Petzer 2017; Sulistiyono et al. 2020b; Suntusia et al. 2019; Tohir et al. 2019; Wahyuni et al. 2020; Wangguway et al. 2020; Wardani et al. 2019).

The first step in RBL requires a contextual and realistic problem and includes at least four scientific studies, namely science, technology, engineering, and mathematics. Therefore, it is necessary to combine RBL with the STEM (Science, Technology, Engineering, and Mathematics) approach so that the students thinking skills can solve some real problems involving four interrelated domains. Scientific literacy is the ability to use scientific knowledge in three main areas science in life and health, science in earth and environment, and science in technology. Technological literacy means the ability to use, manage, understand, and assess ICT (Information, Communication, and Technology). Engineering literacy is the understanding of how technologies are developed via the engineering design process. Engineering design is the systematic and creative application of scientific and mathematical principles to practical ends such as the design, manufacture, and operation of efficient and economic structures, machines, processes, and systems. Mathematical literacy means the ability of students to analyze, reason, and communicate ideas effectively as they pose, formulate, solve, and forecast a solution to the problems in a variety of ways. Some research regarding the application of STEM in class, it can be found in Baharin et al. (2018), Breiner et al. (2012), Leon et al. (2015), Sergis et al. (2017), Siregar et al. (2019), and Soros et al. (2019). Consequently, the STEM classroom shifts students away from learning discrete bits and pieces of a phenomenon and rote procedures and toward having investigating and questioning the interrelated facets of the world (Morrison 2006). By combining the RBL and STEM approach, this study was conducted, thus the research title is "Research Based Learning – STEM Learning Activities: Developing a Secure CryptoKey by Using Antimagic Total Covering of Graph to Improve Students Combinatorial Thinking Skills".

Meanwhile, CryptoKey is an inseparable part of the cryptosystem. A cryptosystem is a system that converts plaintext to ciphertext or ciphertext to plaintext by the application of encryption or decryption algorithm. The strength of the cryptosystem relies on the management of the encryption key. The key should be managed such that it is hard for any intruder to analyze the key. The main issue is how to develop a secure modern cryptosystem such that the key between plaintext and ciphertext is hidden. As an illustration of how the cryptosystem works, see Figure 1. There are many variants to construct a secure CryptoKey such as modified Affine cipher and cipher Feedback Mode (Nisviasari et al. 2021), modified of a block cipher and affine cipher (Maryati et al. 2020) and by using a stream cipher (Prihandoko et al. 2019). However, all of these techniques are relatively conventional, because the keys are easily revealed by the intruders. Therefore, this research will study the use of rainbow antimagic coloring of Graph for the development of a Secure CryptoKey. Research results related to CryptoKey can be seen in Maryati et al. (2020), Nisviasari et al. (2021), and Prihandoko et al. (2019).

Furthermore, by a rainbow antimagic coloring, we mean a bijection $f: V(G) \rightarrow \{1,2,3,..., |V(G)|\}$. The associated weight of an edge $uv \in E(G)$ under $f$ is $w_f(uv) = f(u) + f(v)$. The bijection $f$ is called an edge-antimagic vertex labeling if every edge has a distinct weight. While a path in the vertex-labeled graph $G$ is said to be a rainbow path if for every two edges $uvu'v' \in E(P)$ satisfies $w_f(uv) \neq w_f(u'v')$. If every two vertices $u$ and $v$ of $G$, there exists a rainbow $u$–$v$ path, then $f$ is called a rainbow antimagic labeling of $G$. A graph $G$ is rainbow antimagic if $G$ has a rainbow antimagic labeling. Many results related to this study, can be referred to Chartrand et al. (2008), Dafik et al. (2018), Septory et al. (2021), and Sulistiyono et al. (2020a).

The main objectives of this research are as follows: (1) Describe the framework of the RBL model learning activities with the STEM approach in improving Students Combinatorial Thinking Skills in Developing a Secure CryptoKey by using rainbow antimagic coloring of graph, (2) Describing the framework for the development process of learning materials on RBL model with STEM approach in improving students combinatorial thinking skills in developing a secure CryptoKey by using rainbow antimagic coloring of graph, (3) Describes how learning materials of RBL model with STEM approach can improve students combinatorial thinking skills in developing a secure CryptoKey by using rainbow antimagic coloring of graph.

Figure 1.   The scheme of the cryptosystem.

## 2 METHOD

This type of research is a qualitative method, which is a literature review on the results of previous studies, especially those conducted by the researcher. From the results of the literature review, we develop frameworks related to three research objectives. The learning activities framework development was done by using a qualitative analysis on RBL-STEM syntax. The framework for the process of developing the RBL-STEM learning materials, referred to ADDIE model of the research and development, namely Analyze, Design, Development, Implementation, and Evaluation (Branch 2009).

## 3 RESEARCH FINDINGS

### 3.1 *Framework of RBL-STEM*

In the following, we will present a framework for integrating the RBL learning model in the STEM approach in improving the students' combinatorial thinking skills in developing a secure CryptoKey by using the rainbow antimagic coloring of graph. The framework is developed based on the syntax proposed in Sergis et al. (2019). In the early stages of RBL syntax is posing problems arising from the research group and included in the scope of the research group's study. These problems consider the existence of online transaction data hacked by unauthorized people. Therefore the RBL-STEM model will undertake the following stages: (1) fundamental problems related to the online data transaction abuse, (2) obtain a breakthrough by using the rainbow antimagic coloring of a graph to develop a secure CryptoKey, (3) data collection related to the data type being abused, (4) develop CryptoKey by using the rainbow antimagic coloring of the graph, (5) test the resulting CryptoKey, (6) reporting the research results and observations of students' creative skills. In detail, the framework for this RBL-STEM integration can be seen in Figure 2.

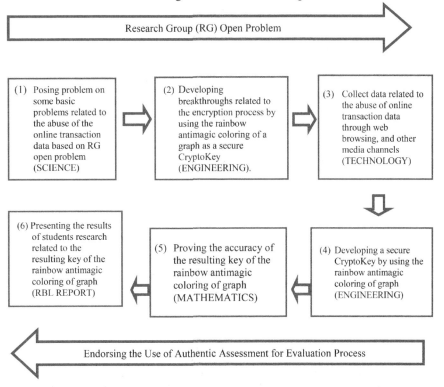

Figure 2. The framework of RBL-STEM in developing a secure CryptoKey.

### 3.1.1 *Learning outcome*

Students can develop a secure CryptoKey by using rainbow antimagic coloring from a graph and analyze whether the rainbow path of the graph can be proven correct. Students can test whether ciphertext encryption using block chaining chipper of rainbow antimagic coloring can be easily decrypted, thus it can turn back to plaintext easily.

### 3.1.2 *Developing a research group*

To achieve the learning outcomes, it cannot be done with an ordinary learning process. Students must be escorted how to develop rainbow antimagic coloring of a graph, secondly, to test whether plaintext encryption using the cipher block chaining algorithm can be easily decrypted. We need a research-based learning model, since the learning activities to achieve the learning outcome require research activities, and analyze the process of encryption and decryption of a real problem is also needed as the problem cannot be solved by one scientific domain. Therefore, the RBL model with a STEM approach is applied.

Furthermore, to carry out effective research-based learning, a research group is needed, thus the implementation of RBL must be preceded by developing a research group. The research group can be at the study program level, faculty, or university level, depending on the scope of the research study, whether it is monodisciplinary, interdisciplinary, or multidisciplinary. If it is monodisciplinary, then the research group is sufficient at the study program level, if it is interdisciplinary, it is necessary to have joint research within the faculty, and finally, if the research study requires a multidisciplinary domain and the research activities started from the invention, innovation, and diffusion, then the research group should be at the university level. In the following section, we present the stages of forming a research group, see Figure 3.

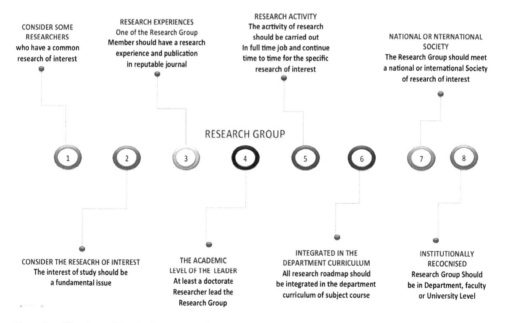

Figure 3. The steps of developing a research group.

Based on these stages, we have succeeded in developing a research group, namely CGANT research group. CGANT stands for Combinatorics, Graph Theory, and Network Topology. The CGANT research roadmap is shown in Figure 4(a). All CGANT research of interest has been integrated into the study program curriculum. Schematically, how the CGANT research study is integrated into the study program curriculum, it can be seen in Figure 4.

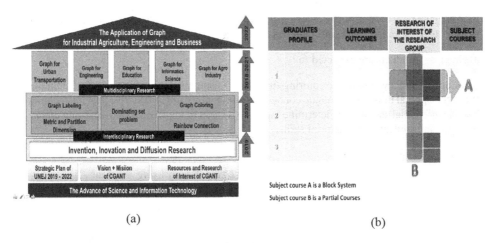

(a)                                                                    (b)

Figure 4. (a) CGANT research roadmap and (b) integrating a research thems of CGANT in the program study curriculum.

### 3.1.3 *Researcher role*
During the implementation of the RBL learning model together with the STEM approach, students who are assisted by researchers as members of CGANT research group will guide the mathematics education students on how to develop a breakthrough related to the encryption process by using the rainbow antimagic coloring of the graph, as a secure CryptoKey. Collecting data related to abuse of online data transactions through web browsing, and other media channels, developing a secure CryptoKey by using the rainbow antimagic coloring of the graph.Proving the accuracy of the resulting key of rainbow antimagic coloring. Presenting the results of student's research related to the resulting key of the rainbow antimagic coloring of a graph.

### 3.1.4 *Learning objective*
This RBL-STEM learning will enable students to develop knowledge and skills in the following fields of Science, Technology, Engineering, and Mathematics.
Sciences – Students are expected to:

– Understand the problem of data abuse that occurs in online transactions carried out by someone
– Analyze the characteristics of the data inputted by the public for the use of online transactions
– Analyzing the online transaction encryption process used by providers

Technology – Students are expected to:

– Use a web browser to identify any online transactions having a potential abuse by hackers
– Use a web browser to find recent studies related to the use of rainbow antimagic coloring of a graph as a secure CryptoKey
– Use the Youtube channel to find out how to develop a secure cryptosystem
– Develop a learning video by using a video maker software to develop a rainbow antimagic coloring of a graph
– Utilize word processing application software as well as inferential statistics software to determine the effectiveness of the RBL-STEM learning materials in improving student combinatorial skills.

23

Engineering – Students are expected to:

– Develop a rainbow antimagic coloring using pattern recognition techniques
– Finding a rainbow antimagic connection number using a qualitative approach
– Applying the rainbow antimagic coloring algorithm in developing plaintext encryption of online transaction data and the decryption process

Mathematics – Students are expected to:

– Develop the rainbow antimagic coloring function by using the piecewise function technique
– Prove the optimal rainbow antimagic connection number by using qualitative proving techniques
– Use the inferential statistics to determine the effectiveness of the RBL-STEM learning materials in improving student combinatorial skills.

### 3.2  *RBL-STEM learning activities on developing a CryptoKey by using rainbow antimagic coloring*

In this section, we will discuss one by one the six stages of the RBL learning model complemented by STEM approach. These six stages will illustrate how students do in learning with RBL-STEM approach regarding the use of rainbow antimagic coloring of graph in developing a secure CryptoKey to improve students' combinatorial thinking skills. Based on Figure 2, the first stage (SCIENCE) is proposing the fundamental problems related to the abuse of the online transaction data, which is done frequently by an authorized people. The activities carried out by the lecturers in the first stage are asking the students about their awareness of the existence of the abuse of the online transaction data. The lecturer will also ask about their knowledge about online transactions. For more details, see Table 2.

The learning activities of RBL model with the STEM approach at the second stage (ENGINEER-ING) are developing breakthroughs related to the use of rainbow antimagic coloring to develop CryptoKey. The activities carried out by the lecturer in the second stage were guiding students to discuss breakthroughs on how to determine the rainbow antimagic coloring. The Lecture also asks students to identify some graph families who admit a rainbow antimagic connection. For more details, see Table 3.

The learning activities of the RBL-STEM approach on the third stage (TECHNOLOGY) are collecting data related to rainbow antimagic coloring and cryptosystem through the Internet and other media channels, see Table 4.

The learning activities by using the RBL model with the STEM approach at the fourth stage (ENGINEERING) is developing rainbow antimagic coloring of graph. This step begins by selecting the graph and expanding its rainbow antimagic coloring. Evaluate the existence of a rainbow path. Later, observe whether the rainbow connection number has been optimum? If yes, then apply it in the encryption process of online transaction data. For more details, see Table 5.

Table 2.  The RBL-STEM learning activities on the online transaction data problems.

| Stage one | Activities |
| --- | --- |
| (1) Posing problem on some basic problems related to the abuse of an online transaction data based on RG open problem (SCIENCE) | 1. The lecturer asks students whether they have ever made online transactions<br>2. The lecturer asks students how confident they are regarding the security assurance of online transaction<br>3. Then the lecturer also provides the opportunity for students to remember what online transactions have been ever used<br>4. Have students ever experienced failure or fraud<br>5. What actions did you take on the unwanted incident |

Table 3.  The RBL-STEM learning activities of rainbow antimagic as a breakthrough.

| Stage two | Activities |
| --- | --- |
| (2) Developing breakthrough related to encryption process by using the rainbow antimagic coloring of graph as a secure CryptoKey (ENGINEERING) | 1. The lecturer guides students to discuss breakthroughs on how to develop rainbow antimagic coloring to build CryptoKey<br>2. The lecturer explains to students how to find rainbow antimagic coloring of graph<br>3. The lecturer and students look for a different graph and find the rainbow antimagic coloring, and finally generalize it<br>4. Lecturers and students are looking for the type of online transaction data to do encryption and decryption using the rainbow antimagic coloring algorithm |

Table 4.  The RBL-STEM learning activities on internet usage.

| Stage three | Activities |
| --- | --- |
| (3) Collect data related to the abuse of online transaction data through web browsing and other media channels (TECHNOLOGY) | 1. Students under the guidance of lecturers carry out data collection activities related to rainbow antimagic coloring and cryptosystem.<br>2. Data collection related to rainbow antimagic coloring and cryptosystem is carried out by browsing scientific journals/articles via research gates or other internet channels.<br>3. Students can use an encyclopedia, research gates (orcid, mendeley), research profile sites (scopus, publons), cloud storage (slideshare, Linkedin, MOOCs), cloud meetings (Google Meet, Zoom, Cisco Webex)<br>4. Develop a learning video using the Camtasia video maker to show a tutorial for the rainbow antimagic coloring process and the encryption process. |

Table 5.  The RBL-STEM learning activities on developing rainbow antimagic coloring for a secure CryptoKey.

| Stage two | Activities |
| --- | --- |
| (4) Developing a secure CryptoKey by using the rainbow antimagic coloring of graph (ENGINEERING) | 1. Lecturers and students choose graphs for rainbow antimagic coloring and test the existence of a rainbow path<br>2. Then proceed with checking whether the rainbow connection number is optimum? If so, proceed with the generalizations<br>3. Lecturers and students develop encryption using this rainbow antimagic coloring of online transaction data (plaintext) to produce a ciphertext<br>4. Lecturers and students develop decryption on obtained ciphertext by using this rainbow antimagic coloring<br>5. Lecturers and students try to generalize for more complex online transaction data and perform the encryption and decryption process by using the obtained rainbow antimagic graph<br>6. Trying to develop a simple algorithm to test the accuracy of CryptoKey |

The learning activities by using the RBL model with the STEM approach at the fifth stage (MATHEMATICS) are proving that the rainbow antimagic coloring of any order and size of graph. Since the plaintext can be in the form of very large data so that the key availability can be easily determined. For more details, see Table 6.

The learning activities by using the RBL model with the STEM approach at the six-stage (RBL REPORT) are carried out by students to do a presentation of the research results related to the use

Table 6. The RBL-STEM learning activities on proving rainbow antimagic coloring of graph of any order and size.

| Stage two | Activities |
| --- | --- |
| (5) Proving the accuracy of the resulting key of the rainbow antimagic coloring of graph (MATHEMATICS) | 1. Define the sets of graph elements to determine the cardinality of the selected graph. Determine the number of vertices and edges to obtain the order and size<br>2. Determine the lower bound of the rainbow antimagic connection number based on the existing lemma<br>3. Determine the upper bound by developing the rainbow antimagic coloring function of the antimagic labeling of vertices<br>4. Evaluate the edge weights whether all edge weights induce the existence of a rainbow path according to the properties of rainbow antimagic coloring<br>5. Check the cardinality of the edge weight set to consider the rainbow antimagic connection number<br>6. Compare the lower and upper bounds, if it is the same then we can set this number as the rainbow antimagic connection number<br>7. Present the table consisting of the data of rainbow antimagic coloring path<br>8. Take an example of a graph with a certain order and size to illustrate its rainbow antimagic coloring |

Table 7. The RBL-STEM learning activities on sharing the student's research results.

| Stage two | Activities |
| --- | --- |
| (6) Presenting the results of on students research related to the resulting key of H-antimagic total graph on $G = Shack(C_n, v, m)$ (RBL REPORT | 1. Students develop a research report on the use of rainbow antimagic coloring to develop CryptoKey<br>2. Students do the presentation in front of the class to do focus group discussion<br>3. Lecturers evaluate and clarify all the results of student's research activities<br>4. Lecturers make observations on the students' combinatorial thinking skills by using observation sheets |

of rainbow antimagic coloring to build CryptoKey. In this case, students will take a focus group discussion (FGD), so that the researcher can observe their combinatorial thinking skills. For more details, see Table 7.

### 3.3 *The framework of learning material process development*

The stage for the learning materials development of this research was carried out based on the ADDIE model. The development stages consist of analysis, design, development, implementation, and evaluation. The first stage: **Analysis**, aims to analyze the characteristics of students, the material and learning process, and the learning media to be used. Doing a literature study to find information about developmental research, learning materials, research-based learning model, STEM approach, a Secure CryptoKey, the rainbow antimagic coloring of graph, Second stage: **Design**, it is carried out by designing and compiling RBL model integrated with the STEM approach. At this stage, the learning materials, namely syllabus, semester learning plan, LKM, pre-test, post-test, and other assessment instruments, is prepared by the researcher. The third stage: **Development**, is carried out by testing the learning materials and instrumentsto check the validity of the learning materials as well as the practicability. The results of the validation are in the form of content validity, format validity, and language validity, and the level of practicability. The fourth stage: **Implementation**, aims to find the effectiveness of learning materials of RB-STEM in improving student's combinatorial thinking skills in developing a secure CryptoKey by using the rainbow antimagic coloring of graph. The fifth stage: **Evaluation,** is a reflection activity to assess whether or not the application of RBL model learning materials with the STEM approach can improve students' combinatorial thinking skills in developing a secure CryptoKey by using the rainbow antimagic coloring of graph. In this stage, the use of inferential statistics is needed.

### 3.4 *Rainbow antimagic coloring for a secure CryptoKey*

Now we will generate CryptoKey by improving variants of a block cipher and affine cipher by using rainbow antimagic coloring. Based on Maryati et al. (2020), the plaintext of a block cipher is normally divided into several blocks with the same length. At the affine cipher, the whole process relies on working *mod m* (the length of alphabet and number used). Our cryptosystem steps can be described as follows.

- The number of the block on the plaintext is taken from the chromatic number of rainbow antimagic Coloring of graphs
- The source of the key system is taken from the edge weights of the rainbow antimagic coloring of graphs
- The key has a length of the cardinality of edges set of graphs

We modify the rainbow antimagic coloring algorithm for constructing a CryptoKey. This algorithm yields a sequence of edge weights taken from rainbow antimagic coloring which is taken from the sum of vertex labels. The sequence is then utilized as an encryption key. The mechanism encrypts each block of plaintext based on the chromatic number of rainbow antimagic coloring. Let us work on 10 numbers and 26 English alphabets, the keystream construction is taken through the following algorithm.

Table 8. The numerical value of 10 numbers and 26 English alphabets of Ciphertext (upper case).

| 0 | 1 | 2 | 3 | 4 | 5 | 6 | 7 | 8 |
|---|---|---|---|---|---|---|---|---|
| 0 | 1 | 2 | 3 | 4 | 5 | 6 | 7 | 8 |
| 9 | A | B | C | D | E | F | G | H |
| 9 | 10 | 11 | 12 | 13 | 14 | 15 | 16 | 17 |
| I | J | K | L | M | N | O | P | Q |
| 18 | 19 | 20 | 21 | 22 | 23 | 24 | 25 | 26 |
| R | S | T | U | V | W | X | Y | Z |
| 27 | 28 | 29 | 30 | 31 | 32 | 33 | 34 | 35 |

**Algorithm 1.** Generating key system

1. Define $w_f$ for edge weights of the rainbow antimagic coloring of graphs
2. Take a certain $b$ for the chromatic number of the rainbow antimagic coloring of graphs
3. Take $z_{ij}$ is the sequence for edge weights of the rainbow antimagic coloring of graphs which $i$ − block and $1 \leq j \leq b$
4. Put $z_{ij}$ and sort the sequence based on the smaller edge weights of rainbow antimagic coloring of graphs
5. Take $k =$ element of sequence $z_{ij}$

Outputs of algorithm 1 are the key $k$. We can use some result of rainbow antimagic coloring obtained in the results (Budi et al. 2021; Jabbar et al. 2020; Kusumawardani et al. 2019). For example, we use rainbow antimagic coloring of $L_{3,n}$ on Budi et al. (2021). This labeling is illustrated in Figure 5. It shows that the vertex labels start from 1 to 9, respectively.

Based on the illustration of Figure 5, we have keys for plaintext, such as the keys for every element of the block are the edge weights of the rainbow antimagic coloring of graphs, consecutively. The CryptoKey, produced by Algorithm 1, is implemented to establish encryption in the mode of affine cipher and block cipher. The encryption process is using Algorithm 2.

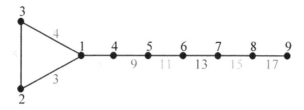

Figure 5.   Rainbow antimagic coloring of $L_{3,6}$.

Table 9.   Encryption process.

| Block 1 | Plaintext | A | D | I | N | A | T | A | D |
|---|---|---|---|---|---|---|---|---|---|
| | $P_i$ | 10 | 13 | 18 | 23 | 10 | 29 | 10 | 13 |
| | $K_i$ | 3 | 4 | 5 | 5 | 9 | 11 | 13 | 15 |
| | $P_i + K_i$ | 13 | 17 | 23 | 28 | 19 | 40 | 23 | 28 |
| | $C_i$ | 13 | 17 | 23 | 28 | 19 | 4 | 23 | 28 |
| | Ciphertext | D | H | N | S | H | 4 | N | S |
| Block 2 | Plaintext | E | W | A | N | D | A | R | U |
| | $P_i$ | 14 | 32 | 10 | 23 | 13 | 10 | 27 | 30 |
| | $K_i$ | 17 | 3 | 4 | 5 | 5 | 9 | 11 | 13 |
| | $P_i + K_i$ | 31 | 35 | 14 | 28 | 18 | 19 | 38 | 43 |
| | $C_i$ | 31 | 35 | 14 | 28 | 18 | 19 | 2 | 7 |
| | Ciphertext | V | Z | E | S | I | J | 2 | 7 |
| Block 3 | Plaintext | 3 | 7 | 8 | 0 | 1 | 5 | 9 | 4 |
| | $P_i$ | 3 | 7 | 8 | 0 | 1 | 5 | 9 | 4 |
| | $K_i$ | 15 | 17 | 3 | 4 | 5 | 5 | 9 | 11 |
| | $P_i + K_i$ | 18 | 24 | 11 | 4 | 6 | 10 | 18 | 15 |
| | $C_i$ | 18 | 24 | 11 | 4 | 6 | 10 | 18 | 15 |
| | Ciphertext | I | O | B | 4 | 6 | A | I | F |

**Algorithm 2.** Encryption in Affine and Block Cipher

1. Let the plaintext $P = (P_i)$, $1 \leq i \leq h$
2. Divide $P$ into blocks of the chromatic number of the rainbow antimagic coloring of graphs $d$
3. For $i = 1$ to $\frac{h}{b}$, compute the ciphertext blocks using equation (3.4.1) and compute the plaintext blocks using equation (3.4.2)

$$C_n = (P_n + K_n)\,mod\,36 \qquad (3.4.1)$$

$$P_n = (C_n - K_n)\,mod\,36 \qquad (3.4.2)$$

where $P_n$, $K_n$, and $C_n$ are the $n$-th block of plaintext, key sequence, and ciphertext, respectively. Tables 8 and 9 exhibit how the keystream was obtained from Algorithm 1. It is utilized to encrypt the plaintext "ADINATADEWANDARU37801594" and yields the ciphertext "DHNSH4NSVZESIJ27IOB46AIF". The decryption process can be done in the reverse direction (Table 10).

### 3.5   *The instruments framework for assessing students' combinatorial thinking skills*

The following will present the instruments framework of combinatorial thinking skills assessment, see Table 11.

Table 10. Decryption process.

| Block 1 | Ciphertext | D | H | N | S | H | 4 | N | S |
|---|---|---|---|---|---|---|---|---|---|
| | $C_i$ | 13 | 17 | 23 | 28 | 19 | 4 | 23 | 28 |
| | $K_i$ | 3 | 4 | 5 | 5 | 9 | 11 | 13 | 15 |
| | $C_i - K_i$ | 10 | 13 | 18 | 23 | 10 | −7 | 10 | 13 |
| | $P_i$ | 10 | 13 | 18 | 23 | 10 | 29 | 10 | 13 |
| | Plaintext | A | D | I | N | A | T | A | D |
| Block 2 | Ciphertext | V | Z | E | S | I | J | 2 | 7 |
| | $C_i$ | 31 | 35 | 14 | 28 | 18 | 19 | 2 | 7 |
| | $K_i$ | 17 | 3 | 4 | 5 | 5 | 9 | 11 | 13 |
| | $C_i - K_i$ | 14 | 32 | 10 | 23 | 13 | 10 | −9 | −6 |
| | $P_i$ | 14 | 32 | 10 | 23 | 13 | 10 | 27 | 30 |
| | Plaintext | E | W | A | N | D | A | R | U |
| Block 3 | Ciphertext | I | O | B | 4 | 6 | A | I | F |
| | $C_i$ | 18 | 24 | 11 | 4 | 6 | 10 | 18 | 15 |
| | $K_i$ | 15 | 17 | 3 | 4 | 5 | 5 | 9 | 11 |
| | $C_i - K_i$ | 3 | 7 | 8 | 0 | 1 | 5 | 9 | 4 |
| | $P_i$ | 3 | 7 | 8 | 0 | 1 | 5 | 9 | 4 |
| | Plaintext | 3 | 7 | 8 | 0 | 1 | 5 | 9 | 4 |

Table 11. The framework of combinatorial thinking skills assessment instruments.

| Indicator | Sub-indicator | Test items |
|---|---|---|
| Identifying some cases | a. Identify the characteristic of the problems<br>b. Find out a breakthrough | a. Explain the types of online transaction data that can be abused<br>b. Discuss breakthroughs on how to avoid the abuse |
| Recognizing the pattern for all cases | a. Identify patterns of the case resolution<br>b. Extend the pattern for solving the bigger order of cases | a. Consider the breakthrough by using a rainbow antimagic coloring of graph<br>b. Choose a graph to find rainbow antimagic coloring of a graph by assigning the vertices of graph with $\{1,2,3,..., n\}$, where $n$ is the order of graph<br>c. Test the existence of a rainbow path, If so, consider the bigger order of graph |
| Generalizing all cases | a. Apply the mathematics symbolization<br>b. Test the accuracy and generalization<br>c. Develop an algorithm | a. Proceed whether the rainbow connection number is optimum? If so, proceed with the generalizations<br>b. Develop encryption using this rainbow antimagic coloring of online transaction data (plaintext) to produce a ciphertext<br>c. Develop decryption on obtained ciphertext by using this rainbow antimagic coloring<br>d. Develop a simple algorithm to handle the encryption/decryption of more complex online transaction data<br>e. Trying to test the accuracy of CryptoKey |
| Proving mathematically | a. Do a counting argument<br>b. Test the validity of the algorithm<br>c. Develop a bijection<br>d. Apply the inductive, deductive, and analytical proof | a. Define the sets of graph elements to determine the cardinality of the selected graph. Determine the number of vertices and edges to obtain the order and size<br>b. Determine the lower bound of the rainbow antimagic connection number based on the existing lemma<br>c. Determine the upper bound by developing the rainbow antimagic coloring function of the antimagic labeling of vertices<br>d. Evaluate the edge weights whether all edge weights induce the existence of a rainbow path according to the properties of rainbow antimagic coloring |

*(Continued)*

Table 12. The framework of combinatorial thinking skills assessment instruments (*Continues*)

| Indicator | Sub-indicator | Test items |
|---|---|---|
| | | e. Check the cardinality of the edge weight set to consider the rainbow antimagic connection number |
| | | f. Compare the lower and upper bounds, if it is the same then we can set this number as the rainbow antimagic connection number |
| | | g. Present the table consisting of the data of rainbow antimagic coloring path |
| | | h. Take an example of a graph with a certain order and size to illustrate its rainbow antimagic coloring |
| Considering the other combinatorial problems | a. Make an interpretation<br>b. Propose an open problem<br>c. Recognize a new problem<br>d. Find a potential conjecture for a new problem | a. Review the obtained results concerning the use of rainbow antimagic coloring of graph for a secure CryptoKey<br>b. Determine an open problem respected to the use of rainbow antimagic coloring of graph for a secure CryptoKey<br>c. Find other studies apart of the use of rainbow antimagic coloring of graph for a secure CryptoKey<br>d. Propose a conjecture regarded to considering another breakthrough for developing a secure CryptoKey |

## 4 DISCUSSION

The development of a framework for STEM-RBL learning activities in developing a secure CryptoKey by using the rainbow antimagic coloring of graphs to improve students' combinatorial thinking skills is very important, and it is as a starting point for R&D research format. This paper will be a guideline for researcher to do further action of the research. There are at least two more research activities that can be done further, namely: (1) developing STEM-RBL learning materials with the ADDIE development model and (2) studying the STEM-RBL learning materials in improvingthe students combinatorial thinking skills in developing a secure CryptoKey by using the rainbow antimagic coloring of graph. We can consider the learning activities that combine RBL-STEM is very effective in cultivating combinatorial thinking skills in students, it is in line with the research result presented in Maylisa et al. (2020), Ridlo et al. (2020a), and Septory et al. (2019). Thus the application in the learning process is very important. We predict that by integrating RBL-STEM for other science and social science problems, it will habituate students to find a good breakthrough toward a complex problem and it is the key for generating a good young generation for the future, namely a generation admitting a good 4C (creative-innovative, critical thinking, collaboration, and communication).

## 5 CONCLUSIONS

We have developed a framework of RBL-STEM learning activities in developing a secure CryptoKey by using the rainbow antimagic coloring of graph to improve students' combinatorial thinking skills. We consider that it is very important to do before carrying out further research activities, namely R& D and experimental research. However, this initial research is not so easy, thus joint research for other STEM cases needs to be explored and as well as the breakthrough for solving the STEM problems needs to be proposed.

## ACKNOWLEDGMENTS

We gratefully acknowledge the support from Combinatorics, Graph Theory, and Network Topology (CGANT) Research Group University of Jember, and the committee of the

6th International Conference on Education in Muslim Society (ICEMS) UIN Syarif Hidayatullah Jakarta Indonesia, of the year 2020.

## REFERENCES

Arifin, P. 2010. *Research-Based Learning, Prosiding Seminar Nasional*. Bandung: Institut Teknologi Bandung.

Baharin, N., Kamarudin, N. & Manaf, U.K.A. 2018. Integrating STEM Education Approach in Enhancing Higher Order Thinking Skills. *International Journal of Academic Research in Business and Social Sciences* 8(7): 810–822.

Branch, R.M. 2009. *Instructional design: The ADDIE approach*. New York: SpringerScience Business Media LCC.

Breiner, J.M., Harkness, S.S., Johnson, C.C. & Koehler, C.M. 2012. What is STEM? A Discussion About Conceptions of STEM in Education and Partnerships. *School Science and Mathematics* 112(1): 3–11.

Budi, H.S., Dafik, Tirta, I.M., Agustin, I.H. & Kristiana, A.I. 2021. On rainbow antimagic coloring of graphs. *Journal of Physics: Conference Series* 1832, 012016.

Chartrand, G., Johns G.L., McKeon, K.A. & Zhang P. 2008. Rainbow Connection in Graphs. *Mathematica Bohemica* 133: 85–98.

Dafik. 2016. *Handbook for the Implementation of RBL (Research-Based Learning) for the Courses*. Jember: University of Jember.

Dafik, Slamin & Muharromah, A. 2018. On The (Strong) Rainbow Vertex Connection of Graphs Resulting from Edge Comb Product. *Journal of Physics: Conference Series* 1008, 012055.

Dafik, Sucianto, B., Irvan, M. & Rohim, M.A. 2019. The analysis of student metacognition skill in solving rainbow connection problem under the implementation of research-based learning mode. *International Journal of Instruction* 12(4): 593–610.

Dini, R.P., Dafik & Slamin. 2019. The Analysis of Generalization Thinking Skills on Solving Local Super H-Decomposition Antimagic Total Coloring Regarding the Application of Research-Based Learning. *J. Phys.: Conf. Ser.* 1211, 012080

Estuhono, Festiyed & Bentri, A. 2019. Preliminary Research of Developing a Research-Based Learning Model Integrated by Scientific Approach on Physics Learning in Senior High School. *Phys.: Conf. Ser.* 1185.

Hastuti, Y., Dafik & Hobri. 2019 The Analysis of Student's Combinatorial Thinking Skill Based on Their Cognitive Style Under the Implementation of Research-Based Learning In The Total Rainbow Connection Study. *J. Phys.: Conf. Ser.* 1211, 012088.

Hidayatul, M., Dafik, Tirta, I.M., Wangguway, Y. & Suni, D.M.O. 2020. The Implementation of Research-Based Learning and The Effect to the Student Metacognition Thinking Skills in Solving H-Irregularity Problem. *J. Phys.: Conf. Ser.* 1538, 012113.

Jabbar, Z.L.A., Dafik, Adawiyah, R., Albirri, E.R., & Agustin, I.H. 2020. On rainbow Antimagic Coloring of Some Special Graph. *J. Phys.: Conf. Ser.* 1465, 012030.

Kusumawardani, I., Kristiana, A.I., Dafik & Alfarisi, R. 2019. On The Rainbow Antimagic Connection Number Of Some Wheel Related Graphs. *International Journal of Academic and Applied Research* 3(12): 60–64.

León, J., Núñez, J.L. & Liew, J. 2015. Self-Determination and STEM Education: Effects of Autonomy, Motivation, And Self-Regulated Learning on High School Math Achievement. *Learning and Individual Differences* 43: 156–163.

Maryati, T.K., Atiqoh, K.S.N., Nisviasari, R., Agustin, I.H., Dafik & Venkatachalam, M. 2020. The Construction of Block Cipher Encryption Key by Using a Local Super Antimagic Total Face Coloring. *Advance in Mathematics: Science Journal* 9(3): 1349–1362.

Maylisa, I.N., Dafik, Hadi, A.F., Wangguway, Y.& Harjito, L.O. 2020. The Influence of Research-Based Learning Implementation in Improving Students' Combinatorial Thinking Skills in Solving Local Irregularity Vertex r-Dynamic Coloring. *J. Phys.: Conf. Ser.* 1538, 012090.

Monalisa, L.A., Dafik, Hastuti, Y., Hussein, S.& Oktavianingtyas, E. 2019. The Implementation of Research-Based Learning in Developing the Students' Mathematical Generalization Thinking Skills in Solving a Paving Blocks Design Problem. *Earth and Environmental Science* 243(1).

Nazula, N.H., Dafik & Slamin. 2019. The Profile of Students' Creative Thinking Skills in Solving Local Antimagic Vertex Coloring Problem in Research-Based Learning. *J. Phys.: Conf. Ser.* 1211, 012109.

Nisviasari, R., Dafik, Agustin, I.H., Prihandini, R.M.& Maylisa, I.N. 2021. Local Super Anti-Magic Total Face Coloring on Shackle Graphs. *J. Phys.: Conf. Ser.* 1836 012022.

Prihandoko, A.C., Dafik & Agustin, I.H. 2019. Implementation of Super H-Antimagic Total Graph on Establishing Stream Cipher. *Indonesian Journal of Combinatorics* 3(1): 14–23.

Rezaie, M. & Zahra, G. 2011. What Do I Mean Combinatorial Thinking? *Procedia Social and Behavioral Sciences*: 122–126.

Ridlo, Z.R., Dafik, Prihandini, R.M., Nugroho, C.I.W. & Alfarisi, R. 2019. The Effectiveness of Research-Based Learning with Computer Programming and Highly Interactive Cloud Classroom (HIC) Elaboration in Improving Higher Order Thinking Skills in Solving a Combination of Wave Function. *J. Phys.: Conf. Ser.* 1211, 012049.

Ridlo, Z.R., Dafik & Nugroho, C.I.W. 2020a. Report and Recommendation of Implementation Research-Based Learning in Improving Combinatorial Thinking Skills Embedded in STEM Parachute Design Activities Assisted by CCR (Cloud Classroom). *Universal Journal of Educational Research* 8(4): 1413–1429.

Ridlo, Z.R., Dafik & Nugroho, C.I.W. 2020b. The Effectiveness of Implementation Research-Based Learning Model of Teaching Integrated with Cloud Classroom (CCR) to Improving Critical Thinking Skills in an Astronomy Course. *J. Phys.: Conf. Ser.* 1563, 012034.

Rohim, M.A., Dafik, Slamin & Sucianto, B. 2019. The Analysis of Implementation of Research-Based Learning Implementation in Developing the Students' Creative Thinking Skill in Solving Dominating Set Problem. *Earth and Environmental Science* 243, 012143.

Septory, B.J., Dafik & Tirta, I.M. 2019. The Analysis of Students' Combinatorial Thinking Skills in Solving r-Dynamic Vertex Coloring Under the Implementation of Problem Based Learning. *J. Phys.: Conf. Ser.* 1211(1).

Septory, B.J., Utoyo, M.I., Dafik, Sulistiyono, B. & Agustin, I.H. 2021. On rainbow Antimagic Coloring of Special Graphs. *J. Phys.: Conf. Ser.* 1836, 012016.

Sergis, S., Sampson, D.G., Rodríguez-Triana, M.J., Gillet, D., Pelliccione, L. & de Jong, T. 2017. Using Educational Data from Teaching and Learning to Inform Teachers' Reflective Educational Design in Inquiry-Based STEM Education. *Computers in Human Behavior* 92: 724–738.

Siregar, Y.E.Y., Rachmadtullah, R., Pohan, N., Rasmitadila & Zulela, M.S. 2019. The Impacts Of Science, Technology, Engineering, And Mathematics (STEM) On Critical Thinking In Elementary School. *J. Phys.: Conf. Ser.* 1175, 012156.

Siregar, N.C., Rosli, R., Maat, S.M. & Capraro, M.M. 2019. The Effect of Science, Technology, Engineering and Mathematics (STEM) Program on Students' Achievement in Mathematics: A Meta-Analysis. *International Electronic Journal of Mathematics Education* 15(1): 1–12.

Soros, P., Ponkham, K. & Ekkapim, S. 2018. The Results of STEM Education Methods for Enhancing Critical Thinking and Problem-Solving Skill in Physics the 10th Grade Level. *AIP Conference Proceedings* 1923(1), p 030045.

Sota, C. & Petzer, K. 2017. The Effectiveness of Research-Based Learning Among Master's Degree Student for Promotion and Preventable Discase. *Faculty of Public health, Khon Kaen University, Thailand Procedia-Social, and Behavioral Sciences* 237: 1359–1365.

Sulistiyono, B., Slamin, Dafik, Wangguway, Y. & Jabbar, A.Z.L. 2020a. Students' Creative-Innovative Thinking Skill in Solving Rainbow Research-Based Learning Model. *J. Phys.: Conf. Ser.* 1538, 012096.

Sulistiyono, B., Slamin, Dafik, Agustin, I.H. & Alfarisi, R. 2020b. On rainbow antimagic Coloring of Some Graphs. *J. Phys.: Conf. Ser.* 1465: 1–8.

Suntusia, Dafik & Hobri. 2019. The Effectiveness of Research-Based Learning in Improving Students' Achievement in Solving Two-Dimensional Arithmetic Sequence Problems. *International Journal of Instruction* 12(1).

Tohir, M.Z., Abidin, Dafik & Hobri. 2018. Students Creative Thinking Skills in Solving a Two Dimensional Arithmetic Series Through Research-Based Learning. *J. Phys.: Conf. Ser.* 1008, 012072.

Wahyuni, S.I., Dafik & Farisi, M.I. 2020. The Analysis of Learning Materials Implementation Based on Research-Based Learning to Improve the Elementary School Student's Creative Thinking Skills in Solving "Polamatika" Problems. *J. Phys.: Conf. Ser.* 1563, 012066.

Wangguway, Y., Slamin, Dafik, Maylisa, I.N. & Kurniawati, S. 2020. The Analysis of Research-Based Learning Implementation andits Effectto The Students Metacognition Skill in Solving a Resolving Domination Number of a Graph. *J. Phys.: Conf. Ser.* 1538, 012087.

Wardani, P.L., Dafik &Tirta, I.M. 2019. The Analysis of Research-Based Learning Implementation in Improving Students Conjecturing Skills in Solving Local Antimagic Vertex Dynamic Coloring. *J. Phys.: Conf. Ser.* 1211, 012090.

# Making choices during disruption – A resilient digital future for education?

J. Mason, K. Khan & F. Badar
*International Graduate Centre of Education, Charles Darwin University, Casuarina, Australia*

ABSTRACT:   The full impact of the 2020 pandemic is still emerging. Until this event, waves of 'digital disruption' also delivered widespread economic and social benefit. With Covid-19, we have been reminded that nature can be more disruptive. How should we respond? Harnessing digital technology for 'emergency remote education' has been an effective response for some; however, the gap of basic access to educational services has widened. We would not want to accept this as the 'new normal' and yet, returning to what was normal was not entirely satisfactory. Moreover, what happens if the next pandemic is digital, triggered by cyberwarfare? Meanwhile, innovation continues with advances in artificial intelligence, deployment of 'smart' systems, and the emergence of Industry 4.0. This paper considers these developments and questions arising such as, what choices must we make to recalibrate our education systems in ways to that align with the sustainable development goals articulated by UNESCO?

## 1  INTRODUCTION

As educational researchers focused on technology enabled learning prior to the outbreak of Covid-19, we were concerned with issues arising from 'post-truth' and the proliferation of misinformation in public discourse globally while recognising how innovations with digital technologies have far-reaching impact that can enable, disrupt, and transform (Khan & Mason 2019). This period has also been described in terms of human adaptability itself being challenged by accelerations and disruptions of technological advancement (Friedman 2016). Indeed, it is arguable that for the past few decades, digital disruption has been normalised. More broadly, global shifts in politics have also been impacted by digital innovations in data manipulation and surveillance, a growing distrust in 'the establishment', emergence of competing 'alternative realities', the normalisation of fake news and different shades of truth. In 2020, everything changed – the pandemic spread quickly, reminding us that we are biological beings living within ecosystems that adjust for disruption and disturbance.

As a direct result of Covid-19, the Australian Computer Society (2020) reported a 67% increase in business hour Internet traffic from the pre-pandemic baseline. Likewise, demand for internet servers increased by 30% globally (Heficed 2020). While 'post-truth' and data manipulation were prominent issues concerning the digital environment pre-Covid, these were largely displaced by the urgency of securing and maintaining connectivity. For the education sector, 'emergency remote education' quickly became the worldwide term describing the transition to online teaching and learning.

Covid-19 has not only disrupted education and economies worldwide but it has also been a catalyst to transform thinking, public policy, and the nature of global research. There is therefore a positive story to tell in relation to the affordances that innovation in digital technology has provided. But while it is true that digital technology has been instrumental in keeping us connected throughout the pandemic, it is also the case that for many young people in the world the opportunity to access education became a lot harder. According to reports from the United Nations (2020),

Table 1. Essential questions in pre- and post-Covid 21st century education.

| | |
|---|---|
| Pre-COVID | *What skills do educators need to develop to teach effectively in a data-driven world cluttered with misinformation?*<br>*What skills and competencies do our students need to function as informed and responsible global citizens?*<br>*How can we build a trustworthy digital infrastructure to support both informal and formal education?*<br>*What 'sensibilities' do we need to cultivate when engaging online as the fourth industrial revolution gets underway?*<br>*How can we draw on 'local wisdom' while embracing global imperatives in solving global problems?* |
| COVID & beyond | *How can we remain meaningfully socially connected while 'socially distanced'?*<br>*What policies are needed to ensure sustainability and resilience in our education systems?*<br>*How can we effectively collaborate across jurisdictions?*<br>*In what ways can we re-calibrate our education systems to minimise the 'digital divide' of educational opportunity?*<br>*How can we use open educational resources and practices to meet the challenge of SDG4 – quality education for all?*<br>*What happens if the next pandemic is digital?* |

nearly 1.6 billion children have been impacted. Such a situation calls for renewed efforts and a recalibration of priorities in public policy. Motivated by 'questions that matter' and a research interest in promoting 'essential questions' in teaching and learning (Wiggins & McTighue 2013) we identify several questions which require deeper investigation. Indicative of these questions are the questions presented in Table 1.

Such questions not only require considered responses but they will likely require us to make choices. There are of course many consequent questions, such as: *What regulatory changes are necessary to smoothly connect different jurisdictions and policies within in a global context that enable solutions? In what ways can we imagine and anticipate the challenges of the post-pandemic era? What will the 'next normal' look like?* Drawing on mixed research methods and supporting a presentation to the 6th International Conference on Education in Muslim Society (ICEMS 2020), this paper discusses several trends associated with the use of digital technology in education and issues emerging from them that might inform how we conceive of and develop our collective futures.

## 2 GLOBAL TRENDS IMPACTING LEARNING

### 2.1 *21st century skills*

Thinking about the future is what we routinely do; predicting it is typically foolish. However, anticipating a range of plausible scenarios informed by discerning options and emerging trends will help us meet it. There are of course many futures and navigating our way to preferred options will depend on the choices we make. In the closing decade of the twentieth century the famous futurist, Alvin Toffler (1991), argued that 'The illiterate of the 21st century will not be those who cannot read and write, but those who cannot learn, unlearn, and relearn'. Such a perspective is already evidenced in various curriculum frameworks all around the world, where the foundations of literacy and numeracy are now supplemented with descriptions of '21st Century Skills', commonly summarised as comprising the four core competencies ('4Cs') – communication, critical thinking, collaboration, and creativity – supplemented by digital literacy and global citizenship skills. Significantly, this terminology is also prominent outside educational literature (Soffel 2016). Thus, when grappling with global issues it is sometimes useful to consider perspectives articulated by agencies such as UNESCO:

> If we are to imagine new ways of knowing, being, living, doing, giving and sharing as well as transforming oneself and society, we must be capable of assessing and bringing about social change, raising consciousness, engaging in critical reflection and discourse. In other words, the learner should be able to think and act "out of the box", rather than merely replicate what is "found in the box." The focus of twentieth century schooling has been on the latter goal, contributing to the great majority of students feeling ultimately frustrated and bored. School systems worldwide have adopted a manipulative instead of an empowering and emancipatory pedagogy and a prescribed, vertically structured and overloaded curriculum that does not reflect what is happening outside the school (2020, p. 144).

Such perspectives are expressed in various ways and the broad discourse on this topic is replete with frameworks and models that aim to communicate the essence of the challenge facing education worldwide. Other important examples are provided by the OECD (2020), in which knowledge, skills, attitudes, and values are conceived as the foundations of a holistic education within and beyond the classroom that supports and promotes well-being. Terminology is of course just an indicator, and each of these four facets is elaborated in detail in the *OECD Learning Compass 2030*. In related research, and in response to the emergence of 'post-truth', we have also identified discernment skills associated with handling and interpreting data and information as essential (Mason Khan & Smith 2016).

## 2.2 *The digital revolution*

Thinking about the future is also informed by reflecting on the past. Literature concerning the transformative impact of digital technologies on education goes back to the early 1980s and is cross-disciplinary in its reach – spanning fields such as educational philosophy, learning theory, computer science, information science, learning science, human computer interaction, data science, and others (Mason & Pillay 2015). This digital revolution began when personal computers first entered classrooms, soon followed by the use of multimedia materials stored on compact discs. Shortly after, the worldwide web was invented and this accelerated the pace of change. Several waves of innovation proceeded and can be characterised in terms of the kinds of technologies driving change: search, social, and smart (Freestone & Mason 2019). In the early phases of each of these periods of change, also commonly described as 'disruption', widespread adoption also signalled widespread empowerment. While it is the case that technological revolution has often been accompanied by dystopian commentaries, such perspective was in the margins of social discourse for much of this period. In other words, most people enjoyed the affordances of digital technology despite the disruption. This has been the case until recent years with the advent of big data, 'post-truth', 'fake news', and misinformation proliferating on the web – as well as the development of surveillance technologies and smart technologies based on 'black box' algorithms (Madsbjerg 2017; Zuboff 2015). These developments have also been a trigger for political turmoil and 'disruption fatigue' (Bryant et al. 2014; Christensen Raynor & McDonald 2015). Quoting Eric Teller, Friedman (2016) describes the historical moment we are entering with exponential disruptions and accelerations that together are widening the gap between the rate of change and human adaptability. It is likely, then, that dystopian accounts of our future will also increase (Selwyn 2016).

## 2.3 *The fourth industrial revolution*

In parallel with the pandemic and the digital revolution has been emergence of the fourth industrial revolution following Klaus Schwab (2016) of the World Economic Forum coining the term. This terminology shifts the focus from the technology to its application and reaches beyond the benefits of automation that preceding industrial revolutions delivered, introducing terms like 'cyberphysical systems' to represent a fusion or blurring of boundaries between biological, physical and digital domains. Of course, technologies are still prominent and are driving the change – technologies such as artificial intelligence, machine learning, the Internet of Things, quantum computing, robotics and even engineered intelligence are representative of this emerging era. Such innovation is sure to disrupt.

Historically, the first industrial revolution delivered mechanization at scale through water and steam power; the second used electricity to drive mass production; the third used computers to control sophisticated tasks and large mechanical systems, transferring physical and repeatable jobs to machines. With the fourth revolution, machines are interoperating with other machines, creating 'smart' and autonomous systems driven by large volumes of data and sophisticated algorithms. This fourth industrial revolution means that machines are also becoming 'learners'. So, it is no surprise that public discourse is turning its attention to the ethics of these developments (Charisi et al. 2017; Firlej et al. 2020; Jobin et al. 2019). Covid-19 has added further complexity into the emerging ethical dilemmas and the choices we make in the near-future will likely have far-reaching consequences for decades.

## 2.4 *Deepening divides*

Not so long ago the 'digital divide' was terminology used to describe inequity of access to the benefits of the digital revolution. With the invention of the smartphone, the trendlines showed some promise for a while with mobile telephony networks enabling rapid entry and access (Summers et al. 2018). Due to Covid-19, however, social and digital divides are widening the gap for the most disadvantaged, diminishing learning outcomes for school-age children in terms of what they learn, know, and do. An estimated 258 million children, adolescents, and youth, or 17% of the global total, were not in school prior to the pandemic. Most of these were from the poorest backgrounds of the world and the worst impacted are underprivileged children (Winthrop & McGivney 2015). Prior to the pandemic it was estimated that by 2030 more than half of the world's 2 billion children will not be able to acquire their basic secondary level learning skills, and approximately 9 out of 10 children from low-income countries are anticipated to reach their adulthood without the skills they need to progress (The Learning Generation 2016). With Covid-19, the numbers are now at alarming levels (Badar & Mason 2020).

In low- and middle-income countries, adolescents from the richest 20% households are three times as likely as those from the poorest to complete lower secondary school and in at least 20 countries, hardly any poor rural young women complete secondary school. The Programme for International Student Assessment (PISA) 2018 results showed that gender and socio-economic status are associated with wide variation in reading and mathematics proficiency among 15-year-olds, primarily due to socio-economic processes that marginalize, disappoint and alienate scores of children, youth and adults (UNESCO 2020).

With over 90% of learners affected worldwide, Covid-19 represents a global crisis that has triggered an unprecedented shift in educational practices on a global scale. The key challenge for policymakers is how to continuity of formal learning during this disruption. The education deprived majority of the world has been pushed further away from their counterparts who continue their learning. Children in many low- and middle-income countries have been left behind as their governments and education systems have not been able to adequately respond to an unprecedented need for a robust digital ecosystem for learning supported by skilled educators. Covid-19 has accentuated the need for real-world technology-assisted learning solutions for the poor. Together with the health crisis of Covid-19 itself, this educational crisis is now emerging as a most urgent global problem (Petrie et al. 2020).

## 2.5 *Open educational resources and practices*

Not long after the change in millennium UNESCO was at the forefront of recognising the significance of 'openness' underpinning the worldwide digital infrastructure when it coined the term 'open educational resources' (OER) to describe educational resources (content and software) freely available on the web. In recent years, discourse in this area has also embrace the notion of Open Educational Practices (OEP) to signify the potential for wider impact on learning (Cox & Trotter

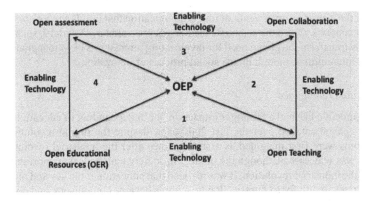

Figure 1.   OEP framework for open education (Huang et al. 2020, p. 10).

2017; DeRosa & Robison 2017; Ehlers 2011; Schuwer & Janssen 2018). OEP implementation, however, is a relatively complex process as it requires transformation of the educational ecosystem – changing mindsets, values and attitudes of stakeholders towards developing a culture of openness. A comprehensive review of OEP definitions by Huang et al. (2020) resulted in emphasis on encouraging flexible learning options for students and five conditions for effective implementation: open educational resources, open teaching, open collaboration, open assessment and enabling technology as show in Figure 1.

UNESCO (2020a) now recommends building open and inclusive knowledge societies to achieve SDG-4 objectives, by shifting the focus from OER to broader implementation and actions with five target areas for action:

   i.   Build the capacity of stakeholders to find, re-use, create and share OER;
  ii.   Develop supportive policy;
 iii.   Ensure inclusive and equitable access to quality OER;
  iv.   Nurture the creation of sustainability business models for OER; and
   v.   Facilitate international cooperation.

The above recommendations and framework can effectively contribute to building open and inclusive knowledge societies and to achieving SDGs, especially SDG4 (inclusive and equitable quality education and promotes lifelong learning opportunities for all). In the following section, we further propose some future directions that may also achieve these objectives.

## 2.6   The web – A local collaborative solution space

With education worldwide moving to a digital space key question arise such as how to deal with learning gaps and cognitive hurdles within the digital environment. How can students develop creative skills to innovate and collaboratively solve problems in local contexts? We suggest using the Web as a local collaborative solution space. The creation of small digital hubs of critical learners within different geographical and physical spaces can create an environment for designing innovative and *local* digital solutions that work (for them). Online communities can thrive as spaces where learners share their (common) struggles, frustrations, ideas, strategies in a risk-free environment. The challenge for educators is to develop the facilitation skills for this to take place. The work of Salmon (2009), for example, represents very practical guidance to achieve such outcomes.

Similarly, the goals of interdisciplinary STEM education could be strengthened through the integration of collaborative problem-solving skills. As such, STEM education can draw strength from the richness of having a variety of learners, varying styles of thinking, and a diversity of cultural and educational backgrounds. We can utilize our students' combined thinking through the potentialities of the web as an open medium for communication that builds a repository of solutions within different contexts. Given the scientific challenges presented by Covid-19, such an approach could potentially transform the global need for invigorating interest in STEM to include a discovery process into an intercultural, more humane social process of innovation.

### 2.7 *The classroom reimagined*

Arguably, the pandemic has had a far larger impact on our understanding of education and schools than any other change catalyst over the last 200 years, despite the digital revolution. Many of today's classrooms were first imagined as assembly lines after the industrial revolution. Prior to 1800, illiteracy was widespread, though the poorest in society had the least opportunity to change this. Following the industrial revolution, it was realized that education is the key and most important driver that generates wealth for a country. Slowly, schools became compulsory, and poorer children could go to school. Classrooms imagined as assembly lines were where future workers were to be prepared. This was a positive economic impact because with education adults became better at work. The system worked well despite challenges such as skills shortages in certain areas. The pandemic has challenged this status quo, in some jurisdictions dramatically. Covid-19 has rendered schools vacant, teachers have lost their physical classrooms, students have lost their social engagement, exercise and sports opportunities. With lockdowns and social distancing, there has been an added impact on mental and health issues. This scenario may again occur in future – so it is imperative we learn from this.

Now that virtual classrooms have gained some real-world traction and acceptance, there is an opportunity to continue to reimagine. Such classrooms urgently need educators skilled in online learning pedagogies. This is a crucial moment in history – the choices we make in responding to the challenges will determine the characteristics of our education systems into the future.

## 3    CONCLUSION

The lockdowns and isolation at home caused by Covid-19 has provided impetus for virtual classrooms to be at least as effective as the classrooms of the past, potentially more so. The widespread disruption of the pandemic has highlighted weaknesses of our existing educational systems while also providing opportunities to change for the better.

In August 2020, the United Nations published a Policy Brief '*Education during COVID-19 and beyond*'. The four recommendations within it are restated here because they bring a concise focus in guiding responses to the issues raised in this paper:

– Suppress Transmission of the Virus & Plan Thoroughly for School Re-openings
– Protect Education Financing & Coordinate for Impact
– Build Resilient Education Systems for Equitable & Sustainable Development
– Reimagine Education & Accelerate Change in Teaching and Learning

REFERENCES

Australian Broadcasting Corporation, 2020. Minister Backflips on MyGov Cyber Attack Claims, As Long Queues Form Outside Centrelink Offices. https://www.abc.net.au/news/2020-03-23/mygov-website-down-centrelink-massive-queues-coronavirus/12080558
Australian Computer Society, 2020. Australia's Digital Pulse 2020. https://www.acs.org.au/insightsand publications/reports-publications/digital-pulse-2020.html
Bryant, P., Coombs, A., Pazio, M. and Walker, S., 2014. Disruption, destruction, construction or transformation? The challenges of implementing a university wide strategic approach to connecting in an open world. University of Greenwich.
Charisi, V., Dennis, L., Fisher, M., Lieck, R., Matthias, A., Slavkovik, M., Sombetzki, J., Winfield, A.F. and Yampolskiy, R., 2017. *Towards moral autonomous systems*. arXiv preprint arXiv:1703.04741

Christensen, C.M., Raynor, M.E. and McDonald, R., 2015. What is disruptive innovation. *Harvard Business Review, 93*(12), 44–53.

Cox, G. and Trotter, H., 2017. Factors shaping lecturers' adoption of OER at three South African universities. Dans C. Hodgkinson-Williams & P. Arinto (Eds.), *Adoption and impact of OER in the Global South*, 287–347.

Ehlers, U.-D., 2011. Extending the territory: From Open Educational Resources to Open Educational Practices. *Journal of Open, Flexible, and Distance Learning, 15*(2), 1–10.

Jobin, A., Ienca, M. and Vayena, E., 2019. The global landscape of AI ethics guidelines. *Nature Machine Intelligence, 1*(9), 389–399.

Mason, J. and Freestone, M.B., 2019. Questions in smart digital environments. *Frontiers in Education 4.*

Mason, J. and Pillay, H., 2015. Opening digital learning for deeper inquiry. *International Handbook of E-Learning Volume 2* 29–38. Routledge.

Friedman, T.L., 2016. *Thank you for Being Late: an Optimist's Guide to Thriving in the Age of Accelerations.* USA: Macmillan.

Heficed, 2020. Internet Infrastructure Demand Rises During COVID-19 Pandemic By 30 Percent https://www.heficed.com/press-releases/internet-infrastructure-demand-rises-during-covid-19-pandemic-by-30-percent.

Huang, R., Liu, D., Tlili, A., Knyazeva, S., Chang, T.W., Zhang, X., Burgos, D., Jemni, M., Zhang, M., Zhuang, R., and Holotescu, C., 2020. Guidance on Open Educational Practices during School Closures: Utilizing OER under COVID-19 Pandemic in line with UNESCO OER Recommendation. Beijing

Khan, K. and Mason, J., 2019. Examining the data to identify essential questions-guilty before innocent. *International Journal of Smart Technology and Learning, 1*(3), 244–266.

Madsbjerg, C., 2017. *Sensemaking: The Power of the Humanities in the Age of the Algorithm.* USA: Hachette Books.

Mason, J., Khan, K. and Smith, S., 2016. Literate, numerate, discriminate—realigning 21st century skills. *Proceedings of the 24th international conference on computers in education* (pp. 609–614). Asia-Pacific Society for Computers in Education.

OECD, 2020. The OECD Learning Compass 2030. The Organisation for Economic Co-operation and Development. http://www.oecd.org/education/2030-project/teaching-and-learning/learning/learning-compass-2030/in_brief_Learning_Compass.pdf.

Ossiannilsson, E., 2018. Ecologies of Openness: Reformations through Open Pedagogy. *Asian Journal of Distance Education, 2*, 103–119.

Ossiannilsson, E., 2019. OER and OEP for access, equity, equality, quality, inclusiveness, and empowering lifelong learning. *International Journal of Open Educational Resources, 1*(2).

Petrie, C., Aladin, K., Ranjan, P., et al., 2020. Spotlight: Quality education for all during Covid-19 crisis. (Report No. #011). Hundred.org. https://hundred-cdn.s3.amazonaws.com/uploads/report/file/15/hundred_spotlight_covid-19_digital.pdf.

Salmon, G., 2009. E-moderating. *Encyclopedia of Distance Learning*, 2nd Edition, 890-897. IGI Global.

Schwab, K., 2016. *Shaping the Future of the Fourth Industrial Revolution.* Great Britain: Penguin.

Selwyn, N., 2016. The dystopian futures. In N. Rushby, & D.N. Surry (Eds), *The Wiley Handbook of Learning Technology*, 542–556.

Soffel, J., 2016. What are the 21st-century skills every student needs? World Economic Forum. https://www.weforum.org/agenda/2016/03/21st-century-skills-future-jobs-students/

Summers, K., Alton, N., Haraseyko, A. and Sherard, R., 2018. Bridging the Digital Divide: One Smartphone at a Time, in A. Marcus, & W. Wang (Eds.), *Design, User Experience, and Usability: Designing Interactions, Lecture Notes in Computer Science.* Springer International Publishing, Cham, 653–672.

Toffler, A., 1991. *Powershift: Knowledge, Wealth, and Violence at the End of the 21st Century.* New York, NY: Bantam Books.

UNESCO, 2020. Global education monitoring report, 2020: Inclusion and education: all means all. https://unesdoc.unesco.org/ark:/48223/pf0000373718

United Nations, 2020. Policy Brief: Education during COVID-19 and beyond. https://www.un.org/development/desa/dspd/wp-content/uploads/sites/22/2020/08/sg_policy_brief_covid-19_and_education_august_2020.pdf

Wiggins, G. and McTighue, J., 2013. *Essential Questions: Opening Doors to Student Understanding.* ASCD: Alexandria, VA.

Zuboff, S., 2015. Big other: surveillance capitalism and the prospects of an information civilization. *Journal of Information Technology, 30*(1), 75–89.

# Emerging trends in technology of education in an uncertain world: Developing digital competences in dealing with the current challenges in education

A. Mu'ti
*Islamic State University of Syarif Hidayatullah, Tangerang, Banten, Indonesia*

R.A. Amirachman
*Sultan Ageng Tirtayasa University, Serang, Banten, Indonesia*

ABSTRACT:    It is inevitable that industry revolution 4.0 has tremendous impact on various aspects of life including education sector. With the evolving artificial intelligence and internet of things, for example, almost everything is now becoming digitalized in order to make the teaching and learning at ease for both teachers and students. While things are getting more positively personalized and pedagogically efficient, shallowness and eclecticism also seem to have become everyday human behavior, which could have an impact on educational outcome. Educational institutions cannot escape from these changing values and must adapt accordingly in order to make the best use of this development and mitigate the unexpected downside. Internet-based distance learning mode, for example, is another development that educational institutions need to prepare both conceptually and practically. Likewise, this might have a further impact on religion education as internalization and practice of religious values and norms could somehow be disrupted. The next task is that there is a need to breakdown what is now called 'digital competence' in order to fittingly utilize this technological development to help face the current challenges in education.

*Keywords*:    educational technology, emerging trends, digital competences.

## 1 INTRODUCTION

It is inescapable that industry revolution 4.0 has tremendous impact on various aspects of life including education sector. With the evolving artificial intelligence and internet of things, for example, almost everything is now becoming digitalized in order to make the teaching and learning at ease for both teachers and students. Even then, since early eighties, educationalists have tried to continuously improve communication technologies as they realize that the interconnectivity offered by these technologies could have promising impact on educational process and outcome if well managed. Furthermore, the Covid-19, which forced millions of students around the world to learn from home to mitigate the deadly impact of the virus, has tremendously accelerated these changes. People seem to have no choice but to embrace educational technologies. While things are getting more positively personalized and pedagogically efficient, shallowness and eclecticism also seem to have become everyday human behavior, which could have an impact on educational outcome. Educational institutions cannot escape from these changing values and must adapt accordingly in order to make the best use of this development and mitigate the unexpected downside. Internet-based distance learning mode, for example, is another development that educational institutions need to prepare both conceptually and practically. Likewise, in the area of religion and character education, for example, this could also have a significant impact as internalization and practice of religious values and norms could somehow be disrupted. Hence, there is a need to elaborate more on what is called 'digital competence' in order to fittingly utilize this technological development

DOI 10.1201/9781003219248-5

to maximize its benefit and to mitigate the unexpected consequences in helping face the current challenges in education.

## 2 HISTORICAL AND CURRENT DEVELOPMENT OF EDUCATIONAL TECHNOLOGY

While there are still persistent challenges with regard to technological access, the benefit of using technology, in this case information and communication technology (ICT), in education sector has so far been proven. Rotolo et al. (2015) elaborated five attributes of educational technology, which is currently being developed: far-reaching innovation, relatively fast development, consistency, conspicuous impact, but also uncertainty and vagueness. Educationalists have increasingly realized that while educational technology has the potential to improve the convenience of teaching and learning, it also demands students' engagement in order to result in useful outcome of learning instruction and process. Hence, what is important is to ensure that educational technology can encourage student's problem-solving skills, critical inquiry and also to make sure that meaningful teaching and learning process are taking place accordingly. While the advantage of using technology in education is incontestable, educationalists need to precisely identify what is useful and what is not suitable in utilizing this technology in order to reach their pedagogical goals (Chanunan & Bruckner 2017).

Nevertheless, there seems to be an increasing gap between research in educational technology and the implementation in the education sector. In developed countries, significant amount of money has been spent in advancing educational technology with the expectation that computer system would function as a frontend to help students in the learning process. As a result, various researches have been conducted in touching advanced issues such as intelligent tutoring, simulation, advanced leaning management system and programmed assessment systems. Unfortunately, educationalists are unable to catch up with fast research development; hence, there is an increasing gap between research and implementation, particularly to make sure that educationalists are taking advantage of these researches to support the pedagogical process. For example, for the last two and three decades, emerging technology research activities have received very little input from educationalists. Educationalists have played insignificant roles as mostly computers scientists and alike who are taking a leading role in the research activities. It is true that academics from other disciplines including educational experts are invited; however, it is mostly done to extract their knowledge to be replaced by the machine (Kinshuk et al. 2013). With this situation, it justifiable to worry that pedagogical aspects such as critical thinking, meaningful learning experience and even character building are not taken into account during the research process.

Despite the apparent gap between the research and implementation, educational technology has been used significantly to support mode of pedagogical deliveries, one of them is distance education. Distance mode of learning itself, which is used to widen educational access and to make teaching and learning more effective and efficient, is not something new to education sector. It has continued to develop in line with the formation of associations at the international and regional levels. At the international level, along with the increasing demands to expand access to education through distance education, the International Council for Distance Education (ICDE) was formed in Norway in 1938. The United Nations Educational, Scientific and Cultural Organizations (UNESCO) since its inception in 1945 has also paid attention to distance education through various technical activities, standard setting, innovative projects, capacity building and networking (Kusmawan & Belawati 2010).

At the regional level, the Asian Association of Open Universities (AAOU) was formed by seven universities in Asia in 1987. Similar organizations were also established such as the African Distance Education Association (ADLA), Canadian Association for Distance Education (CADE), European Association of Distance Teaching Universities (EADTU), Open and Distance Education of Australia (EADTU), United States Distance Education (USDLA). The Southeast Asian Ministers of Education Organization (SEAMEO), which was founded in 1965, also formed the Southeast Asian Ministers of Education Organizations Regional Open Learning Center (SEAMOLEC) which pays attention to the development of distance education in Southeast Asia including in Indonesia (Kusmawan & Belawati 2010).

International Council on Open and Distance Education (ICDE) reported that Asia, as the region with the largest population, needs to respond to global needs. The first issue revolves around access, equity and quality learning outcomes. The second is the rapidly changing working environment, changing skills requirements that are needed by industry and the labor force will have a close relationship between academia and industry. The third is student mobility between countries in Asia, especially at the university level. The fourth is a redefinition of 21st century skills. The deepening of these skills shows that it is necessary to include ethical values, digital citizenship, independent learning, a sense of responsibility, effective time management and integrated learning (Bandalaria 2018).

In ASEAN countries, ICT-based education is also growing rapidly. In Brunei Darussalam, for example, the program, e-Education, consists of Edunet, e-Learning, Education Information System, Digital Library, and Human Capacity Building. One of the pillars of the program, e-Education, is a system that directly helps the implementation of the right technology concepts to enrich new dimensions in the learning and teaching environment (Akbar 2010). In Vietnam, most cities and provinces have implemented digital technology developments in universities and schools. Most schools and hospitals are connected to the internet (Que & Vuong 2010, p. 93–95). In Cambodia, the Open Schools Program (OSP) has changed the map of ICT development in the country. Through this program, the Ministry of Youth and Sports Education of the Government of Cambodia has developed a Master Plan for ICT in Education which will ensure efficient and harmonious development of ICT for education (Sethy 2010, p. 10).

Along with the development of distance education at the international and regional levels, the Government of Indonesia established Open University in 1984. Initially, learning was given in the form of printed modules sent to students and tutorials were held conventionally. With the development of ICT, most of these services are delivered digitally. In one study, it was stated that the participation of students and lecturers was increasing and the administration of open education was more flexible with the use of ICT (Adji et al. 2011, p. 21–40). Not only public universities, e-learning based private universities are also developing. One of them that is currently growing rapidly is Universitas Bina Nusantara, which was established in 1998 (BINUS 2020). In addition, Multimedia Nusantara University was also established in 2006, which was founded by the Kompas Gramedia Group with a main focus on the field of ICT (Panen 2016; UMN 2020).

Not only at the tertiary level, distance education is also developed at the secondary education level. Indonesia's Ministry of Education and Culture introduced distance education at the secondary school level by providing a regulatory basis and guidelines for the implementation of open and long-distance which could be used as a reference for implementing the government's top priorities in developing human resources. The government of West Java province, for example, has massively implemented distance learning program for both regular senior high school and vocational high school in order to increase access and school enrolment. Several schools have used ICT-based distance education to improve the convenience of teaching and learning activities.

Currently, the implementation of ICT-based education is also gaining momentum with the Covid-19 outbreak, where students are required to study from home. According to the UNESCO report (2020) 1,543,446,152 students or 89% of the total students in 188 countries are forced to skip school and study from home. In Indonesia alone, 68,265,787 students are forced to study from home. Therefore, educationalists have no choice but to embrace online-based distance education in order to continue teaching and learning activities. Educational institutions need to prepare both conceptually and practically to make the best use of online learning.

## 3    THE OPPORTUNITIES AND CHALLENGES OF ONLINE LEARNING

Google for Education (2020) reported that there are at least eight emerging trends in educational technology, as which can be deemed as both opportunities and challenges in making the best use of technology for education, namely digital responsibility, life skills and workforce preparation, computational thinking, student-led learning, connecting guardian and schools, innovating pedagogy, and emerging technologies.

## 3.1  *Digital responsibility*

It was reported that even parents who work in Silicon Valles decided to raise their children without gadget and send them to technology free schools. Alarmingly, children under 18 account for approximately one in three Internet users worldwide. In the US, over than 39% of young people registered themselves to have social media account at the age of 12 years old, even more than 46% in the UK. This situation reminded educationalists the importance to create a healthy and sensible relations with technology. In this case, Pederson et al. (2018) proposed a revisit to the concept of digital citizenship by focusing on three interconnected philosophical substructures: "becoming, belonging and the capabilities to do so" (p. 234). Sklar (2017) conceptualizes "digital hygiene", which integrates digital technology into people's lives in "safe, healthy, responsible, and respectful ways" (p. 39).

In Indonesia's context, the government has tried to regulate a number of measures aimed at ensuring the security of individuals' personal data through Government Regulation No. 82 of 2012 on the Implementation of Electronic Systems and Transaction Providers, as well as Ministry of Communication Regulation No. 20 of 2016 concerning Personal Data Protection in Electronic Systems. Socarana …wrote that these regulations cover the concerned stakeholders, particularly corporations, as the controllers of data. The regulatory framework addresses various issues starting from the requirement to provide breach notifications, implement accountable data-polity mechanisms and many more. These regulations work in combination with other provisions including Law No. 8 of 1999 in Consumer Protection (Consumer Protection Law), as well as Law No. 11 of 2008 on Electronic Information and Transactions, which was most amended through the issuance of Law No. 19 of 2016 (EIT Law).

Nevertheless, it is not enough to have only the implementation of mere compliance of the law. A number of complaints deriving from consumers who have become the target or product marketing activities without their consents show the complication of the issue. Greater efforts are needed from the corporations as it reveals that there are cases of face accounts, the non-consensual transfer of personal data and many other incidents, which show the vulnerability of the consumers. It is clear that corporations have an inevitable responsibility to deal with these alarming issues and what they have been currently doing is certainly insufficient. There are principally three areas that corporations need to be responsible: the responsibility to educate, the responsibility to provide adequate safety measures and the responsibility to be accountable (Socarana 2018).

Many countries including Indonesia have invested significantly to equip schools with ICTs. However, mere investment is not enough, ICTs need to be integrated meaningfully into teaching and learning processes and students as well as parents need to be equipped to suitable skills and competences to be efficient and responsible actors in the increasingly digitalized environment. Young people, particularly, need to learn digital skills from the earliest age and continue throughout life. Learning the aspects related to robotics, coding, cybersecurity, blockchain and artificial intelligence will serve as a foundation for their future education. There is a need to establish a minimum level of digital competences among students, underlining the importance of respecting, protecting and fulfilling and the right of the child in the digital environment and the promotion and development of digital literacy (Parliamentary Assembly Council of Europe 2019).

## 3.2  *Life skills and workforce preparation*

Expectation is now much put on soft skills, not only on cognitive aspect, since better leadership and ability to deal with pressure also attribute to emotional intelligence. This means that people are vying for a more holistic education that covers general life skills, which means that academic achievement is no longer regarded as the only road towards success in the future. Borner et al. (2018) finding suggested that there is an "increasing importance of uniquely human skills, such as communication, negotiation, and persuasion... In an increasingly data-driven economy, the demand for 'soft' social skills, like teamwork and communication, increase with greater demand for 'hard' technical skills and tools" (p. 12630).

Social skills are regarded as an assumption of a healthy social life, which are needed to pursue personal sovereignty, ability to adjust to specific social circumstances, to express themselves and comprehend other people Jurevičienė et al. (2018) wrote that with social skills, someone is expected to be able to act effectively in a social environment and an supposition of a successful socialization. Someone's social functionality and the quality of social situation's management are obviously determined by social skills, which also contribute to a great influence on the quality of someone's personal traits and social life. These social skills would enable individuals to communicate and interact effectively and efficiently with other people in various circumstances. Hence, social skills are an important prerequisite for a harmonious existence in a society.

The flawless way of performing actions based on the knowledge, abilities and skills means a competence; hence, skill is regarded as the highest level of performance of the action. The ability to apply the skills is the bridging link between skills and competence. Someone's personal competence is intimately related to the correct social skills and social abilities. Not only in social functioning domains of skills of personal relationships, communication, collaboration; social competence also extends to the area self-management or skills of problem solving. In other words, social competence can be seen as social intuitions skills, successful communication and constructive relations with other people. When people carry out certain roles in society, their social skills become obvious in determining the success of their social interaction. Social skills are also regarded as the degree of personality, in which personal social knowledge and ability to manage social interaction are demonstrated (Jurevičienė, Kaffemanienė et al. 2018).

The development of these social skills is regarded important as part of workforce preparation. The idea of preparing youth for workforce has taken on new meaning as there has been a widespread concern that young graduates are not well equipped with the skills that employers values most such as critical thinking, communication, leadership and collaborative skills. With the shift towards a knowledge economy, adolescents are expected to master these skills to help them with the transitional period to workforce. Almost all attention for the nurturing of these skills focus on mere school-based reforms, but youth programs have the potential to contribute to greater impact by paying more attention to the nature of positive youth development and workforce preparation since learning naturally encompasses both school day and after school hours (Cochran & Ferrari 2009).

## 3.3 *Computational thinking*

There is an increasing demand that students are expected to acquire problem solving besides digital skills to make them more prepared for the future. Science, technology, engineering and mathematics (STEM) education is increasingly regarded as important to prepare students for future technological challenges, in this case educationalists begin to develop toolkit of technical skills such problem solving, coding and adequate comprehension of STEM subjects. For example, Garcia-Penalvo et al. (2018) said that it is important to explore the upshot of the experiences of coding, robots, game-based learning into secondary education students with focus on computational thinking to develop reflective and critical thinking.

Wing (2011) defined computational thinking as "the thought processes involved in formulating problems and their solutions so that the solutions are represented in a form that can be effectively carried out by an information-processing agent" (in Cansu & Cansu 2019, p. 2). Based on the aforementioned definition, Cansu and Cansu (2019) wrote that computational thinking is meant to improve cognitive aspect and support the processes of teaching and learning of both teachers and students. Essentially, computational thinking abilities are the set of skills to translate compli-cated, segregated, partially explained, tangible day-to-day problems into a form that a mechanical computer can handle without human assistance. Among the pertinent components are abstraction, problem decomposition, algorithmic thinking, automation and generalization.

Abstraction is "the process of making an artefact more understandable through reducing the unnecessary detail and number of variable; therefore leading to more straightforward solutions"; problem decomposition is "a method for taking apart problems and breaking them into smaller and more understandable constituents"; algorithmic thinking is "the process of constructing a scheme of ordered steps which may be followed to provide solutions to all constituent problems necessary to solve the original problem"; automation is "the configuration of formed algorithms over computers and technological resources to be efficiently applicable to other problems"; and generalization "is the process of adapting formulated solutions or algorithms into different problem states, even if the variables involved are different" (Cansu & Cansu 2019, p. 4–5).

## 3.4 *Student-led learning*

In order to help students undergo the transition period from schools to larger society, student agency has increasingly become a prerequisite. A study by Gallagher et al. (2016) explored the Learning and Engagement Questionnaire (LEQ), which is used to measure environmental variables to associated with student engagement, to provoke teachers' awareness of the strategies to facilitate inclusive practice via various forms of students engagement. Fifth, collaborative classrooms. Educationalists have begun to redesign classrooms in terms of color, lighting, acoustics and spatial management to match with current schools' focus on openness, flexibility and collaboration. Hod (2017) underlined the importance for school designer to be directed by lessons learned from specific research to ensure that the design meets the pedagogical goal of the innovation age.

The pedagogical power has moved from the teacher to the student as the paradigm shift away from teaching to an emphasis on learning. Criticism has amounted against teacher-focused of information mechanism such as lecturing, paving the way for prevalent development of 'student-centered learning' as an alternative method. However, while many educational institutions have claimed to have adopted this new approach, the reality actually tells otherwise (O'Neill 2005). In this case, much needs to be done to make sure that this new approach has really been adopted by educationalists. Leat et al. (2003, p. 322 in O'Neill 2005) summarizes some of the literature on student-centered learning to cover the following creeds: 1. 'the reliance on active rather than passive learning, 2. an emphasis on deep learning and understanding, 3. increased responsibility and accountability on the part of the student, 4. an increased sense of autonomy in the learner, 5. an interdependence between teacher and learner, 6. mutual respect within the learner teacher relationship, 7. and a reflexive approach to the teaching and learning process on the part of both teacher and learne' (p. 31).

## 3.5 *Connecting guardian and schools*

The involvement of guardian or parents in their child's education is regarded as increasingly impor-tant, particularly to make sure that online distance learning is taking place accordingly during this pandemic. In this case, technology can be used to connect parents and teachers. Willemse et al. (2018) underlined that while cooperation between parents and schools is widely perceived as important, teachers rarely feel adequately prepared for this duty. They pointed out several stud-ies that preliminary teacher education programs strive to deal with this issue of parents-school cooperation.

Parents, who have been regarded as one of the stakeholders of school community, play an imperative role in the child's educational and environmental transformation; hence, their role has always been an important component in education. There should be an effort to expand parental participation in their child's education and school. Many parents are quite active in paying attention to their child's development by communicating frequently with the teachers, assisting their child's homework, getting involved in school program, as well as discussing their child's academic progress with teachers. Nevertheless, there are also parents who are quite passive in their child's education has let schools to deal fully with their child's education.

### 3.6 *Innovating pedagogy*

Reviewing and updating pedagogies that teachers use is important to prepare students to meet new current challenges, since pedagogy is the heart of leaching and learning process. The prime challenge for a research of adaptive teaching lies in analyzing classroom instruction in a more holistic manner. In this case, instead of studying specific teaching approaches, it is important to also identify and study the fundamental principle of adapting teaching, which is the level of adaptivity during the teaching and learning process (Paterson et al. 2018).

Motivated teachers are eager to simplify their administrative task to focus more on teaching to have engaged classes. Teachers usually spend three hours a day for administrative task such as marking and lesson planning and five hours a day for teaching, meaning that their energy was absorbed significantly for administrative task. Teachers who are able to make concerted decision about pedagogy are usually supported by high quality teacher education and resilient proficient infrastructure (Peterson et al. 2018). Hence, schools are striving to find strategies to help teachers focus on teaching and their professional development. In this case, technology has the potential to be utilized to help streamline teachers' administrative burden.

### 3.7 *Emerging technologies*

According to Neira et al. (2017), emerging technology refers to "resources, artifacts, tools, concepts and innovations associated with digital, that have a disruptive potential to transform or generate changes in the processes where they are used, regardless of whether these are new or old technologies" (p. 129). Such technologies have been given various names such as Information and Communication Technologies (ICT), Technologies in Education, Digital Technologies, New Technologies of Information and Communication (NTIC), Technologies of Learning and Knowledge, Technologies for Empowerment and Participation and Emerging Technologies (ETs). But all of them have the same purpose, which is to improve learning process. The competencies or skills that aimed to be improved by incorporating emerging technologies in the classroom were: critical thinking, problem solving, collaborative work, communicative competence, creative thinking, and decision making (Neira, Salinas et al. 2017).

In order to create more innovative and appealing teaching activities, schools are trying to integrate emerging technologies into classroom. Artificial Intelligence (AI), Virtual and Augmented Reality and other emerging technologies are increasingly ubiquitous in everyday lives. For example, in the US, 91% of children between age 4 and 11 use smart voice assistant, while in the UK 70% of children between age 8 to 17. The OECD report suggests that teaching and learning will be significantly affected by emerging technologies such as AI. It should be anticipated too that educational practices, institutions and policies will be under great pressure due to fast speed of technological changes (Tuomi 2018).

Furthermore, while things are getting more positively personalized and pedagogically efficient, shallowness and eclecticism also seem to have become everyday human behavior, which could have an impact on educational outcome. Educational institutions cannot escape from these changing values and must adapt accordingly in order to make the best use of this development and mitigate the unexpected downside. Seckman (2014), for example, in his review of Nicholas Carrs' *The Shallow* wrote that "...technology has both intended and unintended impacts on the psychosocial, social, and cognitive aspects of our lives. Not only are we unquestionably accessing, accepting, and using technology, but we often fail to take time to see the glaring and less than subtle ways that it has consequently changed us." Likewise, in the area of religion and character education this could also have a significant impact as internalization and practice of religious values and norms could somehow be disrupted.

Therefore, in order to deal with the aforementioned challenges there is a need to elaborate on what is called 'digital competence' so that teachers and students can fittingly utilize this technological development to maximize its benefit and to mitigate the unexpected consequences. There are at least five digital competence areas: information and data literacy; communication and collaboration; digital content creation; safety; and problem solving (Carretero et al. 2017). The competences are summarized in Table 1:

Table 1.   The competences are summarized.

1. *Information and Data Literacy*
   1.1 Browsing, searching and filtering data, information and digital content
   To articulate information needs, to search for data, information and content in digital environments, to access and navigate between them. To create and update personal search strategies.
   1.2 Evaluating data, information and digital content
   To analyze, compare and critically evaluate the credibility and reliability of sources of data, information and digital content. To analyze, interpret and critically evaluate the data, information and digital content.
   1.3 Managing data, information and digital content
   To organize, store and retrieve data, information, and content in digital environments. To organize and process them in a structured environment.
2. *Communication and Collaboration*
   2.1 Interacting through digital technologies
   To interact through a variety of digital technologies and to understand appropriate digital communication means for a given context.
   2.2 Sharing through digital technologies
   To share data, information and digital content with others through appropriate digital technologies. To act as an intermediary, to know about referencing and attribution practices.
   2.3 Engaging in citizenship through digital technologies
   To participate in society through the use of public and private digital services. To seek opportunities for self-empowerment and for participatory citizenship through appropriate digital technologies.
   2.4 Collaborating through digital technologies
   To use digital tools and technologies for collaborative processes, and for co-construction and co-creation of data, resources and knowledge.
   2.5 Netiquette
   To be aware of behavioral norms and know-how while using digital technologies and interacting in digital environments. To adapt communication strategies to the specific audience and to be aware of cultural and generational diversity in digital environments.
   2.6 Managing digital identity
   To create and manage one or multiple digital identities, to be able to protect one's own reputation, to deal with the data that one produce through several digital tools, environment and services.
3. *Digital Content Creation*
   3.1 Developing content
   To create and edit digital content in different formats, to express oneself through digital means.
   3.2 Integrating and re-elaborating digital content
   To modify, refine, improve and integrate information and content into an existing body of knowledge to create new, original and relevant content and knowledge.
   3.3 Copyright and licenses
   To understand how copyright and licenses apply to data, digital information and content.
   3.4 Programming
   To plan and develop a sequence of understandable instructions for a computing system to solve a given problem or perform a specific task.
4. *Safety*
   4.1 Protecting devices
   To protect devices and digital content, and to understand risks and threats in digital environments. To know about safety and security measures and to have a due regard to reliability and privacy.

*(Continued)*

Table 1. The competences are summarized. (*Continued*)

---

4.2 Protecting personal data and privacy

To protect personal data and privacy in digital environments. To understand how to use and share personally identifiable information while being able to protect oneself and others from damages. To understand that digital services use a "Privacy policy" to inform how personal data is used.

4.3 Protecting health and well-being

To be able to avoid health-risks and threats to physical and psychological well-being while using digital technologies. To be able to protect oneself and others from possible dangers in digital environments (e.g. cyber bullying). To be aware of digital technologies for social well-being and social inclusion.

4.4 Protecting the environment

To be aware of the environmental impact of digital technologies and their use.

5. *Problem Solving*

5.1 Solving technical problems

To identify technical problems when operating devices and using digital environments, and to solve them (from trouble-shooting to solving more complex problems).

5.2 Identifying needs and technological responses

To assess needs and to identify, evaluate, select and use digital tools and possible technological responses and to solve them. To adjust and customize digital environments to personal needs (e.g. accessibility).

5.3 Creatively using digital technology

To use digital tools and technologies to create knowledge and to innovate processes and products. To engage individually and collectively in cognitive processing to understand and resolve conceptual problems and problem situations in digital environments.

5.4 Identifying digital competence gaps

To understand where one's own digital competence needs to be improved or updated. To be able to support others with their digital competence development. To seek opportunities for self-development and to keep up-to-date with the digital evolution.

---

(Carretero, Vuorikan et al. 2017)

## 5 INDONESIA'S CHALLENGES IN MAKING USE OF EMERGING TECHNOLOGIES IN EDUCATION

It is clear that the competencies described are no longer future trend, they are in demand right now. Indonesi's ministry of education has arranged a newer plan to reconstruct the current curriculum to make sure that it covers the need for students to develop new competencies such as coding, big data and artificial intelligent. A new model of education with appropriate learning format is needed to implement this. Aside from this, up-to-date teacher's professional development is needed. In-house trainings and workshops arranged to improve their academic and pedagogic competences, which would enable them to structure more effective classroom activities, should be in place. Teachers should be encouraged to utilize emerging technologies in making lesson plans and classroom presentation so that they can deliver the lesson more effectively and interactively. Teachers have no choice but to master at least basis skills such as well-planned graphic design, video and power point presentation as well as skills in managing virtual classes. Unfortunately, many teachers involved in the trainings are not really committing to doing great efforts since many of them are only aiming at getting 'certificate', which would bring mere financial benefit as addition to their routine salary. While demanding the government and schools to provide high-tech facilities, teachers have made very few innovations. They tend to deliver lessons with the same method over and over again without serious efforts to enhance their academic and pedagogic competencies (Ghazali 2018).

Indonesia needs to implement the proper use of emerging technologies in order to catch up with other nations and accelerate its economic growth. Various challenges, however, remain in place with regard to policy, curriculum, infrastructure, educational and teacher quality gaps across the country, etc. The government needs to have various strategies to deal with these challenges such as by expanding collaboration with various stakeholders and enacting stronger commitment to information, communication and technology policy and improvement of its management with sustainable evaluation (Hermawan et al. 2018).

## 6 CONCLUSION

The aforementioned digital competences, namely information and data literacy; communication and collaboration; digital content creation; safety; and problem solving, are needed to be nurtured if educationalists are eager to make the best use of the emerging trends in educational technologies and mitigate the unintended consequences in this increasingly uncertain world. For example, competence area of information and data literacy, which requires ability to analyze, compare and critically evaluate the credibility and reliability of sources of data, information and digital content, is needed to deal with the perceived shallowness in online-based teaching and learning. Competence area of communication and collaboration, which requires ability to engage in citizenship and to be aware of behavioral norms and know-how while interacting in digital environments as well as to adapt communication strategies to the specific audience and to be aware of cultural and generational diversity in digital environments, is needed to ensure that character education is addressed and religious-based education is not losing its sacred values. Despite the fact that educational technology has been increasingly used to support mode of teaching delivery such as in distance education, there should be an effort to closer the gap between research of educational technology and its implementation. This means that educationalists should be more involved so that pedagogical aspects are accommodated during the research process; thus, the research outcome would bring the utmost benefit to education.

The Indonesian government has anticipated the use of emerging technologies in education with various program aimed at enhancing teacher academic and pedagogic competencies. The level of achievement is still far from satisfactory as the complexity of education in a huge country like Indonesia is also further affected by Covid-19, which has crippled the country's economy. During this difficult situation, Indonesia government needs to expand partnership with both national and overseas educational institutions through Penta-helix approach to deal with the current challenges and specific programs should be arranged to really make use of the emerging technologies to improve the quality of education of the nation.

## REFERENCES

Adji, S. S., et al. (2011). "The use of e-learning in distance education: Online tutorial in Faculty of Education and Teacher Training Uiversitas Terbuka." Southeast Asian Journal on Open and Distance Learning **V**: 21–40.

Akbar, D. H. K. b. H. (2010). "The development of information and communication technologfy in education in Brunei Darussalam." Southeast Asian Journal on Open and Distance Learning **IV**: 1–15.

Bandalaria, M. d. P. (2018). "Open and distance elearning in Asia: Country initiatives and instructional cooperation for the transformation of higher education in the region." Journal of Learning for Development **5**(2): 116–132.

BINUS (2020). "Sejarah Binus." Retrieved 1 Mei, 2020, from http://web.binus.edu/About.BINUS/Sejarah. BINUS/Indonesia.

Borner, K., et al. (2018). "Skill disrepancies between research, education, and jbs reveal the critical need to supply soft skills for the data economy." PNAS **115**(50): 12630–12637.

Cansu, S. K. and F. K. r. Cansu (2019). "An overview of computational thinking." International Journal of Computer Science Education in Schools **3**(1).

Carretero, S., et al. (2017). The digital competence framework for citizens. Luxemberg, Publication Office of the European Union.

Chanunan, S. and M. Bruckner (2017). "Emerging educational technologies in higher educational institutions: The current trends and impacts from Thailand university's perspectives." New Trends and Issue Proceedings on Humanities and Social Sciences **4**(1): 89–103.

Cochran, G. R. and T. M. Ferrari (2009). Preparing youth for the 21st century knowledge economy: Youth programs and workforce preparation.

Gallagher, T. L., et al. (2016). "Examining learner engagement stratgies: Australia and Canadian teachers' self-report." The Journal of the Teacher Education Division of the Council for Exceptional Children **40**(1): 51–64.

Garcia-Penalvo, F. J. and A. J. Mendes (2018). "Exploring trhe computional thinking effects in pre-university educaion." Computers in Human Behavior **80**: 407–411.

Ghazali, I. (2018). Educational challenges to the 4.0 industrial revolution: Experience from Indonesia. The International Acedemin Seminar 2018. Thepsatri Rajabhat University Thailand.

Google for Education (2020). Futrure of the classroom: Emerging trends in K-12 education Global Edition, Google.

Hermawan, H. D., et al. (2018). Implementation of ICT in education in Indonesia during 2004–2017. 2018 International Symposium on Educational Technology.

Hod, Y. (2017). "Future learning spaces in schiools: Concepts and Designs from learning sciences." Journal of Formative Design in Learning **1**: 99–109.

Jurevičienė, M., et al. (2018). "Concept and structural components of social skills." Baltic Journal of Sport and Health Sciences.

Kinshuk, et al. (2013). "Trends in educational technology througfh the lens of the highly citted articles publoshed in the Journal of Educational Technology and Scciety." Educational Technology and Society **16**: 3–20.

Kusmawan, U. and T. Belawati (2010). "The role of ICT in open and distance education partnership." Southeast Asian Journal on Open and Distance Learning **IV**: 24–36.

Neira, E. A. S., et al. (2017). "Emerging Technologies (ETs) in education: A systematic review of the literature published between 2006 and 2016." International Journal of Emerging Technologies in Learning **12**(5): 128–149.

O'Neill, G. (2005). Student-centred learning: What does it mean for students and lecturers? Emerging issues in the practice of university learning and teaching. G. O'Neill, S. Moore and B. McMullin, Creative Commons licence.

Panen, P. (2016). Kebijakan pendidikan jarak jauh dan e-learning di Indonesia. Kementerian Riset, Teknologi dan Pendidikan Tinggi, Kementerian Riset, Teknologi dan Pendidikan Tinggi.

Parliamentary Assembly Council of Europe (2019) The role of ediucation in the digital world: From "digital natives" to "digital citizens".

Paterson, A., et al. (2018). Understanding innovative pedagogies: Key themes to analyze new approaches to teaching and learning OECD Education Working Paper No 172.

Pedersen, A. Y., et al. (2018). "Patterns of inlcusion: Fostering digital citizenship through hybrid education." International Forum of Educational Technology and Society **21**(1): 225–236.

Peterson, A., et al. (2018). Understanding innovative pedagogies: Key themes to analyse new apporaches to leaching and learning, Directorate for Education and Skills.

Que, P. V. and T. D. Vuong (2010). "ICT-based education for development: The case of Vietnam." Southeast Asian Journal on Open and Distance Learning **IV**: 86–99.

Rotolo, D., et al. (2015). "What is emerging technology?" Research Policy **44**(10): 1827–1844.

Seckman, D. (2014). "Alarmingly shallow: The effects of Internet on our culture, community, and social well being: A review of Nicholas Carr's The Shallows." Retrieved 30 October 2020, from https://elearnmag.acm.org/archive.cfm?aid=2635804.

Sethy, O. (2010). "Open and distance education in Cambodia." Southeast Asian Journal on Open and Distance Learning **IV**: 100–124.

Sklar, A. (2017). "Sound, smart, and safe: A plea for teaching good digital hygiene." Learning Landscape Journal **10**(2): 39–43.

Socarana, B. (2018). Lessons from recent data scandals: A call for corporate digital responsibility.

Tuomi, I. (2018). The impact of Artifical Intelligence on learning, teaching, and education. Luxemburg, European Commission.

UMN (2020). "Universitas Multimedia Nusantara." Retrieved 1 Mei, 2020, from https://www.umn.ac.id/.

UNESCO (2020). "Global monitoring of school closures caused by COVID-19." Retrieved 2 April, 2020, from https://en.unesco.org/covid19/educationresponse.

Willemse, M., et al. (2018). "Teacher education and family–school partnerships in different contexts: A cross country analysis of national teacher education frameworks across a range of European countries." Journal of Education for Teaching **44**(3): 258–277.

*Emerging Trends in Technology for Education in an Uncertain World – Nanto, Rahiem & Khalis Maryati (Eds)*
© 2022 copyright the Author(s), ISBN 978-1-032-11288-6

# The challenges of 21st century teaching after students have experienced learning in an interrupted world

Muhammad Zuhdi
*UIN Syarif Hidayatullah Jakarta*

Stephen Dobson
*Victoria University of Wellington*

ABSTRACT: Learning in the 21st century has increasingly been characterized by online or digital learning in education. However, prior to Covid-19 the uptake was of a much more limited character. In this contribution the authors contend that a key challenge in online learning is the digital bystander where students in schools and universities alike may not actively engage in online and digitally supported learning. This is especially the case if face-to-face pedagogy is transposed in mirror like fashion to the online learning format. A new form of pedagogy is advocated which supports the design of online teaching and learning; it is termed the pedagogy of connectivism.

## 1 INTRODUCTION

As digital communication weaves into every fibre of our existence, it is still the case that an ever increasing number of people across the world are impoverished as digital bystanders. They are not unworldly or naïve. On the contrary, they are rich in experience of other peoples' stories and even their own. Through access to the internet and posting on Facebook, Instagram, twitter or the latest vogue in social media these stories might be shared and communicated. But the voice of the storyteller in terms of complexity and empowerment always risks being limited to sharing and at times a form of narcissistic gratification or simple electronic act of transmission. The fear is that there may be no greater or longer term progress in learning that leads to the development of skills, capacities and a greater sense of both self-determination and inclusion.

This contribution reflects upon how to manage learning and teaching equipped with experiences gained during the period of the pandemic. It asks and answers what it means to learn from and create a culture of inclusion where belonging, wellbeing and a particular kind of voice are clearly evident. Namely, the voice that speaks to and against disadvantage. A central argument is that understanding disadvantage and exclusion should not lead to merely a deficit view of what it means to be a digital bystander. This view suggests that the excluded cannot or are less inclined to intervene and find a way out of the experience; moving from the 'digital bystander' to 'digital upstander' (Wong-Lo & Bullock 2014). A generation before the internet this would have been understood as the Society of the Spectacle mediated by images and voyeurism (Debord 1977). We are thus concerned with how to transcend the experience of the digital bystander and accompanying disadvantage through learning inclusion and finding a voice. A generation has been inspired by Pedagogy of the Oppressed by Freire (2000) and his preference for learning based upon a co-development of skills and knowledge, rather and what he called a banking (one-directional transmission) form of pedagogy. We continue to be inspired by his work, seeking to add contemporary ideas of belonging, wellbeing and voice to an interest in the role of digital resources and digital skills. Freire was an early forerunner for what today is known under the name of appreciative pedagogy or appreciative inquiry (Yballe & O'Connor 2000). Namely, in order to move from a deficit view of lacking education and seeking to fill the empty vessel of the student, the goal is meet the student as already a vessel containing positive learning experiences that constitute a foundation for future directed learning and reflection.

## 2 THE FUTURE IS NOW: PROBLEMS OF DIGITAL BYSTANDER IN LEARNING

Covid-19 has pushed everyone to stay at home. It has been a year since the pandemic was declared and the life of many students has involved learning to learn at home. Digital learning is suddenly an everyday phenomenon. Accompanying this the online classroom has for many become the only option for students and teachers to continue to interact, and this has led to changes in the way students learn. The transformation of learning suddenly taking place has caught participants, both students and teachers unaware and unprepared. The teacher's role has gained added levels of complexity as they have sought to ensure that they can engage students and support their learning.

The main problem that most teachers have faced during the Covid-19 period has been that many teachers at least to being with have simply moved the traditional classroom into a virtual one. The face-to-face classroom teaching has been transposed in mirror like fashion into the online classroom. This has resulted in teachers struggling to gain the attention of students over time and they have found it even more difficult to ensure and ascertain that students have actually been learning from them. As a result, a lot of teachers have been tempted to simply set students weekly assignments as a way of making students learn by themselves. However, in a well-known saying, just because the horse is taken to the water, it does not mean they will drink.

On the other hand, students have felt bored as they are struggling to focus on what their teachers are delivering. Warburton et al. observed that students become digital bystanders in their online classroom (Warburton et al. 2020). They are present in the digital classroom, but they were not really involved in it. Access to premium IT facilities may be of little help, especially when the teaching methods and didactics have not been designed specifically for online delivery e.g. with shorter periods of teaching interwoven with similarly shorter periods of learning and feedback activities.

The issue of learning loss (Hanushek & Woessmann 2020) has now become a worldwide problem as the invisible hand of the involuntary digital classroom makes itself felt (Dobson & Schofield 2020); students are present but do not learn. The question of equity to education, a well-known phenomenon even in face-to-face classrooms is exacerbated still further. Some studies indicate that students are learning less during the pandemic compared with the situation before the pandemic (Engzell et al. 2021).

Despite these problems, the wisdom of pandemic has opened our eyes to the opportunities of well-designed digital learning environments, where learning resources and activities seek to match the characteristics of students at a distance from each other and the teacher. For some teachers this has meant offering some anytime any place learning objects and activities across a week of learning. In such a way teachers have learnt that online learning and digital learning can an applicable model of learning. In fact, a number of schools and universities have developed their own models of online learning. However, for many educators familiarity with the digital world as experienced through their phones, tables or computers, has not been guarantee that they are educationally literate when it comes to teaching online. Many have continued to believe that face-face learning is superior and that they will return to it in due course.

Let us consider New Zealand, where the largest school in this country of 5 million is called Te Kura (https://www.tekura.school.nz/about-us/who-we-are/about-te-kura/). It is the only one of its kind the country and has over 15000 students. As a state financed school it has its roots in the pre-digital correspondence schools (founded 1922) when teaching resources were sent to students in the mail and assignments were likewise returned by mail to the teachers to receive feedback and assessment. Prior to Covid-19, Te Kura had had long since moved to a mix of teachers who would have met their allocated student groups in different models of pedagogy, varying from blended mode face-to-face and online to fully online. When the pandemic hit they were already prepared to move fully online and had deep experience in using learning resources and objects that were only available fully online.

## 3 CONNECTIVISM: TRANSFORMATION IN TEACHING AND LEARNING

Teaching and learning entails, at least in our current technological state where Artificial Intelligence (AI) is limited, teachers and students who interact in the continual and regular act of transferring knowledge, values and skills. While students have to focus their attention on what their teachers explain, teachers have to find ways to ensure that their method of teaching is both motivating, effective and efficient. Siemens suggests that the key is increasingly connectivism (Siemens 2005). Connectivism is a complex theory of learning that involves connecting the different participants in multiple overlapping networks of technologically mediated acts of learning and assessment. These networks can persist over time and at differing levels of intensity. They can offer the opportunity of any time, any place learning and teaching. At other times the networks of teaching and learning can take on the appearance and reality of being limited in time. The digitally mediated learning and teaching encounters in this case lack the anytime, anyplace character.

This online experience is analogous to seaweed that floats in and out with the tides, where the teacher is both seaweed and the tide, while the student is standing on the shore making a decision to pick up the seaweed and make a learning connection or just letting it wash up and wash back into the sea as they remain digital bystanders.

## 4 CONCLUSION

In being interested in education in the time of Covid-10 and the opportunities it offers for the future, we can no longer be satisfied with equipping ourselves with an understanding of cognitive and constructivist learning and teaching models. We must embrace a new form of pedagogy to complement these just mentioned, namely the *pedagogy of connectivism*, where connections are central and learning and teaching is increasingly mediated by digital technology. It is increasingly characterized by the opportunities for anytime, anyplace learning and teaching, as well as its more traditional fixed in time and synchronous variant. The two metaphors we have cited as useful for understanding the interwoven relationship between the horse coming to the water, but they cannot be forced to drink and the view of the teacher as the seaweed washed by the tide onto the shore for the student, who may or may not decide to engage with learning. Straddling both these metaphors is the view that it is desirable for the student to actively cease at times to be merely digital bystanders.

## REFERENCES

Debord, G. 1977. *Society of the Spectacle*. Detroit: Black and Red (first published in French in 1967).
Dobson, S. and Schofield, E. 2020. *The Rush to Online-ness*. https://www.newsroom.co.nz/ideasroom/the-rush-to-online-ness
Engzell, P., et al. 2021. *Learning Loss due to School Closures During the COVID-19 Pandemic*. https://osf.io/preprints/socarxiv/ve4z7/download
Freire, P. 2000. Pedagogy of the Oppressed (30th anniversary ed.). New York: Bloomsbury.
Hanushek, E.A. and Woessmann, L. 2020. *The Economic Impacts of Learning Losses*. OECD. Available at https://www.oecd.org/education/The-economic-impacts-of-coronavirus-covid-19-learning-losses.pdf
Siemens, G. 2005. Connectivism: A learning theory for the digital age. *International Journal of Instructional Technology and Distance Learning*, 2, 1.
Warburton, S., Zuhdi, M., and Dobson, S. 2020. In a world of digital bystanders the challenge is for all of us to design engaging online education. *The Conversation*, Oktober 13, 2020. Available at https://theconversation.com/in-a-world-of-digital-bystanders-the-challenge-is-for-all-of-us-to-design-engaging-online-education-147195

Wong-Lo, M. and Bullock, L. M. 2014. Digital metamorphosis: Examination of the bystander culture in cyberbullying. *Aggression and Violent Behavior*, 19(4).

Yballe, L. and O'Connor, D. 2000. Appreciative pedagogy: Constructing positive models for learning. *Journal of Management Education*, 24(4), 474–483. Available at https://docs.google.com/document/d/1H9Q22j2 EgyHP8_eagILz8cA2M2ERKaQRO2Aysw7dHco/edit

*Technology in math and science education*

*Emerging Trends in Technology for Education in an Uncertain World – Nanto, Rahiem & Khalis Maryati (Eds)*
*© 2022 copyright the Author(s), ISBN 978-1-032-11288-6*

# Islamization of science and its contribution to students' Islamic character building at Islamic universities in Indonesia and Malaysia

Nurbaiti & H.M. Suparta
*Sekolah Pasca Sarjana, Universitas Islam Negeri Syarif Hidayatullah Jakarta*

T.A. Syukur
*Faculty of Education, Universitas Ibnu Khaldun*

D. Nahartini
*English Education Department, Faculty of Education, Universitas Islam Negeri Syarif Hidayatullah Jakarta*

ABSTRACT: This study examined the contribution of the Islamization learning model of science to the student's Islamic character building in Islamic universities in Indonesia and Malaysia. This study employs a quantitative approach. Data were collected by using a survey questionnaire and analyzed by using the SPSS program. A total of a hundred students from 4 faculties in one university in Jakarta, Indonesia, and one university in Gombak, Malaysia have supported this study by answering the distributed questionnaire. The results showed that although there is a positive contribution of the Islamization learning model of Science to the student's Islamic characters building at Islamic universities in Indonesia and Malaysia for 10.40%, this number indicates that the contribution is quite low. Meanwhile, other variables which are 89.6% should call other researchers to do further research in identifying other possible variables that might give more significant influence.

*Keywords*: Islamization learning model of Science, students, Islamic Character Building, Islamic Higher Education, Indonesia, Malaysia

## 1 INTRODUCTION

Educational institutions have an important role in students' Islamic character building. Thus, educational institutions have an obligation to develop student's Islamic character building, although, in fact, a number of students have characters that are contrary to Islamic teachings. Ningrum (2015) stated that there has been a decline in morale among adolescents.

Incorporating religious values into the general science learning process has been mentioned as one of the solutions toward morale declining among adolescents. Incorporating Islamic religious values in general science learning is known as the Islamization learning model of science. The student's Islamic character building can be developed through the Islamization learning model of science in Islamic universities with the aim of producing Islamic scholars that have broad scientific insight and good Islamic character.

So far, there is an assumption that there is a separation between general science and religious knowledge. Science and religion were accepted as two irreconcilable entities. Both have their respective areas, separate from each other, both in terms of formal material objects, research methods, criteria for truth and the role played by scientists. This difference is known as the Dichotomy of Science.

The dichotomy of science is the assumption of separating science and religion. The science dichotomy is identified as the emergence of problems in Islamic education and it is contrary to the true nature of science. Another expression that supports the science dichotomy is the assumption that religion and general science have different ways in terms of approach and experience.

DOI 10.1201/9781003219248-7

However, Kuntowijoyo (2004) stated, science and religion not only need to be combined but even need to be unified. Kuntowijoyo's statement is also in accordance with Mehdi Gulšanī's (2004) theory which unites general science and religion. Furthermore, Hanifah (2018) also said that the Islamization of science has been implemented in several Islamic universities, even though they are still looking for the most appropriate form of learning for each educational institution.

The theory of the Islamization of science contradicts the theory of secularism pioneered by George Jacob Holyoake (13 April 1817–22 January 1906). This theory, according to Kasmuri (2014), there is a difference between world affairs and the hereafter. Thus, general science and religious knowledge do not coalesce. This situation shows that the theory of secularism is a supporter of the science dichotomy theory. O'Brien and Noy (2015) also stated the conflict between general science and religion is often rooted in the theory of secularization which only relies on ratio.

The separation between religious knowledge and general science in learning has been identified to bring several negative impacts on students' characters. Arifuddin (2015) stated, according to al-Faruqi, a result of the secular paradigm, modern knowledge has become dry, even separated from tauhid value. The theory stated by O'Brien and Noy (2015) is a supporter of the theory of secularism which is the originator of the theory of the dichotomy of science. The theory supporting the dichotomy of science. The other secularism as stated by Kasmuri is the theory stated by George Jacob Holyoake. Kasmuri stated that the theory of George Jacob Holyoake (13 April 1817–22 January 1906) was a supporter of the theory of secularism and a supporter of the dichotomy theory of science. This theory states that there is a separation between religious knowledge and general science. The same thing was stated by Naquid Al-Attas (2014) who stated that according to Harvey Coy for the sake of scientific development, general knowledge must be emptied of spiritual or religious values.

Thus, this study opposes the dichotomy theory of science which supports the theory of secularism as stated by O'Brien and Noy, George Jacob Holyoake, and Harvey Coy. This research supports Ashidqi's (2014) theory which states that the emptying of the world or nature from spiritual and religious values (disenchantment of nature), which according to Harvey Cox is an absolute prerequisite for the development of general science is incorrect. This research also supports Naquib Al-Atas' (2001) statement which opposes Harvey Cox's theory of emptying knowledge from religious values and Kuntowijoyo's (2004) statement which is a supporter of Gulšanī's (2004) theory of integration of knowledge which states that knowledge and religion need to be integrated because they both come from the same source.

The learning model with the Islamization of science is implemented in several universities in Indonesia and Malaysia. The implementation is aimed to provide insight to students that basically general science can be viewed from a religious perspective. In addition, the Islamization of knowledge is expected to increase the level of knowledge and level of student piety, so they will become scholars who have broad scientific insights and also have high faith, so it can have implications for their Islamic character.

The students' Islamic character building in this study is the Islamic attitude of students in their daily lives both in fulfilling their wishes and in carrying out their moral habits. However, the research on whether the Islamization of Science can develop students' Islamic character is still scarce. Thus, this study is intended to find out (1) how far is the Islamization of science correlates to students' Islamic character, and (2) ways of Islamization of science approach contribute to students' Islamic character building at the university level.

## 2 LITERATURE REVIEW

### 2.1 Students' Islamic character building

Character education is a way of teaching habits, ways of thinking, and behavior that helps individuals to live and work together as members of the family, community, and state. Islamic character building can be formed through the Islamization learning model of science. The Islamization of science is a learning model by integrating religious knowledge with general science.

Islamic character can be said to be an Islamic character, that is, a character that comes from the teachings of Allah and His Messenger and Islamic character is an open deed so that it can be an indicator of whether a person is a good Muslim or not. According to Kamarudin (2012), a character is a personality that is inherent in a person and is a complex collection of psychological characteristics, partly formed by the growth of cognition that allows a person to act as a moral agent.

## 2.2 *Islamization of science*

The Islamization of science is known as a learning model by combining general science with the science of tauhid. This term is closely related to the phrase of 'Islamization of knowledge' that has been widely used in the late 20th century to address the effort of combining Islamic ethical norms and modern scientific knowledge. According to Nasr, 1991, the phrase Islamization knowledge was first announced by the Malaysian scholar, Syed Muhammad Naquib Al-Atas (2001) in his book, 'Islam and Secularism which first published in 1978'. This idea was proposed by the Palestinian Philosopher, Ismail Al Faruqi in 1982.

Knowledge is not present in empty space but is bound by the context of civilization in the Islamization of science. Islamization of science has a vision of building a more civilized civilization. Al-Attas (1995) as cited in Madani (2016) stated that this new intellectual discipline can be seen as an alternative effort in responding to various problems that he considers to be resolved with principles and values that can create a new reality of civilization. Therefore, the Islamization of science encompasses all aspects of disciplines that build elements of civilization, such as technological developments.

The Islamization of science has given lots of focus on two main areas of knowledge, such as the natural and social sciences. The development of Islamic banks is one example of the emergence of Islamic economics. This example marked the process of the Islamization of science happened in real society. Al-Attas as cited in Daud (1998) stated that the Islamization of science is a real effort to assert humans from mythological traditions that are contrary to Islam and from secular understandings. Islamization of knowledge for al-Attas arises because science is not free of value, but is loaded with certain values. Conventional knowledge is considered a hegemony from the west. He continued by saying that this certainly has implications for western values which are full of animating current knowledge production. Al-Attas viewed that western civilization is not feasible to be consumed before being selected first.

In spite of the heated debate about this idea, there was no large agreement done on neither framework nor a definite methodology plan for the process of Islamization of science in general or in specific (Madani 2016). Madani also pointed out that 'the Islamization of knowledge was still considered to be in its theoretical stage, as each scholar carries a different perspective and different methodology or plan of work.

Despite the fact that the Islamization of Knowledge project has become an attention-seeking phenomenon of many Muslim scholars for the past thirty years, there is no agreement done on neither framework nor a definite methodology plan for the process of Islamization of Knowledge in general or the Islamization of science in specific. The disagreement still presents at extreme until recently, even after thirty years of discussion. The concept of Islamization of Knowledge is still considered to be in its theoretical stage, as each scholar carries a different perspective and a different methodology or plan of work.

## 3 METHODOLOGY

This study has applied a quantitative method which emphasizes objective measurements and the statistical, mathematical, or numerical analysis of data collected through polls, questionnaire, and surveys, or by manipulating pre-existing statistical data using computational techniques (Babbie 2010). The quantitative method research focuses on gathering numerical data and generalizing it across groups of people or explaining a particular phenomenon (Muijs 2010). Quantitative data were collected by using a questionnaire. The questionnaire was distributed to four faculties at two Islamic universities in Malaysia and in Jakarta. The sampling technique used in this research is the purposive sampling technique.

## 4 RESULT AND DISCUSSION

### 4.1 *Correlation analysis*

The correlation coefficient is a statistical measure that calculates the strength of the relationship between the relative movements of the two variables. To measure it, in this study the research hypothesis is: there is a positive and significant correlation (relationship) between the Islamization of science's learning model and the student's Islamic character building.

### 4.1.1 *Correlation between Islamization of science and students' Islamic character building*
This research conducted at the Islamic University of Jakarta, Indonesia, and at the Islamic University of Gombak, Malaysia, and the results are as shown in Table 4.

In Table 1, it can be seen that the value of the correlation coefficient (r) or the degree of closeness of the relationship between the science Islamization learning model and the student's Islamic character building is 0.322, in other words, the degree of closeness of the relationship is positive and low.

While the significance test of the correlation coefficient from the significance value between the science Islamization learning model and the Islamic character of students as shown in Table 5 is 0.001 <0.05, we can conclude that the regression is linear. Likewise, with the t value of 3.364 which is bigger than the value of the t table (0.05; 98) = 0.677, it can be concluded that the application of the science Islamization learning model has a significant degree of closeness to the student's Islamic character building.

From Table 2, it can be seen that the correlation coefficient value between the Islamization of science and student's Islamic character building is 0.322 (positive) and the significance is at $F = 11.320$. These results implied that the Islamization of science and student's Islamic character building has a positive and significant correlation. Thus, the research hypothesis which states that there is a positive and significant correlation between the Islamization of science is tested, it means

Table 1. Correlation coefficient and coefficient of determination between Islamization of science and the students' Islamic character building.

| Model | R | R square | Adjusted R square | Std. error of the estimate | Change statistics | | | | |
| | | | | | R square change | F change | df1 | df2 | Sig. F change |
|---|---|---|---|---|---|---|---|---|---|
| 1 | .322[a] | .104 | .094 | 8.40054 | .104 | 11.320 | 1 | 98 | .001 |

[a]Predictors: (Constant), character.

Table 2. ANOVA of Islamization of science and student's Islamic character building.

| Model | | Sum of squares | Df | Mean square | F | Sig. |
|---|---|---|---|---|---|---|
| 1 | Regression | 798.813 | 1 | 798.813 | 11.320 | .001[b] |
| | Residual | 6915.777 | 98 | 70.569 | | |
| | Total | 7714.590 | 99 | | | |

[a]Dependent variable: Islamization of Science.
[b]Predictors: (Constant), student's Islamic character building.

that the higher the science Islamization value given, the student's Islamic character building will also increase significantly.

## 4.2 *Discussion*

The main objective of this research is to identify the relationship between the Islamization learning model of science and the Islamic character building of students. To achieve this goal, the researcher has set two research objectives.

### 4.2.1 *Discussion on 1st objective: to investigate the correlation level of Islamization and student's Islamic character building*

The interpretation of the degree of closeness of the relationship or the value of the correlation coefficient is as shown in Table 3.

In Table 3, it can be seen that the value of the correlation coefficient (r) or the degree of closeness of the relationship between the science Islamization learning model and the student's Islamic character is 0.322. Thus, if we compare this data to the correlation coefficient interpretation in Table 3, we can conclude that the degree of closeness of the relationship is positive and low. It can be interpreted that the higher the value of the science Islamization learning model, the higher the student's Islamic character building.

While the significance test of the correlation coefficient can be seen from the significance value between the science Islamization learning model and the students' Islamic character building as shown in Table 2 is 0.001 which is (lower than) <0.05, the regression is linear. On the other hand, with the *t* value, from the calculation results obtained a value of 3.364> from the table (0.05; 98) = 0.677, it can be concluded that the application of the science Islamization learning model has a significant degree of closeness to the student's Islamic character.

All in all, it can be summed up that it is important to build students' Islamic character through the Islamization learning model. The character as stated by Suradi (2017) is one of the fundamental attitudes of a person's mindset and behavior to achieve better life success. So, it is appropriate for educational institutions to prepare their students to have better characters that lead to higher culture and ethics as a provision for life in the future.

For Islamic colleges, building the religious aspect and strengthening the character of students is the main task. Apart from transferring knowledge to students, it is also important to transfer good values. The main purpose of character education according to Islam is to shape the personality of students so that they have good ethics and a sense of culture and make it happen in everyday life.

One of the factors that influence students' character is students' understanding of Islamic religious education. As stated by Ainiyah (2013), the role of Islamic religious education is very strategic in realizing character formation, because religious education is a means of transforming religious knowledge (cognitive aspects), as a means of transforming norms and moral values to shape attitudes (affective aspects), which play a role in controlling behavior (psychomotor aspects) so that a complete human personality is created, Thus, the learning model of science Islamization is expected to provide output results that have broad scientific insights both in general and religious sciences and this can be applied in the form of good student attitudes and behavior.

Table 3. Correlation coefficient interpretation.

| Coefficient interval | Relationship level |
| --- | --- |
| 0.00–0199 | Very low |
| 0.20–0.399 | Low |
| 0.40–0599 | Medium |
| 60–0.799 | Strong |
| 0.80–1.000 | Very strong |

### 4.2.2 Discussion on 2nd objective: investigate the contribution of Islamization of science to students' Islamic character building

In this research, the result shows that the learning model only contributes to the Islamic character of students by 10.40%. This is because there are many other factors that can influence the students' Islamic character building besides the science Islamization learning model. As stated by Setiawati (2015) that in character building it is necessary to involve all parties, both household and family; school; and the wider school environment (society) and the formation of character and character education through schools cannot be done solely through learning knowledge, but through the cultivation or education of values, so that to determine success in learning it is necessary to emphasize the affective aspect as well.

Thus, it can be stated that the learning activities which emphasizes more on cognitive aspects only is one of the obstacles in the effort of developing students' Islamic character building at the university level.

## 5 CONCLUSION

Based on the results of the research that has been done, the results show that the science Islamization learning model has a positive and significant correlation with the Islamic character of students in Islamic universities in Indonesia and Malaysia. Thus, the research hypothesis which states that there is a positive and significant relationship between the science Islamization learning model and the formation of the Islamic character of students is accepted.

In spite of the ongoing debate among Islamic and non-Islamic scholars presented in large works of literature about the contribution of the Islamization of science to the students' Islamic character building at the university level, this study result has proved that there is still a place where its contribution still needs to be counted. Other things that should be highlighted include the importance of support from the students' surroundings, i.e., lecturers, parents, peers, and government's supports and the importance of imposing Islamic characters in every possible academic area where students can feel the presence of God in every academic activity that they do.

## REFERENCES

Al-Atas, S.M.N. 2001. *Risalah untuk kaum muslimin*. Kuala Lumpur: ISTAC.
Al-Attas, S.M.N. 2014. *Islam and secularism*. Kuala Lumpur: IBFIM.
Ainiyah, N. 2013. "Pembentukan Karakter Melalui Pendidikan Agama Islam." *Al.Ulum*. 13(14).
Arifuddin, A. 2015. "Konsep Integrasi Ilmu dalam Pandangan Ismail Raji Al-Faruqi." *SYAMIL J. Pendidik. Agama Islam J. Islam. Educ.* 3(1).
Babbie, Earl R. 2010. *The Practice of Social Research*. 12th ed. Belmont, CA: Wadsworth Cengage.
Daud, W.M. 1998. *Filsafat dan Praktik Pendidikan Islam Syed M. Naquib al-Attas*. Bandung: Mizan.
Gulšanī, M. 2004. Issues in Islam and science. Tehran, New York: Institute for Humanities and Cultural Studies; Global Scholarly Publications.
Hanifah, U. 2018. "Islamisasi Ilmu Pengetahuan Kontemporer (Konsep Integrasi Keilmuan di Universitas-Universitas Islam Indonesia." *Tadris Jurnal Pendidikan Islam* 13(2).
Kasmuri, K. 2014. "Fenomena Sekularisme." *Al-Araf J. Pemikir. Islam Dan Filsafat* 11(2):89.
Kuntowijoyo. 2004. *Islam Sebagai Ilmu: Epistemologi, Metodologi, dan Etika*. 1st ed. Jakarta: Mizan Media Utama.
Madani, R.A. 2016. "Islamization of Science." *International Journal of Islamic Thought* 9(6).
Muijs, D. 2010. *Doing Quantitative Research in Education with SPSS*. 2nd ed. London: SAGE Publications.
Ningrum, D. 2015. "Kemerosotan Moral Di Kalangan Remaja: Sebuah penelitian Mengenai Parenting Styles dan Pengajaran Adab." *Unisia* 37(82):18–30.
O'Brien, T.L., and Noy, S. 2015. "Traditional, Modern, and Post-Secular Perspectives on Science and Religion in the United States." *Am. Sociol. Rev.* 80(1):92–115.
Setiawati, R. 2015. "Integritas Ilmu dalam Perpekstif Pendidikan." *Jurnal Penelitian* 9(2):295.
Suradi, S. 2017. "Pembentukan Karakter Siswa melalui Penerapan Disiplin Tata Tertib Sekolah," *Briliant: Jurnal Riset Dan Konseptual* 2(4):522.

*Emerging Trends in Technology for Education in an Uncertain World – Nanto, Rahiem & Khalis Maryati (Eds)*

# Physics learning in distance: Teacher observation reports and students' learning performance

D.R. Romadhon

*Department of Physics Education, Faculty of Educational Sciences, Universitas Islam Negeri Syarif Hidayatullah Jakarta, Tangerang Selatan, Banten, Indonesia*

ABSTRACT: The Covid-19 pandemic has caused schools to change their strategy for implementing face-to-face learning to distance learning. Meanwhile, no school has faced a pandemic like this before, so it is difficult for schools to find the best example of implementing distance learning. Likewise, physics teachers must quickly adapt and learn various digital tools to carry out active, interactive, and creative distance learning. This paper aims to provide an overview of how physics teachers react and adapt to the changes in terms of the conditions of learning. The method used in this study was mixed method. Twenty-five physics teachers at seven schools in various cities on Java and Sumatra were observed, mainly focusing on planning and organization of the lesson, the instructional process, classroom management, and professionalism. Observations were done twice, before the pandemic and during the pandemic. The learning performance of 1,399 students in physics during the pandemic were also collected and discussed.

*Keywords*: Distance learning; Learning achievement; Teaching strategies

## 1 INTRODUCTION

The COVID-19 pandemic has fundamentally affected the education system, which had to a shift to distance learning (Dhawan 2020). Teachers all over Indonesia were pushed to change strategies from face to face learning to online learning (Teräs et al. 2020). The entire educational community was swiftly pushed in March 2020 into unprepared and undesirable remote teaching (Bozkurt et al. 2020). Distance teaching requires careful thinking, planning, and the development of technical and human resources to complete expected learning outcomes successfully (Cheawjindakarn et al. 2012). Nevertheless, in the present situation caused by the COVID-19 pandemic, the preparation time became short. In the process, the educators had support from their schools in providing e-learning platforms, other digital learning management systems, and communication tools. However, the instructors' main burden was adapting their teaching methods and resources to have an online format (Klein et al. 2021). This study aimed to observe teaching and learning processes during the COVID-19 pandemic in the context of physics courses at junior and high schools across Indonesia.

Students were doing online courses before the COVID-19 pandemic, and in some countries, like Indonesia, distance education already existed before the pandemic, such as in the Universitas Terbuka. New learning platforms offer a new teaching model, and an initial study has shown that student progress is similar to the traditional face-to-face lesson but is drastically lower than the interactive face-to-face lesson (Seaman et al. 2018). Online education changes all components of teaching and learning, and numerous educational researchers are trying to assess the results of these changes (Chopra & Syazwani 2020). The problems faced during the initial phase of pandemic by teachers are that they have to learn many new tools to start online learning, they have to apply the tools, and they need to troubleshoot the technical problem by experiencing the problem directly (Rasmitadila et al. 2020). How the teachers react to the shift learning is important to learn during the beginning of the pandemic era. This article focuses on synchronous teaching activities and the learning achievement of the students. It is structured as follows: First, a short overview about online teaching and learning in the context of physics was provided, mainly focusing on planning and organization of lesson, instructional process, classroom management, and professionalism, which were considered essential for the study. in Section II, we describe data collection methods, an appraisal form for online learning, online summative assessment using the methods by Latihan.id, followed by the results, their discussion and conclusion.

## 2 RESEARCH METHODS

This study used a mixed method methodology. Two aspects were being assessed, the teaching and learning process during the pandemic and the students' learning achievement. There were 25 teachers across Indonesia being observed, 14 male teachers and 11 female teachers. The schools where they teach are private schools which implement the Cambridge curriculum. The profiles of the teachers observed are shown in Table 1.

There are only two certified teachers from the Ministry of Education who are from Sem School Semarang.

The observation was done once before the pandemic and once during the pandemic. The observation focused on the lesson's planning and organization, instructional process, classroom management, and professionalism. The criteria for each aspect are shown in Table 2.

Table 2 shows the four aspects of teaching along with the criteria that the teacher should fulfill. The score given for each aspect follows a Likert scale from one to five with one as never, two as rarely, three as often, four as most of the times, and five as always. In addition to this observation form, the author wrote the lesson process in the journals. There were critical activities observed, such as the opening, main activity, and closing activities.

The students' learning performance were assessed using the summative online assessment platform Latihan.id. The platform used was designed to provide real exam results. Latihan.id requires the students to turn on the camera and microphone during the exam. The camera records the student during the exam session and the exam proctor sees what is going on in front of the computer. The interface of Latihan.id is shown as Figure 1.

Table 1. Teachers profile.

| School | City | Gender | | Education | | Teaching year | | | |
|---|---|---|---|---|---|---|---|---|---|
| | | Male | Female | Bachelor | Master | <2 | 2–5 | 5–10 | >10 |
| Fatih | Banda Aceh | 3 | – | 2 | 1 | 1 | – | 2 | – |
| TNA | Banda Aceh | – | 2 | 2 | – | – | 1 | 1 | – |
| Kharbang | Tangerang Selatan | 3 | 1 | 4 | – | 2 | – | 2 | – |
| PD | Depok | 2 | 1 | 2 | 1 | 1 | 1 | – | 1 |
| PB | Bandung | – | 3 | 3 | – | – | 1 | 1 | 1 |
| CRIBS | Bogor | 1 | – | 1 | – | – | 1 | – | – |
| Sem | Semarang | 1 | 2 | 3 | 1 | – | 1 | – | 3 |
| Sem 3 | Semarang | – | 1 | 1 | – | – | 1 | – | – |
| Kesbang | Jogjakarta | 4 | 1 | 5 | – | 1 | 1 | 2 | 1 |
| Sum | | 14 | 11 | 22 | 3 | 5 | 6 | 8 | 6 |
| Total | | 25 | | 25 | | 25 | | | |

Table 2.  The appraisal form for teacher's observation.

| Aspects | Score |
|---|---|
| **Planning and organization of the lesson** | |
| prepares lesson plans | ... |
| prepares lesson plans that are well laid out and sequenced | ... |
| writes objectives that are clear | ... |
| writes objectives that are level appropriate | ... |
| selects objectives that are achievable | ... |
| plans activities that are well differentiated | ... |
| prepares instruction with opportunities for individual and/or group work | ... |
| **Instructional process** | |
| welcomes/settles and check the readiness of the class appropriately | ... |
| makes objectives explicit to students at the start of the lesson | ... |
| presents correct information | ... |
| gives students opportunities to respond to questions | ... |
| engages students in activities that are appropriate | ... |
| engages students in activities that are meaningful | ... |
| uses appropriate instructional materials in the teaching/learning environment | ... |
| uses appropriate questioning techniques | ... |
| ensures that all students participate in instructional activities | ... |
| ends lessons appropriately | ... |
| **Classroom management** | |
| demonstrates an awareness of what is happening in the classroom | ... |
| takes a class register and report it | ... |
| creates an atmosphere conducive to learning | ... |
| manages time effectively | ... |
| **Professionalis** | |
| reports for work regularly | ... |
| submits required information (reports, data, etc.) on time | ... |
| adheres school dress code for teacher | ... |
| adheres to the code of ethics | ... |

Figure 1.  Latihan.id user interface.

The exam consisted of 40 multiple choice questions from Cambridge's past paper exam questions. The Cambridge Education International Assessment is provided to schools and is affiliated with past paper resources that the teacher can use to examine students' progress. The questions were taken from exam paper from past five years. The questions were prepared by a team of teachers using several processes. They were selecting questions, proofreading the questions, and taking the exam by themselves to check if the exam time was appropriate.

The number of students in each grade from different schools is shown in Table 3.

Table 3. Students' distribution.

| School | City | Grade 7 | Grade 8 | Grade 10 | Grade 11 |
|--------|------|---------|---------|----------|----------|
| Fatih | Banda Aceh | 25 | 23 | 36 | 31 |
| TNA | Banda Aceh | 32 | 29 | 27 | 22 |
| Kharbang | Tangerang Selatan | 42 | 47 | 80 | 72 |
| PD | Depok | 28 | 32 | 36 | 26 |
| PB | Bandung | 37 | 36 | 50 | 55 |
| CRIBS | Bogor | 58 | 22 | 22 | 18 |
| Sem | Semarang | 39 | 26 | 93 | 78 |
| Sem 3 | Semarang | 27 | | | |
| Kesbang | Jogjakarta | 35 | 35 | 81 | 99 |
| Total | | 323 | 250 | 425 | 401 |

## 3 RESULTS AND DISCUSSION

### 3.1 *Observation results*

The results collected from the observation form showed that the online teaching did not alter the habit of teachers during lesson planning and organization. Most of the teachers prepared the lesson plan, similar to before the pandemic. The differences in the lesson plans were that the learning activities were accompanied by digital learning tools such as Google Meet, Zoom Meeting, Edpuzzle, Google Slide, Google Form, Mentimeter, Nearpod, Jamboard, OneNote, and Peardeck. The teachers who were always preparing the lesson plan would prepare the lesson plan similar to before the pandemic. In comparison, teachers who rarely prepared the lesson plan did not improve and became less productive in lesson planning.

For the instructional process, there was a unique finding. Teachers who scored high during offline teaching were scored low during online teaching. Teacher with digital backgrounds who scored medium before the pandemic got high score during online teaching. The teachers' technological savviness helped the teacher navigate different mediums easily, switching from one platform to another without problems. Teachers who were very engaging during the offline teaching had difficulty applying the same strategy during online learning since the teachers' experience of using interactive online teaching application was limited.

For classroom management, it was found that teachers could not control the classroom during online sessions as quickly as offline. The teachers' character and the imposed rules during class were found to be important in conditioning the classroom. The aspects of professionalism that were observed before and after pandemic were not different.

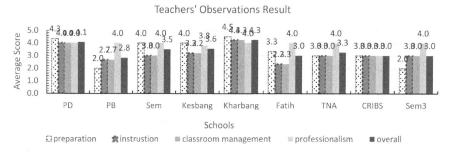

Figure 2. Online instruction teachers' observation results.

In Figure 2 the data showed the teachers' observation results. Kharbang overall scored the highest in every aspect of the teaching and followed by PD in the second position. While according to the overall score the rank from third to the last were Kesbang, Sem, TNA, Fatih, Cribs, Sem3 and PB.

## Grade 7 Physics Summative Exam Results

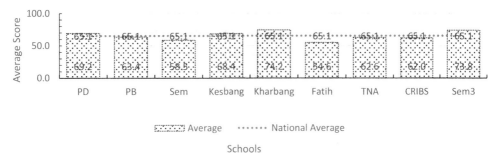

Figure 3.   Grade 7 summative exam results.

## Grade 8 Physics Summative Exam Results

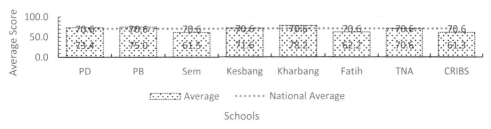

Figure 4.   Grade 8 summative exam results.

### 3.2   *Students' learning performance*

The exam was conducted on 11th of June 2020 and was taken by 1,399 students. There were 323 7th grade students, 250 8th grade students, 425 10th grade students, and 401 11th grade students. The topics for 7th grade students were speed and sound. The questions consisted of 40 multiple choice items with Revised Blooms' Taxonomy cognitive aspect recalling or abbreviated as C1 up until analyzing or abbreviated as C4 type questions for all grades. The curriculum was Cambridge secondary checkpoint science (Figure 3).

The national average score for grade 7th was 65.1 There were four schools that scored above the national average, which are PD, Kesbang, Kharbang, and Sem3. Those four schools were in Java and other big cities which had good infrastructure for online learning. While for PB, Sem, and CRIBS, even though they are in Java, the schools were located in areas with signal difficulty from cellular internet provider. For Fatih and TNA, they are in Banda Aceh, which have different condition as in Java.

The topics for 8th grade students was temperature and thermal expansion, heat energy transfers, and world energy needs. The curriculum was Cambridge secondary checkpoint science (Figure 4). The national average score for grade 8th was 70.6, with five 5 schools who had the same or above the national average, which are PD, PB, Kesbang, Kharbang, and TNA. Three schools comprised the top five, which came from big cities that had good infrastructure for online learning. Two schools with infrastructure problem placed in the top five, which are PB, and TNA. This had to do with the students' intake and experience with the teacher the 7th grade.

The topics for 10th grade students were properties of waves, sound, and. The curriculum was Cambridge International General Certificate of Secondary Education or abbreviated as IGCSE (Figure 5).

The national average score for the 10th grade was 68.2, with four schools that had results above the national average, which are PD, PB, Sem, and Kharbang. Two schools placed in the top five,

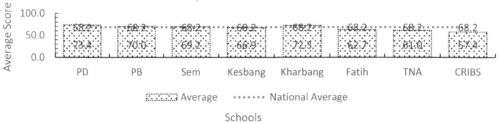

Figure 5.   Grade 10 summative exam results.

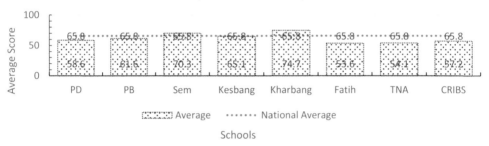

Figure 6.   Grade 11 summative exam results.

and were found in big cities which had good infrastructure for online learning. Three schools with infrastructure problems placed at the bottom, which are Fatih, TNA, and CRIBS. This had to do with the students' intake in the 10th grade.

The topics for 11th grade students were particle physics, motion in a circle, and oscillations (Figure 6). The curriculum was Cambridge Advanced Subsidiary Level.

The national average score for the 11th grade was 65.8, with only two schools that were above the national average, which are Sem, and Kharbang. Kharbang was above average for all grades and according to the observation result. The teacher for Sem for the 11th grade is a very seasoned teacher with science Olympiad medal experience.

## 4   CONCLUSION

The teaching aspect of planning and organization of the lesson was similar to that as before the pandemic, which means the pandemic did not alter teachers' habit in planning and organization. Teachers with a digital background had outstanding performances during online teaching for the instructional process. For classroom management, the teachers' character and class rules imposed were found to be an essential aspect for controlling the students. The professionalism aspect before and during the pandemic were the same. The schools which are located in Java and other big cities scored above the national average. Schools with high-performing teachers were also ranked the highest among other schools.

ACKNOWLEDGEMENTS

Thanks to International Conference of Education in Moslem Society (ICEMS) 2020 FITK UIN Syarif Hidayatullah Jakarta for publication support.

# REFERENCES

Bozkurt, A., Jung, I., Xiao, J., Vladimirschi, V., Schuwer, R., Egorov, G., Lambert, S.R., Al-Freih, M., Pete, J., Olcott, D., Rodes, V., Aranciaga, I., Alvarez, A.V., Roberts, J., Pazurek, A., Raffaghelli, J.E., de Coëtlogon, P., Shahadu, S., Brown, M., Asino, T.I., Reyes, T.R., Ipenza, E.B., Ossiannilsson, E., Bond, M., Irvine, V., Sharma, R.C., Adam, T., Janssen, B., Sklyarova, T., Olcott, N., Ambrosino, A., Lazou, C., Mocquet, B., Mano, M., 2020. A global outlook to the interruption of education due to COVID-19 Pandemic: Navigating in a time of uncertainty and crisis 15, 126.

Cheawjindakarn, B., Suwannatthachote, P., Theeraroungchaisri, A., 2012. Critical Success Factors for Online Distance Learning in Higher Education: A Review of the Literature. Creat. Educ. 03, 61–66. https://doi.org/10.4236/ce.2012.38B014

Chopra, A., Syazwani, A., 2020. Investigating the common factor of drop out based on learner's perspective and dropout rate in MOOCs in Malaysia. Int. Res. J. Eng. Technol. IRJET 7, 5317–5326.

Dhawan, S., 2020. Online Learning: A Panacea in the Time of COVID-19 Crisis. J. Educ. Technol. Syst. 49, 5–22. https://doi.org/10.1177/0047239520934018

Klein, P., Ivanjek, L., Dahlkemper, M.N., Jeličić, K., Geyer, M.-A., Küchemann, S., Susac, A., 2021. Studying physics during the COVID-19 pandemic: Student assessments of learning achievement, perceived effectiveness of online recitations, and online laboratories. Phys. Rev. Phys. Educ. Res. 17, 010117. https://doi.org/10.1103/PhysRevPhysEducRes.17.010117

Rasmitadila, R., Aliyyah, R.R., Rachmadtullah, R., Samsudin, A., Syaodih, E., Nurtanto, M., Tambunan, A.R.S., 2020. The Perceptions of Primary School Teachers of Online Learning during the COVID-19 Pandemic Period: A Case Study in Indonesia. J. Ethn. Cult. Stud. 7, 90. https://doi.org/10.29333/ejecs/388

Seaman, J.E., Allen, I.E., Seaman, J., 2018. Grade Increase: Tracking Distance Education in the United States. Babson Surv. Res. Group.

Teräs, M., Teräs, H., Arinto, P., Brunton, J., Subramaniam, T., 2020. COVID-19 and the push to online learning: reflections from 5 countries. Digit. Cult. Educ. 8.

*Emerging Trends in Technology for Education in an Uncertain World – Nanto, Rahiem & Khalis Maryati (Eds)*
*© 2022 copyright the Author(s), ISBN 978-1-032-11288-6*

# Integration of Islam and science in biochemistry course

S. Suryaningsih, B. Muslim & V. Fitriani
*Departement of Chemistry Education, Faculty of Educational Sciences, Universitas Islam Negeri Syarif Hidayatullah Jakarta, Tangerang Selatan, Banten, Indonesia*

ABSTRACT: The integration of Islam and science is an important idea to create quality education. The Chemistry Education Study Program of UIN Syarif Hidayatullah Jakarta has not optimized the study of Islamic integration in all subjects. The purpose of this research is to conduct an Islamic integration with biochemistry courses. The research method used 4-STMD. The subjects of this study were 60 chemistry education students class of 2016. The instruments used were characterization instruments, expert validation sheets and book feasibility testing instruments. Data analysis using the Guttman scale. The results showed that all concepts had high understanding with a proportion of 92.8%, and all concepts were categorized as easy. The integration of Islam in the material of amino acids and proteins produces a draft of integrated Islamic amino acid and protein material that is suitable for use in learning that can foster faith in Allah SWT.

*Keywords*: Amino Acid and Proteins, Biochemistry, Integration of Islam and Science

## 1 INTRODUCTION

Biochemistry is the study of chemical reactions that occur in living things (Poedjiadi et al. 2012). As for the material in biochemistry courses that can be studied regarding the integration of Islam, one of them is an amino acid and protein material (especially protein-based on function). Amino acids are the building blocks of protein. The protein is a component of living things that performs many functions in the body, including as a driving force, building body structure, transportation of substances, defense, and as an enzyme (Lehninger 2005). This is closely related to Islam because there are many verses of the Al-Quran and hadiths that discuss living things and the features in them. How mighty Allah SWT who has created the human body with many features and various functions. As according to Azhar (2017) in his research entitled "Humans and Science in the Perspective of the Qur'an" states that the human body is so balanced and perfect, these features are mentioned in the Al-Qur'an letter At-Tin verse 4 which means: we have created humans in the best possible form". So the study of Islamic integration referred to in this research is an effort to combine Islamic and scientific sciences, but not in the sense of "being mixed" between the sources of knowledge in Islam, namely the Al-Qur'an and hadiths with science, because both have the same function, namely to understand nature and this life (Suprayogo 2016) The integration of Islam in this study is adjusted to the integration guidelines written in the 2017 chancellor's decree which states that the integration of natural and Islamic sciences is carried out by making the text of the Qur'an and hadith as a source of inspiration or a reference source for the development of knowledge, providing Islamic values. as a basis and reference in the application of science.

Based on this explanation, the purpose of this research is to conduct a study on the integration of Islam (based on the study of the Koran and hadith) with amino acids and proteins based on function, and to analyze students' understanding of the material of amino acids and proteins integrated with Islam so that the results the study in the form of a draft of this material can later be used by students and educators in studying biochemistry courses on amino acids and protein in Islamic aspects, so

DOI 10.1201/9781003219248-9

that not only knowledge of chemical materials will be obtained, but also can enrich knowledge in terms of Islam which is expected to increase devotion to Allah SWT.

## 2 METHODS

The method used is the research and development method (Research and Development/R&D) with the Four Steps Teaching Material Development (4-STMD) development model which consists of four stages, namely the stages of selection, structuring, characterization, and reduction (Chasanah et al. 2019).

The selection stage is the stage of a literature study to collect information related to document studies, curriculum, sources of teaching materials, and information related to the material (Hendri & Setiawan 2016). At this stage, the researchers carried out several activities consisting of analyzing the Learning Outcomes (PLO) and Course Learning Outcomes (CLO) Programs in the Semester Learning Plan (RPS) for biochemistry courses, analyzing Islamic integration models, collecting teaching materials and other sources related to the material. amino acids and proteins as well as sources of Islamic studies, developing learning indicators, making concept analysis, and drafting the suitability of amino acid and protein material with Islamic integration, validating the material at the selection stage.

The structuring stage is the stage of arranging the material didactically. Some of the activities carried out at this stage are making a concept map based on all drafts of the material that has been made, creating a macrostructure, compiling multiple representations, and drafting the material according to the material collected at the didactic selection stage.

At the characterization stage, all concepts that had been compiled from the previous stage were tested on the 2016 batch of chemistry education students using the main idea writing test. The purpose of conducting the characterization stage is to determine the level of student understanding of the concepts that have been compiled (Bartlett 2013). At the bottom of the test instrument, there is also a feedback column for students to provide an assessment of the difficulty level of the concept (Hendri & Setiawan 2016).

The reduction stage is carried out to reduce the difficult concepts contained in the draft material that has been prepared. So this stage can be done if the results of the characterization stage find difficult concepts.

The object of this research is a draft/collection of amino acids and protein materials (based on their function) which is integrated with Islam based on studies sourced from the Al-Qur'an and hadith. The subjects of this research are expert interpreters, chemistry lecturers, and as many as 60 chemistry education students class of 2016, of which all students have received biochemistry courses, value integration, and Islamic and science (IIP) courses.

The data from this research were obtained from the validation sheet and the main idea writing test. Validation sheets are carried out at the selection stage to determine the suitability of amino acid and protein material (based on their function) with Islamic integration (Al-Qur'an verses and hadith). The results obtained were analyzed using the Guttman scale with a score of 1 for the answer "yes" and a score of 0 for the answer "no" (Riduwan 2010). The results of the calculation of the score are then calculated using the formula:

$$Percentage = \frac{Total\ Score}{Maximum\ Score} \times 100\%$$

(Riduwan 2010).

The percentage obtained is then interpreted according to the eligibility criteria according to Riduwan (2010), in Table 1.

The second data collection is in the form of a main idea writing test that is tested on students at the characterization stage. The data generated from the main idea writing test were analyzed by giving a score of 1 for each correct answer, and a score of 0 for wrong answers. The total value obtained is

71

Table 1. Feasibility categories.

| Percentage | Criteria |
|---|---|
| 0–20 | Very Infeasible |
| 21–40 | Infeasible |
| 41–60 | Fair |
| 61–80 | Feasible |
| 81–100 | Very Feasible |

Table 2. Text comprehension level.

| Text Comprehension Criteria | Text Comprehension Level |
|---|---|
| $60 < K \leq 100\%$ | High (Independent Category) |
| $40 < K \leq 60\%$ | Fair (Instructional Category) |
| $K \leq 40\%$ | Low (Hard Category) |

calculated as a percentage as in the previous data collection, then the percentage results obtained can be identified the level of student understanding of the text presented based on the classification of text comprehension criteria according to Rankin and Culhane (Arifin 2016, Table 2).

## 3 RESULT

The results of the research were obtained from several stages that have been carried out based on the Four Steps Teaching Material Development (4-STMD) development model. At the selection stage, the initial activity carried out is an analysis of the competencies to be achieved, so that the draft material developed is following the curriculum (Rahman et al. 2019). The achievement of lecture competencies is formulated by the terms Program Learning Outcomes (PLO) and Course Learning Outcomes (CLO).

The results of the PLO and CLO analysis in the biochemistry course show that biochemistry learning is expected to be able to increase the devotion to God and religious attitudes of students, and be able to master biochemical concepts and be able to relate them to everyday life, as for the biochemical concepts that are the focus of this research, namely the concept biochemistry on the matter of amino acids and proteins based on their function.

The results of the search for reference sources used by researchers to determine the breadth of concepts to be discussed in the material of amino acids and proteins based on their function, which is organized into a form of concept analysis according to Herron et al. (1977) which consists of identifying concept labels, concept definitions, concept attributes, concept hierarchy, examples, and non-examples. The concepts that have been determined are then developed into indicators of amino acid and protein material based on the integrated functions of Islam.

This indicator becomes a reference in developing the draft material for amino acids and proteins based on integrated functions of Islam, to be subsequently reviewed by chemist lecturers and validated by expert commentators. Expert validation was carried out to determine whether the relationship between chemical concepts and aspects of Islamic integration was appropriate or not (Chasanah et al. 2019) Material validation resulted in percentage value of 100% with a slight improvement in the writing of the hadith translation. This shows that the concept of amino acid and protein material based on function is in accordance with its integration in the Al-Qur'an and hadith. The concept and integrated aspects can be seen in Table 3.

In the structuring stage, the suitability of the amino acid and protein material with the validated Islamic integration from the selection stage was arranged in a didactic manner. This stage will

Table 3. Suitability of the concept of chemistry with the aspect of Islamic integration.

| Aspect | Islam Intregation Aspects |
| --- | --- |
| **Amino Acids based on the body's ability to Synthesize** | |
| Essential and Non-Essential Amino Acid | Al-Qur'an |
| **Amino Acids Based on Their Side Chains** | |
| Non-Polar Amino Acid (Hydrophobic) | Al-Qur'an and Hadits |
| Negatively Charged Amino Acids | Al-Qur'an and Hadits |
| Positively Charged Amino Acids | Al-Qur'an |
| **Protein Based on Their Functions** | |
| Enzyme | Al-Qur'an and Hadits |
| Structural Protein | Al-Qur'an |
| Movement Protein | Al-Qur'an |
| Antibody (Defensive Protein) | Al-Qur'an |
| Transport Protein | Al-Qur'an |

facilitate students in connecting one concept to another (Syamsuri et al. 2017) making it easier for students to build cognitive structures. The concepts in the material that have been validated are made into the form of concept maps, macrostructures, and multiple representation tables.

The concept map that has been compiled is used as a reference in presenting the concepts on validated material because by making a concept map it will be seen the relationship of one concept to another (Arifin 2016). The macrostructure generated from this stage serves to determine the outline of the concepts that will be presented in the draft material. The third result at the structuring stage is an explanation of all concepts based on 3 levels of representation, namely macroscopic, submicroscopic, and symbolic, which are referred to as multiple representation tables. Windayani et al. (2018) have also made multiple representations in their research intending to minimize student misconceptions in learning material, so it must be seen the completeness of several levels of chemical representation. The three results of making the material structure are then used as a reference for researchers in drafting the material so that it is easily understood by students.

The characterization stage is carried out to determine the level of student understanding of the concepts in the draft teaching materials and to determine the character of the concepts presented in the teaching materials whether they are included in easy or difficult concepts.

Based on the results of the main idea writing test tested on students, it shows that the average percentage value is 92.8%, with a high level of understanding according to Arifin (2016) as shown in the table. So it can be seen that all the concepts contained in the draft material have a high level of understanding (can be understood easily by the students). This strengthens the existence of the draft material that has been produced to be used by students in studying amino acid and protein material in biochemistry courses, as according to (Bartlett 2013) which states that good teaching materials can be understood by users (Table 4).

At the bottom of the main idea writing test, there is a feedback column or concept characterization for students to provide their assessment of the concepts presented in the material. The results show that the average student gives an assessment that the concept presented has an easy category.

## 4 DISCUSSION

The material coverage that has been known from the results of the CLO analysis in the biochemistry course is used as a reference in collecting teaching material sources. To explore the material in more depth, researchers collected teaching material sources in the form of biochemistry textbooks, journals, and other references related to amino acid and protein material based on function. The main references used are the textbook Biochemistry, Basics of Biomolecules, and the Concept of

Table 4. Results of the main idea writing test.

| Concept Label | Percentage of Concept Understanding (%) | Level of Understanding | Category |
|---|---|---|---|
| Essential and Non Essential Amino Acid | 82 | High | Easy |
| Non-Polar Amino Acid (Hydrophobic) | 87 | High | Easy |
| Negatively Charged Amino Acid | 90 | High | Easy |
| Positively Charged Amino Acid | 93 | High | Easy |
| Enzyme | 97 | High | Easy |
| Struktural Protein | 100 | High | Easy |
| Movement Protein | 92 | High | Easy |
| Antibody | 98 | High | Easy |
| Transport Protein | 97 | High | Easy |
| **Median** | **92.8** | **High** | **Easy** |

Metabolism (Sumarlin 2018), Basics of Biochemistry (Poedjiadi 1994), and Basics of Biochemistry (Lehninger 2005). Because the draft material that was developed contains Islamic values that can be extracted based on the Al-Qur'an and Hadith, the researchers used references that support Islamic content in the form of Al-Qur'an and Hadith Tafsir, including Tafsir Al-Misbah, Tafsir Al- Lubab, Tafsir Ibnu Katsir, Encyclopedia of Islam and Science, Encyclopedia of Hadits and Its Translations. This research was also carried out by Chasanah et al. (2019) namely using interpretation as a reference source for Islamic integration.

This reference is used by researchers because the integration model of this research refers to the Integration Guidelines in the 2017 UIN Jakarta Chancellor's Decree, which is to make the Al-Qur'an and hadith as a reference source for the application of science. It is also supported by several kinds of research on the integration of Islam and science that have been carried out, including the dialogue model for integration of the dialogic girls according to Hamzah (2016) which is an integration model involving two disciplines, namely natural science and religion, Islamic integration according to Fauzan (2017) and Suprayogo (2016) which states that the integration of science and Islam can be carried out if science is presented in an integrated manner with Islam which is based on the qauliyah verse (Al-Qur'an and Hadith). So it can be concluded that the material of amino acids and proteins based on their function is integrated with Islamic aspects, namely the Al-Qur'an and hadith.

The concepts and aspects of integration presented in Table 3 can be explained as follows:

### 4.1 Essential and non-essential amino acid

Based on the body's ability to synthesize amino acids, amino acids are divided into two major parts, namely essential amino acids, which are amino acids that cannot be synthesized by the body, so that these amino acids are obtained from food ingredients derived from animals or plants. The benefits of animals and plants as food for humans have also been explained by Allah in the Al-Qur'an Sura At-Tur verse 22.

The non-essential amino acids are amino acids that can be produced by the body. Glory to Allah who has created humans in the best possible form, so that in the body some non-essential amino acids can be produced which are useful for the body.

### 4.2 Non-polar amino acid (hydrophobic)

Research by Damayanthi et al. (2014) has identified the dominant amino acid content in buffalo milk, namely the amino acids histidine, isoleucine, leucine, lysine, methionine, phenylalanine, threonine, valine, alanine, and tyrosine which are amino acids with nonpolar side chains and beneficial for the body. The specialty of milk for human consumption has also been explained by Allah in Al-Qur'an Surah An-Nahl verse 66. In the hadith narrated by Abu Dawud, the Prophet Muhammad. also mentioned the benefits of milk as medicine.

### 4.3  *Negatively charged amino acid*

Aspartic acid and glutamic acid are amino acids that have negative side chains. Glutamic acid was first found in wheat (Lehninger 2005) which has many benefits in it. So much for the benefits of wheat, at the time of the Prophet Yusuf, wheat was used as a staple food as mentioned in the Al-Qur'an, Yusuf verses 47-48. The benefits of consuming wheat-based foods have also been mentioned by the Prophet Muhammad in the hadith narrated by Bukhari.

### 4.4  *Positively charged amino acid*

Lysine, arginine, and histidine are amino acids that have positively charged side chains. Research conducted by Purwaningsih et al. (2013) showed that fresh Ipong-Ipong snail meat contained dominant lysine and arginine content. This amino acid content is beneficial for the growth and defense of the body. The benefits of sea animals have also been provided by Allah SWT. mention in the Al-Quran Surah Al-Maidah verse 96, namely Allah SWT. has legalized marine animals as delicious food for humans.

### 4.5  *Enzyme*

Protein functions as an enzyme, which functions as a catalyst (speeds up chemical reactions). One example of an enzyme is found in the digestive system to help break down food so that it is easily absorbed by the body. Digestive enzymes will work properly according to their function if humans eat the right way and not in excess. This good eating procedure has also been described in the Al-Qur'an surah Al-A'raf verse 31, the Prophet Muhammad. has also recommended it as stated in the hadith narrated by Tirmidhi.

### 4.6  *Movement protein*

Movement protein is a protein required for all forms of movement or coordination of movement, one of which is the dine-in protein which functions as a flagellum activator in sperm, so that the sperm is able to penetrate the egg in the process of human reproduction, then the results of the fusion of the sperm and egg are stored in the uterus. Sperm, which was used as the basic material for human creation and stored in the womb, has also been explained by Allah in the Al-Qur'an Surat Al-Mursalat verses 20 and 21.

### 4.7  *Structural protein*

Protein functions to provide mechanical support and outer covering, so it is called a structural protein, one of which is the structural protein in bone for movement and body support. Allah Most High has arranged human bones since human development in the form of a fetus in a mother's womb, as explained in the Al-Qur'an surah Al-Mu'minum verse 14.

### 4.8  *Antibody (protein as a defensive measure)*

Antibodies as the body's immune system are very specific proteins and can recognize and combine with foreign bodies. AIDS, which is caused by HIV, is a disease that attacks the immune system, which until now is still destroying humans. HIV is transmitted in various conditions of sexual intercourse. So by staying away from adultery is not only keeping yourself away from the disease, but also a proof of obedience to stay away from the prohibitions in Islam, because of Allah SWT has previously prohibited people from committing adultery as stated in the Al-Qur'an chapter Al-Isra 'verse 32.

### 4.9 *Transport protein*

Protein also functions as a means of transportation in the body. Hemoglobin is a transport protein that carries oxygen in the blood to diffuse into body cells. Hemoglobin carries oxygen to the capillaries of the systematic circuit, capillaries to the veins, and veins return blood to the heart. Because of the important role of the heart and blood vessels that spread in the human body, in the Al-Qur'an surah Al-Haqqah verses 44-47, Allah SWT makes the heart and veins (to be cut) a threat to people who deviate.

The reduction stage is carried out on the results of the comprehension test which has a medium and low level of understanding. According to Munawwarah and Anwar (2016) which states that the reduction stage is a stage that is carried out to reduce difficult concepts so that they are easy to understand. The results of the characterization stage in this study indicate that all concepts in the draft material have a high understanding of the easy category, so in this study, the reduction stage was not carried out. The final result of the 4-STMD development process is in the form of teaching materials that have easy concept criteria (Hendri & Setiawan 2016), so in line with these objectives, the whole draft material of Islamic integrated amino acid and protein material produced in this study is easy to understand so it is feasible to use.

## 5  CONCLUSION

Based on the research that has been carried out, the conclusion is that the study of the integration of Islam with amino acid and protein material (based on function) can be carried out to produce a collection of integrated Islamic amino acid and protein material (based on the results of the study of the Qur'an and hadith) which is appropriate to be presented as a collection of materials for teaching materials. It is said to be feasible because based on the results of validation by expert commentators, all concepts are following the aspects of Islamic integration, namely the Al-Qur'an and hadith. The collection of integrated Islamic amino acid and protein material that is produced also has a high level of understanding that is easily understood by students, so it is suitable for use by students in studying biochemistry courses on amino acids and protein, as well as its integration with the Al-Qur'an and hadiths can enrich the treasury of religious knowledge. The material studied for its integration in this study only focused on amino acids and proteins (based on function). In the biochemistry course, many other materials can be studied regarding its integration with Islam based on the Al-Qur'an and hadith. So with this research, it is hoped that it can give birth to the study of Islamic integration with other materials in biochemistry courses so that learning can be delivered in its entirety from the point of view of science and Islam.

## ACKNOWLEDGMENT

We acknowledgement that thank to International Conference of Education in Moslem Society (ICEMS) 2020 FITK UIN Syarif Hidayatullah Jakarta for publication support.

## REFERENCES

Arifin, A. S. (2016). the Development of Earth Quake Teaching Material for Junior High School By Four Step Teaching Materials Development Method Pengembangan Bahan Ajar Tema Gempa Bumi Menggunakan Four Step Teaching Materials Development. *Jurnal Pendidikan Fisika Indonesia, 12*(1), 8–18.

Azhar, A. (2017). Manusia Dan Sains Dalam Perspektif Al-Qur'an. *Lantanida Journal, 4*(1), 72. https://doi.org/10.22373/lj.v4i1.1869

Bartlett, J. (2013). 济無 *Journal of Chemical Information and Modeling, 53*(9), 1689–1699.

Chasanah, G., Suryaningsih, S., & Fairusi, D. (2019). ANALISIS INTEGRASI KEISLAMAN PADA MATERI KIMIA PANGAN (Sumber, Manfaat, dan Keterpahamannya). *JTK (Jurnal Tadris Kimiya), 4*(2), 168–176. https://doi.org/10.15575/jtk.v4i2.5197

Damayanthi, E., Yopi, Hasinah, H., Setyawardani, T., Rizqiati, H., & Putra, S. (2014). Karakteristik Susu Kerbau Sungai dan Rawa di Sumatera Utara. Jurnal Ilmu Pertanian Indonesia. *Jurnal Ilmu Pertanian Indonesia, 19*(2), 67–73.

Fauzan, F. (2017). Integrasi Islam Adan Sains Dalam Kurikulum Program Studi Pendidikan Guru Mi Berbasis Kkni. *JMIE (Journal of Madrasah Ibtidaiyah Education), 1*(1), 1–13. https://doi.org/10.32934/jmie.v1i1.21

Hamzah, F. (2016). Studi Pengembangan Modul Pembelajaran Ipa Berbasis Integrasi Islam – Sains Pada Pokok Bahasan Sistem Reproduksi Kelas Ix Madrasah Tsanawiyah. *Adabiyah: Jurnal Pendidikan Islam, 1*(1), 41. https://doi.org/10.21070/ja.v1i1.163

Hendri, S., & Setiawan, W. (2016). *The Development of Earth Quake Teaching Material for Junior High School By Four Step Teaching Materials Development Method Pengembangan Bahan Ajar Tema Gempa Bumi Menggunakan Four Step Teaching Materials Development, 12*(1), 65–76. https://doi.org/10.15294/jpfi

Herron, J. D., Cantu, L. L., Ward, R., & Srinivasan, V. (1977). Problems associated with concept analysis. *Science Education, 61*(2), 185–199. https://doi.org/10.1002/sce.3730610210

Lehninger. (2005). *Dasar-dasar Biokimia*. Jakarta: Erlangga

Munawwarah, P., & Anwar, S. (2016). The Development of Interactive E-Book Learning Materials Through 4S TMD. *Enriching Quality and Providing Affordable Education Through New Academia*, 402–408.

Poedjiadi, Anna, & Supiyanti, Titin. (1994). *Dasar-Dasar Biokimia*. Jakarta: UI Press.

Purwaningsih, S., Salamah, E., & Apriyana, G. P. (2013). PROFIL PROTEIN DAN ASAM AMINO KEONG IPONG-IPONG (Fasciolaria salmo) PADA PENGOLAHAN YANG BERBEDA. *Jurnal Gizi Dan Pangan, 8*(1), 77. https://doi.org/10.25182/jgp.2013.8.1.77-82

Rahman, D. F., Chandra, D. T., & Anwar, S. (2019). Development of an integrated science teaching material oriented ability to argue for junior high school student. *Journal of Physics: Conference Series, 1157*(2). https://doi.org/10.1088/1742-6596/1157/2/022056

Riduwan. (2010). *Dasar-Dasar Statistika*. Bandung: Alfabeta.

Sumarlin, La Ode. (2018). *Biokimia Dasar-dasar Biomolekul dan Konsep Metabolisme*. Jakarta: UIN Jakarta Press.

Suprayogo, I. (2016). Membangun Integrasi Ilmu dan Agama: Pengalaman UIN Maulana Malik Ibrahim Malang. *Batusangkar International Conference, 1*(October), 27–46.

Syamsuri, B. S., Anwar, S., & Sumarna, O. (2017). Development of Teaching Material Oxidation-Reduction Reactions through Four Steps Teaching Material Development (4S TMD). *Journal of Physics: Conference Series, 895*(1). https://doi.org/10.1088/1742-6596/895/1/012111

Windayani, N., Hasanah, I., & Helsy, I. (2018). Analisis Bahan Ajar Senyawa Karbon Berdasarkan Kriteria Keterhubungan Representasi Kimia. *JTK (Jurnal Tadris Kimiya), 3*(1), 83–93. https://doi.org/10.15575/jtk.v3i1.2682

*Emerging Trends in Technology for Education in an Uncertain World – Nanto, Rahiem & Khalis Maryati (Eds)*

# Metacognition as an approach to overcome mathematical anxiety

Z. Amir, Risnawati & L.M. Rizki
*Universitas Islam Negeri Sultan Syarif Kasim, Pekanbaru, Riau, Indonesia*

ABSTRACT:   Mathematics is a subject that is often feared and makes students anxious. It requires thinking skills as known as metacognitive. To improve these thinking skills, each student must reduce anxiety in learning mathematics. This article reviewed 45 articles that related to the metacognition approach and mathematical anxiety. This article explored the characteristics of mathematical anxiety, the causes of mathematical anxiety, and the correlation between mathematical anxiety and the metacognition approach. The result shows that: 1) mathematical anxiety has various characteristics that could be divided into physical, behavioral, and cognitive characteristics; 2) the cause factors of mathematical anxiety are from students' cognitive and students' affective self and social or environment of the student; 3) mathematical anxiety can be reduced by the metacognition approach. These results suggest that the metacognition approach needs to be introduced to students as early as possible.

## 1 INTRODUCTION

Anxiety comes from Latin (*anxious*) and from German (*anst*), which is a word used to describe the adverse effects and physiological stimuli (Bellack & Hersen 1988). Singer (1980) says that anxiety refers to a tendency to perceive situations as threatening or stressful (*stressful*). Anxiety occurs when a specific condition is perceived as scary or threatening.

*Pathophobia* is a synonym for mathematics anxiety as "an irrational and impeditive fear of mathematics" (Lazarus 1974). Lazarus (1976) distinguishes feelings of anxiety based on the causes. First, *state anxiety* is a temporary emotional reaction. Second, *trait anxiety* is a condition that exists in an individual. Besides that, mathematical anxiety is a belief that cannot solve math problems, and they even avoid math lessons (Hembree 1990; Oxford & Vordick 2006; Scarpello 2007; Sheffield & Hunt 2006; Richardson & Suinn 1972). Also, Bessant (1995) explains that the concept of mathematical anxiety has two dimension which is cognitive dimension and affective dimension. The cognitive dimension contributes to explore students' difficulties in learning mathematics. The affective dimension contributes to examine the influence of mathematics, attitudes, and larger and clearer anxiety concepts. Fiore (1999) found that mathematical anxiety as an emotional and cognitive fear.

Furthermore, mathematical anxiety generally comes from negative encounters from teachers, tutors, classmates, parents, or siblings (Yenilmez et al. 2007). Mathematics anxiety can also happen at all level of school or education. Once it is formed, it will persistently interfere with daily activities, especially when it involves numeracy skills and learning mathematics.

Mathematical anxiety is a hot topic in mathematics education research. Some research states that students feel anxious when learning mathematics (Amir 2015; Desai et al. 2018; Irfan 2017). According to the Ministry of Health of the Republic of Indonesia in Anita (2014), anxiety is tension, insecurity, and worry that arise because of something unpleasant. She further explained that each student faces a different kind of anxiety depending on the students' preferences and tendencies towards certain subjects. The higher a student's anxiety in learning mathematics will certainly impact the process and learning outcomes. If it is not taken seriously, it will affect

DOI 10.1201/9781003219248-10

students' psychological and emotional conditions while studying mathematics, a source of anxiety. Therefore, it is necessary to conduct a study regarding the causal factors of mathematical anxiety and reduce mathematical anxiety.

In learning mathematics, metacognition can play a role in solving problems. Schoenfeld (2016) says that there are three various aspects of metacognition in mathematics learning, namely: 1) *beliefs and intuitions*; 2) a person's knowledge about his thinking process, in this case how a person describes his thinking appropriately; 3) consciousness *(self-awareness)* or setting yourself *(self-regulation)*. Through these three aspects, it is expected that students have self-confidence in learning, are aware of what difficulties are being experienced, and can control the way they learn. Thus, it is hoped that the metacognition approach can reduce anxiety in learning mathematics.

Metacognition is an essential concept of cognition theory, simply defined as rethinking what has been thought. It is defined as knowledge and activities that regulate cognition (Lockl & Schneider 2007; Murti 2012). Neisser (1976) explains that the term cognition refers to the whole interaction where tactile information is changed, diminished, deciphered, put away, recovered, and utilized. It can be seen as thinking about one's thinking or cognition about a person's cognition. In other words, metacognition is cognition at the second level (Anggo 2011). To sum up, metacognition is a thinking process that a person does about his mind.

Based on the description above, metacognitive can be used as a mathematics learning approach since a long time ago. There are so many studies that investigate the relationship between math anxiety and the metacognition approach. So, it is crucial to conduct a literature study on metacognition as an approach to overcome mathematical anxiety.


## 2 METHOD

This study is a document survey. The data was collected by the library research method. The sources were tracked by websites such as EBSCO, ScienceDirect, Proquest, Google Scholar, and Sinta within five decades. It is carried out by reading, recording, and comparing several journals, scientific articles, books, documents, and other information that is considered relevant. Three main things need to be considered in this research are: 1) the authors are faced directly with text/numerical data; 2) sources from the library are interpreted as a second source, it means that the authors obtained information from the second party, not directly from the field survey; 3) the data obtained is ready-to-use; 4) the library material obtained is not limited by space and time. This study reviewed 45 papers, including books and articles with the keywords "mathematical anxiety" and "metacognition." The data were analyzed and summarized in systematic paragraphs and produced conclusions to explore: 1) what are the characteristics of mathematical anxiety? 2) what is the cause factor of mathematical anxiety? 3) what is the metacognition approach? And 4) how is the relationship between math anxiety and metacognition approach?


## 3 RESULTS AND DISCUSSION

### 3.1 *Characteristics of mathematical anxiety*

Mathematical anxiety can disturb a student physically, behaviorally, and cognitively. Table 1 shows several previous studies that explained the characteristics of mathematical anxiety from 1972 to 2019.

Table 1 shows that not all studies on mathematical anxiety have the same characteristics. Only two of six researchers stated that mathematical anxiety could be seen from cognitive traits. The contents will be discussed in detail as follow.

Richardson and Suinn (1972) say that mathematics anxiety involves disturbing feelings of tension and anxiety and is associated with number manipulation and mathematical problem-solving in various situations. Hembree (1990) also conducted a meta-analysis of 151 studies that used the

Table 1. Characteristic of mathematical anxiety.

| Name | Year | Characteristics | | |
|---|---|---|---|---|
| | | Physical | Behavioral | Cognitive |
| Richardson & Suinn | 1972 | √ | | √ |
| R. Martinez | 1987 | | √ | |
| Aksu & Saygi | 1988 | | √ | |
| Hembre | 1990 | √ | √ | |
| Annisa & Ifdil | 2016 | √ | √ | √ |
| Paudel | 2019 | √ | √ | |

construct math anxiety, stating that one of his research results was that common fears were related to mathematics, including classes, homework, and tests. Thus, mathematical anxiety symptoms can occur in students while doing homework at home or doing tests. Also, anxiety can be seen as a physical problem characterized by erratic heart movements (Hembree 1990; Richardson & Suinn 1972).

Moreover, Martinez (1987) says that the symptoms of people experiencing math anxiety include experiencing delays in final math assignments, avoiding class frequently, and saying negative things about math. According to Aksu and Saygi (1988), these feelings and thoughts about math anxiety include incorporate strain, alarm, powerlessness, dread, sorrow, disgrace, and a failure to adapt.

Annisa and Ifdil (2016) also says that anxiety characteristics can be seen from physical traits, behavioral characteristics,and cognitive characteristics. They further explained that from the physical aspects. There will be nervousness, trembling hands or limbs, the sensation of a tight band that binds around the forehead, tightness in the skin pores of the stomach or chest, excessive sweating, sweaty palms, fainting, dry mouth, difficulty speaking, difficulty breathing, or shortness of breath, heart racing, cold fingers or limbs, feeling weak or numb, neck or back feeling stiff, there is upset stomach or nausea, fever cold, frequent urination, face flushed and feeling sensitive or irritable. Behavior characteristics can be seen by avoidance behavior, attached and dependent behavior, and shaken behavior. Then, the characteristics of anxiety in the cognitive aspect are worrying about something, feeling disturbed by fear of something that will happen in the future, the belief that something terrible will happen soon without a clear explanation, feeling threatened, fear of losing control, fear of losing overcoming problems, thinking that everything is out of control, worrying about trivial things, difficulty in concentrating, and focusing your mind (Annisa & Ifdil 2016). Arem in Paudel (2019) adds that people who experience math anxiety have feelings of disorder, confusion, insecurity, and experience of hard to breath, muscle shortness, or other physical ailments.

## 3.2 *Causes factor of mathematical anxiety*

Mathematical anxiety is a feeling of tension, discomfort, and a sense of inability to solve problems related to mathematics that can be caused by three factors, namely: 1) *Cognitive factors,* as a process factor in obtaining knowledge and understanding of mathematics have a significant role because anxiety can arise due to a lack of understanding of the concept of mathematics itself; 2) *Affective factors,* it is related to feelings and attitudes towards mathematics, where these feelings and attitudes will affect the understanding of mathematics itself; 3) *Social or environmental factors,* it is related to treatment from the surrounding student that can influence the anxiety of student in learning. The summary of expert studies that have been discussed before can be seen in Table 2.

Table 1 shows that 9 of 14 experts found that cognitive is one factor that can cause mathematical anxiety, while 10 of 14 are affective factors. Only 2 of 14 experts said that social or environmental factors could cause it. In this paper, the cognitive aspect will be explicitly discussed.

Table 2. Expert's studies on causes factor of mathematical anxiety.

| Name | Year | Factor | | |
|------|------|-----------|-----------|------------------------|
| | | Cognitive | Affective | Social or environmental |
| Richardson & Suinn | 1972 | ✓ | ✓ | |
| Lazarus | 1976 | ✓ | ✓ | |
| Mathison | 1977 | | ✓ | |
| Singer | 1980 | | ✓ | |
| Bellack & Hersen | 1988 | | ✓ | |
| Hembree | 1990 | ✓ | ✓ | |
| Bessant | 1995 | ✓ | ✓ | |
| Fiore | 1999 | ✓ | ✓ | |
| Trujillo & Hadfield | 1999 | ✓ | ✓ | ✓ |
| Shiffield & Hunt | 2006 | ✓ | | |
| Scarpello | 2007 | ✓ | | |
| Yenilmez | 2007 | | | ✓ |
| Arigbabu | 2012 | ✓ | | |

Mathematical anxiety should be taken seriously. Experts have conducted several studies to deal with anxiety, especially mathematics anxiety. Some experts used brain imaging technology for the first time on people who experience anxiety in doing math problems. Scientists have learned how some students can overcome their fears and succeed in mathematics (Saputra 2017; Wicaksono & Saufi 2013). Researchers from the University of Chicago found a strong relationship between success in solving math problems and activity in the brain area network in the frontal and parietal lobes that are involved in controlling attention and regulating adverse emotional reactions (Siregar & Lisma 2018).

According to Freedman (2012), there are ten method to diminish mathematical anxiety, namely: 1) defeat negative self-talk; 2) propose some questions; 3) think that mathematics is a foreign language – it must be practiced; 4) do not use memorization methods in studying mathematics; 5) read your math text; 6) study math depend upon your learning style; 7) ask someone else in the same day if you don't understand; 8) be enjoy while studying math; 9) talk mathematics, 10) develop the responsibility for your successes and failures.

From the description of the opinion above, several things that might overcome math anxiety are as follows. A teacher must eliminate students' negative prejudice against mathematics by providing rational explanations to students why they should learn mathematics. For example, the teacher provides simple models to complex models. Besides, teachers can also use various learning innovations so that students feel interested and impressed with mathematics. Teachers can build a student's self-confidence while doing math problems. For example, the teacher gives easy questions first so they can work on these questions. Then, students will have confidence that they can do math problems, and students will be challenged to solve the following problem. Also, Friedman's ten methods are close to the metacognitive approach, namely, thinking about what is being thought, which will then be discussed in the next section.

### 3.3 The relationship between metacognition approach and mathematical anxiety

Metacognition is someone's ability to regulate and control his/her thinking process. According to the metacognition theory, students who have this ability can handle and retain what they learn. This ability differs someone from other individuals according to their thinking process abilities. So, by using this metacognition approach, it is expected that students can control themselves well in understanding what they are learning so that there is no excessive fear that causes anxiety in learning. This approach could develop students' abilities in learning cognitive strategies such as asking themselves and gaining awareness control over themselves.

According to Fauzi (2012), students who learn with Metacognition Training (MT) are more flexible in using vocabulary, fluency, and metacognition explanation strategies than students who learn without MT. It can be concluded that metacognition learning is an alternative that can foster students' self-confidence so that it can reduce mathematical anxiety because mathematics anxiety is closely related to feelings of fear, anxiety, the tension in participating in mathematics learning.

The metacognition approach will increase the students' self-confidence because they are trained to describe their thinking activities. It will also reduce anxiety in learning mathematics. With this approach, students can control their thinking processes so that there is no tension in carrying out learning. The metacognitive approach could be used to investigate the effects of mathematics anxiety on mathematics learning and problem-solving (Morsanyi et al. 2019).

There is so much previous research that relates to the metacognition approach and mathematical anxiety. Legg and Locker (2009) say that metacognition moderated math anxiety. It also predicted performance would decrease as anxiety increased, except at high metacognition levels. Other research by Saricam and Ogurlu (2015) and Anggoro et al. (2019) show a negative correlation between metacognitive awareness and math anxiety. The results indicated that the metacognition approach mediated the effect of mathematical anxiety (Lai et al. 2015). The metacognition approach has an important role in learning mathematics and reducing mathematical anxiety (Özcan & Eren 2019; Trigueros et al. 2020).

Overall, the metacognition approach can reduce students' mathematical. It needs to be taught to students as early as possible.

## 4   CONCLUSION

Mathematical anxiety involves disturbing feelings of tension and anxiety. It is associated with number manipulation and mathematical problem-solving in life and academic situations caused by cognitive factors, affective factors, and social or environmental factors. It can happen to students ranging from elementary to tertiary education. The metacognition approach is an alternative that can be used to implement mathematics learning to reduce mathematical anxiety experienced by students. Through the metacognition approach, students are trained to find, obtain, store, and recall the information they have received in mathematics learning. So, it can reduce students' fear and grow students' motivation to take part in learning. It also fosters self-confidence in facing mathematics learning. Hopefully, it can overcome students' mathematical anxiety. Therefore, the metacognitive approach should be introduced to students early on.

## ACKNOWLEDGMENT

The authors would like to express our gratitude to International Conference of Education in Moslem Society (ICEMS) 2020 FITK UIN Syarif Hidayatullah Jakarta for publication support.

## REFERENCES

Aksu, M., & Saygi, M. 1988. Turkeyfostersects of Feedback Treatment on Math-Anxiety Levels of Sixth Grade Turkish Students. *School Science and Mathematics*, *88*(5), 390–396.

Amir, Z. 2015. Mengungkap seni bermatematika dalam pembelajaran. *Suska Journal of Mathematics Education*, *1*(1), 60–78.

Anggo, M. 2011. Pelibatan metakognisi dalam pemecahan masalah matematika. *Edumatica: Jurnal Pendidikan Matematika*.

Anggoro, B.S., Agustina, S., Komala, R., Komarudin, K., Jermsittiparsert, K., & Widyastuti, W. 2019. An Analysis of Students' Learning Style, Mathematical Disposition, and Mathematical Anxiety toward

Metacognitive Reconstruction in Mathematics Learning Process Abstract. *Al-Jabar: Jurnal Pendidikan Matematika*, *10*(2), 187–200.

Annisa, D.F., & Ifdil, I. 2016. Konsep kecemasan (anxiety) pada lanjut usia (lansia). *Konselor*, *5*(2), 93–99.

Arigbabu, A.A., Balogun, S.K., Oladipo, S.E., Ojedokun, O.A., Opayemi, S.A, Enikanoselu, O.A., & Oluwafemi, OJ. 2012. Examining Correlates of Math Anxiety Among Single-Sex & Co-Educational Schools in Nigeria. *Global Journal of Human Social Science Linguistics & Education*, *12*(10), 1–14.

Bellack, & Hersen, M. 1988. Behavioral Modification: An Introductory. *Text Book Oxford University*.

Bessant, K.C. 1995. Factors associated with types of mathematics anxiety in college students. *Journal for Research in Mathematics Education*, 327–345.

Desai, W.I., Dariyo, A., & Basaria, D. 2018. Hubungan Antara Kecemasan Matematika dan Self-Efficacy Dengan Hasil Belajar Matematika Siswa SMA X Kota Palangka Raya. *Jurnal Muara Ilmu Sosial, Humaniora, dan Seni*, *1*(2), 556–568.

Fauzi, K.M.A. 2011. Peningkatan kemampuan koneksi matematis dan kemandirian belajar siswa dengan pendekatan pembelajaran metakognitif di sekolah menengah pertama.

Fiore, G. 1999. Math-abused students: are we prepared to teach them? *The Mathematics Teacher*, *92*(5), 403–406.

Freedman, Ellen. 2012. *Do You Have Math Anxiety? A Self-Test.*

Hembree, R. 1990. The nature, effects, and relief of mathematics anxiety. *Journal for Research in Mathematics Education*, 33–46.

Irfan, M. 2017. Analisis Kesalahan Siswa dalam Pemecahan Masalah Berdasarkan Kecemasan Belajar Matematika. *Kreano, Jurnal Matematika Kreatif-Inovatif*, *8*(2), 143–149.

Lai, Y., Zhu, X., Chen, Y., & Li, Y. 2015. Effects of mathematics anxiety and mathematical metacognition on word problem-solving in children with and without mathematical learning difficulties. *PloS One*, *10*(6), e0130570.

Lazarus, M. 1974. Pathophobia: Some personal speculations. *The National Elementary Principal*.

Lazarus, R.S. 1976. *Patterns of Adjustment and Human Effectiveness*. Tokyo: Mcgraw-Hill Kogakusha, Ltd.

Legg, A.M., & Locker J.L. 2009. Math performance and its relationship to math anxiety and metacognition. *North American Journal of Psychology*, *11*(3).

Lockl, K., & Schneider, W. 2007. Knowledge about The Mind: Links Between Theory of Mind and Later Metamemory. *Child Development*, *78*(1), 148–167.

Mathison, M. 1977. Curricular interventions and programming innovations for the reduction of mathematics anxiety.

Morsanyi, K., Cheallaigh, N.N., & Ackerman, R. 2019. Mathematics anxiety and metacognitive processes: Proposal for a new line of inquiry. *Psihologijske teme*, *28*(1), 147–169.

Neisser, U. 1976. Cognition and Reality WH Freeman. *New York*.

Oxford, J., & Vordick, T. 2006. Math anxiety at Tarleton State University: An empirical report. *Tarleton State University*.

Özcan, Z. Ç., & Eren Gümüş, A. 2019. A modeling study to explain mathematical problem-solving performance through metacognition, self-efficacy, motivation, and anxiety. *Australian Journal of Education*, *63*(1), 116–134.

Paudel, K.C. 2019. Mathematics Anxiety among Secondary Level Students in Nepal. *The Eurasia Proceedings of Educational and Social Sciences*, *14*, 34–40.

R. Martinez, J.G. 1987. Preventing math anxiety: A prescription. *Academic Therapy*, *23*(2), 117–125.

Richardson, F.C., & Suinn, R.M. 1972. The mathematics anxiety rating scale: psychometric data. *Journal of Counseling Psychology*, *19*(6), 551.

Saricam, H., & Ogurlu, Ü. 2015. Metacognitive Awareness and Math Anxiety in Gifted Students. *Cypriot Journal of Educational Sciences*, *10*(4), 338–348.

Scarpello, G. 2007. Helping students get past math anxiety. *Techniques: Connecting Education and Careers (J1)*, *82*(6), 34–35.

Schoenfeld, A.H. 2016. Learning to think mathematically: Problem-solving, metacognition, and sense-making in mathematics (Reprint). *Journal of Education*, *196*(2), 1–38.

Sheffield, D., & Hunt, T. 2006. How Does Anxiety Influence Math Performance and What Can We Do About It? *MSOR Connections*, *6*(4), 19–23.

Singer, R.N. 1980. *Motor learning and human performance: An application to motor skills and movement behaviors*. New York: Macmillan.

Siregar, M.A.P., & Lisma, E. 2018. Pengaruh Rasa Cemas Terhadap Prestasi Belajar Matematika Siswa di SMP Negeri 28 Medan. *AXIOM: Jurnal Pendidikan dan Matematika*, *7*(2).

Trigueros, R., Aguilar-Parra, J.M., Mercader, I., Fernández-Campoy, J.M., & Carrión, J. 2020. Set the Controls for the Heart of the Maths. The Protective Factor of Resilience in the Face of Mathematical Anxiety. *Mathematics*, 8(10), 1660.

Trujillo, K.M., & Hadfield, O.D. 1999. Tracing the roots of mathematics anxiety through in-depth interviews with preservice elementary teachers. *College Student Journal*, 33(2), 219–232.

Wicaksono, A.B., & Saufi, M. 2013. Mengelola kecemasan siswa dalam pembelajaran matematika. In *Prosiding Seminar Nasional Matematika dan Pendidikan Matematika* (Vol. 9).

Yenilmez, K., Girginer, N., & Uzun, O. 2007. Mathematics anxiety and attitude level of students of the Faculty of Economics and Business Administrator; The Turkey Model. *International Mathematical Forum*, 2(41), 1997–2021.

# The use of Matlab to compute the total vertex irregularity strength of generalized uniform cactus chain graphs with pendant vertices

I. Rosyida
*Department of Mathematics, Faculty of Mathematics and Natural Sciences,*
*Universitas Negeri Semarang, Semarang, Indonesia*

ABSTRACT: Given a graph $G(V, E)$ which consists of the sets $V$ (set of vertices) and $E$ (set of edges), respectively. In this article, we study the "vertex irregular total k-labeling" of $G$ and the "total vertex irregularity strength of $G$" (tvs($G$)). Based on the formulas that was initiated in the previous results, we construct algorithms to calculate the tvs of $C_r C_n^{n-2}$, i.e., the generalized uniform cactus chain graphs which have $(n-2)r$ vertices of degree one and the length of the chain is $r$. According to the formulas that have been published, the algorithms are constructed into two cases, i.e. the cycle on each chain is an odd cycle or an even cycle. Further, we evaluate the algorithm through Matlab programming. We choose Matlab to compute the tvs because it is better in constructing and programming mathematical formulas. Therefore, it could be an interactive media in the labeling process so that the students could learn the labeling concept easily.

## 1 INTRODUCTION

Assume $G$ is simple, finite, and each edge does not have orientation. The concept of graph labeling was given in (Wallis 2001) as follows: A labeling $h$ of $G$ is called total $k$-labeling if it maps the union of $V$ and $E$ into a set $\{1, 2, \ldots, k\}$ which are mentioned as labels. Further, the total labeling $h$ is called a vertex irregular if each pair of vertices has distict weights, i.e., $wt_h(x) \neq wt_h(y)$ for different vertices $x, y \in V$ where $wt_h(x) = h(x) + \sum_{xv \in E} ht(xv)$. A minimum number $k$ for which $G$ has a "vertex irregular total $k$-labeling" is called "a total vertex irregularity strength of $G$", symbolized by tvs($G$) (Bača et al. 2007, 2015).

Bača et al. (2007), Anholcer et al. (2009), also Nurdin et al. (2010) initiated the lower bounds to determine the tvs of $G(V, E)$. In this paper, we use the bound proved in Nurdin et al. (2010). Many researchers have studied the tvs of various graph classes, such as in Ahmad et al. (2014), Bača et al. (2015), Indriati et al. (2016), Nurdin et al. (2010), Rosyida et al. (2019b, 2020a, 2020b), etc. For more results on tvs of any graphs, the readers could see in the survey of Gallian (2018). The concepts of cactus graphs and cactus chain graphs were studied in Borissevich and Došlić (2015), Rosyida and Indriati (2019a), Sadeghieh et al. (2017), and others. In this paper, we focus on the class of uniform cactus chain graphs $C_r(C_n^{n-2})$ of the length $r$ that contain $(n-2)r$ vertices of degree one (Rosyida et al. 2020b). The uniqueness of the $C_r(C_n^{n-2})$ graphs compared to other uniform cactus chains is the existence of $(n-2)$ pendants vertices connected to $(n-2)$ vertices of cycle $C_n$ on each chain.

Based on the theorems given in (2020b), we construct algorithms to determine labels of elements of the generalized uniform cactus chains $C_r(C_n^{n-2})$ and compute the tvs. Recently, the use of technology is needed on all aspects, such as in research, education, bussines, etc. Matlab is better in constructing, visualizing, and programming mathematical formulas ("What is MATLAB" 2020). Therefore, we choose Matlab to verify the algorithms through Matlab programming and show some experimental results of the program. Also, many students we familiar with Matlab in other course before. Hopefully, the Matlab programming for the labeling could motivate the students to learn the labeling concept easily and also could help the lecturer to teach the labeling concept interactively.

## 2  METHODS

We use the steps as follows.

1. Presenting definition $C_r(C_n^{n-2})$ as given in Rosyida et al. (2020). The notion of the cactus graph is referred from (Borissevich & Došlić 2015; Rosyida & Indriati 2019a; Sadeghieh et al. 2017). A cactus graph that contains cycles with the same size $n$ (for any natural number $n$) is mentioned as an $n$-uniform cactus graph. Meanwhile, an $n$-uniform cactus chain graph is a uniform cactus graph in which each cycle has maximally two cut-vertices and each of them belongs to precisely two-cycle. The length of the cactus chains is the number of cycles in the chains. The generalized uniform cactus chain graphs of length $r$ that have $(n - 2)r$ pendant vertices is symbolized by $C_r(C_n^{n-2})$. The cactus chains $C_r(C_n^{n-2})$ have vertex and edge sets as follows:

$$V(C_r(C_n^{n-2}))$$
$$= \{a_1, a_2, \ldots, a_{r+1}\} \cup \{b_{1i}, b_{2i}, \ldots, b_{pi}\} \cup \{b'_{1i}, b'_{2i}, \ldots, b'_{pi}\} \cup \{c_{1i}, c_{2i}, \ldots, c_{qi}\}$$
$$\cup \{c'_{1i}, c'_{2i}, \ldots, c'_{qi}\}$$

and

$$E(C_r C_n^{n-2})$$
$$= \{a_i b_{1i}, b_{1i} b_{2i}, \ldots, b_{(p-1)i} b_{pi}, b_{pi} a_{i+1}, a_i c_{1i}, c_{1i} c_{2i}, c_{2i} c_{3i}, \ldots, c_{(q-1)i} c_{qi}, c_{qi} a_{i+1}\}$$
$$\cup \{b_{1i} b'_{1i}, b_{2i} b'_{2i}, \ldots, b_{pi} b'_{pi}, c_{1i} c'_{1i}, c_{2i} c'_{2i}, \ldots, c_{qi} c'_{qi}\}$$

$\forall i = 1, 2, 3, \ldots, r$. If $n$ is even, the values of $p$ and $q$ are $\frac{n-2}{2}$. When $n$ is odd, $p = \lceil \frac{n-2}{2} \rceil$ and $q = \lfloor \frac{n-2}{2} \rfloor$.

2. Determining the lower bound for the tvs by using the formulas below (Nurdin et al. 2010):

$$tvs\left(C_r\left(C_s^{s-2}\right)\right)$$
$$\geq \max \left\{ \begin{array}{c} \left\lceil \frac{1+(s-2)r}{2} \right\rceil, \left\lceil \frac{3+(s-2)r}{3} \right\rceil, \left\lceil \frac{(s-2)r+(s-2)r+3}{4} \right\rceil, \\ \left\lceil \frac{2(s-2)r+3+(r-1)}{5} \right\rceil \end{array} \right\}$$
$$\geq \left\lceil \frac{2(s-2)r+3}{4} \right\rceil$$

3. Showing that the upper bound is $\frac{2(n-2)r+3}{4}$ by constructing two algorithms based on the values $n$, i.e., $n$ is odd or even.
4. Constructing the Matlab programming to evaluate the algorithms.
5. Showing some experimental results.

## 3  MAIN RESULTS

### 3.1  *An algorithm to find the tvs of $C_r(C_n^{n-2})$*

Given the graphs $C_r C_n^{n-2}$ of length $r$ where $n$ is the cardinality of $V(C_n)$ on each chain.

The formulas of the labels of elements of $C_r C_n^{n-2}$ have been proved in Rosyida et al. (2020). Since the pattern of the labels is different based on the even cycle or the odd cycle on each chain, we differentiate the algorithm to determine the tvs of $C_r C_n^{n-2}$ into two algorithms. The first algorithm holds for even number $n$ (Table 1).

Further, we can use the second algorithm if the cycle on each chain is an odd cycle (Table 2).

Based on evaluation of vertex and edge-labels, we can see that the labels are less than or equal to $\lceil \frac{2(n-2)r+3}{4} \rceil$. Further, no vertices have a same weight. Hence, we get tvs$(C_r C_n^{n-2}) = \lceil \frac{2(n-2)r+3}{4} \rceil$.

Table 1.  Algorithm 1: Algorithm for computing tvs of $C_r C_n^{n-2}$ where $n$ is even.

| Step | Commands |
|------|----------|
| | **Input** r = the length of chains |
| | **Input** n = the number of vertices of cycle $C_n$ |
| | **Input** vertices $a_i, i=1,2,\ldots,r+1; b_{ji}, b'_{ji}, c_{ji}, c'_{ji}, i=1,2,\ldots,r, j=1,2,\ldots,\frac{n-2}{2}$ |
| | **Output** fv=Labels of vertices |
| | **Output** fe=Labels of edges |
| | **Output** Wv=weights of vertices |
| 1 | **Set label** $\mathrm{fv}(a_{r+1}) = 2$ |
| 2 | **for** i = 1 : r |
| 3 | $\mathrm{fv}(a_i) = \mathbf{i}$ |
| 4 | $\mathrm{fe}(a_1 b_{1i}) = \alpha - 1$, where $\alpha = \lceil \frac{2(n-2)r+3}{4} \rceil$ |
| 5 | $\mathrm{fe}(a_1 c_{1i}) = \alpha$ |
| | $\mathrm{fe}(b_{(\frac{n-2}{2})i} a_{i+1}) = \alpha - 1; \ \mathrm{fe}(c_{(\frac{n-2}{2})i} a_{i+1}) = \alpha$ |
| 6 | **for** $j = 1 : \frac{n-2}{2}$ |
| 7 | $\mathrm{fv}(b_{ji}) = j + 2 + ((n-2)/2) * i - ((n-2)/2)$ |
| 8 | $\mathrm{fv}(b'_{ji}) = j + ((n-2)/2) * i - ((n-2)/2)$ |
| 9 | $\mathrm{fv}(c_{ji}) = j + ((n-2)/2) * i - ((n-4)/2))$ |
| 10 | $\mathrm{fv}(c'_{ji}) = j + ((n-2)/2) * i - ((n-4)/2))$ |
| 11 | **end** |
| 12 | **for** $j = 1 : \frac{n-2}{2} - 1$ |
| 13 | $\mathrm{fe}(b_{ji} b_{(j+1)i}) = \alpha - 1$, where $\alpha = \lceil \frac{2(n-2)r+3}{4} \rceil$ |
| 14 | $\mathrm{fe}(c_{ji} c_{(j+1)i}) = \alpha$ |
| 15 | **end** |
| 16 | **for** $j = 1 : \frac{n-2}{2}$ |
| 17 | $\mathrm{fe}(b_{ji} b'_{(j)i}) = 1$ |
| 18 | $\mathrm{fe}(c_{ji} c'_{(j)i}) = \alpha - 1$ |
| 19 | $\mathrm{fe}(b_{(j-1)i} b_{ji}) = \alpha - 1; \ \mathrm{fe}(c_{(j-1)i} c_{ji}) = \alpha$ |
| 20 | $\mathrm{Wv}(b'_{ji}) = \mathrm{fv}(b'_{ji}) + \mathrm{fe}(b_{ji} b'_{(j)i})$ |
| 21 | $\mathrm{Wv}(b_{ji}) = \mathrm{fv}(b_{ji}) + \mathrm{fe}(b_{(j-1)i} b_{ji}) + \mathrm{fe}(b_{ji} b_{(j+1)i}) + \mathrm{fe}(b_{ji} b'_{(j)i})$ |
| 22 | $\mathrm{Wv}(c_{ji}) = \mathrm{fv}(c_{ji}) + \mathrm{fe}(c_{(j-1)i} c_{ji}) + \mathrm{fe}(c_{ji} c_{(j+1)i}) + \mathrm{fe}(c_{ji} c'_{(j)i})$ |
| 23 | $\mathrm{Wv}(c'_{ji}) = \mathrm{fv}(c'_{ji}) + \mathrm{fe}(c_{ji} c'_{(j)i})$ |
| 24 | **end** |
| 25 | **end** |
| 26 | $\mathrm{fe}(b_{(\frac{n-2}{2})r} a_{r+1}) = \alpha - 1; \ \mathrm{fe}(c_{(\frac{n-2}{2})r} a_{r+1}) = \alpha$ |
| 27 | $\mathrm{Wv}(a_1) = \mathrm{fv}(a_1) + \mathrm{fe}(a_1 b_{1i}) + \mathrm{fe}(a_1 c_{1i})$ |
| 28 | $\mathrm{Wv}(a_{r+1}) = \mathrm{fv}(a_{r+1}) + \mathrm{fe}(b_{(\frac{n-2}{2})r} a_{r+1}) + \mathrm{fe}(c_{(\frac{n-2}{2})r} a_{r+1})$ |
| 29 | **for** i = 1 : r − 1 |
| 30 | $\mathrm{fv}(a_{i+1}) = \mathbf{i} + 1$ |
| 31 | $\mathrm{fe}(a_{i+1} b_{1(i+1)}) = \alpha - 1;$ |
| 32 | $\mathrm{fe}(a_{i+1} c_{1(i+1)}) = \alpha;$ |
| 33 | $\mathrm{Wv}(a_{i+1}) = \mathrm{fv}(a_{i+1}) + \mathrm{fe}(a_{i+1} b_{1(i+1)}) + \mathrm{fe}(b_{(\frac{n-2}{2})i} a_{i+1}) + \mathrm{fe}(c_{(\frac{n-2}{2})i} a_{i+1}) + \mathrm{fe}(a_{i+1} c_{1(i+1)})$ |
| 34 | **end** |

## 3.2  *Using Matlab to evaluate the algorithms*

We evaluate the algorithms through computer based experiment using Matlab. In the first part, we present experimental results of Algorithm 2 for $C_r C_{11}^9$. The illustration of the cactus chain for $r = 5$ is given in Figure 1.

When $n = 11$ and $r = 5$, the vertex set of $C_5 C_{11}^9$ is $\{a_1, a_2, \ldots, a_6\} \cup \{b_{j1}, b_{j2}, \ldots, b_{j5}\} \cup \{b'_{j1}, b'_{j2}, \ldots, b'_{j5}\}$ for $j = 1, 2, \ldots, \lceil \frac{9}{2} \rceil$, and $\{c_{j1}, c_{j2}, c_{j3}, c_{j4}\} \cup \{c'_{j1}, c'_{j2}, c'_{j3}, c'_{j4}\}$ for $j = 1, 2, \ldots, \lfloor \frac{9}{2} \rfloor$. Based on the algorithm, we get the tvs$(C_5 C_{11}^9) = \lceil \frac{18.5+3}{4} \rceil = 24$. The execution of the Matlab program file shows the labels of elements and the weights of vertices of the cactus chains:

Table 2. Algorithm 2: Algorithm for determining tvs of $C_r C_n^{n-2}$ where $n$ is odd.

| Step | Commands |
|---|---|
| | **Input** r = the length of chains |
| | **Input** n = the number of vertices of cycle $C_n$ |
| | **Input** vertices $a_i, i = 1, 2, \ldots, r + 1$; $b_{ji}, b'_{ji}, c_{qi}, c'_{qi}, i = 1, 2, \ldots, r.; j = \lceil \frac{n-2}{2} \rceil, q = \lfloor \frac{n-2}{2} \rfloor$ |
| | **Input** $\alpha = ceil(\frac{2(n-2)r+3}{4})$ |
| | **Output** fv = Labels of vertices |
| | **Output** fe = Labels of edges |
| | **Output** Wv = weights of vertices |
| 1 | **Set label** fv$(a_{r+1}) = $ **2** |
| 2 | **for i = 1: r − 1** |
| 3 | **if mod(r,2) == 0** |
| 4 | fe$(a_{i+1}b_{1(i+1)}) = \alpha - 1$; fe$(a_{i+1}c_{1(i+1)}) = \alpha$ |
| 5 | **end** |
| 6 | **if mod(r,2) ==1** |
| 7 | fe$(a_{i+1}b_{1(i+1)}) = \alpha - 1$; fe$(a_{i+1}c_{1(i+1)}) = \alpha - 1$ |
| 8 | **end** |
| 9 | **end** |
| 10 | **for i = 1: r** |
| 11 | fv$(a_i) = $ **i** |
| 12 | **if mod(r,2) ==0** |
| 13 | fe$(a_i b_{1i}) = \alpha - 1$; fe$(a_i c_{1i}) = \alpha$ |
| 14 | fe$(b_{(\frac{n-2}{2})i} a_{i+1}) = \alpha - 1$; fe$(c_{(\frac{n-2}{2})i} a_{i+1}) = \alpha$ |
| 15 | **end** |
| 16 | **if mod(r,2) == 1** |
| 17 | fe$(a_i b_{1i}) = \alpha - 1$; fe$(a_i c_{1i}) = \alpha - 1$ |
| 18 | fe$(b_{(\frac{n-2}{2})i} a_{i+1}) = \alpha - 1$; fe$(c_{(\frac{n-2}{2})i} a_{i+1}) = \alpha - 1$ |
| 19 | **end** |
| 20 | Wv$(a_{i+1}) = $ fv$(a_{i+1}) + $ fe$(a_{i+1}b_{1(i+1)}) + $ fe$(b_{(\frac{n-2}{2})i} a_{i+1}) + $ fe$(a_{i+1}c_{1(i+1)}) + $ fe$(c_{(\frac{n-2}{2})i} a_{i+1})$ |
| 21 | **end** |
| 22 | Wv$(a_1) = $ fv$(a_1) + $ fe$(a_i c_{1i}) + $ fe$(a_i b_{1i})$; Wv$(a_{r+1}) = $ fv$(a_{r+1}) + $ fe$(b_{(\frac{n-2}{2})r} a_{r+1}) + $ fe$(c_{(\frac{n-2}{2})r} a_{r+1})$ |
| 23 | **if mod(r,2) == 0** |
| 24 | **for i = 1: r** |
| 25 | **for j = 1**:$ceil((n-2)/2)$ |
| 26 | fv$(b_{ji}) = ceil((\text{n}-2)/2) * \text{i} - ceil((\text{n}-2)/2) + \text{j} + 2$ |
| 27 | fv$(b'_{ji}) = ceil((\text{n}-2)/2) * \text{i} - ceil((\text{n}-2)/2) + \text{j}$ |
| 28 | fe$(b_{ji}b'_{(j)i}) = 1$; fe$(b_{(j-1)i}b_{(j)i}) = \alpha - 1$ |
| 29 | **end** |
| 30 | **for q = 1**:$floor((n-2)/2)$ |
| 31 | fv$(c_{qi}) = floor(\frac{\text{n}-2}{2}) * \text{i} - floor((\text{n}-2)/2) + (\text{q} + 3)$ |
| 32 | fv$(c'_{qi}) = floor(\frac{\text{n}-2}{2}) * \text{i} - floor((\text{n}-2)/2) + (\text{q} + 3)$ |
| 33 | fe$(c_{qi}c'_{(q)i}) = \alpha - 1$; fe$(c_{(q-1)i}c_{(q)i}) = \alpha$ |
| 34 | **end** |
| 35 | **for j = 1**:$ceil((n-2)/2) - 1$ |
| 36 | fe$(b_{ji}b_{(j+1)i}) = \alpha - 1$ |
| 37 | **end** |
| 38 | **for q = 1**:$floor((n-2)/2) - 1$ |
| 39 | fe$(c_{qi}c_{(q+1)i}) = \alpha$ |
| 40 | **end** |
| 41 | **end** |
| 42 | **end** |
| 43 | **if mod(r,2) == 1** |
| 44 | **for i = 1: r** |

*(Continued)*

88

Table 2. Algorithm 2: Algorithm for determining tvs of $C_r C_n^{n-2}$ where $n$ is odd. (*Continues*)

| Step | Commands |
|---|---|
| 45 | **for** j = 1: *ceil*$((n-2)/2)$ |
| 46 | fv$(b_{ji})$ = ceil$((n-2)/2)*i -$ ceil$((n-2)/2) + (s+1)$ |
| 47 | fv$(b'_{ji})$ = ceil$((n-2)/2)*i -$ ceil$((n-2)/2) + s$ |
| 48 | fe$(b_{ji}b'_{(j)i})=1$; fe$(b_{(j-1)i}b_{(j)i})=\alpha-1$ |
| 49 | **end** |
| 50 | **for** q = 1floor$((n-2)/2)$ |
| 51 | fv$(c_{qi})$ = floor$((n-2)/2)*i -$ floor$((n-2)/2) + (q+3)$ |
| 52 | fv$(c'_{qi})$ = floor$((n-2)/2)*i -$ floor$((n-2)/2) + q + 2$ |
| 53 | fe$(c_{qi}c'_{(q)i})=\alpha$; fe$(c_{(q-1)i}c_{(q)i})=\alpha-1$ |
| 54 | **end** |
| 55 | **for** j = 1:*ceil*$(\frac{n-2}{2})-1$ |
| 56 | fe$(b_{ji}b_{(j+1)i})=\alpha-1$ |
| 57 | **end** |
| 58 | **for** j = 1:floor$((n-2)/2)-1$ |
| 59 | fe$(c_{ji}c_{(j+1)i})=\alpha-1$ |
| 60 | **end** |
| 61 | **for** j = 1:*ceil*$((n-2)/2)$ |
| 62 | Wv$(b'_{ji})$ = fv$b'_{ji}$ + fe$(b_{ji}b'_{(j)i})$ |
| 63 | Wv$(b_{ji})$ = fv$(b_{ji})$ + fe$(b_{(j-1)i}b_{(j)i})$ + fe$(b_{ji}b_{(j+1)i})$ + fe$(b_{ji}b'_{(j)i})$ |
| 64 | **end** |
| 65 | **for** q = 1:floor$((n-2)/2)$ |
| 66 | Wv$(c_{qi})$ = fv$(c_{qi})$ + fe$(c_{(q-1)i}c_{(q)i})$ + fe$(c_{qi}c_{(q+1)i})$ + fe$(c_{qi}c'_{(q)i})$ |
| 67 | Wv$(c'_{qi})$ = fv$(c'_{qi})$ + fe$(c_{qi}c'_{(q)i})$ |
| 68 | **end** |
| 69 | **end** |
| 70 | **end** |

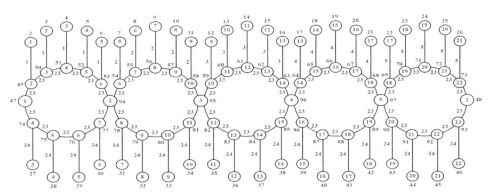

Figure 1. The uniform cactus chain graph $C_5 C_{11}^9$.

The first screenshot in Figure 2 shows the label $f(a_i)$ and the weight $W(a_i)$ for i=1, 2, ..., 6.

Further, the screenshots in Figure 3 depict the labels and the weights of $b_{ji}, b'_{ji}$ for i = 1, 2, 3, 4, 5, and the labels and the weights of $c_{ji}, c'_{ji}$ for i = 1, 2, 3, 4. In all screenshots above, we can see that the labels are not more than $\lceil \frac{18.5+3}{4} \rceil = 24$. It describes the tvs$(C_5 C_{11}^9) = \lceil \frac{18.5+3}{4} \rceil = 24$.

In the second part, we give an illustration of numerical results of Algorithm 1 for $n = 12$. Let us consider the uniform cactus chain graphs $C_r C_{12}^{10}$. For $r = 6$, the vertex set

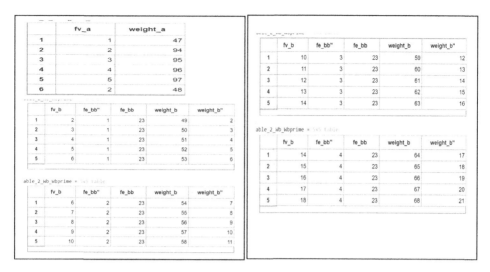

Figure 2. Output of Matlab program file for the labels and the weights of $a_i$, $b_{ji}$, and $b'_{ji}$ in $C_5C_{11}^9$.

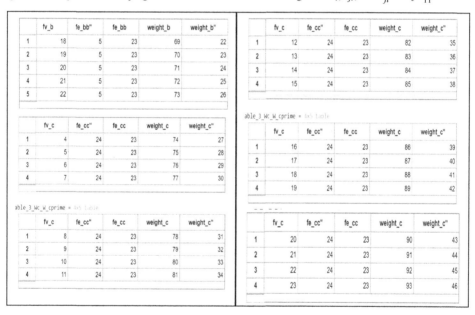

Figure 3. The screenshot of output of Matlab program file for $f_v(b_{ji})$, $f_e(b_{ji}b'_{ji})$, $f_e(b_{ji}b_{(j+1)i})$, $f_v(c_{ji})$, $f_e(c_{ji}c'_{ji})$, $f_e(c_{ji}c_{(j+1)i})$, $W(b_{ji})$, $W(b'_{ji})$, $W(c_{ji})$, and $W(c'_{ji})$ in $C_5C_{11}^9$.

is $\{a_1, a_2, \ldots, a_7\} \cup \{b_{j1}, b_{j2}, \ldots, b_{j6}\} \cup \{b'_{j1}, b'_{j2}, \ldots, b'_{j6}\} \cup \{c_{j1}, c_{j2}, \ldots, c_{j6}\} \cup \{c'_{j1}, c'_{j2}, \ldots, c'_{j6}\}$ for $j = 1, 2, \ldots, \frac{n-2}{2}$ and the edge set is

$E(C_6C_{12}^{10})$

$= \{a_ib_{1i}, b_{1i}b_{2i}, b_{2i}b_{3i}, b_{3i}b_{4i}, b_{4i}b_{5i}, b_{5i}b_{6i}, b_{6i}a_{i+1}, a_ic_{1i}, c_{1i}c_{2i}, c_{2i}c_{3i}, c_{3i}c_{4i}, c_{4i}c_{5i}, c_{5i}c_{6i}, c_{6i}a_{i+1}\}$

$\cup \{b_{1i}b'_{1i}, b_{2i}b'_{2i}, b_{3i}b'_{3i}, b_{4i}b'_{4i}, b_{5i}b'_{5i}, b_{6i}b'_{6i}, c_{1i}c'_{1i}, c_{2i}c'_{2i}, c_{3i}c'_{3i}, c_{4i}c'_{4i}, c_{5i}c'_{5i}, c_{6i}c'_{6i}\}$.

for i=1,2,...,6.

| | fv_a | weight_a |
|---|---|---|
| 1 | 1 | 62 |
| 2 | 2 | 124 |
| 3 | 3 | 125 |
| 4 | 4 | 126 |
| 5 | 5 | 127 |
| 6 | 6 | 128 |
| 7 | 2 | 63 |

Figure 4.    Output of Matlab program file for the label and the weights of $a_i$ in $C_6C_{10}^{12}$.

Figure 5.    Output of Matlab program file for the labels $f_v(b_{ji})$, $f_e(b_{ji}b'_{ji})$, $f_e(b_{ji}b_{(j+1)i})$, $f_v(c_{ji})$, $f_e(c_{ji}c'_{ji})$, $f_e(c_{ji}c_{(j+1)i})$, and the weights $W(b_{ji})$, $W(b'_{ji})$, $W(c_{ji})$, and $W(c'_{ji})$ in $C_6C_{10}^{12}$.

Based on the algorithm, we know that the $tvs(C_6C_{12}^{10}) = \lceil \frac{20.6+3}{4} \rceil = 31$. The experimental results show the weights of vertices as in the screenshots above.

The screenshot in Figure 4 depicts the labels and the weights of vertices: $a_i$ for $i = 1, 2, \ldots, 7$. Meanwhile, Figure 5 describes the labels and the weights of $b_{ji}$, $b'_{ji}$, $c_{ji}$, and $c'_{ji}$ for $i = 1, 2, \ldots, 5$. It is shown that the labels are not more than $\lceil \frac{20.6+3}{4} \rceil = 31$. It indicates that tvs $(C_6C_{12}^{10}) = 31$.

By using the Matlab programming, we could determine the pattern of labels of elements of $C_r C_n^{n-2}$ and compute the tvs in an easy way. Also, it is more efficient (in time) for simulating the pattern of labels of elements of the graph compared with the manual calculation. For example, the elapsed time for $n = 11$ and $r = 5$ is around 0.33 seconds. Meanwhile, the average elapsed time for $n = 12$ and $r = 6$ is 0.43 seconds. It can be an interactive media in the learning process of the graph labeling and it will help the students to learn the concept in an easy way.

## 4 CONCLUSIONS

In this paper, have constructed algorithms to determine "vertex irregular total k-labeling" of the uniform cactus graphs $C_r C_n^{n-2}$ which contain $(n - 2)r$ pendant vertices where the tvs is $\lceil \frac{2(n-2)r+3}{4} \rceil$. Further, we evaluate the performance of the algorithm through Matlab programming. The experiments show that the computation of tvs of $C_r C_n^{n-2}$ could be done in an easy way. The Matlab programming could be an interactive media in learning the graph labeling, especially the vertex irregular total labeling.

In future research, we can construct the algorithms to find the tvs of subdivisions of the "generalized uniform cactus graphs" $C_r C_n^{n-2,t}$, where $t$ indicates the number of subdivision vertices on each pendant edge. Also, we can develop the Matlab programming to determine the tvs of $C_r C_n^{n-2,t}$.

## REFERENCES

Ahmad, A., Bača, M., & Bashir, Y. 2014. Total vertex irregularity strength of certain classes of unicyclic graphs. *Bulletin mathematiques de la Societe des sciences mathematiques de Roumanie* 57(2): 147–152.

Anholcer, M., Kalkowski, M., & Przybyło, J. 2009. A new upper bound for the total vertex irregularity strength of graphs. *Discrete Mathematics* 309: 6316–6317.

Bača, M., Jendrol, M., Miller, S. & Ryan, J. 2007. On irregular total labellings. *Discrete Mathematics* 307: 1378–1388.

Bača, M., Jendrol, S., Kathiresan, K., Muthugurupackiam, K. & Semaničová-Fenovcikova, A. 2015. Survey of Irregularity Strength. *Electronic Notes in Discrete Mathematics* 48: 19–26.

Borissevich, K. & Došlić, T. 2015. Counting dominating sets in cactus chains. *Filomat* 29(8): 1847–1855.

Gallian, J.A. 2018. A dynamic survey of graph labeling. *Electronic Journal of Combinatorics* 1: #DS6.

Indriati, D., Widodo, Wijayanti, I.E., Sugeng, K.A., Bača, M. & Semaničová-Fenovcikova, A. 2016. The total vertex irregularity strength of generalized helm graphs and prisms with outer pendant edges. *Australasian Journal of Combinatorics* 65: 14–26.

Nurdin, Baskoro, E.T., Salman, A.N.M. & Gaos, N.N. 2010. On the total vertex irregularity strength of trees. *Discrete Mathematics* 310(21): 3043–3048.

Rosyida, I. & Indriati, D. 2019a. On total edge irregularity strength of some cactus chain graphs with pendant vertices. *Journal of Physics: Conference Series* 1211: 012016.

Rosyida, I., Mulyono & Indriati, D. 2019b. Determining total vertex irregularity strength of Tr(4,1) tadpole chain graph and its computation. *Procedia Computer Science* 157: 699–706.

Rosyida, I., Ningrum, E., Setyaningrum, A. & Mulyono. 2020a. On total edge and total vertex irregularity strength of pentagon cactus chain graph with pendant vertices. *Journal of Physics: Conference Series* 1567: 022073.

Rosyida, I., Mulyono & Indriati, D. 2020b. On total vertex irregularity strength of generalized uniform cactus chain graphs with pendant vertices. *Journal of Discrete Mathematical Sciences and Cryptography* 23(6): 1369–1380.

Sadeghieh, A., Alikhani, S., Ghanbari, N. & Khalaf, A.J.M. 2017. Hosoya polynomial of some cactus chains. *Cogent Mathematics* 4(1): 1305638.

Wallis, W.D. 2001. *Magic Graphs*, 1st ed. Boston: Birkhäuser Basel.

What is MATLAB?. (2020, November 16). Retrieved from https://cimss.ssec.wisc.edu/wxwise/class/aos340/spr00/whatismatlab.htm#.

*Emerging Trends in Technology for Education in an Uncertain World – Nanto, Rahiem & Khalis Maryati (Eds)*

# Students' profile on higher order mathematical thinking skill at Islamic Junior High School (MTsN) in Indonesia

G. Satriawati, G. Dwirahayu, Afidah & M. Hafiz

*Department of Mathematics Education, Faculty of Tarbiya and Teaching Sciences, Universitas Islam Negeri Syarif Hidayatullah Jakarta, South Tangerang, Banten, Indonesia*

ABSTRACT: The development of mathematics learning that is oriented towards higher order thinking is a program developed in an effort to improve the quality of learning and graduates. The method used in this study was quantitative with descriptive analysis. It was conducted for the purpose of analyzing and describing the higher order mathematical thinking (HOMT) of MTsN students after the learning process was implemented in the classroom. The subjects in this study were 563 students in South Sulawesi, South Sumatra, West Java, East Java, DKI Jakarta, and Banten. The instrument used in this study was a HOMT test consisting of three indicators : problem solving, reasoning, and communication. The results showed that the HOMT of MTsN students are still in the low category. The highest indicator is in reasoning while the lowest is in communication. Based on results, it is necessary to provide assistance to students in improving HOMT.

*Keywords*: Higher Order Mathematical Thinking; Problem Solving; Reasoning; Communication

## 1 INTRODUCTION

Education 4.0 is a response to the needs of the 4.0 industrial revolution, humans and technology are aligned to create new opportunities creatively and innovatively (Delipiter 2019). Learning in the era of the industrial revolution 4.0 requires students to have higher order thinking skills, that is skills in processing information so that they can control quite large challenges (Yumanhadi 2018). Higher order thinking skills in mathematics consist of logic and reasoning skills, the ability to analyze, evaluate and create, solve problems, and make decisions (Brookhart 2010). Mathematical high-order thinking skills are the ability to obtain new information stored in memory and related to each other, rearrange each other, expand each other on an information problem to achieve goals or find possible answers in confusing conditions (Dinni 2018; Hidayati 2017). Students' high-order thinking skills include aspects of concept formation, problem solving, analytical thinking (Goethals 2013; Rubin & Rajakaruna 2015) connection concepts, obtaining big ideas, visualization skills, asking questions, generalizing ideas, practical, and creative (Goethals 2013). Furthermore, Brookhart (Hidayati 2017) divides higher-order thinking skills into three categories, namely 1) as a form of transfer of learning outcomes, 2) as a form of critical thinking, and 3) as a problem-solving process.

In the 2013 curriculum, education in Indonesia is implemented to train students' critical thinking, problem-solving, communication and collaboration skills creativity and innovation skills, information and communication technology literacy, contextual learning skills, information and media literacy skills (Gradini 2019). The purpose of learning mathematics is to form an intellectual person, be able to solve problems and to think or give reason (Atmadi & Setyaningsih 2000). The general objectives of learning mathematics are formulated by NCTM (National Council of Teachers of Mathematics) which is known as mathematical power, i.e. 1) problem solving, 2) reasoning, 3) communication, 4) connection, 5) representation. The five processes according to

Utari (Sumarmo 2003) are not routine mathematical thinking processes but it also should develope high-order mathematical thinking.

Mathematical high-order thinking skills can not be separated from mathematical power. Mathematical power according to NCTM (1989), namely, Mathematical power includes the ability to explore, conjecture, and reason logically; to solve non-routine problems; to communicate about and through mathematics; and to connect ideas within mathematics and between mathematics and other intellectual activity. Mathematical power is the student's ability to explore, make conjectures and reason logically to solve non-routine problems in mathematics. There are three aspects that need to be considered in developing students' mathematical power, including: 1) standard processes which include problem solving, argumentation, communication, connection and representation, 2) content standard, material what is meant in Indonesia is a mathematics subject written at k-13 in Junior High School education units in the scope of algebra, geometry, statistics, opportunities and social arithmetic, and 3) mathematical abilities, namely basic knowledge and skills required to be able to perform mathematical manipulation includes understanding procedural concepts and knowledge. This opinion is reinforced in the Process Standards in KTSP (2006) in Indonesia, NCTM (2000), and Elliot (NCTM 1989) that mathematics learning must include five mathematical abilities which are standards namely problem solving, reasoning and evidence, communication, connection, and representation.

However, in this study, the studens' HOMT to be measured is 1) Problem Solving, The ability of students to implement various mathematical concepts to solve problems using various solving strategies both in mathematics itself and problems outside mathematics. Mathematical problem solving according to Polya (Sumarmo 2003) includes activities: Understanding the problem; Choosing a strategy and implementing a strategy; Carry out calculations or solve mathematical models; and Interpret the solution (result) to the original problem and check the correctness of the solution. 2) Reasoning, the concept of thinking that tries to link known facts to conclusions. Mathematical reasoning activities include: formulating conjectures, making logical deductions based on assumptions and special rules, and maintaining results (Mullis & Martin 2017; Sumarmo 2003). 3) Communication Skills, namely the ability of students to convey abstract mathematical ideas to others, both orally and in writing. According to Mullis and Martin (2014), Mathematical communication skills are indicated by the following: Students are able to express mathematical situations or problems or everyday life in the form of images, diagrams, language or metematic symbols, or mathematical models; Students are able to explain a mathematical idea with pictures, expressions, or their own language orally or in writing; Students are able to make a story based on a given picture, diagram, or mathematical model; Students are able to compose questions about the given mathematical content.

So far, the success of the learning process in the classroom is only measured by the achievements reached by students, even though as previously described, students' high-level thinking abilities also need to be prepared to face mathematics learning in the era of the industrial revolution 4.0. For this reason, it is necessary to conduct in-depth research on students' higher order thinking skills in mathematics learning. This study analyzes and describes the Mathematical Thinking ability of MTsN Students in Indonesia.

## 2 METHODS

The method used in this study was descriptive analysis method with a quantitative approach. The design used is a type of survey with the aim of knowing a general description of the characteristics of the population (Hamdi & Bahruddin 2014). It was conducted in 2019 from 6 provinces in Indonesia. The subjects of this study were 563 students of MTsN consisting of 108 students in South Sulawesi, 87 students in South Sumatra, 94 students in East Java, 95 students in West Java, 76 Students in Banten, and 103 students in DKI Jakarta.

The procedure in this study consists of three stages, i.e. the preparation, the activity implementation, and the data collection. Data were collected through a written test in essay form of HOMT and it was worked individually. The test instrument for students' HOMT consists of 10 items, i.e. 4 problem solving questions, 3 reasoning questions and 3 communication questions which cover the scope of algebra, geometry, statistics, opportunity and social arithmetic. The instrument has been tested for validation through an expert test consisting of six lecturers from the mathematics education program UIN Syarif Hidayatullah Jakarta and has a reliability value of 0.556 which is included in the medium category. The steps for analyzing the written test result data were 1) sorting the data based on the score or value on each indicator, 2) analyzing the data on each indicator, 3) determining the student's test scores and determining the students' higher order thinking categories, 4) concluding the percentage of students' higher order thinking in terms of indicators and overall. An explanation of the results of the analysis based on the category of students' HOMT is as follows (Prasetyani et al. 2016).

Table 1. Categories of students' Higher Order Mathematical Thinking (HOMT).

| Score | Level |
|---|---|
| 81–100 | Very High |
| 61–80 | High |
| 41–60 | Medium |
| 21–40 | Low |
| <20 | Very Low |

## 3 RESULTS

There are three indicators of HOTM, namely mathematical problem solving, mathematical reasoning, and communication. The results of students' higher order thinking skills can be shown in Figure 1.

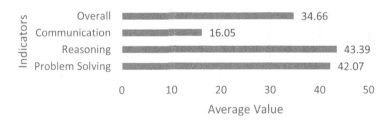

Figure 1. Students' higher order mathematical thinking.

Based on Figure 1, the overall HOMT of MTsN students is still low, only reaches an average of 34.66. The highest HOMT is reasoning ability, and the lowest ability is communication ability.

### 3.1 Problem solving

The mean value of the overall problem-solving test results was 42.07. This shows that the students' mathematical problem solving are in the low category. Indicators of problem-solving include:

identifying problems, formulating problems, implementing strategies by answering correctly, with an assessment score between 0 to 4 with details in Table 2.

Table 2. Students' mathematical problem solving levels.

| Score | Problem Solving Indicators | The number of students | Percentage |
|---|---|---|---|
| 4 | Students are able to identify problems, formulate problems, apply strategies by answering correctly | 67 | 11.8 |
| 3 | Students are able to identify problems, formulate problems, implement strategies with wrong answers | 182 | 32.3 |
| 2 | Students are only able to identify problems, formulate problems | 22 | 3.9 |
| 1 | Students are only able to identify problems | 66 | 11.6 |
| 0 | No answer | 227 | 40.4 |

Based on the data in Table 2, the number of students who were able to answer the problem solving questions well was 11.8%. 40.4% students did not answer. This shows that students do not have good mathematical problem solving.

## 3.2  Reasoning

The mean value of the mathematical reasoning test results in this study was 43.39. It can be concluded that students' mathematical reasoning are in the low category. Indicators of mathematical reasoning, namely students are able to solve problems correctly and with the right reasons, with an assessment score between 0 to 4 with details in Table 3.

Table 3. Percentage of students' mathematical reasoning levels.

| Score | Reasoning Indicators | The number of students | Percentage |
|---|---|---|---|
| 4 | Students are able to solve problems correctly and for the right reasons | 66 | 11.8 |
| 3 | Students are able to solve problems correctly however, do not give the right reasons | 86 | 15.3 |
| 2 | Students have not been able to solve the problem correctly however, and give inappropriate reasons | 183 | 32.6 |
| 1 | Students have not been able to solve the problem correctly, but do not give reasons | 82 | 14.5 |
| 0 | No answer | 146 | 25.9 |

Based on the data in Table 3, the number of students who were able to answer questions with indicators of mathematical reasoning well was 11.8%. Meanwhile, there were 25.9% students who did not answer. This shows that students do not have good reasoning.

## 3.3  Communication

The mean value of the test results of mathematical communication in this study is as a whole is 16.05. This shows that students' mathematical communication are in the very low category. Indicators of mathematical communication skills, namely students are able to explain ideas, situations and mathematical relations with real objects, pictures, graphics and algebra by answering correctly, with an assessment score between 0 to 4 with details in Table 4.

Table 4. Percentage of students' mathematical communication levels.

| Score | Communication Ability Indicator | The number of students | Percentage |
|---|---|---|---|
| 4 | Students are able to explain ideas, situations and mathematical relations with real objects, pictures, graphs and algebra by answering them correctly | 10 | 1.8 |
| 3 | Students are able to explain ideas, situations and mathematical relations with real objects, pictures, graphics and algebra by answering incorrectly | 12 | 2.1 |
| 2 | Students are only able to explain ideas, and pictures or graphs and algebra | 102 | 18 |
| 1 | Students are only able to explain ideas or pictures | 66 | 12 |
| 0 | No answer | 373 | 66 |

Based on the data in Table 4, the number of students who were able to answer questions with indicators of mathematical communication skills well was 1.8%. Meanwhile, the percentage of students who did not answer was 66%. This shows that students do not have good mathematical communication skills.

4 DISCUSSION

Higher order thinking skills are defined as the use of the mind broadly to find new challenges (Yee et al. 2011). This higher order thinking skill requires a person to apply new information or previous knowledge and manipulate information to reach possible answers in new situations. Woolfolk (2008) states that students who have higher order thinking skills are able to distinguish between facts and opinions, identify relevant information, solve problems, and be able to conclude the information they have analyzed.

4.1 *Problem solving*

Brookhart (2010) suggests that higher-order thinking can be seen as problem solving. In problem solving activities students can use various strategies, for example understanding problems, planning strategies, implementing strategies, and looking back (Polya 1985). These activities require students' ability to analyze information on problems, plan and synthesize solving strategies and evaluate the results obtained. The following is an example of the test items for mathematical problem solving abilities used in this study.

Question:
Mr. Ahmad has a home yard whose ground level is as shown below

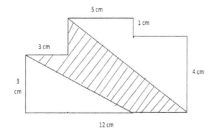

Mr. Ahmad plans to build a road in the shaded area as shown in the picture and the remaining land area will be planted with grass. Find:

a. The area of land to be planted with grass
b. The area of land to be made the road
c. The cost that must be paid by Mr. Ahmad to buy grass if the price of grass is IDR 40,000/m$^2$

To answer the problem of problem solving abilities, students must be able to identify the problem, namely students need to identify what is known, what is there, the number, relationships and values associated with what is being asked. To formulate a problem, students need to identify the operations involved and the strategies needed to solve the given problem and apply the strategy by answering correctly. However, based on the research results, only 11.8% of students were able to do problem solving problems well, 32.3% of students were only able to determine the strategy used but it was wrong in its application, 3.9% of students were only able to formulate problems, 11.6% of students were only able to identify the problem, and as many as 40.4% of students did not answer the questions given. This shows that students have not been able to understand the problems given. The results of this study are in line with the results of research conducted by Fitri (Amaliah 2019) and Adityawarmah (Hidayat & Irawan 2017) which concluded that the most mistakes made by students were indicators of understanding the problem.

## 4.2 *Reasoning*

Shurter and Pierce (Sumarmo 2003) define the terms of reasoning similar to the notion of propositional reasoning or logical reasoning, namely as a thinking process that includes activities to draw conclusions based on existing data and events. The following shows an example of the mathematical reasoning ability test items used in this study.

Question:
BERKAH Bookstore provides 25% discount to every buyer for every purchase of an item. The price tag for a Math book is IDR 100,000.00. After deducting the discount, it turned out that the shop was still making a profit of 20%. Determine the purchase price of the item in advance!

To answer reasoning questions, students first solve the problems given and provide a logical explanation of the answers. Based on the research results, as many as 183 students or 32.6% of students have not been able to solve the problem correctly and provide inaccurate reasons. Students are only able to determine the amount of discount and selling price, but it is difficult to determine the purchase price. 146 students or 25.9% could not answer this question. This is because students have not been able to understand the questions given. The results of this study are in line with research conducted by Hariawan (Aziz & Hidayati 2019) which concluded that the low understanding of students was due to the students not understanding the problems given.

## 4.3 *Communication*

According to Mullis and Martin (2014), Mathematical communication skills are indicated by the following: Students are able to express mathematical situations or problems or everyday life in the form of images, diagrams, language or metematic symbols, or mathematical models; Students are able to explain a mathematical idea with pictures, expressions, or their own language orally or in writing; Students are able to make a story based on a given picture, diagram, or mathematical model; Students are able to compose questions about the given mathematical content. Through mathematical communication students exchange and explain their ideas or understandings to their friends. The communication process helps students construct the meaning of a series of mathematical processes and make generalizations. In an effort to explore and develop students' mathematical communication skills, teachers should expose students to various contextual problems and invite them to communicate their respective ideas. The following is an example of the test items for mathematical communication skills used in this study.

Question:
Mother gave a sponge cake with the same size to Fatimah, Zainab, and Aminah. Fatimah cut the cake into 12 equal pieces and ate 5 pieces. Zainab ate 0.375 parts of the cake, while Aminah ate 40% of the cake. Who do you think eats the most cakes? Explain your reasons using pictures of the part of the cake that each one ate!

To answer communication questions, students first state the problem, explain ideas, situations and mathematical relations with real objects, pictures, graphs and algebra by answering correctly. Based on the results of the study, of the 563 students, only 10 students or 1.8% were able to solve communication problems well, some of the students, namely 102 students, were only able to explain ideas in the form of pictures or symbols, but they were not correct in solving them. As many as 363 students or 66% were unable to answer communication questions, it can be concluded that students' mathematical communication skills were low. The results of this study are in line with the results of research by Annisa (Maulidya & Hidayati 2019) which state that mathematical communication explaining ideas, situations, writing with real objects, pictures, graphics and algebra is low.

The three indicators of students' higher order mathematical thinking skills, namely problem solving, reasoning and communication are abilities that must be trained by students in solving mathematical problems. Kusumaningrum (Situmorang 2017) which states that higher order thinking skills can be developed and optimized through solving mathematical problems. This means, through solving problems in which there is a process of identifying the problem, which is followed by analyzing the relationship between existing patterns which determines the students' next thinking ability. In addition, Newman Wehlage (Abdullah et al. 2015) states that in solving high-level math problems students go through the stages of manipulating data, information, and ideas to break down meanings and implications, synthesize, generalize, explain, make temporary conclusions, and finally make a conclusion. Thus, students' higher thinking abilities have a mutual relationship.

## 5 CONCLUSIONS

Based on the results of research that has been conducted by researchers on the Mathematical Thinking of MTsN Students in Indonesia, it can be concluded that the Mathematical Thinking of MTsN Students is in the low category. Of the three indicators of Students' HOMT, namely problem solving, reasoning and communication. Reasoning is the highest ability with a value of 43.39 and the lowest ability is communication, with a value of 16.05.

## 6 RECOMMENDATION

The results of this study recommend: a) It is necessary to provide assistance to students in improving HOMT, b) providing modules that contain non-routine questions to all students c). There is a need for technical guidance to all students by doing collaboration between Schools and Universities.

## ACKNOWLEDGEMENTS

The authors gratefully acknowledge the financial support of the Puslitpen and LP2M UIN Syarif Hidayatullah. We would like to offer our special thanks to Math Teachers and students of MTsN in 5 provinces for their assistance with the collection of our data. Thanks are also due to 6th International Conference on Education in Moslem Society (ICEMS) committee for the support on publishing this article.

## REFERENCES

Abdullah, Abdul Halim, Nur Liyana Zainal Abidin, and Marlina Ali. 2015. Analysis of students' errors in solving Higher Order Thinking Skills (HOTS) problems for the topic of fraction. *Asian Social Science* 1(1): 1–10.

Amaliah, Fitri. 2019. Kemampuan pemecahan masalah matematis siswa pada materi luas dan volume kubus balok. *Sesiomadika* 2(1a): 194–199.

Atmadi, A., and Y. Setyaningsih. 2000. *Transformasi pendidikan memasuki millenium ketiga*. Yogyakarta: Kanisius.

Aziz, Hariawan Estu, and Nita Hidayati. 2019. Analisis kemampuan penalaran matematis siswa SMP pada materi aritmatika Sosial. *Sesiomadika* 2(1c): 824–828.

Brookhart, Susan M. 2010. *How to assess higher-order thinking skills in your classroom*. Alexandria. ASCD.

99

Delipiter, Lase. 2019. "Pendidikan Di Era Revolusi Industri 4.0." *SUNDERMANN: Jurnal Ilmiah Teologi, Pendidikan, Sains, Humaniora Dan Kebudayaan* 1(1): 28–43.

Dinni, Husna Nur. 2018. "HOTS (High Order Thinking Skills) dan kaitannya dengan kemampuan literasi matematika. *Proc. PRISMA* 1: 170–176.

Goethals, P.L. 2013. *The pursuit of higher-order thinking in the mathematics classroom*: A Review. Review submitted in partial fulfillment of the Master Teacher Program, a 2-year faculty professional development program conducted by the Center for Faculty Excellence, United States Military Academy, West Point, NY, 2013.

Gradini, Ega. 2019. Menilik konsep kemampuan berpikir tingkat tinggi (higher order thingking skills) dalam pembelajaran matematika. *Jurnal Numeracy* 6(2): 189–203.

Hamdi, Asep Saepul, and E. Bahruddin. 2014. *Metode penelitian kuantitatif aplikasi dalam pendidikan*. Yogyakarta: Deepublish.

Hidayat, Adityawarmah, and Indra Irawan. 2017. Pengembangan LKS berbasis RME dengan pendekatan problem solving untuk memfasilitasi kemampuan pemecahan masalah matematis siswa. *Jurnal Cendekia: Jurnal Pendidikan Matematika* 1(2): 51–63.

Hidayati, Arini Ulfah. 2017. Melatih keterampilan berpikir tingkat tinggi dalam pembelajaran matematika pada siswa Sekolah Dasar. *Terampil* 4(2): 143–156.

Maulidya, Annisa Nurul, and Nita Hidayati. 2020. Analisis Kemampuan Komunikasi Matematis Siswa SMP Pada Soal Himpunan. *Sesiomadika* 2(1b): 327–334.

Mullis, Ina V.S., and Michael O. Martin. 2017. *TIMSS 2019 Assessment Frameworks*. Boston: TIMSS & PIRLS International Study Center.

NCTM. 1989. *Curriculum and Evaluation Standards for School Mathematics*. Reston: VA: NCTM.

NCTM. 2000. *Principles and Standards for School Mathematics*. Reston: VA: NCTM.

Polya, George. 1985. *How To Solve It*. 2nd ed. New Jersey: Princeton University Press.

Prasetyani, Etika, Yusuf Hartono, and Ely Susanti. 2016. Kemampuan berpikir tingkat tinggi siswa kelas XI dalam pembelajaran trigonometri berbasis masalah di SMA Negeri 18 Palembang. *Jurnal Gantang* 1(1): 31–40.

Rubin, Jim, and Manikya Rajakaruna. 2015. Teaching and assessing higher order thinking in the mathematics classroom with Clickers. *Mathematics Education* 10(1): 37–51.

Situmorang, Adi Suarman. 2017. Efektivitas model pembelajaran creative problem solving dan contextual teaching and learning terhadap kemampuan pemahaman konsep matematis mahasiswa FKIP UHN. *JURNAL Suluh Pendidikan FKIP-UHN* 4(1): 1–13.

Sumarmo, Utari. 2003. *Berpikir dan disposisi matematik serta pembelajarannya*. Bandung: UPI.

Woolfolk, A. 2008. *Educational psychology active learning edition* 10th ed. Pearson Education, Inc.

Yee, Heong Mei, Widad Othman, Jailani Md Yunos, and Tze Kiong Tee. 2011. The level of Marzano higher order thinking skills among technical education students. *International Journal of Social Science and Humanity* 1(2): 121–125.

Yumanhadi, Aripin Fajar. 2018. Perbedaan keterampilan berpikir tingkat tinggi (HOTS) siswa dengan menggunakan metode Learning CYCLE 7E Dan Learning Cycle 5E pada pembelajaran IPA. *Prosiding Seminar Dan Diskusi Nasional Pendidikan Dasar*, 6–11.

*Emerging Trends in Technology for Education in an Uncertain World – Nanto, Rahiem & Khalis Maryati (Eds)*
© 2022 copyright the Author(s), ISBN 978-1-032-11288-6

# The analysis of "HOTS" in mathematic of Indonesia's Madrasah Tsanawiyah students

Maifalinda Fatra
*Faculty of Educational Sciences, Syarif Hidayatullah State Islamic University of Jakarta, Jakarta, Indonesia*

M. Anang Jatmiko
*Faculty of Educational Sciences, Syarif Hidayatullah State Islamic University of Jakarta, Jakarta, Indonesia*

ABSTRACT:   Mathematical high order thinking skills are abilities must be possessed by students of Madrasah Tsanawiyah. High-level thinking skills referred to in this study include aspects of analysis and evaluation. The population in this study were all students of Madrasah Tsanawiyah in DKI Jakarta and West Java. The sample consisted of 141 students of Madrasah Tsanawiyah DKI Jakarta and 166 students of Madrasah Tsanawiyah Bandung. High-order thinking skills of Madrasah Tsanawiyah students use the TIMSS design with an Islamic context seen from the average value of the test results given. The results showed that 1) the high order mathematical thinking skills of Madrasah Tsanawiyah students of both regions who have analysis and evaluation skills with application and reasoning indicators are still low and 2) there are no differences in the ability of HOTS mathematical abilities using the TIMSS design with the Islamic context of Madrasah Tsanawiyah students in DKI Jakarta and Bandung.

*Keywords*:   Mathematical Skills, High Order Thinking Skilss (HOTS), TIMSS Design.

## 1  INTRODUCTION

Mathematics as part of the basic education curriculum plays a strategic role in improving the quality of Indonesian human resources. The ability to think mathematically, especially high-level mathematical thinking, is necessary for students and is related to the need for students to solve the problems they face in their daily lives. Some of the thinking skills that can improve processing intelligence are critical thinking skills, creative thinking skills, brain organizing skills, and analytical skills.

Mathematics learning is usually done partially, not as an integrated part of other subjects included in Islamic Religious Education. As a result learning mathematics has becomes rigid, seems difficult, is alienated from the reality of life, which eventually becomes a scourge. Mathematics contributes less to character formation and is less able to provide the planting of Islamic values. In addition, students' math achievements tend to be low.

The Trend in International Mathematics and Science Study (TIMSS) survey, conducted by the Amsterdam-based International Association for the Evaluation of Educational Achievement (IAE), focuses on the domain of math content and students' cognitive abilities. The domains content include Numbers, Algebra, Geometry, Data and Opportunity, while cognitive domains include knowledge, application, and reasoning (Mullis et al. 2012). The survey conducted every four years was conducted starting 1999 and placed Indonesia at 34th out of 48 countries, in 2003 at 35th out of 46 countries, in 2007 at 36th out of 49 countries, in 2011 at 40th out of 45 countries, and in 2015 at 45th out of 50 countries.

DOI 10.1201/9781003219248-13

Indonesia's involvement in the TIMSS program is one of the efforts to evaluate the extent of the success of Indonesia's education program compared to other countries in the world as well as an effort to catch up with other, more developed countries. In reality, however, Indonesians have a low mathematical ability compared to other countries.

Indonesian students still experience difficulties in dealing with math problems, especially math problems with the TIMSS model. As the results of Jailani and Wulandari's research show, the mean ability of students in solving TIMSS model questions is 22.30 from the highest ideal score of 52 and the lowest ideal score of 0. Of the 400 students who were part of the research sample, 3% of students had the ability to solve the TIMSS model questions, which are included questions in the very high category of 22%, high category of 28%, medium category of 28%, the low category, and 20% in the very low category (Jailani & Wulandari 2017). Prasetyo and Rudhito's research (2016) also found almost similar results where the study showed that 22.6% of students were categorized as having high or good ability to solve the TIMSS model questions. With these difficulties, students need to be trained in working on TIMSS model questions.

TIMSS questions not only demand ability in applying concepts, but also how the concept is applied in various conditions as well as the students' ability to think critically and argue about how the problem can be solved. In solving similar problems, TIMSS requires critical thinking from students. Critical thinking is the ability to think at a complex level and use an analysis and evaluation process. Critical thinking involves inductive thinking skills such as recognizing relationships, analyzing open problems (with many possible solutions), determining cause and effect, making conclusions and taking into account relevant data (Gunawan 2004).

The TIMSS assessment framework (Mullis & Preuschoff 2009) is divided into two dimensions; namely the content dimension that determines the subject matter and the cognitive dimension determines the thought process that learners use when it comes to content. Mathematical studies in eighth grade for content dimensions there are four domains: Numbers, Algebra, Geometry, and Data and Opportunities with percentages of 30%, 30%, 20%, and 20%, respectively. While the cognitive domain is knowledge, application, and reasoning with consecutive percentages of 35%, 40%, and 25%, respectively. The instrument form used in TIMSS utilizes multiple choice and description. Valuations for multiple-choice items are worth one point, while instrument form descriptions are generally worth one or two points. These multiple choice questions include analyzing, generalize, integrating, justifying, and solving non-routine problems (Ina et al. 2013: 46). In addition, TIMSS-like questions not only use formulas but also require students to use critical thinking skills in the completion process, requiring students to write a description of the answer before selecting the option provided.

This is in accordance with those presented by Yunengsih (2008: 36) and cognitive ranahs in Trend in International Mathematics and Science Study (TIMSS) have emphasised on breaking the problem so that it can be used as a mould to summarize the questions of measuring the level of cognitive ranah. Therefore, the TIMSS is used as a mould for the development of questions on the materietical questions of TIMSS, almost all of which are found on the curriculum in Indonesia. Likewise, the cognitive aspects are the target of learning mathematics in accordance with the content standards (Permen Dikbud 2016). These are important for formulating content standards in the mathematics curriculum for junior high school education units covering cognitive abilities up to a high level or up to a high order thinking skill level.

These high order thinking skills include problem-solving skills, creative thinking skills, critical thinking, argumentation skills, and decision-making abilities. According to King, high-order thinking skills include critical, logical, reflective, metacognitive, and creative thinking, while according to Newman and Wehlage (Widodo 2013: 162), high-order thinking skills will allow students to be able to distinguish ideas or ideas clearly, argue well, able to solve problems, be able to construct explanations, able to hypothesize and understand complex matters more clearly. According to Vui (Kurniati 2016: 62) high-order thinking skills will occur when someone associates new information with information that is already stored in his/her memory. The ability of students at this level is still very low, as the results of the study (Tanudjaya & Dorman 2020) show that around

14% of students conduct proportional reasoning by giving consideration and only 1% of students conduct proportional reasoning with some considerations built on an adequate mathematical basis.

As an Islamic educational institution, Madrasahs have distinctive features compared to other schools. The distinctive feature of these madrasas is that they contain Islamic education materials which include Al Quran Hadith, Fiqh, Akidah Akhlak and Islamic Cultural History (SKI). The material in these subjects is presented partially without presenting the connection with the natural sciences such as science, mathematics, social sciences and other sciences. Therefore, to avoid the scientific dichotomy between the religious sciences (Qauliyah) and the world sciences (Kauniyah), it is necessary to make connections that integrate these sciences. Mulyadi (Akbarizan 2014) explained that scientific integration is a process of linking a person to the principle of tawhid. In this case, the object of the integration of knowledge is not science itself but someone who seeks knowledge. Meanwhile Ali defines scientific integration as: "Integration of sciences means the recognition that all true knowledge is from Allah and all sciences should be treated with equal respect whether it is scientific or revealed". The essence of the above definition is that all true knowledge comes from Allah. In the Koran, it says "the truth comes from Allah, and you should never doubt it," therefore Muslim scientists agree that Allah is the original source of knowledge, the truth (Mulyadi 2005: 47).

One form of scientific connection can be done by familiarizing students with solving math problems related to the material of the Al-Quran, Hadith, Fiqh, Akidah and Islamic Cultural History. Ma'rif stated that it is necessary to continuously develop the analysis of mathematical material by linking it with the verses of the Al-Quran (Ma'rif 2015). The process of linking Islamic and mathematical contexts has been carried out by many teachers in learning mathematics at Madrasah. For this reason, a study of the mathematical HOTS abilities of madrasah students in Indonesia is needed which is integrated with the Islamic context.

The main purpose of this research is to describe and analyze the mathematical HOTS ability of madrasah students in Indonesia. Specifically, this study aims to: (1) Describe and analyze the mathematical HOTS ability of Madrasah Tsanawiyah students in Indonesia who use the TIMSS design within the Islamic context, and (2) Knowing the difference in the mathematical HOTS ability of Madrasah Tsanawiyah students who use TIMSS design within the Islamic context in DKI Jakarta and Bandung.


2 METHOD

This study uses a type of survey research, aimed at generalizing the population based on sample data so that temporary conclusions can be made about the characteristics, behaviors, or attitudes of the population. The survey method was chosen to facilitate the obtaining of mathematical HOTS capability data with TIMSS design and Islamic context of Madrasah Tsanawiyah students (Madrasah Tsanawiyah (MTs) in Jakarta area, and Madrasah Tsanawiyah (MTs) in Bandung area).

The population in this study were all students of Madrasah Tsanawiyah in DKI Jakarta and West Java. The sample consisted of 141 students of Madrasah Tsanawiyah DKI Jakarta and 166 students of Madrasah Tsanawiyah Bandung, which were taken from all participants of the mathematics olympiade, which was held by students of the UIN Jakarta Mathematics Education Departement. The data were collected using a HOTS ability test using the TIMSS design and Islamic context. Mathematical HOTS ability test with the TIMSS design and the Islamic context of Madrasah Tsanawiyah students (MTs) consisted of 10 questions with the subject of Numbers, Algebra, Geometry, Data and Opportunities that had previously been tested for validity and reliability. Data obtained from the test results given to students of Madrasah Tsanawiyah (MTs) and was then analyzed using descriptive statistics and hypothesis testing using the One-way ANOVA test and continued with the Scheffe test.

Table 1. Comparison of mathematical HOTS capabilities with TIMSS design and the context of Islam.

|  | MTS JAKARTA | MTS BANDUNG |
| --- | --- | --- |
| N | 141 | 166 |
| Mean | 58.48 | 58.83 |
| Std. Error of Mean | 1.330 | 1.168 |
| Median | 58.00 | 60.00 |
| Mode | 48 | 55 |
| Std. Deviation | 15.793 | 15.045 |
| Variance | 249.408 | 226.339 |
| Skewness | .044 | .004 |
| Std. Error of Skewness | .204 | .188 |
| Kurtosis | −.448 | −.303 |
| Std. Error of Kurtosis | .406 | .375 |
| Range | 70 | 70 |
| Minimum | 23 | 23 |
| Maximum | 93 | 93 |
| Sum | 8245 | 9765 |

## 3  RESULTS AND DISCUSSION

The research was conducted in DKI Jakarta and Bandung and aimed to analyze and determine the differences in mathematical HOTS ability with TIMSS design and Islamic context of Madrasah Tsanawiyah students by sampling madrasah Tsanawiyah students from both regions. To find out and see the difference in the ability of HOTS mathematically given a description test consisting of 10 points of question. The test has been tested on Madrasah Aliyah students and analysis its characteristics in the form of validity test, reality test, difficulty level test, and problem differentiating power test.

Based on the results of the mathematical HOTS ability test with TIMSS design and Islamic context of Madrasah Tsanawiyah students, there are differences in average, median, mode, variance, standard deviation, slope level, and sharpness. A description of data comparing mathematical HOTS capabilities with TIMSS design and Islamic context is presented in Table 1.

Data of HOTS ability test results mathematically with TIMSS design and Islamic context of Madrasah Tsanawiyah students in DKI Jakarta area had the highest score of 93 and the lowest score of 23. The average score of HOTS test results mathematically with TIMSS design and Islamic context of Madrasah Tsanawiyah students in DKI Jakarta area was 58.48. There was a standard error of the mean, which reflects the accuracy of the sample selected against the population. The standard value of error of the mean of 1.33 minimal. This indicates that the average obtained can be said to be representative or can represent well the average value of the population. The median value obtained is 58, the mode is 48, and has a slope/skewness value of 0.044 (positive), meaning the curve has a positive model. This illustrates that the data spreads to below-average values. The students of Madrasah Tsanawiyah in DKI Jakarta area were more likely to get below average grades than students who get above average grades. While sharpness or kurtosis of −0.448 which means pointed curve or leptokurtis. The graph of the data distribution of the mathematical HOTS ability values with the TIMSS design and the Islamic context of Tsanawiyah Madrasah Students in the DKI Jakarta area can be seen in Figure 1.

For the Bandung area, data of HOTS ability test results are mathematical with TIMSS design and Islamic context of Madrasah Tsanawiyah students in Bandung area with the highest score of 93 and lowest score of 23. This data shows the range of HOT abilities of students from these two regions is the same. The average score of a mathematical HOTS capability test with TIMSS design and Islamic context is 58.83. The standard error of the mean reflects the accuracy of the sample

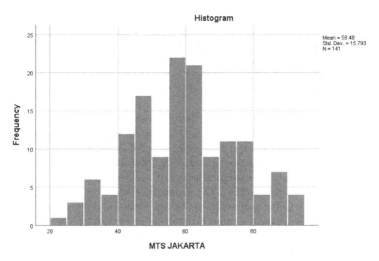

Figure 1.  Data distribution of students' mathematical HOTS ability values, Madrasah Tsanawiyah DKI Jakarta.

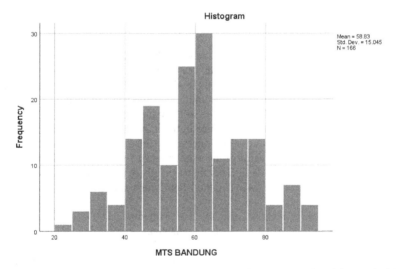

Figure 2.  Data distribution of students' mathematical HOTS ability values, Madrasah Tsanawiyah Bandung.

we choose against the population, as evidenced by the standard value of error of mean of 1,168, which is small. This indicates that the average obtained can be said to be representative or can represent well the average value of the population. The median value obtained is 60, the mode is 55, and has a slope value of/skewness of 0.004 (positive), meaning that the curve has a positive model that is the tail extending to the right. This illustrates that the data spreads to below-average values. This shows that students of Madrasah Tsanawiyah in Bandung area are more likely to get below average grades than students who get above average grades. While sharpness or kurtosis of −0.303 which means pointed curve or leptokurtis. The graph of the distribution of data on the value of the mathematical HOTS ability value of the TIMSS design with the Islamic context of Tsanawiyah Madrasah Students in the Bandung area can be seen in Figure 2.

To find out the difference in the average mathematical HOTS ability with the TIMSS design and the Islamic context of Madrasah Tsanawiyah students in these two areas, the hypothesis will be significantly tested. The results of hypothesis testing can be seen by looking at the significance value obtained. If the significance value > 0.05 then Ho is accepted. The significance value is 0.549 > 0.05. So it can be concluded that there is no difference in mathematical HOTS abilities with the TIMSS design and the Islamic context of Madrasah Tsanawiyah students in DKI Jakarta and Bandung.

The results of the research that have been described above show the low mathematical HOTS skills of Madrasah Tsanawiyah students in the DKI Jakarta and Bandung areas using the TIMSS framework. This can be seen from the average score of 58.48 for MTs DKI Jakarta students and 58.83 for MTs students in Bandung from a score range of 0–100. The questions given consisted of items that can be used to apply the reasoning aspects in accordance with the TIMSS domain whose content is related to the Islamic context. The material for Islam referred to in this case includes material on the Qur'an, Hadith, Jurisprudence, Akidah Morals and the History of Islamic culture. Students' mistakes in solving the questions here are not due to the aspects of Islamic material but in their mathematical abilities. The results of this study are in line with the findings of Tanudjaya and Dorman (2020) which state that the ability to give considerations or reasons is still very low. In addition, the results of this study are also supported by findings of Jailani and Wulandari (2017) and Prasetyo and Rudhito (2016), which state that students' ability to solve TIMSS questions is still low.

## 4 CONCLUSION AND RECOMMENDATIONS

Based on the results of research and discussion of mathematical HOTS abilities with the TIMSS design and the Islamic context of Madrasah Tsanawiyah students in Indonesia, the following conclusions can be drawn: (1) Mathematical HOTS abilities in the aspects of analysis and evaluation with the TIMSS design of applying and reasoning indicators and the Islamic context of Students Madrasah Tsanawiyah Jakarta and Bandung are still low and the abilities of students in both regions are almost the same. (2) There is no difference in the mathematical HOTS ability of the TIMSS design and the Islamic context of Madrasah Tsanawiyah students in DKI Jakarta and Bandung. The test results show the significance value of the mathematical HOTS ability with the TIMSS design and the Islamic context of 0.549 > 0.05. This shows that there is no difference in the mathematical ability of HOTS with the TIMSS design and the Islamic context of Madrasah Tsanawiyah students in DKI Jakarta and Bandung.

Based on the results of research and discussion of mathematical HOTS abilities with the TIMSS design and the Islamic context of Madrasah Tsanawiyah students in Indonesia, the following conclusions can be drawn: (1) Mathematical HOTS abilities in the aspects of analysis and evaluation with the TIMSS design of applying and reasoning indicators and the Islamic context of Students Madrasah Tsanawiyah Jakarta and Bandung are still low and the abilities of students in both regions are almost the same. (2) There is no difference in the mathematical HOTS ability of the TIMSS design and the Islamic context of Madrasah Tsanawiyah students in DKI Jakarta and Bandung. The test results show the significance value of the mathematical HOTS ability with the TIMSS design and the Islamic context of 0.549 > 0.05. This shows that there is no difference in the mathematical ability of HOTS with the TIMSS design and the Islamic context of Madrasah Tsanawiyah students in DKI Jakarta and Bandung.

ACKNOWLEDGMENTS

The authors would like thank to International Conference on Education in Muslim Society (ICEMS 2020) committee for their financial support, as well as participated Madrasah Tsanawiyah students in DKI Jakarta and Bandung for their participation in this study.

# REFERENCES

Akbarizan. 2014. *Integrasi Ilmu.* Suska Press.

Departemen Pendidikan Nasional. 2016. *Kurikulum Tingkat Satuan Pendidikan.* Jakarta: Pusat Kurikulum Balitbang Depdiknas.

Gunawan and Adi W. 2004. *Genius Learning Strategy.* Jakarta: Gramedia Pustaka Utama.

Ina V S, Mullis, Michael O M and Editors. 2013. *TIMSS 2015 Assessment Framework.* Chestnut Hill: Boston College, p 19.

Jailani and Wulandari. 2017. *Kemampuan Matematika Siswa Kelas VIII di Daerah Istimewa Yogyakarta dalam Menyelesaikan Soal Model TIMSS. Jurnal Pengajaran MIPA* vol 22, pp 1–8.

Kurniati D. 2016. *Kemampuan Berpikir Tingkat Tinggi Siswa SMP Di Kabupaten Jember Dalam Menyelesaikan Soal Berstandar PISA. Jurnal Penelitian dan Evaluasi Pendidikan* vol 2, pp 142–155.

Maarif S. 2015. *Integrasi Matematika Dan Islam Dalam Pembelajaran Matematika. Jurnal Infinity* vol 4.

Mullis, Ina V S, Martin, Michhael O, Ruddock, G J, O'Sullivan and Preuschoff C. 2009. *TIMSS 2011 Assessment Frameworks.* Chestnut Hill: Boston College.

Mullis, Ina V S, Martin, Michael O, Foy P and Arora A. 2012. *TIMSS 2011 International Results in Mathematics.* Chestnut Hill: Boston College.

Mulyadi K. 2005. *Integrasi Ilmu.* Bandung: PT Mizan p 2.

Prasetyo D A B and Rudhito M A. 2016. *Analisis Kemampuan dan Kesulitan Siswa SMP dalam Menyelesaikan Soal Bilangan Model TIMSS. Jurnal Pengajaran MIPA* vol 2, pp 122–128.

Rudhito M A and Prasetyo D A B. 2016. *Pengembangan soal Matematika model TIMSS untuk mendukung pembelajaran Matematika SMP kelas VII Kurikulum 2013. Cakrawala Pendidikan* vol 35, pp 88–97.

Tanudjaya C P and Doorman M. 2020. *Examining Higher-Order Thinking in Indonesian Lower Secondary Mathematics Classrooms. Journal on Mathematics Education* vol 11, pp 277–300.

Widodo T and Kadarwati S. 2013. *High Order Thinking Berbasis Pemecahan Masalah Untuk Meningkatkan Hasil Belajar Berorientasi Pembentukan Karakter Siswa. Cakrawala Pendidikan* vol 3, pp 161–171.

Yunengsih Y Widiatmika I M A and Candrasari A. 2008. *Hasil Kajian Ujian Nasional Matematika Pada Sekolah Menengah Pertama.* Jakarta: Departemen Riset Putera sampoerna Fundation.

*Social and humanities*

*Emerging Trends in Technology for Education in an Uncertain World – Nanto, Rahiem & Khalis Maryati (Eds)*
*© 2022 copyright the Author(s), ISBN 978-1-032-11288-6*

# Model of IVAM for enhancing responsibility of young citizens in Pancasila education

Z. Slam
*Faculty of Educational Sciences, UIN Syarif Hidayatullah Jakarta, Jakarta, Indonesia*

ABSTRACT: Low learning responsibility affects student learning outcomes of Pancasila Education, so to overcome this problem, a model of IVAM (Initial Stage of Character Building, Values Clarification Stage, Application Stage, and Stage of Meaning) is applied. The purpose of this study is to describe the model of IVAM to increase student responsibility in Pancasila Education. This research uses a qualitative approach with a case study method. Research informants were students with data collection techniques in the form of interviews, observations, questionnaires and document studies. The results showed that model of IVAM has succeeded in increasing student learning responsibilities, namely: completing assignments well, obeying campus regulations and studying diligently. This success from the point of view of Pancasila Education is the development of the potential of students to become young citizens who are responsible as part of the goals of Pancasila Education.

*Keywords*: model of ivam, pancasila education, rresponsibility, young citizens

## 1 INTRODUCTION

The fourth wave of civilization, which we currently call the industrial revolution 4.0, makes the world of education challenged to make curriculum changes by focusing on incubation so that graduates can contribute to be players to take part in the world of star-ups and also in developing strong soft skills (Adi 2020). No exception in learning as part of curriculum change, it must instill the responsibility of students as the nation's next generation.

Learning should include developing morally responsible character and implementing ethical and moral behavior (Isfihani 2017). Responsibility is the attitude and behavior of a person to carry out his duties and obligations as he should, towards himself, society, the natural environment, the social and cultural environment, the State and God Almighty (Mustari 2019). Responsibility in learning is an obligation to complete a task that has been received completely through maximum effort and to be brave enough to bear all the consequences. Responsible individualsare individuals who can fulfill their own duties and needs, and can fulfill their responsibilities to the surrounding environment properly. Individuals must be trained continuously, so that they become responsible individuals (Syafitri 2017).

In learning, there is no more important task, namely the development of human resources for young citizens who are responsible, effective, and educated (Budimansyah 2010). The importance of a person having a responsible attitude is that he will be trusted, respected, appreciated and liked by others, stronger and stronger in facing various problems and successfully completing tasks throughly with quality and is the key to success in life (Ministry of Education and Culture 2016).

Developing the potential of students to become responsible citizens is one of the goals of national education (Chapter II, Article 3 of Law Number 20 of 2003 on the National Education System).

Conversely, someone who is not responsible for learning will get less than optimal results, so he cannot know how much the results of his ability (Syafitri 2017). In the context of learning, responsibility can be a tool to avoid negative behavior such as neglect, verbal and non-verbal aggression and also disciplinary actions such as not doing school work.

Pancasila education has a strategic and significant role in the development of responsible citizens. The Ministry of Research, Technology and Higher Education of the Republic of Indonesia (2016) states that one of the competencies that Pancasila Education must achieve is by delivering students so that they have the ability to take a responsible attitude according to their conscience.

In this case, the role of the lecturer is needed to teach responsibility in everyday life by providing learning assignments and emphasizing students to be responsible for doing assignments as well as possible so that students can improve and show an attitude of responsibility optimally in various environments (Septyani et al. 2020).

If you look at the substance of the material taught in Pancasila Education, it should be able to build the responsibility of students, but so far this course has not been able to build student responsibility so it is undeniable that some young citizens are currently experiencing the fragility of responsibility (Widiatmaka 2016). The fragility of responsibility among students is no less worrying, such as crashing ethics, morals, laws from mild to severe ones, which are often demonstrated by students. The habit of cheating on exams is still being done. The desire to pass the easy way without working hard on the exam causes them to try to find answers in an unethical way. Plagiarism of scientific papers among students is still massive (Slam 2014).

The social phenomenon that has recently occurred is very worrying, such as the phenomenon of violence in solving problems that has become commonplace. Policy coercion occurs at almost every level of the institution. Information manipulation is commonplace. Emphasis and imposition of the will of one group on another group is considered normal. The law is so observant of mistakes, but blind to justice (Hasanah in Isfihani 2017). These behaviors are antiresponsibility behavior.

Regarding this problem, we do not want to lose the opportunity to continue to develop the potential of students to become responsible citizens. Therefore, the source of the various weakening of the responsibilities of these students needs to be studied and it seems that one of the causes is that the current education praxis is running in a "business as usual" state (Tilaar 2002). Current educational praxis tends to still use the old paradigm of education, in which lecturers provide knowledge to passive learners. This old paradigm also means that if a person has knowledge and expertise in a field, he will definitely be able to teach. He does not need to know about the proper teaching and learning process. He only needs to pour what he knows into an empty bottle that is ready to receive it (Lie 2007).

According to Adisusilo (2012) that lecturers must change the paradigm from being a teacher to being an educator. In each lesson or face-to-face, the teacher shows that "behind the material being studied, there is at least one value/character of life that is good for students to know, think about, ponder on and believe to be good and true, thus encouraging them to implement it in their lives".

There is no guarantee that moral or character such as responsibility will be formed just because of the "label" "Religious Education" or Moral Education", if the process and approach is not different from other subjects, therefore educating the true character with a character learning model (Suryadi 2010).

If the aforementioned problems are not immediately resolved, it will certainly make it more difficult for opportunities to present responsible young citizens. Therefore, a values approach is needed that emphasizes the development of students' ability to think logically, by analyzing problems related to social values (Windrati 2011). According to Suwarna and Jatirahayu (2013), to teach values/characters, lecturers need to be supported by the selection of content, methods, and media effectively. Furthermore, Sukitman (2016) states that the value analysis approach can emphasize the development of the ability of students to think logically, by analyzing problems related to social values. Seeing the conditions of learning management like this and projections of better learning in the future, it is very reasonable, especially in this case, to develop the potential of students to become responsible young citizens.

One of the models for developing the potential of students to become responsible citizens of Pancasila Education is the IVAM (Initial Stage of Character Building, Values Clarification Stage, Application Stage, and Stage of Meaning) model. Kohlberg, Marline Lockheed and Andrian

Verspoor as cited by Suryadi (2010), the character of responsibility can only be grown after going through four stages, namely: 1) Initial Stage of Character building, 2) Value Clarification Stage, 3) Application Stage and 4) Meaning Stage.

This kind of development model has been carried out by Suwarna and Jatirahayu (2013) that in order to teach character, steps from seeding to culture are needed to become habituation. Finally, character education is internalized in the learner.

This study aims to increase the responsibility of young citizens in Pancasila education through the IVAM model.

## 2 RESEARCH METHODS

This research uses a case study method, which is an empirical inquiry that investigates phenomena in the context of real life, whenever; boundaries between phenomena and contexts are not clearly visible and where: multiple sources of evidence are utilized (Yin 2013).

The case study method used in this research aims to describe how the IVAM Model is in developing the responsibilities of students through Pancasila Education.

The characteristics of the responsibility of students in this study are the attitudes and behaviors of students that reflect a sense of responsibility in a college environment, namely: completing tasks well, obeying rules and regulations, and studying diligently.

Research participants are sources who can provide information, selected purposively and implemented according to specific objectives. Participants in this study were 30 students in semester 6 of class B consisting of 2 boys and 28 girls in Madrasah Teacher Education study program.

Data collection techniques in this study, namely observation, interviews, and documentation Observations made by researchers in this study were to observe the process and results of implementing the IVAM model to increase the responsibility of students in learning Researchers used unstructured interviews about how students responded to the application of the IVAM model in increasing the responsibility of young citizens in Pancasila Education. What are the added and weak points, if you become a citizen who is responsible for studying on campus? The indicators of theresponsibility of young citizens in this context are (1) completing campus assignments well; (2) obey campus rules and regulations; (3) study diligently.

Documentation in the form of semester learning plans, student learning outcomes, photos, group discussion reports and so on. All data were collected in accordance with the formulation of the research problem, then data reduction, data presentation and conclusion drawing were carried out.

## 3 RESULT AND DISCUSSION

The implementation of the IVAM model uses four stages, namely: (1) Initial Stage of Character Building, (2) Values Clarification Stage, (3) Application Stage, (4) Stage of Meaning or abbreviated as the IVAM Model, successfully developing students to become young citizens responsible.

### 3.1 *Initial stage of character building (I)*

The development of responsibility at this stage is through habituation. Students familiarize themselves with responsibilities in completing campus assignments properly, obey campus rules and regulations, and study diligently.

The development of the responsibility of students through the habituation stage is relevant to the results of research by Nasih (2013) that the habituation method contributes to the formation of the character of responsibility. The added value of habituation according to Amri (2014), can encourage and provide space for students on theories that require direct application, so that heavy theories can be light for students if they are often used to it.

## 3.2 *Values clarification stage (V)*

The Values Clarification Stage (V) is the second stage of developing students to become responsible young citizens. The development of the character of responsibility at this stage is carried out through cooperative learning of the jigsaw technique, with the division of task group discussion among experts to discuss the importance or danger of students completing or not completing campus assignments properly. The second group of experts discussed the importance or dangers of obeying/disobeying campus rules and regulations. Expert group three discusses the importance or danger of studying diligently/not studying diligently.

The results of one expert group discuss the importance or dangers of carrying out or not carrying out campus assignments properly. According to them, campus assignments are always considered an important component in student learning activities. Through assignments such as given papers or book reports, students are expected to be able to practice the skills needed to be more familiar and understand a teaching material. The more practice, the more proficient it is so that it can improve students' understanding of a science. By regularly doing campus assignments, students become accustomed to managing study time, and in the end they can foster self-discipline. When analogoused, like a relationship, the more we meet, the closer it will be.

Why do students have to carry out tasks well? Because by carrying out tasks properly it will make it easier for students to achieve success in the future. The benefits of carrying out tasks well are as follows: (1) getting better learning achievement; (2) provide convenience/brightness to achieve success in the future; (3) broader insight and mindset; (4) making a quality campus. Then what if students do not carry out their duties properly? Failure to carry out tasks properly can lead to the following things: (1) getting bad grades automatically does not pass; (2) difficulty achieving goals (bleak future); (3) Low Human Resources; (4) become unemployed; (5) adding to the state problem/state burden.

The results of the discussion from two expert groups discussing the importance or dangers of obeying/not obeying campus regulations. According to them, every student who is studying at university is obliged to obey the regulations of the institution where they study. In addition, they must also have the skills, attitudes, and ethics to support success during their studies. According to them, there are several skills, attitudes, and ethics that students must have, namely: (1) dress neatly and politely. Using clothes according to campus regulations, namely wearing neat, clean, unobtrusive clothes and so on; (2) taking part in lecture activities, students are required to attend courses according to a predetermined schedule and fill out the available attendance list. It is during lectures that useful knowledge is obtained; (3) respect lecturers and campus staff. Every student is required to always respect the lecturers and staff who work on the campus where they study; (4) maintaining order and security, that is, it is prohibited to carry out various actions that cause noise, disturbance, riot, fights, brawls, inconvenience, hatred, terror, fear, and so on. Learning activities must not be disturbed by anyone, either from within or from outside. At the time of learning, students are required to follow the existing procedures so that learning runs comfortably and as expected; (5) obeying the applicable regulations, students are required to comply with campus regulations for the sake of smooth and orderly studies. Everything went according to the rules. Legal sanctions are imposed for those who violate rule (6) of not committing fraud. Any act of cheating is not allowed in any activity. Cheating activities, copying other people's work, working together during exams, etc. need to be sanctioned according to the applicable regulations.

Why do students need to obey campus regulations? Because by obeying campus regulations, students in learning become orderly, safe, and comfortable. The benefits of obeying campus regulations are: (a) life becomes more disciplined; (b) life becomes more responsible; (c) avoid punishment; (d) appreciated by friends and lecturers; (e) the creation of a peaceful, serene and safe environment. Then what are the consequences if you do not comply with campus regulations? Failure to comply with campus regulations can result in the following: (1) sanctions are ensured; (2) is considered someone who is not disciplined/has a negative view; and (3) missing lecture materials.

Obeying campus/disciplinary regulations has the aim of directing students so that they learn about good things that are preparation for adulthood, when they are very dependent on themselves.

Thus, obeying campus regulations is very important to make someone more focused in living their life. Students as the nation's next generation, from an early age, need to be grown to comply with campus regulations that regulate the lives of students that are useful for themselves and have an impact on society, nation, and country.

The results of the discussion group of three experts discuss/discuss the importance or danger of studying diligently/not studying diligently. According to students there is no task more important than them than responsible citizen development, namely to study diligently. Study diligently as a student to get achievements and achieve their goals. Without diligent learning from students, presenting superior Human Resources would not be possible.

Why is it necessary to study diligently? Because by studying diligently you will get achievements and achieve your goals. The benefits of diligent learning include the following: (1) growing patience in students, namely by studying diligently for the sake of achieving goals, so they can endure a situation or in a difficult situation and they will go through it without complaining. In this way, patience will grow in them, because they will not give up even if they encounter an obstacle while on their way to that goal; (2) the work that students do will feel more fun. There is no job that feels difficult when they do it diligently, instead the work they do will feel more enjoyable. Why? Because persistence teaches us to live it sincerely. In addition, their diligent attitude will make them continue to try and study them when they have difficulty learning. In contrast to those who are not diligent due to being lazy, the work they do will feel much heavier; (3) students can complete their work with optimal results. When students study diligently with a happy feeling, try to the best of their abilities and with the intention of continuing to try, it will make you complete tasks with optimal results. Then there will be a sense of satisfaction in yourself because you have given the best results; (4) there will be motivation to continue to grow. A diligent attitude will make students have a strong will, so that they become the focus to achieve their goals. This strong will will generate motivation to continue to develop so that he will continue to learn and eventually gain more knowledge, both self-taught and knowledge he gets from other people's experiences; (5) good work results will make people trust their performance. The diligent attitude that students have makes them have a wellstructured, neat and clear plan, so that it will give good work results. After other people see the results of his work, their trust will arise in him. They do their own assessment of the performance that he did. He will also maintain their trust by establishing good cooperation if it is a team with his co-workers; (6) the more skilled and thorough in carrying out a job/task. Get used to being diligent so that the habit will eliminate the feeling of being afraid to try. Thus, he becomes more courageous in trying to complete his job/task in other ways to be more effective and efficient. He didn't even hesitate to double-check his work. So, he will be more skilled and thorough in doing his job. These are the six benefits that will be obtained when students have a diligent attitude. Students who have a diligent attitude will have a better and more advanced life. Because diligence becomes a trigger to be serious in achieving what you aspire to. So, do not hesitate every student to have a diligent attitude if they have a dream that they want to achieve.

Then what if you don't have the attitude of being diligent in studying? Without persistence in learning, it can have the following impacts: (1) low grades, learning is the most important thing if you want to get high or above average scores, without learning he will not get anything. Lazy studying usually causes oneself to be lazy to do assignments and lazy to go to school, causing a person to get low grades. It should be noted that low scores are not only influential on campus but will make it difficult for them to be accepted for success in entering the competitive world of work, because the value is one of the important points and one of the requirements for whether to accept it or not in the world of work; (2) disappoint many people. The impact of being lazy to study for others will certainly be obvious when someone is lazy to learn, namely the two parents who have worked hard to send to school but all they get is disappointment. Apart from parents, lecturers on campus will also feel disappointed with someone's lazy nature and will feel that they have not been successful in educating students so far. People who are lazy, of course, will be shunned and disliked by others, for example when there is a group assignment, but because they are lazy to come to study, of course it will cause a negative impression from classmates; (3) to be stupid. When someone decides to be lazy, he must accept the consequences of not learning, namely ignorance and of course the main cause is laziness to learn. In addition, he who is stupid likes to blame others for their own mistakes, often feels the most right and wants to always be right, becomes more aggressive when facing problems or conflicts, tends to ignore others and is selfish, feels the best and right of others, and all it is due to laziness; (4) difficult to get the best performance index. Class achievement is certainly the hope of every student, especially parents. When he gets the best class achievement, it will not only be his own pride, but his family is also proud, especially his parents. However, to get the highest class achievement, of course, cannot be separated from effort and hard work and prayer. But if he is still struggling and comfortable in the world of laziness, how can he excel? Of course, the main key to the end result is to learn, learn and keep learning. Maintained lazy nature will make it difficult to get the best performance; (5) being naughty, when he is lazy to learn, of course it will cause a lack of knowledge and the importance of education and tend to be naughty students. Plus, today's relationships are increasingly becoming both urban and rural. There are a lot of juvenile delinquencies that can be seen and lead to things that are not desired. For example brawls between students, consuming alcohol openly, smoking, consuming illegal drugs and the severity of adultery everywhere. This, of course, could be the cause of the destruction of a future which should be the nation's next generation which is a valuable asset. Besides being able to boast of both parents, it can be the pride of the country and the nation; (6) lazy to worship, even though it is known about the importance of studying religion and how to be able to implement it in everyday life. A person who is lazy, of course, will feel heavy hearted in doing whatever is meant in worship. When he is lazy to worship, be prepared to get a negative impact, namely weak faith, not getting grace from God Almighty, the heart becomes unsettled and always overshadowed by fear, irritability, easily indulges in Satan's invitation and tends to be difficult to tolerate.

In developing the responsibility of students through the Values Clarification stage, this stage emphasizes by fostering emotional awareness of students' values through clarification, rational critical study, and testing truth, goodness, justice, feasibility, and accuracy (Adisusilo 2012; Subur 2007). Education about values means that the educational process undertaken puts more emphasis on values debates, not how to make those values come true within the lives of students (Suryanto et al. 2019). With this technique, it is able to foster and instill moral values, be able to classify or explore moral messages and then convey these moral messages, be able to assess the quality of the moral values of students, be able to develop the potential that exists in students, be able to provide a number of learning experiences in various lives, able to ward off the pressure of moral values in a person, and able to provide an acceptable picture of moral values.

It is also in line with the research results of Martoni et al. (2019) that the application of the value clarification technique is proven to improve the learning understanding of class V students in Islamic Education subjects at Primary School 003 Lubuk Kebun, Logas Tanah Darat District. This can be seen from the results of the Pre-Cycle test, only 25% of students have a good understanding of Islamic Education learning, Cycle I rises to 41.7% students who have good learning understanding, Cycle II rises to 75% of students who have a good understanding of learning good and it turns out that in Cycle III grade V students who have a good understanding of learning have reached 87.5% in Islamic Education subject at Primary School 003 Lubuk Kebun, Logas Tanah Darat District.

## 3.3 *Application stage*

At this stage students are involved in habituation activities and an understanding of the character of responsibility in real situations in Pancasila Education lectures with an online model. Previously, students were assigned in groups to write papers and power points. Furthermore, during the online model lecture, each group presented their paper presentation. The results of this application stage students are able to make papers, presentations, and be active in lectures. These results prove that students have a responsible attitude. This is in line with the results of research by Martoni et al. (2019) that the application of the stage application is proven to increase the learning responsibility of students.

### 3.4 *Meaning stage*

The Meaning Stage is the final stage where students are able to feel the meaning of positive values, attitudes and behaviors that have been understood and carried out so far, both in matters relating to or not related to learning. This stage has a long-term impact, and if students have reached this stage, students can get institutionalized values and can benefit from what they do. The attitudes and behavior of students which are included in the meaning stage if they continue to show responsible behavior consistently or begin to cultivate. This condition is what quality Pancasila Education wants to create because it will be the basis for the growth and development of the character of responsibility of young citizens. This "meaning" stage is also the most decisive stage in any quality education process which will become the basis for the sustainable growth of character and personality.

According to Lickona (1992), without these three aspects, the character education would not be effective. With a systematical and continuous character education, a student would be emotionally intelligent. This emotional intelligent is the important foundation for the student's future, therefore the student will be more successful in facing every life challenge, including the academic challenge. There are nine fundamental characters based on the universal noble values: the first is the character of loving God and all of God's creation, second is independence and responsibility, the third is honesty and diplomacy, fourth is respect fullness and politeness, the fifth is generosity and helpfulness, the sixth is confidence and hard working quality, the seventh is leadership and fairness, the eight is good manner and humble, and the ninth is tolerance, peace and unity.

These nine fundamental characters are systematically teach in a holistic education model using the method of knowing the good, feeling the good, and acting the good.

According to Agung (2011) that knowing the good is easy to be taught because it is only about the cognitive knowledge. After the knowing the good we have to grow the feeling of loving the good, that is how to feel and love the good deeds as an engine that make people always wanted to do the good. As the result, it will develop awareness that a person is willing to do the good because that person loves the good manner. After getting used to do the good things, then acting the good will be a habit.

## 4   CONCLUSION

The model of IVAM can increase student responsibility as young citizens in Pancasila Education. The increase in students who reflect responsibility is evidenced by completing college assignments, obeying campus regulations, and studying diligently.

The responsibility that has been formed reflects the success of Pancasila Education as a vehicle that makes students aware, intelligent, and responsible in learning.

This IVAM model is an alternative model of responsibility character education in Pancasila Education. For this reason, it is suggested that the application of the model of IVAM can be used in Pancasila Education, value education,moral education or character education to develop the responsibilities of students.

ACKNOWLEDGMENT

It's my pleasure to acknowledge to thank for International Conference of Education in Moslem Society (ICEMS) 2020 on the opportunity to share this article.

REFERENCES

Adi, F.P. 2020. Arah Pendidikan Karakter Pancasila Era Covid-19. *Jurnal Pendidikan Indonesia*, 6(4):1–9.
Adisusilo, S. 2012. *Pembelajaran Nilai-Karakter.* Jakarta: PTRaja Grafindo Persada.

Agung, L. 2011. Character Education Integration In Social Studies Learning. *Journal International Journal of History Education*, 9 (2): 392–340.

Amri, U.S. 2014. *Pendidikan Karakter Berbasis Alqur'an*. Jakarta: Rajawali Pers.

Budimansyah, D. 2010. *Penguatan Pendidikan Kewarganegaraan Untuk Membangun Karakter Bangsa*. Bandung: Widya Aksara Press.

Isfihani. 2017. Pembentukan Karakter Bangsa Melalui Paradigma Pendidikan. *Jurnal Kependidikan Al-Riwayah*, 9(2) : 375–406.

Kementerian Pendidikan dan Kebudayaan. 2016. *Mengembangkan Tanggung Jawab Kepada Anak*. Jakarta: Kemdikbud.

Kementerian Riset, Teknologi dan Pendidikan Tinggi Republik Indonesia. 2016. *Pendidikan Pancasila Untuk Perguruan Tinggi*, Jakarta: Kemristekdikti.

Lickona, K. 1992. *Educating for Character*. New York: Bantam Books.

Lie, A. 2007. *Cooperative Learning*. Jakarta: Grasindo.

Martoni, *et al.* 2019. Penerapan Teknik Mengklarifikasi Nilai Untuk Meningkatkan Pemahaman Belajar Siswa Pada Mata Pelajaran Pendidikan Agama Islam. *Jurnal Pendidikan Agama Islam*, 5 (2): 93–101.

Mustari. 2019. *Nilai Karakter Refleksi Untuk Pendidikan*. Depok: PT RajaGrafindo Persada.

Nasih, A.U. 2013. *Pendidikan Anak Dalam Islam*. Jakarta: Khatulistiwa Press.

Septyani, N.L.P.Y., Suniasih,N.W., Negara, I.G.A.O. 2020. Pengaruh Interaksi Sosial dan Sikap Tanggung Jawab Terhadap Sikap Peduli Lingkungan. *Jurnal Ilmiah Pendidikan Profesi Guru*, 3 (1): 84–97.

Slam, Z. 2014. *Pengembangan Karakter Kerjasama Berdasar Pancasila Melalui Pembelajaran Pendidikan Kewarganegaraan*. (Disertasi). Sekolah Pasca Sarjana Universitas Pendidikan Indonesia. Bandung.

Sukitman. 2016. Internalisasi Nilai dalamPembelajaran: Upaya Menciptakan Sumber Daya Manusia yang Berkarakter. *Jurnal Pendidikan Sekolah Dasar*, 2(2): 86–96.

Suryadi, A. 2010. *Sebuah Model Pendidikan Karakter Dalam Sistem Persekolahan Di Indonesia*. Bandung: Universitas Pendidikan Indonesia.

Suryanto, Jumintono, Pambudi, Dholina,I.P., Mardati, A., Wantini. 2019. Strategy of Values Education in the Indonesian Education System. *International Journal of Instruction*, 12 (1): 607–624.

Suwarna dan Jatirahayu. 2013. Pembelajaran Karakter Yang Menyenangkan. *Jurnal Pendidikan Karakter*, 3 (3): 274–287.

Syafitri, R. 2017. Meningkatkan Tanggung Jawab Belajar Melalui Strategi Giving Questions And Getting Answer Pada Siswa. *Jurnal Penelitian dan Pengembangan Pendidikan*, 1 (1): 57–63.

Tilaar, H.A.R. 2002. *Perubahan Sosial dan Pendidikan*. Jakarta: Grasindo.

Undang-Undang Nomor 20 Tahun 2003 Tentang Sistem Pendidikan Nasional.

Windrati. 2011. Pendidikan Sebagai Suatu Strategi Dalam Pembentukan Kepribadian Siswa. *Jurnal Formatif*, 1 (1): 40–47.

Widiatmaka, P. 2016. Kendala Pendidikan Kewarganegaraan Dalam Membangun Karakter Peserta didik Di Dalam Proses Pembelajaran. *Jurnal Civic*, 13 (2): 188–198.

Yin, R.K. 2013. *Study Kasus: Desain dan Metode*. Jakarta: PT RajaGrafindo Persada.

*Emerging Trends in Technology for Education in an Uncertain World – Nanto, Rahiem & Khalis Maryati (Eds)*
© 2022 copyright the Author(s), ISBN 978-1-032-11288-6

# Evaluation of learning in the pandemic era in the PGMI study program in Indonesia

Fauzan, Fatkhul Arifin & Neli Rahmaniah
*Faculty of Educational Sciences, Syarif Hidayatullah State Islamic University of Jakarta, Jakarta, Indonesia*

Maulana Arafat Lubis
*Faculty of Educational Sciences, Padangsidimpuan State Islamic Institute, Sumatera Utara, Indonesia*

ABSTRACT: The purpose of this study is to determine the adaptation of lecturers and students in using technology as a learning medium, as well as what technologies are often used in learning. The research method used is quantitative research by analyzing the data found descriptively. The instruments used were observation, literature study and questionnaires. The population in this study were all students of the Madrasah Ibtidaiyah Teacher Education Study Program (PGMI) in Indonesia, and the sample was more than 40 Madrasah Ibtidaiyah Teacher Education Study Programs (PGMI) in Indonesia with 1294 students as respondents. The results obtained from this study, including the effectiveness of the application of distance learning methods during the pandemic which were well responded to by students, and the mastery of lecturers in using PJJ learning media was quite good. Of course, this is homework for lecturers to be more creative and innovative in using media during PJJ.

*Keywords*: Learning, pandemic era, learning media, PGMI Study Program

## 1 INTRODUCTION

Corona Virus Disease 2019 (COVID-19) has infected millions of people in more than 200 countries in the world, causing many to die (Lin et al. 2020; Shereen et al. 2020). The emergence of the COVID-19 pandemic has greatly affected the education process in higher education. Since the birth of the COVID-19 pandemic, universities have driven the education system from face to face to e-learning. Some of the facts have resulted from the emergence of the Covid-19 pandemic such as (1) close to 7.5 million students are required to carry out education at home; (2) the network availability in the student residence area is not completely sufficient; (3) learners and learners are not yet fully prepared for the imposition of online learning; (4) routine patterns, changes in educational procedures make some learners and students shock. Even with the current state of the COVID-19 pandemic, the education process must not stop. Until this is a challenge for the Indonesian nation, the challenge is not an eternal obstacle, but the Indonesian nation must be ready to face it. Many paths lead to Rome, many methods lead to hope. Therefore, all of them need to innovate in education during the COVID-19 era.

Based on UNESCO's information, 112 countries have practiced learning from home policies, including Malaysia, Thailand, Germany, Austria, Mexico, South Africa, Yemen, and Zambia. Of these 112 countries, 101 have nationwide learned from home policy. Meanwhile, 11 other countries, listed Indonesia, practice studying at home. In Indonesia, learning from the home policy has been implemented near 28.6 million students from SD to SMA/Vocational High School (SMK) in various provinces. As of March 18, 2020, as many as 276 state and private universities in Indonesia have practiced online lectures (Sirri & Lestari 2020, p. 67). The consequence of closing learning institutions physically as well as changing learning at/from home as a government policy is the replacement of the teaching and learning system (Arora & Srinivasan 2020).

The Ministry of Learning and Culture of the Republic of Indonesia has produced a policy on the application of learning in the emergency period of the spread of the COVID-19 virus. The policy describes the application of the learning process from home by changing face-to-face education which is usually carried out in schools or on campus to be online or online. Education is carried out remotely using an internet network and assisted by intermediary equipment such as gadgets (Mesran et al. 2020). Kuntarto said that the term online learning was originally used to describe a learning system that utilizes internet technology (Fauzi & Khusuma 2020, p. 59).

After the birth of the 20th century, we are still invited to be literate towards technology, to facilitate the implementation of innovative education. I wish, but after the birth of the 21st century and the emergence of the COVID-19 pandemic, technology has become equipment that you don't want to use or use. 21st-century education known as 6C (Critical thinking, Communication, Collaboration, Citizenship, Creativity, and Connectivity). 21st-century education must be tried in the education process in any condition listed during the COVID-19 pandemic (Gusty et al. 2020).

Critical thinking is the critical thinking process of students. There are efforts to search for data and cases experienced to obtain a good scientific construction. Communication is the process of communicating students to the areas they face. Students must be able to speak well anywhere with anyone. Collaboration is a collaboration that students should try. Cooperation is meaningful because humans cannot live without the encouragement of other humans. Citizenship, students can participate in civic activities, and resolve cases contained in these residents. Creativity, a student is someone who pursues the highest knowledge in an official institution. So, a student must be creative and skilled to experience a competitive life. Connectivity, allows students to be connected with anyone related to the case they are experiencing. Regarding this, the lecturer can facilitate student connections with related parties to provide insight into the cases they are experiencing.

The arrival of the COVID-19 pandemic requires lecturers and students to continue learning. Learning is a process of changing one's behavior with the interaction of one person with another so that education for students can be referred to as teaching and learning activities where there is access to transfer knowledge from lecturers to students accompanied by interactions between the two (Mustakim 2020, p. 43).

The form of lectures that can be used as a solution during the COVID-19 pandemic is online education. The research that was tried by Sadikin and Hamidah (2020) obtained results that education was efficient to overcome allowing lecturers and students to connect in virtual classes so that they could be accessed anywhere and anytime. Online education can make students learn independently and increase motivation. However, there are drawbacks to online education if students are not well supervised throughout the online education process. One of them is the weak internet signal as well as the high payment of information packages which is a particular challenge in experiencing online education. However, online education can emphasize the spread of COVID-19 in universities.

Research related to learning in the era of the COVID-19 pandemic was also conducted by Annur and Hermansyah (2020) with the title "Analysis of the Difficulties of Mathematics Education Students in Online Learning During the COVID-19 Pandemic". The results of his research show that students experience some difficulties which are classified as technical difficulties, difficulties in adjusting themselves, and teacher unpreparedness. To overcome these difficulties, it is necessary to develop an educational strategy that can support the acceleration of student adaptation in online education. Not only that, but lecturers are also required to improve their ICT skills so that they can use online educational media that are more varied according to the technical difficulties they experience.

Changing the educational model during the COVID-19 pandemic is a demand not only to be free from the spread of the epidemic, social and physical distancing, as well as to ensure that students are served the right to learn while studying at home and control their activities and social attitudes as an evaluation model for cognitive, affective, and psychomotor cooperation (Purnomo et al. 2020, p. 92).

E-learning is an application formed to overcome limitations between educators and student participants, most importantly in matters of space and time. Through e-learning, lecturers and students are not required to be in one size of space and time so that education can run well (Kusuma in Ismawati & Prasetyo 2020, p. 666). Online learning is open, sharing learning area that uses the internet and the web to facilitate learning as well as building knowledge through meaningful action and interaction. Distance learning is formal institution-based learning where study groups are separated and a telecommunications system is used to connect learners, instructors, and learning resources. Virtual learning is education through electronic mediation that bridges gaps that are caused by the separation of instructors and learners in time or place. Electronic mediation includes sound, video, information, and print via formats such as radio, TV, website-based programming, streaming audio and video, and various other recording technologies.

Continuity of learning throughout the COVID-19 pandemic will depend on various aspects, such as the level of learning preparation, the readiness of parents/families, and the readiness of teachers. Consideration must be given to the needs of all students to continue to share learning throughout the COVID-19 pandemic. Universities can use various technology-based solutions to make it possible for students to continue their educational activities (Wahyono et al. 2020, p. 54).

The fact that has existed throughout the COVID-19 pandemic is shown that the death of students in South Sulawesi is just for searching the internet network in fulfilling online college obligations. Like what Ishak posted, if one of the 2nd-semester students of the PGSD Study Program, Faculty of Teacher Training and Education, Muhammadiyah University of Makassar, faced a motorcycle accident while searching for an internet network while studying online. The same incident occurred by the hospital, one of the students of Hasanudin University Makassar. Djaman's article on the news portal, Hospital died after falling from the mosque tower after trying to find an internet signal to do college assignments (Karim 2020, p. 108).

Students need lecturers who are creative, innovative, and adaptive. Therefore, lecturers must first master several various technologies, so that later they will be able to teach them to students. The following are various technologies that are currently widely used around the world in Tables 1 and 2.

Table 1. Online learning technology.

| No. | Technology name | Various types of technology |
| --- | --- | --- |
| 1. | Web-based hypermedia technology | Graphics, audio, video, visual text, and hyperlinks |
| 2. | Web-based multimedia technology | A combination of text, audio, images, animation, video, and interactive content |
| 3. | Synchronous communication tools | Chat, video/teleconference, audio call |
| 4. | Asynchronous communication equipment | Email, web, URL, discussion forum, quiz, assignment |
| 5. | Presentation equipment | PowerPoint, online PowerPoint, google slides, Prezi, keynote |
| 6. | Online meeting equipment | *Zoom Cloud Meeting, Skype, Cisco Webex Meeting, Jitsi Meet, Google Hangout, Google Meet, Microsoft Teams* |
| 7. | *Learning management system* | *Moodle, Blackboard course sites, Schoology, SEVIMA EdLink, Google Classroom, Edmodo* |

Table 2. Audio and visual applications.

| No. | Application name | Website |
| --- | --- | --- |
| 1. | Audacity | https://audacity.id.softonic.com/download |
| 2. | Ocenaudio | https://www.ocenaudio.com/ |
| 3. | WavePad | https://www.nch.com.au/wavepad/downloadnow.html |
| 4. | Bear Record | https://voice-recorder-online.com/id/ |
| 5. | Bubbl.us | https://bubbl.us/ |

The two tables above show several types of technology and their websites that are often used in universities. It's just that it takes a habit of using this application in the era of the COVID-19 pandemic. This is because the success of lecturers in conducting online learning lies in their ability to be creative in designing teaching materials, learning procedures, and applications that are suitable for teaching materials as well as procedures for learners' ability to use them.

## 2  METHODS

This research uses quantitative methods, where the researcher makes observations on the research object and then performs a descriptive analysis. The research in this article uses descriptive analysis method. Where this method takes problems or focuses attention on problems as they are when the research is carried out, the results of the research are then processed and analyzed to draw conclusions. The scattered questionnaires cover 25 questions from 3 aspects of learning, namely planning, implementing, and evaluating learning.

The data collection technique is carried out in several steps: (1) Observation, (2) Questionnaire, and (3) Literature Study. Observations were made by researchers on learning in PGMI Study Program students in the pandemic era, where 100% learning was done virtually. Of course there are many obstacles faced by students, so that researchers are motivated to evaluate how the learning process is carried out in a pandemic era like this. The questionnaire was given to determine the response of PGMI study program students to learning in the current pandemic era. A ketket is distributed via google form to PGMI students of the Private Islamic Religious College (PTKIS) and State Islamic Religious College (PTKIN) throughout Indonesia. Furthermore, the researcher identifies the results and comments of the respondents and then gives a conclusion. Literature study is used as supporting data, where the findings are combined with appropriate theories. Data analysis techniques make use of n SPSS with the following steps: data selection, data tabulation, the response of the students.

The population in this study were all students of the PGMI Study Program in Indonesia. While the sample in this study were some PGMI Study Program students who were determined by researchers and students involved in filling out this questionnaire as many as 1294 people.

## 3  RESULTS AND DISCUSSION

Learning during the pandemic was felt to be less effective by both lecturers and students. The researcher gave out questionnaires to more than a thousand students. The components that researchers want to know about learning responses during a pandemic include curriculum planning, lecture implementation and process, and assessment. There are several criteria for respondents in this study as in Table 3.

Respondents involved in this study were PGMI students in Indonesia. Among them 155 or 12% of male respondents and 1139 or 88% of female respondents, the total is 1294 respondents. The research was conducted using Google form which is distributed to PGMI study programs throughout Indonesia.

Respondents involved were PGMI PTKIN and PTKIS students in Indonesia as in Table 4.

Table 3.  Respondent gender.

|  |  | Frequency | Percent | Valid percent | Cumulative percent |
|---|---|---|---|---|---|
| Valid | Male | 155 | 12.0 | 12.0 | 12.0 |
|  | Female | 1139 | 88.0 | 88.0 | 100.0 |
|  | Total | 1294 | 100.0 | 100.0 |  |

Table 4. Respondent college status.

| | | Frequency | Percent | Valid percent | Cumulative percent |
|---|---|---|---|---|---|
| Valid | State | 947 | 73.2 | 73.2 | 73.2 |
| | Private | 346 | 26.7 | 26.8 | 100.0 |
| | Total | 1293 | 99.9 | 100.0 | |
| Missing | System | 1 | .1 | | |
| Total | | 1294 | 100.0 | | |

Of the total 1294 respondents, 947 or 73.2% of them were PGMI students from PTKIN, 346 or 26.7% of them were PGMI PTKIS students, and 1 or 0.1% of respondents did not provide information. The table above shows that the respondents involved in this study were mostly PGMI students from PTKIN, meaning that some of the respondents should have been established in terms of learning facilities and of course have lecturers who are experts in their respective fields.

## 3.1 Curriculum planning

Based on the data that has been filled in by respondents, the majority of respondents considered that the Semester Learning Plan (RPS) prepared by the lecturer in distance learning has been in a Good category (B), as well as the Study Contract that has been prepared before starting learning, the Assignment Plan, the assessment formulation offered, the Activity Design Plan to be implemented, the course teaching material plan, and the suitability of learning outcomes with the planned courses. The average overall score is Good, which is 43.2%. Meanwhile, those who rated Very Good were 26.4%, 20.2% answered Normal or Regular, while those who answered Poor were 6.3%, and only 3.8% answered Very Poor.

This shows that for an educator (lecturer), planning appropriate learning, it must be carefully prepared. The role of learning planning is very important because it is one of the absolute requirements for any learning activity. Without planning, the implementation of a lesson will experience difficulties and may even experience failure of the goals to be achieved.

The results of most respondents' responses related to curriculum planning are good, but some student comments need to be evaluated. One of these comments is as follows:

> **Comment 1**: *"The implementation of the PJJ curriculum is still new for us due to a pandemic that has come to our lives so that inevitably educators and students must be able to use other alternatives to continue learning. However, not all elements of learning can be achieved perfectly, it can be said that learning with this curriculum is still at moderate values and has not been able to achieve real success and you have to learn a lot about this curriculum so that educators and students are better and achieve perfect scores in any aspect of learning. Consider all circumstances if this curriculum is to be continued."*

These comments came from several PGMI Study Program students who were involved in this research. There needs to be special attention from the study program and the lecturers themselves related to curriculum planning and design. In this distance learning many possibilities occur from both students and lecturers, so there need to be several alternatives so that it can run optimally.

## 3.2 Lecture implementation and process

Furthermore, in the category of lecture implementation, the majority of respondents also answered that the suitability of the material taught by the lecturers with the learning outcomes was good, in the Good category (B).

Regarding the implementation of learning, with the success of a good learning plan, the process of implementing or implementing learning becomes easier, more focused, and controlled. This is achieved because there is a match between the material provided to achieve learning outcomes, namely mastery of attitudes, knowledge, and skills. This is directly proportional to the mastery of lecturers in the use of learning resources through Distance Learning (PJJ) which can be seen from the responses in the highest Good category. As for the composition and structure of lecture materials, although in the good category, the percentage is lower, namely 35.2% compared to other components which reach 46.9%, such as mastery of the use of teaching material sources, selection of lecture media, availability of teaching materials that have been prepared. , the majority of lecturers have prepared teaching materials in the form of PPT, Modules, Learning Videos, and others. This supports the process of distance learning activities between lecturers and students to be balanced.

Even though the student response to the implementation or implementation of the learning was good, there were some student comments regarding the implementation that was still not good, including:

**Comment 1**: *"Understanding the material that has been given by the lecturer by applying PJJ curriculum for some students is still difficult to understand, it takes a long time to say while time is sometimes limited according to the SKS or the agreed time so that students' understanding is still half while learning. It's ended."*
**Comment 2**: *"Students still do not understand the material presented because many students are constrained by internet networks, lack of interaction between teachers, students are often confused with the material that is almost similar to before".*

From these comments, it can be concluded that when PJJ's understanding of students is not the same as direct learning, it takes time to digest what is explained by the lecturer. Also, network constraints and quotas are very influential, because not all students are in urban areas, so when the lecturer explains they are disconnected. There needs to be a dispensation by the lecturer so that the material can be conveyed to all students.

### 3.3 *Curriculum evaluation*

In the lecture evaluation category, the majority of respondents also stated that they were in a good category (B) with the highest score achievement of 46.8%, namely in terms of the ability of the lecturers to make assessments. Assessment includes aspects of attitude, knowledge, and skills, which are carried out online and transparently following the course objectives contained in the lesson plan. The implementation is carried out both during the learning process, for example by giving interactive quizzes, polls, and others, and is done as feedback on the achievements of the process. Assessment is also carried out at the end of learning in the form of a Semester Final Examination to determine the level of learning achievement during the semester. The total average of respondents' statements, namely 39.2%, stated that the curriculum evaluation carried out in this distance learning process was carried out in the good category (B).

However, this average is inversely proportional to some student comments regarding the assessment. Following are some student comments regarding assessment/evaluation:

**Comment 1**: *"Assessment, assignments to students must be following current conditions. More and more assignments are given when conditions like this do not become better understood, instead, they do not understand a subject."*
**Comment 2**: *"Less efficient online learning is as good as any, but the knowledge gained is not as good as face to face."*
**Comment 3**: *"Implementation of learning through applications that are not conducive so that it affects the achievement of the final goal of learning"*

From some of these comments, the researchers considered that excessive assignment was not effective in providing more understanding for students. Some of the students are not comfortable doing online learning, it could be due to a lack of understanding of the students' application or their learning styles that are not suitable so that the effect can be less than optimal learning outcomes.

## 4 CONCLUSION

From the results and discussion, it can be concluded that learning during the pandemic shows several responses to students regarding curriculum planning, implementation, and the lecture process, and assessment. From the three aspects of learning, the response of most students was on average Good. This shows learning during the pandemic, even though it is done remotely, the lecturers still carry out their duties properly to prepare, carry out, and evaluate lectures.

## ACKNOWLEDGMENTS

Thanks to International Conference of Education in Moslem Society (ICEMS) 2020 FITK UIN Syarif Hidayatullah Jakarta for publication support.

## REFERENCES

Annur, M. F., & Hermansyah. (2020). Analisis Kesulitan Mahasiswa Pendidikan Matematika dalam Pembelajaran Daring Pada Masa Pandemi Covid-19. *Paedagoria: Jurnal Kajian, Penelitian Dan Pengembangan Pendidikan, 11*(2), 195–201. Retrieved from https://journal.ummat.ac.id/index.php/paedagoria/article/view/2544/pdf.10.31764

Gusty, S., Nurmiati, Muliana, Sulaiman, O. K., Ginantra, Manuhutu, …Sahabuddin. (2020). *Belajar Mandiri: Pembelajaran Daring di Tengah Pandemi Covid-19* (J. Simarmata, Ed.). Medan: Yayasan Kita Menulis. Retrieved from https://books.google.co.id/books?hl=en&lr=&id=HSz7DwAAQBAJ&oi=fnd&pg=PA85&dq=PEMBELAJARAN+DI+ERA+PANDEMI&ots=QncHGnwjPh&sig=-MSs_Z-jRZt_b4JiXLP1HDFCJ9M&redir_esc=y#v=onepage&q=PEMBELAJARAN DI ERA PANDEMI&f=false

Karim, B. A. (2020). Pendidikan Perguruan Tinggi Era 4.0 Dalam Pandemi Covid-19 (Refleksi Sosiologis). *Education and Learning Journal, 1*(2), 102. https://doi.org/10.33096/eljour.v1i2.54

Lin, Q., Zhao, S., Gao, D., Lou, Y., Yang, S., Musa, S. S., …He, D. (2020). A conceptual model for the coronavirus disease 2019 (COVID-19) outbreak in Wuhan, China with individual reaction and governmental action. *International Journal of Infectious Diseases, 93*, 211–216. https://doi.org/10.1016/j.ijid.2020.02.058

Mesran, Sulaiman, O. K., Wijoyo, H., Putra, S. H., Watrianthos, R., Sinaga, R., …Indarto, S. L. (2020). *Merdeka Kreatif di Era Pandemi Covid-19*. Medan: Green Press. Retrieved from https://books.google.co.id/books?hl=en&lr=&id=Nxv5DwAAQBAJ&oi=fnd&pg=PA55&dq=PEMBELAJARAN+DI+ERA+PANDEMI+COVID-19&ots=GKouyeWCO4&sig=aLDUpE3JdVhVD7jMFbT9mu95RT8&redir_esc=y#v=onepage&q=PEMBELAJARAN DI ERA PANDEMI COVID-19&f=false

Mustakim, U. S. (2020). Efektivitas Pembelajaran di Era New Normal Terhadap Hasil Belajar Mahasiswa Pada Mata Kuliah Matematika Diskrit. *UJES: Uniqbu Journal of Exact Sciences, 1*(1), 41–45. Retrieved from http://ejournal-uniqbu.ac.id/index.php/ujes/article/view/15/20

Purnomo, H., Mansir, F., Tumin, & Suliswiyadi. (2020). Pendidikan Karakter Islami pada Online Class Management di SMA Muhammadiyah 7 Yogyakarta Selama Pandemi Covid-19. *Jurnal Tarbiyatuna, 11*(1), 91–100. Retrieved from http://journal.ummgl.ac.id/index.php/tarbiyatuna/article/view/3456/1846

Sadikin, A., & Hamidah, A. (2020). Pembelajaran Daring di Tengah Wabah Covid-19. *BIODIK, 6*(2), 109–119. https://doi.org/10.22437/bio.v6i2.9759

Shereen, M. A., Khan, S., Kazmi, A., Bashir, N., & Siddique, R. (2020). COVID-19 infection: Origin, transmission, and characteristics of human coronaviruses. *Journal of Advanced Research, 24*, 91–98. https://doi.org/10.1016/j.jare.2020.03.005

Sirri, E. L., & Lestari, P. (2020). Implementasi Edpuzzle Berbantuan WhatsApp Group Sebagai Alternatif Pembelajaran Daring Pada Era Pandemi. *Jurnal Pendidikan Matematika Indonesia, 5*(2), 67–72. Retrieved from https://journal.stkipsingkawang.ac.id/index.php/JPMI/article/view/1830/pdf#

Wahyono, P., Husamah, H., & Budi, A. S. (2020). Guru Profesional di Masa Pandemic COVID-19: Review Implementasi, Tantangan, dan Solusi Pembelajaran Daring. *Jurnal Pendidikan Profesi Guru, 1*(1), 51–65. Retrieved from http://ejournal.umm.ac.id/index.php/jppg/article/view/12462/pdf

*Emerging Trends in Technology for Education in an Uncertain World – Nanto, Rahiem & Khalis Maryati (Eds)*

# Compromise between traditionality and modernity (study on utilization of information and communication technology in the Kasepuhan Ciptagelar community)

M. Arif
*UIN Syarif Hidayatullah Jakarta, Jakarta, Indonesia*

ABSTRACT:   The main problem that is often faced by traditional societies, especially regarding their attitude towards modernity. There are those who reject modernity so that they become backward societies. Some are too eager to adopt a modern lifestyle so that they are deprived of their customs and traditions. The research was conducted on the Kasepuhan Ciptagelar community to obtain a model of a society that maintains tradition, while at the same time adopting the values of modernity. This study used a qualitative descriptive approach with data collection techniques including literature review, observation, and interviews. An important finding from this study is the occurrence of social changes in the Kasepuhan Ciptagelar community which makes information and communication technology-based community media as information media related to customary and traditional activities. Community media is used by the Kasepuhan Ciptagelar community to compromise the traditional system with modern lifestyles.

*Keywords*:   The Kasepuhan Ciptagelar community, information and communication technology, community media, traditional values, modernity values.

## 1   INTRODUCTION

The dynamics of modernity provide two choices for traditional societies. *First,* respond negatively by rejecting modernization in order to maintain the uniqueness of the traditional system inherited from their ancestors from generation to generation. The *Baduy Dalam* community, for example, chose to reject modernization because of their commitment to maintaining the traditional system while preserving the natural environment. In this case, the *Baduy Dalam* traditional leaders play a significant role, especially in creating communication to future generations in the context of inheriting the traditional system (Setyanto, 2019). Such a choice causes the *Baduy Dalam* community to be more backward compared to modern society which has made advances in science and technology.

*Second,* respond positively by accepting modernization in order to achieve the desired advances. As happened to the Samin community in Tapelan Village, Ngraho District, Bojonegoro Regency. Since the independence era they have undergone significant changes in which all the children of the Samin community have taken formal education, not even a few are trying to continue to higher education (Arif & Ghofur 2020: 98–99). However, this attitude has caused the Samin community to be uprooted from traditional values as inherited by their predecessors. Currently, the portrait of the Samin community is changing like society in general and does not reflect the character of being a Saminist.

Is there a model of society that is able to compromise the values of traditionality with the values of modernity so that it develops as a society with character and at the same time as a modern society?

In contrast to the two extreme attitudes above, the Kasepuhan Ciptagelar community has a unique attitude. They choose an attitude of compromise between remaining committed to maintaining the

DOI 10.1201/9781003219248-16

traditional system while at the same time adopting a new culture that suits their personalities, so as to create socio-cultural harmony in their lives. Their efforts to adopt modern culture are carried out by synchronizing their traditional systems.

Basically, this compromise is an old phenomenon in the life of the Ciptagelar community. As an Islamic community, they carry out Islamic law while maintaining the traditional system side by side. They are very enthusiastic in carrying out worship such as praying in mosques, following Islamic studies, *tahlilan,* and commemoration of Islamic holidays such as *Sedekah Mulud* (commemoration of the birth of Prophet Muhammad SAW which was held in the month of Rabiul Awal), *Sedekah Ruwah* (commemoration of the death of Prophet Muhammad SAW), *Prah-prahan* (ritual requests to avoid illnesses carried out in the month of Safar), *Nyimur* (procession welcoming the birth of babies and toddlers held at Rabiul-Tsani, *Berebes Bengkong* (circumcision processions for boys and girls), and so on at the Mosque Jami' that they build (Firmansyah 2019).

Along with the implementation of these Islamic activities, they also still carry out various kinds of traditional ceremonies that have been passed down from generation to generation, especially those related to agricultural activities, including *Ngaseuk* (rice planting procession), *Sapangjadian Pare* (ritul requesting permission from *Ibu Pertiwi* to plant rice), *Sawenan* (upaca gives treatment to rice to avoid pests), *Beberes Mager* (ritual to protect rice from pest attacks), *Ngarawunan* (request ritual so that the rice contents grow perfectly), *Mipit* (rice harvesting ritual), *Nutu* (rice pounding ritual the first harvest), *Nganyaran* (the ritual of cooking the first rice harvest), *Tutup Nyambut* (the final ritual of agricultural activities), *Turun Nyambut* (the ritual of starting the plowing period as a sign of the planting season), and of course *Seren Taun* as the culmination of the tradition of the whole series. Agricultural activities carried out every year (Firmansyah 2019).

So, do not be surprised if the Kasepuhan Ciptagelar community choose the attitude to compromise their traditional system with modern culture in their life. This research focuses on the activities of the Kasepuhan Ciptagelar community in utilizing information and communication technology as information media related to customary and traditional activities. This research raises the question: how can the use of information and communication technology be compromised with the customary systems and traditions of the Kasepuhan Ciptagelar community?

The attitude of the Kasepuhan Ciptagelar community in adopting modern technology to support their daily activities indicates that there is social change even though it is still at the level of material culture. Therefore, one of the tools of analysis in this research is the theory of social change proposed by W.F. Ogburn. Furthermore, their commitment to maintaining the customary and traditional systems will be analyzed using the Tri-Kon theory put forward by Ki Hajar Dewantara. At least according to the perspective of the Tri-Kon Principle, it can be said that the Ciptagelar Kasepuhan community is a true model of Indonesian society.

## 2  RESEARCH METHODOLOGY

This qualitative descriptive study was conducted to obtain an overview of how the compromise model made by the Kasepuhan Ciptagelar community in maintaining the traditional system and at the same time adopting modern culture, especially those related to the use of information and communication technology to build community media. Various information related to the commitment of the Kasepuhan Ciptagelar community in maintaining the traditional system, as well as utilizing information and communication technology by building community media as a means to instill traditional values in the young generation of Kasepuhan Ciptagelar. The phenomenological approach is used to analyze the experiences of the Kasepuhan Ciptagelar community in everyday life (Endraswara 2006; Moleong 2014: 15; Sujana & Ibrahim 2001: 64). This study uses an ethnographic approach that refers to an ethnic approach model, which views socio-cultural phenomena based on the perspective of the community being the object of research (Spradley 1997). In this way, an understanding of the various concepts found during the research process will be obtained (Denzim & Yvonna 1996: 207).

The researcher initiated the data collection process through literature review, especially for collecting data through documents, both written and electronic, which supported the research process. On the positive side, the research results are increasingly credible because they are supported by existing academic papers (Sugiyono 2005: 83). Furthermore, the researcher made observations to obtain real data and what it is (Moleong 2002: 118; Usman & Akbar 2017: 56). The data collection process was continued with interviews to gather complete information (Moleong 2010: 186). These three data collection techniques are very useful for capturing and understanding empirical phenomena found during the research process (Denzim and Yvonna 1996: 207).

The data validity test was carried out through triangulation which included triangulation of sources, methods, and theories. In this case the researcher tries to check (a) the results of the literature review, (b) the results of the observations, and (c) the results of the interviews conducted with various resource persons. In addition, peer review is one of the verification techniques so that an intersubjective agreement is obtained (Miles & Huberman 1992: 19).

Furthermore, all data will be analyzed using an argumentative descriptive approach, by providing a description of a condition as it actually happens. Thus, during research activities the researcher does not provide special treatment, manipulation, or alteration to the existing variables (Sukmadinata 2005: 73).

## 3 RESULT AND DISCUSSION

### 3.1 *Result*

The use of information and communication technology in the Kasepuhan Ciptagelar community cannot be separated from the role of traditional leaders who have advanced insight. Various innovations in the technology sector have been carried out, among others, by creating community media, such as community television, community radio, and internet networks that are managed independently under Kasepuhan's control (DeVito 2011: 587–588). The community media is used as a tool and media for Traditional Leaders and Baris Kolot to carry out their duties and responsibilities, especially in instilling the traditional values possessed by the Kasepuhan Ciptagelar community (West & Turner 2008: 67–74).

Media komunitas dibangun sebagai ruang publik, sekaligus sebagai media informasi dan komunikasi di antara warga Kasepuhan Ciptagelar.

### 3.1.1 *Community television*

Kasepuhan Ciptagelar community formed Ciptagelar-Televisi (Ciga-TV) as community television. The main objective of Ciga-TV is to anticipate the domination of information from outside, as well as to prevent the erosion of traditional and traditional values. On the basis of such thoughts, Ciga-TV broadcasts content taken from local traditions. In addition, Ciga-TV has also developed as a medium of information related to the daily activities of Kasepuhan Ciptagelar residents (Arigi 2017).

Apart from being an information medium, Ciga-TV is also used as an educational medium for Kasepuhan Ciptagelar residents. The contents broadcast by Ciga-TV are focused on agricultural issues, traditional children's toys, angklung art, and traditional activities. Usually the content that is raised is in accordance with the season that is happening. Given that the Kasepuhan Ciptagelar community is an agrarian society, the content that is regularly broadcast is related to agriculture, such as the planting season, the summer season, the harvest season, to the peak of the *Seren Taun* event. Ciga-TV managers are taken from local residents. They learn self-taught television management, starting from finding and processing information to editing and broadcasting the information. The managers of Ciga-TV are also diligent in adding knowledge and skills in managing television from anyone who is competent in television management and journalistic work. In fact, Abah Ugi as the leader of Kasepuhan Ciptagelar, assembled his own drones to support coverage activities and area mapping activities.

Interestingly, the use of modern technology is only carried out for non-traditional activities. The use of technology in customary activities is considered taboo by the Kasepuhan Ciptagelar community. In this case, Abah Ugi emphasized that even though he has used technology, the customary system must not be faded. This means that all activities related to tradition do not involve technology at all. For example, agricultural activities that start from land cultivation, rice cultivation, fertilization, harvesting, storage of crops, and so on, do not use modern technology at all. Modern technology is only used for public activities outside traditional activities, such as the use of power generation turbines, television and radio media support technology, the internet, and the like. Even more importantly, modern technology must still be aligned with the values and norms of the Kasepuhan Ciptagelar community.

### 3.1.2 *Community radio*

In 2004 the Kasepuhan Ciptagelar community established a radio broadcast called Radio Swara Ciptagelar (RSC-FM). Yoyo Yogasmana, the spokesperson for the Kasepuhan Ciptagelar community, explained that the content broadcast by the radio is not much different from Ciga-TV, but the format is more dominant as a conversation regarding the life of the Kasepuhan Ciptagelar community. In 2018, RSC-FM, which was originally a community radio, received a license from the local government, as well as becoming the Ciptagelar FM Commercial Radio. However, the manager is still committed to displaying local wisdom up to at least 60 percent of the total content broadcast.

### 3.1.3 *Internet networks*

Currently, the people of Kasepuhan Ciptagelar have an internet network that can be accessed by all residents. The internet network has had a positive impact, including the increased activity of citizens in using the internet network, both for seeking information and for communication. They are accustomed to using cell phones and computers.

Apart from using the internet, the Kasepuhan Ciptagelar community has also started to develop media literacy activities. The goal is that citizens are not only active in communicating, but also have skills in selecting information according to the media platforms they use on a daily basis. Furthermore, the information that has been selected will be processed and uploaded to the internet network. The content uploaded on the internet network is also related to the traditional system.

The inculcation of these traditional values can also be seen on the developed website, namely https://ciptagelar.info/tentang/, with the following menus:

a. *Beranda:* Displays general and important information, for example regarding news, tweeter info, streaming radio info, Ciptagelar Facebook info, and so on.
b. *Tentang Kasepuhan Ciptagelar:* Describe the Kasepuhan Ciptagelar community in general, both related to the environment they live in, history, traditional systems, and so on.
c. *Berita:* As an information medium, both internal related to agricultural activities, traditional activities, and so on, as well as external ones such as the corona pandemic, and so on.
d. *Kegiatan Warga:* As a media of information related to the Kasepuhan community's' activities, such as the annual development schedule to welcome *serentaun,* handing over *ponggokan, tandur, ngangler, prah-prahan* every 4th of the month of *Sapar, ngaseuk, opat belasan, ngaruwat imah ki putri, nganyaran,* and so on.
e. *Galery:* To store various documents related to the activities of the Kasepuhan Ciptagelar community, especially those related to the traditional system.
f. *Lokasi:* To describe the position of the Kasepuhan Ciptagelar community village, which is located in Sirnaresmi Village, Cisolok District, Sukabumi Regency, West Java.
g. *Kontak:* As a medium for outsiders who want further information about the Kasepuhan Ciptagelar community, by filling in the contact form provided. In this feature, a column is provided that contains the full name, email address, message theme, message content, and send.

## 3.2 *Discussion*

The existence of Ciga-TV and RSC-FM which are used as community media shows a change in the dimension of material culture. This fact is in line with Ogburn's statement that "the rate of change in material culture is like a geometric series, while the rate of change in immaterial culture is like an added series" (Del Sesto 2002; Ogburn 1947; Volti 2004). The influence of material culture such as technology is faster in driving social change, in contrast to immaterial culture such as social institutions, values, norms, and the like which are slower in driving social change (Ogburn 1947; Soekanto 1993: 102)

Currently, more and more people of Kasepuhan Ciptagelar use information and communication technology. Not only limited to Ciga-TV and RSC-FM, but they also use the internet network. In fact, they have also started to develop literacy activities, not only as a medium of communication, but also to have skills in selecting information according to traditional values. This is in line with Ogburn's statement that the rate of social change is influenced by new discoveries. On the other hand, there is a tendency that new inventions have a higher level of sophistication than the culture of society in general. This shows the importance of understanding certain cultural bases. That a new discovery requires a background of cultural transmission from previous discoveries (Ogburn 1947; Rudi Volti 2004). For example, there is no internet information without the preceded discovery of computers and micro-electronics.

In this case, it is really interesting to study the changes that have occurred in the Kasepuhan Ciptagelar community. This is where, as an agrarian society that is full of customary systems and traditions, they have now adopted very sophisticated information and communication technology. Remarkably, they have successfully compromised traditional values with modern values. This also shows that a cultural basis will lead to the essence of an ideal culture. That the findings that occur accumulatively will encourage changes in a cultural basis towards its increasingly perfect form. This is also evidence that changes in the dimensions of material culture will lead to changes in the dimensions of immaterial culture (Ogburn 1947; Soekanto 1983: 99). Because changes in material culture occur more rapidly than changes in immaterial culture, it is better if a society takes advantage of ever-changing technology, while adapting customary systems and traditions in their lives (Henslin 2007).

The results of the innovation gave rise to community media that have an important function in maintaining existence while spreading customary values and norms widely, thus helping the role of *Baris Kolot* to socialize the agenda of customary activities to the community. Community media broadcasts, in this case, facilitate the delivery of Ciptagelar's cultural identity to the public. Through the presentation of various kinds of traditions in community media, there is a process of instilling traditional values among the next generations of the Kasepuhan Ciptagelar community (West & Turner 2008: 65).

The use of information and communication technology has also opened the widest possible way for the entry of the culture of the outside community. However, the cultural values of the outside community do not necessarily penetrate the Kasepuhan Ciptagelar community. They will always filter out the culture of the outside community that is not appropriate, as well as adopt the positive sides that are not yet owned so that the acculturation process occurs. In this case, the Kasepuhan Ciptagelar community has achieved mindfulness, in the form of the ability to adapt to the culture of the outside community without reducing their socio-cultural identity at all (Ting-Toomey 1999).

The Tri-Kon theory put forward by Ki Hajar Dewantara is also interesting to use to analyze the strong commitment of the Kasepuhan Ciptagelar community in maintaining the customary and traditional systems. That the intercultural meeting is a necessity that takes place naturally and in turn opens the possibility for a process of cultural adaptation (Dewantara 2011: 227). The question is how can a society take the maximum possible profit and at the same time reduce the loss to the minimum? Such questions are what prompted Ki Hadjar Dewantara to formulate the following basic principles of Tri-Kon.

It is very important for every society to inherit traditions and at the same time perfect the cultural heritage of foreign cultural elements. This requires activation of the "Tri-Kon Principle", which includes: (1) continuity *(konsentris),* that the existence of a society today is a continuation of the life of a society in the past, is not merely an imitation of the life of an outside society, (2) convergence *(konvergensi),* that a society needs to adapt to an outside society in order to bring together the positive dimensions of the existing culture, to then formulate a new culture that is beneficial for the continuity of a society, and (3) concentric *(konsentris),* that it is important to keep the values of inherited characters ancestors as the center of the life cycle (Dewantara 2011: 227–228).

The traditional system of the Kasepuhan Ciptagelar community which was inherited from their ancestors *(karuhun)* is a traditional system based on rice culture. It is not surprising that the Kasepuhan Ciptagelar community have a set of supernatural views on the rice entity that are reflected in the values, thought systems, and practices in everyday life as a peasant society. One of the main principles of the Kasepuhan Ciptagelar community is the view that rice is a living entity like humans who have a soul and are related to life (Kusdiwanggo 2003: 37–42). For the Kasepuhan Ciptagelar community, farming activities are seen in such a way as to be worship activities, so that they are always accompanied by sacred ritual traditions (Kusdiwanggo & Sumardjo 2016: 310).

The strong commitment of the Kasepuhan Ciptagelar community in maintaining the traditional system cannot be separated from the role of traditional elders who are committed to maintaining their traditional system. In addition, the Kasepuhan Ciptagelar community also develop community media to show and/or spread the existence of their identity to the outside community. In fact, through the community media the Kasepuhan Ciptagelar community creates a hegemony that can match the influences of dominant outside cultures. In this way, the Kasepuhan Ciptagelar community has the ability to survive and simultaneously interact in a balanced manner with the dominant outside culture (Dalil & Rahardjo 2019: 59–71). The elders of the Kasepuhan Ciptagelar community try to pass on the traditional system to their children. The elders are worried that their children will violate the traditional system as they will be subject to customary sanctions. Phenomena like this are the determining factors for the existence of the Kasepuhan Ciptagelar community to this day (Samovar 2010: 71).

More than that, the Kasepuhan Ciptagelar community are not only committed to maintaining the traditional system, but also committed to perfecting it by adopting a new culture that is not yet owned. The new culture that is adopted must of course be in accordance with their personalities and at the same time according to the needs of their daily lives. Such a commitment becomes the background for a compromise between the dimensions of traditionality and the dimensions of modernity in the life of the Kasepuhan Ciptagelar community. This compromise is not something that is impossible because of the perspective of the Kasepuhan Ciptagelar community which emphasizes the harmony of nature. As seen in the *sakuren* concept during the *mabay* activity. *Sakuren* is a term for a pair of rice as a form of harmonization of two different but mutually supporting traits in the fairy of life. Sakuren is a complementary relationship in a harmonious existence (Kusdiwanggo & Sumardjo 2016: 310). The habit of putting up these two different characteristics has at least provided a foundation for the Kasepuhan Ciptagelar community to carry out the traditional system while adopting a new culture, as seen in the following technological developments.

The adoption of a new culture as above has made the Kasepuhan Ciptagelar community develop as a society that is committed to improving their traditional system. Even though their position is in a mountainous environment, it does not mean that they are left behind with various modern information. In practice, the Kasepuhan Ciptagelar community are very selective in absorbing new technology. They do not take technology that is against tradition, but technology that is appropriate and supports their daily lives (Tim 2020). Specifically related to the tradition of planting rice, the Kasepuhan Ciptagelar community is committed to strictly maintaining the mandate of their ancestors.

## 4 CONCLUSSION

Based on the research results described above, the following conclusions were obtained. *First,* as an agrarian society, the Kasepuhan Ciptagelar community has a very high commitment to maintaining the customary systems and traditions inherited from previous generations, especially those related to agricultural activities. *Second,* the commitment to inheriting customary systems and traditions does not prevent the adoption of information and communication technology. Instead, they created this sophisticated technology-based community media to inform their customary activities. *Third,* the use of information and communication technology in the Kasepuhan Ciptagelar community is a manifestation of their compromise to the values of traditionality and the values of modernity, so that they develop as a society with strong character and at the same time as a modern society.

## REFERENCES

Arif, M. & Ghofur, A., (2020), *Islam dan Transformasi Sosial pada Gerakan Saminisme (Kajian Historis dan Sosiologis terhadap Penganut Saminisme di Desa Tapelan, Kecamatan Ngraho, Bojonegoro),* Depok: PARA CITA MADINA.

Arigi, F., (2017), *TELEVISI KOMUNITAS: Kajian Kritis pada Ciga-TV di Kasepuhan Ciptagelar,* Thesis, Bandung: Universitas Pendidikan Indonesia.

Dalil, F. & Rahardjo, T., (2019), Peran Sesepuh Adat dan Media Komunitas Masyarakat Kasepuhan Ciptagelar dalam Menjaga Identitas Kebudayaan Asli, *Interaksi Online,* Vol. 7, No. 3, Juni 2019, Semarang: UNDIP.

Del Sesto, S.L., (2002), Teccnology an Social Change: William Fielding Ogburn Revisited, *Technological Forecasting and Social Change,* Volume 24, Issue 3, November 1983, p. 183–196 (https://doi.org/10.1016/0040-1625(83)90014-8, available online 11 April 2002).

Denzim, N.K. & Yvonna, S.L. ed, (1996), *Handbook of Qualitatif Research,* California: Sage Publication.

DeVito, J.A., (2011), *Komunikasi Antarmanusia,* Tangerang: KARISMA.

Dewantara, K.H., (2011) *Karya Ki Hadjar Dewantara Bagian Pertama (Pendidikan)* (Cetakan Keempat), Yogyakarta: Majelis Luhur Persatuan Taman Siswa.

Endraswara, S., (2006), *Metode, Teori, dan Teknik Penelitian Kebudayaan: Ideologi, Epistemologi, dan Aplikasi,* Yogyakarta: Pustaka Widyatama.

Firmansyah, E.K., dkk, (2019), *Sistem Religi dan Kepercayaan Masyarakat Kasepuhan-Kasepuhan banten Kidul, Cisolok, Sukabumi, Jurnal Pengabdian kepada Masyarakat,* Sumedang: Direktorat Sumber Daya Akademik dan Perpustakaan Universitas Padjadjaran.

Kusdiwanggo, S., (2003), *Membaca Ngalalakon pada Komunitas Adat Ciptagelar sebagai Masyarakat Peladang,* Prosiding Temu Ilmiah IPLBI.

Miles & Huberman, (1992), *Analisis Data Kualitatif.* Cet. I, Jakarta: UI-Press.

Moleong, L., (2002), *Metodologi Penelitian Kualitatif,* Bandung: Rosdakarya.

Moleong, L., (2010), *Metodologi Penelitian Kualitatif,* Bandung: Rosdakarya.

Moleong, L, (2014), *Metodologi Penelitian Kualitatif: Edisi Revisi,* Bandung: Remaja Rosdakarya.

Ogburn, W.F., (1947), *How Technology Changes Society,* The ANNALS of the American Academy of Political and Social Science, First Published January 1, 1947, https://doi.org/10.1177/000271624724900111.

Samovar, L.A., dkk, (2010), *Komunikasi Lintas Budaya,* Jakarta: Salemba Humanika.

Setyanto, Y., dkk, (2019), *Komunikasi dan Peran Pemimpin Adat dalam Menjaga Tradisi pada Masyarakat Baduy,* Jakarta: Universitas Taruma Negara.

Spradley, P., (1997), *Metode Etnografi,* Yogyakarta: PT Tiara Wacana.

Sugiyono, (2005), *Memahami Penelitian Kualitatif,* Bandung: Alfabeta.

Sukmadinata, N.S., (2005), *Metode Penelitian Pendidikan,* Bandung: PT Remadja Rosdakarya.

Tim, (2020), *Kasepuhan Ciptagelar: Setia Mempertahankan Budaya Tanam Padi,* (Sumber: https://kebudayaan.kemdikbud.go.id/ditwdb/kasepuhan-ciptagelar-setia-mempertahankan-budaya-tanam-padi/), tersedia: Ahad, 20 September 2020.

Ting-Toomey, S., (1999), *Communicating Across Cultures,* New York: The Guilford Press.

Usman, H. & Akbar, P.S., (2017), *Metodologi Penelitian Sosial Edisi Ketiga,* Jakarta: Bumi Aksara.

Volti, R., (2004), Classics Revisited: Wiliam F. Ogburn, Social Change with Respect to Culture and Original Nature, *Technology and Culture,* Vol. 45, No. 2, April 2004, doi: 10.1353/tech.2004.0107

West, R. & Turner, L.H., (2008), *Pengantar Teori Komunikasi: Edizi 3,* Jakarta: Salemba Humanika.

*Emerging Trends in Technology for Education in an Uncertain World – Nanto, Rahiem & Khalis Maryati (Eds)*
*© 2022 copyright the Author(s), ISBN 978-1-032-11288-6*

# The euphoria of webinar during the Covid-19 pandemic in Indonesia

W. Susiawati & K. Umbar
*Department of Arabic Education, Faculty of Educational Sciences, Universitas Islam Negeri Syarif Hidayatullah Jakarta, Tangerang Selatan, Banten, Indonesia*

ABSTRACT:   There was an interesting phenomenon during the Covid-19 pandemic. The phenomenon not only appeared with a fantastic number but also the participation rate in webinars increased drastically compared to before the pandemic. This research used a survey research method approach with a questionnaire using Google Form. The number of respondents involved in this study was 1698 respondents. The data collection is verified, classified, and analyzed in diagrammatic form. This research reveals that many seminars are triggered by various government policies. Online seminars are the only media for learning and sharing knowledge that is conducted without having to meet. The participation of lecturers, students, teachers, and students in participating in webinars has increased rapidly more than 10 times in one semester. The reasons are between; insight, the fulfillment of institutional obligations, obtain certificates for promotion for lecturers, teachers, and graduation requirements for students.

*Keywords*:   webinars, Covid-19 pandemic, learning, government policy

## 1   INTRODUCTION

The year 2020 will be memorable as one of the dark years in the history of human life in the world because of coronavirus disease 2019 (Covid-19) or SARS-CoV-2 (Wawan Mas'udi 2020). Online seminars (webinars) have sprung up almost every day in Indonesia, some are free or paid. Based on the observations of researchers, in one of the groups on Facebook that publish webinars with the Webinar Indonesia group account, there are 18–19 webinars per day. Even more than that, the findings of researchers on the Instagram account @webinarzoom, this October alone, can reach 58–63 online seminars per day. Researchers term this phenomenon the euphoria of online seminars, because researchers see this phenomenon as something out of the ordinary and happen just like that, naturally, and coincidentally. Supporting applications used are also various, ranging from zoom, YouTube, google meet, google classroom, WeBex. The participants are also diverse, from students, teachers, college students, lecturers, and staff. Note the distribution of the following data in Table 1.

The results of tracking researchers related to webinars during this pandemic from April to October with samples from August to September and September to October were fantastic. In the period August 12th–September 12th 2020, data from the Facebook Webinar Indonesia group contained 565 webinar information advertisements for a month, with 18 webinars on average per day. In contrast to the data from the @webinarzoom Instagram account, in the same period, there were 1750 webinars, with an average of 58 webinars per day, both paid and free.

Meanwhile in the second period, which is September 13th–October 13th, the Facebook group of Indonesia Webinar data shows that about 613 webinars or 20 webinars on average a day. Moreover, the @webinarzoom's Instagram data shows that 1890 webinars a month, or 63 webinars on average per day.

Researchers see this is an unusual phenomenon. When the dynamics of education are constrained and affect learning patterns, there are many open forums that provide the widest possible opportunity

Table 1. Result of the number of webinars during the 2020 pandemic.

| Keyword | | |
| --- | --- | --- |
| Webinar Nasional, Seminar Onlie, Seminar Virtual, Bincang Online, Workshop Online, Kuliah Tamu, Online Talkshow, Sharing Online, Konferensi Nasional Online, Workshop Daring, Lokakarya Online, Zoom Seminar, FGD Online, Desiminasi Online, Seminar Daring, Webinar Series, *an-nadwah al-iftiradhiyyah*, pandu digital daring, zoom webinar, | 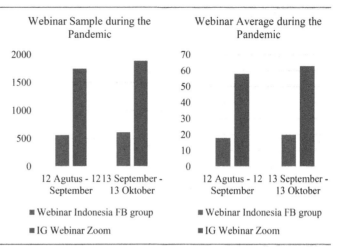 | |

The data were processed from researcher investigations in the Webinar Indonesia Facebook group and @webinarzoom IG on 12–14 October 2020.

to access useful knowledge from experts in their fields. It could be that this is one part of the era of the digital education revolution to become an electronic university (e-university) (Pujilestari 2020) because it is based on its changes.

This research is held to provide an answer to this unique phenomenon. What is the reason for webinars that have sprung up? For the webinar participants what has motivated them to join webinars.

## 2 THEORETICAL FRAMEWORK

### 2.1 *Euphoria in perspective*

The word euphoria comes from the Greek word euphoria (EU + pherein), which means 'more resilient' or 'healthier' (Longman 2020a). The word is absorbed by English into euphoria which means 'joy' or 'feeling better'. The word euphoria is more often used in the world of psychology and medicine to describe a feeling of happiness that is overflowing and occurs continuously over a while. "A mental and emotional condition in which a person experiences intense feelings of well-being, elation, happiness, excitement, and joy" (Maniacci & Sperry 2014). This is very relevant to the proliferation of online seminar activities and is attended by enthusiastic participants and occurs within the planned time frame.

### 2.2 *Webinar*

The word "webinar" is a combination of the word 'web + seminar' which means a seminar via the internet. In Longman, webinars mean lectures, lessons, etc. provided on the Internet, where everyone who takes part sees the same information on their computer screen and can talk to each other, usually using a telephone (Longman 2020b). The main feature of webinars is their potential for discussion and sharing of information using zoom, YouTube, Facebook, and other applications (Verma & Singh 2010).

## 3 METHOD

Researchers used survey research methods to answer the above problem questions with a questionnaire using Google Form. The number of respondents involved in this study was 1698 respondents with a classification of 396 lecturers, 558 teachers, 711 college students, and 33 students. Researchers distributed questionnaires using the google form platform twice. The first questionnaire distributed on June 18th 2020 at the National Webinar and Book Review held by the Arabic Language Education (PBA) study program UIN Syarif Hidayatullah Jakarta, received 764 respondents with a classification of 178 lecturers, 189 teachers, 390 college students, and 7 students. The second questionnaire was distributed on August 13th, 2020, at the Virtual Conference for the PBA S2 Study Program at UIN Sultan Maulana Hasanuddin Banten, which received 934 respondents, 218 lecturers, 369 teachers, 321 college students, 26 students. As supporting data, researchers also made observations on online media that publish, announce, and advertise online seminar activities.The data collected from these respondents is verified to ensure the completeness of the respondent's answers and the data can be used. Furthermore, the data is classified based on criteria to facilitate analysis. Furthermore, the researcher tabulated the data, calculated the percentage, and visualized it in tabular form accompanied by its interpretation.

## 4 RESULT AND DISCUSSION

This survey research involved a total of 1698 respondents who were verified. The respondents consist of lecturers and teachers, as well as college students and students. The data will be classified and tabulated based on the questions in the questionnaire, then the percentage is calculated and analyzed carefully. Based on the first questionnaire, the number of valid respondents was 764 respondents. Respondents were dominated by students reaching 51%, then 25% of teachers, 23% of lecturers, and 1% of students. Meanwhile, the second questionnaire found 934 respondents with 40% from teachers, 34% from students, 23% from lecturers, and 3% from students. Furthermore, the data that has been obtained is described in detail according to the question items in the questionnaire given (Figure 1).

### 4.1 *Experience taking webinar*

Based on Figure 2, the researcher knows that the quantity of the participation of lecturers, college students, teachers, and students in webinars, online seminars, virtual seminars before the COVID-19 pandemic, the majority ranges from 1 to 5 with a percentage of 69%. There were 21% of those who participated in webinars in the range of 6–10 times, and the rest of those who attended webinars more than 10 times were only 10%. If we look in more detail based on the classification

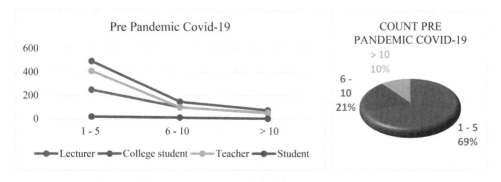

Figure 1.  Quantity pre-pandemic webinar participation Covid-19.

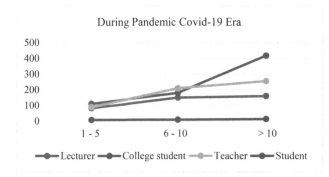
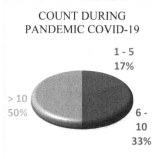

Figure 2.  Webinar participation quantity during the Covid-19 pandemic.

of researchers, 248 lecturers take part in the webinar 1–5 times; those who follow 6–10 times 98, and those who are more than 10 times there are only 50 people. With the same pattern, the majority of students also participated in webinars 1–5 before the pandemic with a total of 493 people, 145 people participated in 6–10 times, and the rest were over 10 times there were 73. From the teacher group, those who took webinar 1–5 times there were 409 people, 6–10 times there were 97 people, and for those who attended the webinar more than 10 times, there were 52. For this student item, at first, the researchers were hesitant to include the item, but it turns out that their participation in the webinar also exists, those who follow 1–5 are 20 people, for 6–10 people there are 11 people, and the rest >10 there are 2 students.

Based on data from Figure 3, researchers found a drastic increase in the participation of lecturers, college students, teachers, and students during the Covid-19 pandemic. Those who participate >10 dominate with a percentage of 50%, then followed by 6–10 reaching 33%, and the remaining 1–5 times there is 17%. The data from Figure 3 shows a contrast with the data in Figure 2 which asked about their participation in the webinar before the covid-19 pandemic.

There are only 85 lecturers who took part in webinars 1–5 times during the Covid-19 pandemic, 151 lecturers who attended webinars 6–10 times, and mostly 161 lecturers who attended webinars >10 times. From the college student, 112 students attended 1–5 times, 211 people participated in 6–10 times, and 418 students participated in the webinar >10 times. From the teacher, 91 people attended the webinars 1–5 times, 211 teachers attended 6–10 times, and 256 teachers attended >10 webinars during this pandemic. From the student, there were 9 people participated in webinars 1–5 times, 10 people participated in 6–10 times, and 14 people attended webinars >10 times.

All of this data shows the opposite of the number of webinars that followed before the pandemic. Before the pandemic, the majority attended webinars 1–5 times, and those who attended webinars >10 times were not that many. Whereas during this pandemic, the majority of all elements studied, lecturers, students, teachers, and students, many attended webinars >10 times, even the percentage 50%, while those who attended webinars 1–5 times were limited to 17% only.

### 4.2  *Motivation to join webinars*

To address the changes in participation in pre-pandemic and post-pandemic webinars, researchers also offered participants a question item that motivated them.

Based on respondent data compiled by researchers, 83% of respondents answered that their motivation was simply to add knowledge, 7% of respondents whose motivation was to increase credit rank and gain knowledge, 4% of respondents answered because it was required by the institution where they worked, and other motivations were to increase rank credit and gain knowledge, 2% of respondents said only institutional obligations, 2% of other respondents answered institutional obligations and gained knowledge, and 2% of other respondents answered for credit increases in rank (Figures 3 and 4).

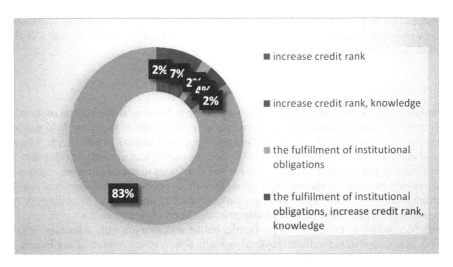

Figure 3.   Motivations of participants to take part in webinars during the Covid-19 pandemic.

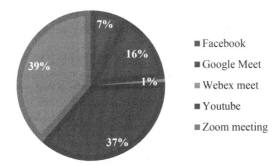

Figure 4.   Application used in webinars during the Covid-19 pandemic.

### 4.3   *Media applications for online seminars*

The media frequently used by respondents in attending webinars is quite diverse. There are 39% of respondents who use zoom meetings, while who use YouTube are almost the same in quantity, 37%. The use of Google Meet is far from the two media mentioned, only 16%. There are 7% who use Facebook, while respondents who use the WeBex meet applications are only 1% or about 17 people of the total response.

### 4.4   *Constraints and advantages of online seminars*

Based on these findings, researchers categorized these constraints in two ways. First, related to infrastructure such as the uneven internet network and had been discussed by many researchers (Suni Astini 2020). Second, related to the need for the quota to increase drastically to take part in live webinars or join the meeting application directly. However, this problem was helped a little with the help of quota from the government (Kompas.com 2020).

Behind these constraints, respondents also found several advantages in participating in online seminars. Researchers classify these advantages as follows: easy access to knowledge from national and international figures without being limited by long distances; the time to take part in online seminars is flexible, some respondents attend more than one seminar in a while; respondents also learned to adapt to technology. When the material presented in the online seminar has not been understood, the respondent can play it back because the material is a recording. This advantage is also widely mentioned in the results of research abroad (Garfin 2020; Tartavulea et al. 2020; Verma & Singh 2010).

### 4.5 *Discussion*

The number of webinars during the Covid-19 pandemic is the same as the interest of the academic community in gaining knowledge. For participants, many webinars that were held provided the widest possible opportunity to access useful knowledge from experts in their fields. Moreover, it is noted that most of the webinars can be followed for free by participants, whether they provide e-certificates or not. Another advantage, in normal conditions to attend seminars requires a lot of costs, ranging from transportation, registration fees are expensive, limited time, and not flexible. In online seminars by utilizing technology, participants play audio-visual recordings of material from seminars that are not understood independently (Verma & Singh 2010).

In the conditions of the Covid-19 pandemic, online seminars are truly a solution for distance learning that can continue without physical contact. It is very appropriate if organizers such as campus, expertise groups, workgroups, communities, and other educational institutions organize online seminars to share knowledge. This online seminar offers several advantages, the organizer can hold seminars with a panel of several speakers without having to meet, allowing them to communicate via voice, writing, and send documents. Some online seminar applications also offer the smallest number of participants for a limited circle up to thousands of participants in meetings (Verma & Singh 2010).

This phenomenon is not just a trend in the era of the Covid-19 pandemic, webinars have provided many benefits. For educators such as lecturers and teachers, webinars can promote a better understanding of e-learning and create a constructive e-portfolio that helps students learn productively. Many teachers and trainers have expressed satisfaction with the webinars as a means of disseminating concepts or knowledge as per the author's search results. Another positive aspect of using webinars as an effective tool in training is flexibility in gaining knowledge anywhere and easy access to training materials (Toquero & Talidong 2020). In other words, this euphoria provides an opportunity or a new alternative form of implementation of the 4.0 industrial revolution in education (Syah 2020).

## 5 CONCLUSION

Based on the analysis of the respondent's data and the researcher's investigation for the online seminars, the researcher can conclude the following:

The euphoria of online seminars arises because offline seminars that usually attended by many people and face-to-face cannot be held on the Covid-19 pandemic.

The number of webinars is same as the number of webinars interested in the Covid-19 pandemic. Before the pandemic, the standard of the academic community following webinars in the last six months was limited to 1–5 times. In the pandemic in Indonesia since April has changed, the majority of the academic community is >10 times.

The motivation of the participants is knowledge from the experts, obtained certificates that could be used for promotion and also graduation requirements for students, as well as fulfilling the demands of the institutions.

## ACKNOWLEDGMENTS

The author would like to thank ICEMS 2020 committee, UIN Syarif Hidayatullah Jakarta, LPDP (Indonesia Endowment Fund for Education) for supporting and funding to publish this research.

# REFERENCES

Garfin, D. R. 2020. 'Technology as a coping tool during the COVID-19 pandemic: Implications and recommendations', *Stress and Health*, (May), pp. 555–559.

Hasanah, A. *et al.* 2020. 'Analisis Aktivitas Belajar Daring Mahasiswa Pada Pandemi COVID-19', *Karya Tulis Ilmiah (KTI) Masa Work From Home (WFH) Covid-19 UIN Sunan Gunung Djati Bandung Tahun 2020*, pp. 4–8.

Herliandry, L. D. *et al.* 2020. 'Transformasi Media Pembelajaran Pada Masa Pandemi Covid-19', *Jurnal Teknologi Pendidikan*, 22(1), pp. 65–70.

Kompas.com. 2020. *Ini Syarat Penerima Bantuan Kuota Internet Gratis dari Pemerintah Halaman all - Kompas.com*. Available at: https://money.kompas.com/read/2020/09/25/150200926/ini-syarat-penerima-bantuan-kuota-internet-gratis-dari-pemerintah?page=all (Accessed: 22 October 2020).

Longman. 2020a. *Euphoria | meaning of euphoria in Longman Dictionary of Contemporary English | LDOCE, https://www.ldoceonline.com/dictionary/euphoria*. Available at: https://www.ldoceonline.com/dictionary/euphoria (Accessed: 21 October 2020).

Longman. 2020b. *Webinar | meaning of webinar in Longman Dictionary of Contemporary English | LDOCE*. Available at: https://www.ldoceonline.com/dictionary/webinar (Accessed: 21 October 2020).

Maniacci, M. P. and Sperry, L. 2014. *Neurocognitive disorders, Psychopathology and Psychotherapy: DSM-5 Diagnosis, Case Conceptualization, and Treatment*.

Mansyur, A. R. 2020. 'Dampak COVID-19 Terhadap Dinamika Pembelajaran Di Indonesia', *Education and Learning Journal*, 1(2), p. 113.

Pujilestari, Y. 2020. 'Dampak Positif Pembelajaran Online Dalam Sistem Pendidikan Indonesia Pasca Pandemi Covid-19', *Adalah*, 4(1), pp. 49–56.

Suni Astini, N. K. 2020. 'Tantangan Dan Peluang Pemanfaatan Teknologi Informasi Dalam Pembelajaran Online Masa Covid-19', *Cetta: Jurnal Ilmu Pendidikan*, 3(2), pp. 241–255.

Syah, R. H. 2020. 'Dampak Covid-19 pada Pendidikan di Indonesia: Sekolah, Keterampilan, dan Proses Pembelajaran', *SALAM: Jurnal Sosial dan Budaya Syar-i*, 7(5).

Tartavulea, C. V. *et al.* 2020. 'Online teaching practices and the effectiveness of the educational process in the wake of the Covid-19 pandemic', *Amfiteatru Economic*, 22(55), pp. 920–936.

Toquero, C. and Talidong, K. 2020. 'Webinar Technology: Developing Teacher Training Programs for Emergency Remote Teaching amid COVID-19', *Interdisciplinary Journal of Virtual Learning in Medical Sciences*, 11(3), pp. 200–203.

Tuwu, D. 2020. 'Kebijakan Pemerintah Dalam Penanganan Pandemi Covid-19', *Journal Publicuho*, 3(2), p. 267.

Verma, A. and Singh, A. 2010. 'Webinar - Education through digital collaboration', *Journal of Emerging Technologies in Web Intelligence*, 2(2), pp. 131–136.

Wawan Mas'udi, P. S. W. 2020. *Tata Kelola Penanganan COVID-19 di Indonesia: Kajian Awal*. UGM Press.

Wijayanti, M., Yunita, T. and Dharmanto, A. 2020. 'Pembelajaran Perguruan Tinggi Dalam Jaringan (Daring) Masa Pandemi Covid-19', *Jurnal Kajian Ilmiah*, 1(1), pp. 31–38.

*Emerging Trends in Technology for Education in an Uncertain World – Nanto, Rahiem & Khalis Maryati (Eds)*
© 2022 copyright the Author(s), ISBN 978-1-032-11288-6

# Relationship of the role of teacher class and national character value in primary school

P. Islamiati & A.E. Latip
*Department of Primary Teacher Education, Faculty of Educational Sciences, Universitas Islam Negeri Syarif Hidayatullah Jakarta, Tangerang Selatan, Banten, Indonesia*

ABSTRACT: This study aims to determine students perceptions of the relationship between the role of classroom teachers in the formation of national character values in Grade V students at MI Al Husna Lebak Bulus. The research method used is a quantitative method. The research instrument used was a questionnaire with a scale of 1–5. The sampling technique was total sampling. The data analysis technique used is the product moment correlation. The results showed that there was a positive relationship between the role of classroom teachers on the formation of the national character of students. This is shown by obtaining $r_{count}$ of 0.640. Meanwhile, the $r_{tabel}$ at the 5% significance level with N = 49 was obtained for 0.2816. From the results of the analysis, it can be seen that $r_{count}$ is greater than $r_{tabel}$ (0.640 > 0.2816) and because the $r_{count}$ is positive, the relationship is positive.

*Keywords*: The Role of Class Teachers, National Character, and Correlation Research

## 1 INTRODUCTION

Today the educational process places more emphasis on cognitive abilities and less emphasis on very basic aspects, namely aspects of character. Character is a very important aspect in assessing the quality of human resources. If a person has good character with high intellectual abilities, he can be a useful person for himself and the surrounding environment. With the influence of foreign cultures in society, it also influences the behavior of the population of this nation, and so far many have forgotten that education is about education, not just teaching.

### 1.1 *Research background*

Today the educational process places more emphasis on cognitive abilities and less emphasis on very basic aspects, namely aspects of character. Character is a very important aspect in assessing the quality of human resources. If a person has good character with high intellectual abilities, he can be a useful person for himself and the surrounding environment. With the influence of foreign cultures in society, it also influences the behavior of the population of this nation, and so far many have forgotten that education is about education, not just teaching.

Several years earlier the government introduced a government program called Strengthening Character Education (PPK), PPK was an attempt to cultivate character education in schools. The PPK program will be implemented in stages and as needed. The PPK program aims to promote quality and moral education that is evenly distributed throughout the nation. Issuance of Presidential Regulation number 87 article 2 of 2017 concerning Strengthening Character Education (PPK), PPK has the following objectives:

1. Build and equip students as Indonesia's golden generation in 2045 with the spirit of Pancasila and good character education to face the dynamics of change in the future.

   DOI 10.1201/9781003219248-18

2. Developing a national education platform that places character education as the main soul in the delivery of education for students with the support of public involvement through formal, non-formal, and informal education by taking into account the diversity of Indonesian cultures and
3. Revitalizing and strengthening the potential and competence of educators, education staff, students, the community, and the family environment in implementing PPK.

## 1.2 *Literature review*

The role of the classroom teacher, namely the role of the teacher as a facilitator, motivator, communicator, evaluator, informator, mediator, and demonstrator (Mally 2010). The indicators of the role of classroom teachers that the authors have concluded are as follows:

1. The role of the teacher as a facilitator
   Based on some of the opinions above, it can be concluded that the indicators of the role of classroom teachers as facilitators in character building are:
   a) Provide facilities and infrastructure that support character building activities.
   b) Listening to every complaint about the problems faced by students.
   c) Using learning resources (resource persons, books, texts, magazines, newspapers) which facilitate the teaching and learning process (Iskandar 2017).
2. The teacher's role as motivator
   It can be concluded that the indicators of the classroom teacher's role as a motivator are:
   a) Clarify the goals to be achieved.
   b) Generating interest in students to always have a positive character.
   c) Adjusting the material with the experiences and abilities of students.
3. The role of the teacher as a communicator
   Indicators of the role of classroom teachers as communicators are:
   a) Skilled in communication.
   b) Pack yourself attractively.
   c) Provide views on the majesty of various stories about life.
4. The role of the teacher as an evaluator
   Indicators of the role of classroom teachers as evaluators, namely:
   a) Assessing the learning process of students.
   b) Assessing the learning outcomes of students.
5. The role of the teacher as an informator
   Indicators of the role of the classroom teacher as an informator, namely:
   a) Provide information related to character values related to oneself.
   b) Describe the character values that will be achieved in school.
   c) Explain the benefits of having a positive character to students.
6. The role of the teacher as a mediator
   The teacher as a mediator is defined as a mediator in the learning activities of students, such as providing a solution in student discussion activities. Mediator is also defined as providing media, how to use and organize media usage. Indicators of the role of the classroom teacher as a mediator, namely:
   a) Provide a way out in student discussion activities.
   b) Knowing and understanding educational media.
   c) Using educational media properly.
7. Teacher's role as demonstrator
   Indicators of the role of the classroom teacher as a demonstrator are:
   a) Enriching himself with various knowledge.
   b) Can play its role as a teacher well.
   c) Behave and behave that can be role models.

We can understand that national character is a measured activity of a person to respond to social conditions in his country in a good and wise way (Lita 2017). Individual responses are also in the form of loving the country and defending themselves when there are threats from outside/other countries (Tabah 2017). The national character of Indonesia is rooted in the Pancasila ideology (Akmal 2018).

## 2 METHODS

This research is a quantitative correlational type. Quantitative methods are often referred to as traditional, positivistic, scientific and discovery methods.

Researchers used correlational research because it is in accordance with the purpose of this study, namely to see the relationship between two variables, namely between the role of the classroom teacher and the national character of students. So the research method that is suitable for use in this study is a correlational research model.

### 2.1 *Population and sample*

Population is a generalization area consisting of objects/subjects that have certain qualities and characteristics that are determined by the researcher for study and then draw conclusions (Sugiyono 2013).

The sample is part of the number and characteristics of the population. If the population is large and it is impossible for the researcher to study everything in the population, for example because of limited funds, manpower and time, the researcher can use a sample drawn from the population. Samples taken from the population must be truly representative (represent). Because of what is learned from the sample, the conclusions will be applicable to the population (Sugiyono 2013).

The population in this study were students of class V MI Al Husna Lebak in the 2020/2021 school year. There were 49 students in class V. The class can be said to be heterogeneous because there are students with good, sufficient, and less character. Based on the characteristics that have been described, the sample selection is carried out by the Saturated Sampling technique, which is to take all members of the population into a sample because of the small population.

### 2.2 *Data collection technique*

The research data was collected through a questionnaire, namely the questionnaire is a number of written questions used to collect data or information (Sartika 2010). The number of questionnaire instruments in this study were 20 items to measure the national character of students and 20 items to measure the role of the classroom teacher, each item having 5 alternative answers. The questionnaire was given to students who were used as a unit of analysis in the study to determine the role of the classroom teacher in the formation of the national character of students at MI Al Husna Lebak Bulus.

This questionnaire uses a Likert scale where the respondent is provided with alternative answers.

### 2.3 *Hypothesis*

The statistical hypothesis in this study is as follows:

$H_0$: $\rho = 0$
$H_1$: $\rho \neq 0$

Information:

$H_0$ is accepted if rho is equal to zero, it means that there is no significant relationship between the role of the classroom teacher on the formation of the national character of students.

$H_1$ is accepted if rho is not equal to zero (less than or more than zero), it means that there is a significant relationship between the role of the classroom teacher on the formation of the national character of students.

## 3 DISCUSSION AND RESULTS

This research was conducted at MI Al Husna Lebak Bulus. In this study, it was conducted to describe the correlation between the X variable (the role of the classroom teacher) and the Y variable (the national character). In this study, data collection used a questionnaire which was distributed to 25 students in class VA and 24 students in class VB, so that the total number of respondents was 49 people. Questionnaires were distributed from July 13 to 18 using the google form application.

The distributed questionnaire consisted of 40 statements regarding the role of the classroom teacher and the national character of students. The data was declared valid by expert judgment with a note of improvement, namely by correcting the sentence. Then an external test was carried out by distributing instruments to grade V students at MI not the target of the study, namely MI Nurul Huda using the google form application. After the questionnaire was filled in by 39 grade V students, then the distribution of the questionnaire answers was made, then determined the answer scores according to the predetermined score provisions. Each statement item has five alternative answers consisting of always, often, sometimes, ever, and never which the respondent can choose. The scoring of each item is done by giving a score of 1 to 5 according to the type of item. The answer scores of each respondent are then tabulated. After the external test, the validity and reliability were tested. As for the results of the instrument validity test, there was one invalid statement from 14 statements in the class teacher role variable (X), then in the national character variable (Y) there were six invalid statements from 26 statements.

1.  Test prerequisite analysis
    The prerequisite analysis tests carried out were the normality test, linearity test and homogeneity test. The normality test is carried out to determine whether the data obtained is normally distributed or not.
    a)  Normality test
        The results of the calculation of the normality test using the Kolmogorov Smirnov are given in Table 1.
            Based on the results of the normality test, the value on the classroom teacher role variable (X) was 0.139 and the value on the national character variable (Y) was 0.728. Each variable has a significance value greater than 0.05, thus the two variables can be stated as normally distributed.
    b)  Linearity test
        The results of the linearity test calculation are given in Table 2.
        Based on the results of the linearity test above, the deviation from linearity value is 0.101, this value is greater than 0.05. Thus it can be concluded that the two variables are stated to run linearly.

Table 1.  Tests of normality.

|  | Kolmogorov-Smirnov[a] | | | Shapiro-Wilk | | |
|---|---|---|---|---|---|---|
|  | Statistic | df | Sig. | Statistic | df | Sig. |
| National character | .105 | 49 | .200* | .964 | 49 | **.139** |
| The role of the classroom teacher | .065 | 49 | .200* | .984 | 49 | **.728** |

*This is a lower bound of the true significance.
[a]Lilliefors significance correction.

143

Table 2. ANOVA table.

| | | | Sum of squares | df | Mean square | F | Sig. |
|---|---|---|---|---|---|---|---|
| National character* The role of the classroom teacher | Between groups | (Combined) | 4193.718 | 27 | 155.323 | 3.362 | **.003** |
| | | Linearity | 2112.753 | 1 | 2112.753 | 45.731 | **.000** |
| | | Deviation from linearity | 2080.966 | 26 | 80.037 | 1.732 | **.101** |
| | Within groups | | 970.200 | 21 | 46.200 | | |
| | Total | | 5163.918 | 48 | | | |

Table 3. Test of homogeneity of variances.

The role of the classroom teacher

| Levene statistic | df1 | df2 | Sig. |
|---|---|---|---|
| 2.479 | 12 | 20 | **.035** |

Table 4. Correlations.

| | | The role of the classroom teacher | National character |
|---|---|---|---|
| The role of the classroom teacher | Pearson correlation | 1 | **.640**\** |
| | Sig. (2-tailed) | | **.000** |
| | N | 49 | **49** |
| National character | Pearson correlation | .640** | 1 |
| | Sig. (2-tailed) | .000 | |
| | N | 49 | **49** |

**Correlation is significant at the 0.01 level (2-tailed).

c) Homogeneity test

The homogeneity test was carried out to determine whether the variance between the tested groups was different or not, the variance was homogeneous or heterogeneous. The expected data is homogeneous. Data is said to be homogeneous if the significance value obtained is less than 0.05, on the other hand, if the significance value is greater than 0.05, the data is said to be not homogeneous or heterogeneous. The results of the homogeneity test are given in Table 3.

Based on the results of the homogeneity test above, the significance value is 0.035, this value is less than 0.05. Thus it can be concluded that the two variable data spread homogeneously.

2. Hypothesis testing

a) Product moment correlation analysis

Based on the results of the analysis and the existing analysis requirements test, the distribution of each variable is normal and has a good linear relationship, then it can be continued with hypothesis testing. Hypothesis testing is done to find out whether the hypothesis proposed in this study can be accepted or rejected. Testing the hypothesis in this study using the product moment correlation test with the help of the IBM SPSS Statistics 20 program. The hypothesis proposed is that there is a positive relationship between the role of the classroom teacher on the national character formation of grade V students at MI Al Husna Lebak Bulus. The explanation of the results of hypothesis testing in this study is given in Table 4.

Based on the table above, the correlation value is 0.640, it can be concluded that there is a relationship between the role of the classroom teacher and the national character of students.

Table 5. Model summary.

| Model | R | R square | Adjusted R square | Std. error of the estimate |
|---|---|---|---|---|
| 1 | .640[a] | .409 | .397 | **8.057** |

[a] Predictors: (constant), classroom teacher.

The two asterisk indicates that the correlation of significance lies at the 0.01 level. The positive correlation number shows a positive relationship, that is, if the role of the classroom teacher increases, the national character of students will also increase. The significance value obtained is 0.000, the value is less than 0.01, so there is a significant relationship.

Thus considering the resulting $r_{count}$ is 0.640 which is in the range 0.61 to 0.80, this shows that between variable X and variable Y there is a strong correlation.

b) Coefficient of determination

The analysis of the coefficient of determination used in this study is with the help of the IBM SPSS Statistics 20 program. The results of the analysis of the following coefficient of determination are given in Table 5.

Based on the results of the coefficient of determination above, the R square value is 0.409. This shows that the classroom teacher role variable has a relationship to the national character of students by 0.409 and the rest has a relationship with other factors that are not discussed in this study.

In this study, the aim of this research is to describe the relationship between the role of the classroom teacher and the formation of the national character of the fifth grade students at MI Al Husna Lebak Bulus in the 2020/2021 academic year. Data were collected using a questionnaire. Based on the results of the product moment correlation analysis calculated using the help of IBM SPSS Statistics 20, the relationship between the role of the classroom teacher and the formation of the national character of students was obtained $r_{count}$ of 0.640. Meanwhile, the $r_{tabel}$ at the 5% significance level with N = 49 was obtained for 0.2816. From the results of the analysis, it can be seen that $r_{count}$ is greater than $r_{tabel}$ (0.640 > 0.2816) and because the $r_{count}$ is positive, the relationship is positive, which means that if the role of the class teacher is high, the national character of the students is also high. So it can be stated that, there is a positive relationship between the role of classroom teachers on the formation of the national character of students. And the results of hypothesis testing state that H0 is rejected and H1 is accepted. H1 accepted in this study, namely: there is a positive relationship between the role of classroom teachers on the formation of the national character of grade V students at MI Al Husna Lebak Bulus Academic Year 2020/2021.

Then in line with the opinion expressed by Siti Sholiha Nurfaidah, Efforts to solve this problem are to increase the ability of educators to shape the values of the national character of students. One of them is through the role of the teacher in the use of learning media, such as traditional game media (Siti 2018).

This research is in line with research conducted by Imam Suwardi Wibowo, and Ririn Farnisa shows that $r_{count}$ 2.289498 > $r_{tabel}$ 1.7081 thus there is a relationship between teacher roles. in the learning process with student achievement (Imam & Ririn 2018).

Dini Palupi Putri research in 2017 the results of the study can be known that the efforts to establish the character of the nation reflected in the individual character of the citizens are determined by the quality of the educational process of families, schools and communities (Dini 2018).

In this study the results of the product moment correlation test stated that $r_{count}$ was greater than $r_{tabel}$ (0.640 > 0.2816) and because the $r_{count}$ was positive, the relationship was positive, which meant that if the role of the class teacher was high, the national character of the students was also high.

## 4 CONCLUSION

The conclusion of the results of this study is that there is a strong relationship between the variable role of the classroom teacher on the formation of the national character of the fifth grade students at MI Al Husna Lebak Bulus. This is evidenced by the results of the hypothesis test which states that $H_0$ is rejected and $H_1$ is accepted. As indicated by the value of rhitung is greater than $r_{tabel}$ ($0.640 > 0.2816$), which means that in forming national characters consisting of religious, honest, tolerance, discipline, hard work, creative, independent, democratic, curiosity, national spirit, love homeland, respect for achievement, friendly/communicative, peace-loving, fond of reading, caring for the environment, social care, and responsibility required the role of classroom teachers as facilitators, motivators, communicators, evaluators, informators, mediators, and demonstrators.

## REFERENCES

Akmal Rizki Gunawan Hsb dan Siti Aisah, *Attadib Journal Of Elementary Education* 3, no. 2 (2018): 90–104.

Dini Palupi Putri, "Pendidikan Karakter Pada Anak Sekolah Dasar Di Era Digital," *AR-RIAYAH: Jurnal Pendidikan Dasar* 2, no. 1 (2018): 37.

Imam Suwardi and Ririn Farnisa, "Hubungan Peran Guru Dalam Proses Pembelajaran Terhadap Prestasi Belajar Siswa," *Jurnal Gentala Pendidikan Dasar* 3, no. 2 (2018): 181–202.

Iskandar Agung. "Peran Fasilitator Guru Dalam Penguatan Pendidikan Karakter (Ppk)," *Perspektif Ilmu Pendidikan* 31, no. 2 (2017): 106–119.

Lita Ariyanti. "Membangun Pendidikan Karakter Di Sekolah Dasar Melalui 6 Kebajikan Positif Universal," ELSE (Elementary School Education Journal): *Jurnal Pendidikan dan Pembelajaran Sekolah Dasar* 1, no. 3 (2017): 107–113.

Mally Maeliah, "Peran Guru Dalam Menyiapkan Kompetensi Kerja Siswa Sesuai Tuntutan Dunia Kerja Di Industri Busana," *APTEKINDO: Asosiasi Pendidikan Teknologi dan Kejuruan Indonesia* (2010): 173–178.

Sartika Putri Wardana, "Hubungan Intensitas Layanan Bimbingan Dan Konseling Dengan Motivasi Belajar Siswa (Studi Kasus Siswa Kelas XI SMA Negeri 3 Kota Tangerang Selatan)" (UIN Syarif Hidayatullah Jakarta, 2010), h. 46.

Siti Sholiha Nurfaidah, "The Role of Teachers in Building National Character Values through Traditional Games for Elementary School Students," *International Journal of Community Service Learning* 2, no. 4 (2018): 297–301.

Sugiyono, Metode Penelitian Pendidikan (Pendekatan Kuantitatif, Kualitatif, Dan R&D) (Bandung: Alfabeta, 2013), h. 13–118.

Tabah Sumarlam dan Subekti, "Nilai Karakter Kebangsaan Dalam Buku Teks Bahasa Indonesia Sekolah Dasar," 9, no. 1 (2017): 70–80.

*Emerging Trends in Technology for Education in an Uncertain World – Nanto, Rahiem & Khalis Maryati (Eds)*

# Building good character for children during the Covid-19 pandemic

E.R. Yuliyanti
*Department of Islamic Education, Faculty of Educational Sciences, Universitas Islam Negeri Syarif Hidayatullah Jakarta, Tangerang Selatan, Banten, Indonesia*

M.D. Pratama
*Department of English Education, Faculty of Educational Sciences, University Islam Negeri Sultan Syarif Kasim Pekanbaru, Riau, Indonesia*

ABSTRACT: The Covid-19 outbreak has produced a tremendous impact on education. Learning usually carried out in the classroom must be distance learning at home. The community still views schools as the most effective places for education. The government policy to study at home requires parents to participate in cultivating a positive character for students. This study aims to reveal (1) Parent's methods to build good character, (2) The growth character at home. The research subjects were 5 the parents of SDIT Al-Azhar Kemang Pratama Bekasi students. The design of this research is a qualitative studies. Data collection techniques were interview and documentation. Data analysis technique was based on three concepts; data reduction, data presentation, and verifying the conclusions.The results of this research were (1) The parents methods to build good character were role model, intervention, and habituatuon, (2) The growth character during distance learning were independent, discipline, creativity and religious.

*Keywords*: character, character education, the Covid-19 pandemic

## 1 INTRODUCTION

Today, all countries in the world are facing the Covid-19 pandemic (Shereen et al. 2020). All activities are restricted to prevent the spread of the Covid-19, including educational activities. The world is encountering problems in which the government's policy to stay at home, work from home, etc. UNESCO has recommended distance learning programs and other education platforms (UNESCO 2020). In Indonesia, The Ministry of Education and Culture has instructed all educational institutions to carry out the learning process using e-learning with the Indonesian Minister of Education and Culture Circular No. 3 of 2020 concerning the Prevention of Covid-19 in the Education Unit on March 9, 2020. Changes that need to be adopted by all parties. It is undeniable that distance learning is one answer in the educational process. With distance learning, students can still learn and gain knowledge without having to come to school.

For the Indonesian people, the classroom is still seen as true education (Arifin 2012). The community still sees the classroom as an actual school. As a result of government policy to study at home, people must be able to think clearly, learning and working at home policies prevent teachers from monitoring the development of student behavior. Every adult obliges to foster positive character in students during the pandemic. Character education that has been implemented in schools during the pandemic is the responsibility of parents to replace teachers. Various studies have written character education during a pandemic can grow in a family environment, even though there are many obstacles faced by parents. Abdusomad said the family was the principal medium for shaping character values during distance learning in the pandemic (Abdusomad 2020). The student's positive character attitude can grow in him during distance learning from home (Alif et al. 2020; Enika & Sutama 2020; Maman et al. 2020). Hence, parents have to continue to shape character values in conveying knowledge and tasks during the learning process in the network. However, parents play a role in shaping the affective and psychomotor aspects of children at home.

Meanwhile, the study of character received attention from scientists. According to Lickona, the character is related to moral concepts (moral knowing), moral feelings, and moral behavior (moral behavior) (Lickona 2013). Character is the quality of someone's rational thought, approaching a need, task, or idea from a new perspective, producing, causing existence, imagination, and the ability to imagine something. There are 18-character components identified as coming from religion, culture, and national education goals. These characters are honesty, tolerance, discipline, hard work, creativity, independence, democracy, curiosity, national spirit, satisfactory achievement, friendliness, peace-loving, fondness of reading, environmental care, social care, responsibility, and religion (Kemendiknas 2011).

Character building in education is distinguished as character education. Various character education discourses according to experts and several studies conclude the character education is particularly related to individual moral behavior and personal development that is expressed in students' life (Pattaro 2016). Character education represents a growing discipline, with deliberate efforts to optimize students' ethical behavior (Agboola & Tsai 2012; Kisby 2017; Walsh 2018; Wibowo 2012). It is the process of supplying demands on students to become completely human beings with character in the dimensions of heart, mind, body, taste, and desire (Samani et al. 2011). According to Thus, character education becomes a conscious effort to appreciate virtue, namely objectively outstanding human qualities, not only good for individuals but also good for society as a whole (Lickona 2012). By providing character education, students are expected to be more sensitive and reflective about their humanity, themselves, their environment, their surroundings, and their God (Suryanto 2017).

Currently, children are 24 hours with their parents at home, so it opens up invaluable opportunities for children to get care and education from parents. Parents become role models for children in carrying out activities (Koesuma 2012). Parents can apply various models in constructing the character of their children. The quality of communication between parents and children will increase children's trust in their parents (Badudu 2019). Modeling is intertwined with character education. How parents treat their children will affect behavior development.

According to Gunadi, there are three key roles that parents can play with developing children's character: (1) Obliged to create a warm and serene atmosphere, because, without such an atmosphere, the child will be stunted by the growth of his soul. As a result, children live in tension and fear. (2) Become a positive role model for children, because children learn the most from what they see, not from what they hear. The character of the parents shown through proper behavior is a learning material that will be absorbed by the child. (3) Educating children, meaning that teaching moral character will discipline children to behave under what it has taught (Gunadi 2016).

## 2 METHODS

This research was designed as a qualitative descriptive study in which the conditions and situations were direct data. The researcher was positioned as central actors of all existing instrumens (Gerring 2007). This research was conducted for 3 months from May 2020 to July 2020. The subjects of this study were 5 parents of SDIT Al-Azhar Kemang Pratama Bekasi. The data collection techniques were interview methods and documentation. The research conditions in the midts of the COVID-19 outbreak changed data techiques as usuall through the Video Call and Messenger of WhatsApp application. The data obtained from parents to answer questions were also strengthened by data from interviews with teachers.

The interviews were conducted which aimed to get information from parents about building good character during distance learning. The aspects asked to parents: (1) How are the efforts of parents in building children's character during pandemic? (2) What good characters were growth during distance learning in pandemic? The data analysis technique that the researcher used during the study was based on the Miles-Huberman approach, which comprised three concepts; data reduction (conducted directly at the time of data collection), data presentation, and verifying the conclusions (Sugiono 2019). After the data was obtained, the analysis was carried out as an investigation interactively and simultaneously until all the problems in this study were answered and the answers were obtained. Data reduction was to retrieve the required data according to the problem of research.

## 3 RESULT

### 3.1 *Parent's methods*

#### 3.1.1 *Independent character*
The application of the most basic role model in the character education process is to place parents as agents of role modeling. Therefore, showing good behavior will be the primary requirement for parents. Role modeling activities were shown by parents carrying out worship at home. Predominantly, parents routinely performed worship during prayer hours. Based on the data, many parents reminded and invited their children to pray. During the pandemic, parents demonstrated examples to be disciplined with health protocols, namely washing hands, wearing masks, and making distance.

Learning from home is challenging for parents. At the start of the Covid-19 pandemic, three of five felt troubled to adapt as an educators for their children. Many working parents have been instructed to work from home. The task was given by teacher through WhatsApp group to support the learning process. From the results of interiew by Video Call, respondents stated that they were most likely to experience difficulties in home schooling, feeling stress and under pressure. They have to do parenting full time. Every day during school hours, there were always assignments administered by the teacher to be conducted through Google Form and submitted the next day. This information became the attention of parents to consistently remind and assist children in performing these tasks. From the results of interviews with parents, many of them always forgot to read the information in WA. As a result, children did not complete the assignments that the teacher assigns them. However teacher still monitors through WhatsApp. Teachers provided a more detailed explanation of the assigment. Parents try to be good parents for their children. Based on the results of interview, two families tried to get more knowledge about the materials by reading boooks or watching Youtube. This condition has a positif impact and makes it more easier for parent to be with their children.

One effort in shaping the character in this research is habituation. Habituation is a psychological learning process wherein there is a decrease in response to a stimulus after being repeatedly exposed to it. Many examples that have been exercised and developed through the conditioning activities should be done by parents. Spiritual activities in general become in front line in the habituation process. The learning process in the from of habituation is initiated by praying, greeting, revide the holy.

According parents in assigning assignments to their childern, the teacher does not necessarily impose a massive series of tasks, let alone the face-to-face online learning process using Zoom. So, the childrem were asked to get used to performing daily activities independently. The task assigned by the teacher required parental assistance so that children could carry out these physical activities. It was not uncommon for the tasks assigned to do adult activities like helping childern watering flowers, sweeping the yard, and washing dishes. Various efforts had been made by parents so that children could complete the tasks. As proof that students had worked on assignments, parents took photos when active students submit them to the teacher through the Google Classroom application.

### 3.2 *Children's character*

#### 3.2.1 *Independent character*
The character suitable for distance learning is independent. The results of the study reported that independence was very important for students themselves. So, students were asked to get used

to performing daily activities independently. The task assigned by the teacher required parental assistance so that children could carry out these physical activities. Activities include tidying up bed, textbooks, toys, using your own clothes, going back and forth by yourself to eating yourself. It was not uncommon for the tasks assigned to do adult activities like watering flowers, sweeping the yard, and washing dishes. Activities include tidying up bed, textbooks, toys, using your own clothes, going back and forth by yourself to eating yourself.

### 3.2.2 *Creativity*

Based on the interviews that the researchers gave parents, it was revealed that the parents and teachers were proud of seeing the students' work from the assignments they were given. From the tasks given, the children preferred physical activities like drawing, coloring, and sports. This activity was great fun for children. According to their parents, they were happy to do physical activities with their parents at home. In contrast to memorizing lessons, students were bored and bored with sitting for long in front of the laptop. This condition was understandable by the teacher, and students may change their sitting position with their legs stretched out, sitting in a different place. The evidence of creativity in distance learning was that children are encouraged to make videos of activities they enjoy. For female students, make cooking videos at home with their mothers, and for male students to make video playing with their fathers. Even though they were children, the ability of students to use devices was quick compared to their parents.

### 3.2.3 *Discipline character*

From the results of review parents via WhatsApp, parents stated that disciplined attitudes during the pandemic were very important for students and families. According to parents a disciplined attitude was formed when their children began to learn. Parents provided a Zoom link form teacher a day before activity. Children became accustomed to activating the Zoom application five minutes before studying because the teacher would take the names of the students. Although studying in front of the screen, the school's rules for children to wear school uniforms like normal conditions were also carried out by parents and students. As if what children did was not much different from what they did in school. In addition to discipline while studying, the teacher also always reminded students to be disciplined in dealing with pandemic conditions. The development of a disciplined attitude was applied by parents at home, namely following the rules of health protocols such as wearing masks when hanging out with crowded people, washing hands after interacting outside. If traveling for a long time, children were required to take a shower and take off all clothes, and made some distance when gathering.

### 3.2.4 *Religious character*

From the results of the interview by Video Call, the parents stated that in the efforts they did, both in the form of thoughts, words, and actions, all were oriented to religious values. Their existence as Muslims who sent their children to Al-Azhar aimed so that their children were planted with a firm foundation for their beliefs. One year earlier, their children were in first grade were believed to had achieved significant progress in implementing the obligatory prayers and the Sunnah. During a pandemic, this habit had effects like reading prayers before studying, reading prayers before eating. Every morning before starting class, the children always checked by teacher to pray. Continue reading the Prophet Muhammad's vows and prayers. Every student, every day took turn to become an officer in reading the Prophet's vows and prayers, and hoping learning would be blessed by Allah SWT. The results of interviews that researchers conducted by parents accompanying, supervising, and doing worship together with the child. In their worship, they ask Allah SWT to consistently provide health and avoid the Covid-19 outbreak and other dangers.

## 4 DISCUSSION

Humans with character are humans whose behavior and everything related to their life activities are filled with good values. This type of human does not mean he never makes mistakes, but always tries to correct all forms of his mistakes and continuously improves himself (Surasman 2020). Asrori said that creativity was a useful new idea (Asrori 2020; Ngalimun.dkk 2013) and has the same understanding that creativity is the ability to create new ones. Cultivating creative abilities in children from an early age will make children become resilient individuals. Another aspect of character education is the value of independence, namely the ability to organize and control thoughts, feelings, and actions freely and try to determine oneself without the help of others to complete tasks. Independent character values represent attitudes and behaviors that do not depend on others. It uses all your energy, thoughts, time to recognize hopes, dreams, and ideals. Students who have independence will make the learning process smooth so that teachers can also enjoy teaching. Independent students will serve their own needs and be responsible for themselves. Erikson said that independence is a development towards a steady and standing individuality (Raul 2016).

One strategy or method used in shaping religious character is the formation of good habits and leaving bad ones through guidance, training, and hard work. The formation of this habit will enhance a person's character. Therefore, a strong character is usually constructed by planting values that emphasize good and bad. This value is established through appreciation and experience. The formation of a religious character towards children can be conducted if all educational stakeholders, including parents and families, participate and take part. As for religious values in daily life consistently and continuously will establish a habit. Habit is a method used to accustom children to think, behave, and act in accordance with the guidance of Islamic teachings. Habit is a process of forming attitudes and behaviors relatively settled through an iterative learning process. Habit also encourages and provides space for children on theories that require a direct application, so that theories that are initially heavy become light for children if they are often implemented.

Distance learning during this pandemic, parents have a big enough role to create character values at home. During the Covid-19 pandemic, the communication effectiveness of parents and children was exceptionally high, because of almost 24 hours of parents together with children in carrying out various activities. In developing character values at home, parents act as the primary role models that support children to develop character effectively. The parental examples that students see and feel are the main key to character education at home. Apart from acting as role models, parents must also be able to act as filters that help children filter out various negative influences that are bad for their development. Parents are also able to act as a liaison for children with various sources of learning that are close daily.

## 5 CONCLUSION

The man finding from of this study is a parents methods to build good character are role model, intervention and habituation. The children's character were growth are independent, creativity, discipline and religious.

## ACKNOWLEDGMENT

The author would like to thank to International Conference of Education in Moslem Society (ICEMS) 2020 FITK UIN Syarif Hidayatullah Jakarta for publication support.

## REFERENCES

Abdusomad, A. 2020. Pengaruh COVID-19 terhadap penerapan pendidikan karakter dan pendidikan Islam, Qalamuna: Jurnal Pendidikan Sosial dan Agama 12(2), 107–115.
Agboola, A., & Tsai, K.C. 2012. Bring character education into classroom, Europian Journal of Educational Research, 1(2), 163–170.

Akpunar, Burhan & Dogan, Yunus. 2011. Decipering The Theory of Multiple Intelligences: An Islamic Perspective, International Journal of Business and Social Science, 2(11), 224–231.

Arifin, Z. 2012. Evaluasi pembelajaran. Bandung: Remaja Rosdakarya

Asrori, M. 2013. Psikologi pembelajaran. Bandung: Wacana prima.

Bania, A.S., Nuraini, & Ulfa, Maria. 2020. Character and student ability of Covid-19: Understanding in Digital Era in 2020. Available of https://doi.org/10.33258/birci.v.1156, Budhapest International Research and Critics Institue Journal, 3(3), 2233–2240.

Gerring, J. 2007. Case Study Research: Principle & Practices. New York: Cambridge University Press.

Intania, V.E., & Sutama. 2020. The role of character education in learning during the COVID-19 pandemic, Jurnal Penelitian Ilmu Pendidikan, 13(2), 129–136.

Kemendiknas. 2011. Pedoman pelaksanaan pendidikan karakter. Jakarta: Pusat Kurikulum Perbukuan.

Kisby, B. 2017. Politics is ethics done in public: Exploring linkages and disjunctions between citizenship education and character education in England. Journal of Social Science Education, 16(3), 7–20.

Koesuma, D. 2012. Pendidikan karakter: Strategi membidik anak di zaman global. Jakarta: Grasindo.

Lickona, T. 2012. Educating for character: Mendidik untuk membentuk karakter. Jakarta: Bumi Aksara.

Ngalimun, Fadillah, H., Ariani, Alpha. 2013. Perkembangan dan pengembangan kreatifitas. Yogyakarta: Aswaja Presindo.

Pattaro, C. 2016. Character Education: Themes and researches: an academic literature review. Italian Journal of Sociology of Education, 8(1), 6–30.

Raul, C. 2016. Psychososial development factors associated with occupational and vocational identity between infancy and adolescence. Springer International Publishing DOI 10.1007/s408954-016-0027-y

Shereen, M., Khan, S., Kazmi, A., Bashir, N., & Siddique, R. 2020. Covid-19 Infection: Origin transmission and characteristics on human Coronaviruses. Journal of Advanced Research, 4(7), 91–98.

Sugiyono. 2018. Metode penelitian kuantitaif kualitatif dan R&D. Bandung: Alfabeta.

Surasman, O. 2020. Karakter building upaya harmonisasi interaksi manusia modern. Jurnal Qira'ah, 10(1), 45–66.

Suryaman, M., Cahyono, Y., Muliansyah, D., Bustani, O., Suryani, P., Fahlevi, M., Pramono, R., Purwanto, A., Purba, J., Parhehean, A., Munthe, Juliana, Harimurti, S. 2020. Covid-19 pandemic and home online learning systemL does it affect the qualitu of pharmacy school learning. Systematic Reviews in Pharmacy, 11(8), 524–530.

WHO. (2020). Retrieved 16 March 2020, from http://www/who.int/dpcs/defaultsource/coronaviruses/getting-workplace-ready-forcovid-19.pdf6.

*Emerging Trends in Technology for Education in an Uncertain World – Nanto, Rahiem & Khalis Maryati (Eds)*
*© 2022 copyright the Author(s), ISBN 978-1-032-11288-6*

# Instructional video in e-learning: Assessing the impact of motivation on student achievement

Zaharah Indrayanto
*Syarif Hidayatullah Islamic State University, Jakarta, Indonesia*

Ibnu Sina
*University of Pamulang, Jakarta, Indonesia*

ABSTRACT: The main objective of this research is to explore the results of using video as a helpful educational tool increase students' motivation. The study was based on several streaming videos created as supporting material for learning and used by 45 students in the Department of Social Sciences, Syarif Hidayatullah Islamic State University, Jakarta. This research explains these various areas and provides innovative ways learning tools that can be used and emphasizes the skills developed in every application. Lastly, it presents the impact results use of videos on student motivation.

## 1 INTRODUCTION

E-learning has recently become a promising alternative to traditional classroom learning, helping society move towards a vision of lifelong and on-demand learning (Zhang et al. 2004). It has become one of the fastest moving trends (Wang 2003) and aims to provide a configurable infrastructure that integrates learning materials, tools, and services into a single solution to create and deliver training or educational content quickly, effectively, and economically (Ong & Wang 2004). Thousands of online courses are now offered. Not only are instructional materials made available on the Internet but online collaborative learning and discussion can also take place. Videos are a rich and powerful medium used in e-learning. It can present information in an attractive and consistent manner. Previous studies have investigated the effect of instructional videos on learning outcomes (Sorensen & Baylen 1999).

However, the instructional videos used in the early studies were mainly broadcasted via TV programs or stored on CD-ROMs. The linear nature of the video instructions produced inconsistent results (Kozma 1986). Recent advances in multimedia and communication technology have resulted in robust learning systems with instructional video components. The emergence of non-linear interactive digital video technology allows students to interact with learning videos. This can increase learner engagement, and thereby increase learning effectiveness. The main "media attribute" of interactive video is random access to video content (Salomon et al. 1991) — the user can select or play a segment with minimal search time. This concept is not new but takes a new form. However, the effect of interactive video on e-learning is still not well understood.

Instructional tools for delivering material to learners have increased since the conception of the Internet and the World Wide Web (WWW or Web). Students now have greater access to teaching materials that have been traditionally distributed in the classroom. Materials such as lecture notes, communication tools, assignments, visual graphics, etc. are now easily available via the internet. In addition, the Internet can provide a media-rich environment such as digital video (Garrison 2001). With advances in network software and technology, digital video streaming on the Internet has become easier and more effective.

Streaming media, such as video and audio, can help students understand complex concepts and procedures that are difficult to explain using just text and graphics (Klass 2003). This capability is important for distance learning as most online courses still use text-based material to convey instruction, and multimedia can add interactivity to this stagnant text-based material (Michelich 2002). Most online courses today lack creativity and/or interactivity when it comes to delivering instructional materials. There is a cognitive belief that the addition of multimedia can help improve and enhance students' learning processes because they see concepts in action [10]. By using visual and auditory messages, students can process information more quickly, which in turn, helps promote the acquisition of material in their learning. The old adage that "a picture is worth a thousand words" applies in this case because moving images add authenticity and reality to the context of learning (Joint Information System Committee 2002). Face-to-face video contexts engage students, and can effectively capture cultural contexts to enhance learning experiences (Stilbore & MacGibbon 2001). In addition, moving pictures can help students visualize a process or see how something works. Videos can take information or tacit knowledge that may be too difficult to describe in text into clear and clear descriptions through the use of images. In addition, videos have a visual appeal that can evoke emotional reactions from students which will help in increasing motivation (Stilbore & MacGibbon 2001). With these benefits in mind, video streaming is a new opportunity for educators to bring online courses to life.

It is widely accepted that student motivation is a key element in the learning process (Pintrich 1999). Existing educational literature has proven the positive effects of using new technology as a support tool to increase learning efficacy (Barford & Weston 1997; Targamadza & Petrauskiene 2010). This technology attracts students' attention when students get used to it and they can easily use this tool.

Among these tools, video has been used "off-line" for many years to support student learning in a variety of settings (Green et al. 2003). Today, a new concept called "low-cost educational video" has been defined as a short demonstration stream video that has a very specific purpose and has been created in a very short time, with few resources and which can be incorporated or embedded in other material or course (Simo et al. 2010). This kind of video enables lecturers to eliminate a large number of common problems associated with video, such as the required resources (both budget and time), which are reduced, the simplification of the video enhancement process, and the possibility to efficiently fit videos into courses according to the lecturer paradigm. This shows that learning is created from the interaction between motivation and cognitive variables (Valle et al. 2003). Authors analyzing the use of video streaming as a learning tool have focused their research efforts on analyzing the advantages and disadvantages of using this new technological tool (Fernandez & Sallan 2009; McKinney & Page 2009; Palmer 2007). However, none of these studies qualitatively examined the effect of using these tools on student motivation. In-depth analysis of these effects can help lecturers develop content that is compatible with the new technology, which in addition to meeting the objectives of understanding education, independent and efficient learning must also exploit the full potential of motivation, as one of the most important factors for obtaining positive results in the learning process.

This research mainly focused on investigating the impact of interactive video on e-learning effectiveness through an empirical study. Learning by asking (LBA), a multimedia based e-learning system, integrates multimedia instructional material including video lectures, PowerPoint slides, and lecture notes.

## 2 MATERIALS AND METHODS

Our research design uses data from open-ended questions a list of questions. The research was conducted with one course of three different classes: Department of Social Sciences, Faculty of Tarbiya and Teaching Trainer taught full-distance, at Syarif Hidayatullah Islamic State University, Jakarta, Indonesia. The purpose of this study is to identify positive and negative aspects associated with the use of low-cost educational videos in learning process in order to gain a better understanding of the effects of this innovative learning tool. This research conducted during the 2020/2021 academic year during the Covid-19 pandemic by introducing cheap educational videos with high graphic content and a duration time of approximately 5.5 minutes. Videos focused specific content or techniques from a specific subject, as for example, a video about the management of classes for the subject of micro-teaching or a video about competitiveness conceptualizations used in strategic management classes. These videos were broadcasted in various ways, such as web integrated using the university's teaching platform (based on google classroom), or through the YouTube channel for later reproduction. The questionnaires are intended to clarify pedagogical purposes pursued in each session. Each interview took place approximately 30 minutes. Next, data was taken from these interviews and from that, we developed a questionnaire which includes two open-ended questions, so that students can express their opinion about the positive and negative aspects related to use of video as a learning tool.

The questionnaires were distributed to 45 students, who were undertaking different subjects and different degrees. Data are categorized and codified according to interpretation and reduction of data regarding effects use of low-cost educational videos to motivate students. This study follows a whole grounded theory process for data coding and analysis, including theoretical sampling (Fend & Sachs 2008). Code was developed incrementally during the first phase of the data memory. The data are validated during the second stage interview. Following the suggestion of Miles and Huberman (1994), first we transcribed the data coming from the questionnaire and further obtained data from the interviews. Next, we analyzed the results and discuss any differences until we reach a consensus, after multiple iterations. In this work, we present relevant student quotes to illustrate the effect of video on student motivation.

## 3 RESULTS

Our exploratory analysis reveals that participants' opinions emphasize that low-cost video is an innovative teaching a tool that has a positive effect on student motivation. These effects are discussed and described in the following sections. For this purpose, we present several applications and the results obtained some of the subjects involved in this experiment were based on use of low-cost video. These results were further analyzed. These data were based on the results of a questionnaire distributed to 40 respondents with 15 questions each for each indicator. There are three indicators used as aspects of the assessment, namely (1) Student learning motivation; (2) Student achievement; and (3) Understanding and using learning technology (video learning). The three indicators are to determine the relationship between motivation, student achievement, and teaching media and technology, especially video media, in learning teaching tool. The following assessment indicators are given in Table 1.

Several students decided to present their final project video instead of a written document followed by a verbal presentation. They believe that videos make it possible for them to more

Table 1. Assessment indicators in distributing questionnaires.

| No. | Assessment aspects | Indicator | No. item questions | **Total** |
|---|---|---|---|---|
| 1 | By utilizing learning technology, it is able to complete work and assignments quickly. | Understanding and using learning technology (video learning) | 1–15 | 15 |
| 2 | The use of technology-based learning media in learning media subjects attracts attention so that it fosters interest in learning. | Student's motivation to study | 1–15 | 15 |
| 3 | Utilizing learning technology so that in the learning media course the learning outcomes get satisfactory grades. | Student achievement | 1–15 | 15 |

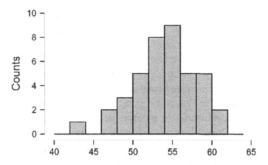

Figure 1. The video usages among students.

efficiently explain some parts of their job. Students also commented via video from lecturers that videos give them better feedback than via email if the complicated problem of technology has been resolved. Based on the results of questionnaires distributed to students, student motivation was 35.09% while student achievement based on test results was 85%, which was favorable. While students' knowledge of learning technology was 52.07%, a percentage of the students considered that the use of teaching media, especially video, was supportive of learning achievement in-class lectures, especially in social studies for learning media subjects. Descriptive analysis shows the mean of using video 54.55 with a standard deviation of 4.01, and student motivation in taking social studies learning media was 56.27, with a standard deviation of 3.78 and the mean of student achievement in social studies learning media lectures is 51.82, with a standard deviation of 3.054.

Based on the results of questionnaires distributed to students, student motivation was 35.09% while student achievement based on test results was 85%, which was favorable. While students' knowledge of learning technology was 52.07%, a high percentage of students considered that the use of teaching media, especially video, was very supportive of learning achievement in-class lectures, especially in social studies for learning media subjects. Descriptive analysis shows the mean of using video was 54.55, with a standard deviation of 4.01, and student motivation in taking social studies using learning media was 56.27, with standard deviations of 3.78. The mean of student achievement in social studies learning media lectures is 51.82, with a standard deviation of 3.054. This shows that students' motivation to learn by using learning media is significant (Figure 1).

## 4  DISCUSSION

Motivation in an academic context has been defined as the motivational value of the content itself without providing external incentives to push participation (Rieber 1991). In the context of knowledge economics, Marx and Frost (1998) suggested that video can be strong motivators and context-setters for student learning, quoting the example of Martin Luther King "I have a dream" speech or the Challenger shuttle disaster. Moreover, most educational experts agree that videos are best shown briefly segment to maximize learner concentration. A student stated:

> "The videos are entertaining and help me learn some technical concepts which difficult to understand without a graphical representation".

Most of the students used the allocated space to fill positive aspects regarding using videos to thank professors for their efforts to prepare the video. By using different tools for presenting content, the lecturers succeeded in improving intrinsic motivation and encourage them to increase its learning outcomes. As a student explains:

> "The use of various learning tools such as videos, PowerPoint presentations and scientific papers shows the lecturers' interest in supporting and improving the student learning process".

Sellani and Harrington (2002) emphasized that motivated students can access videos in their own time. Therefore, teaching tools should approach students from an angle that seems interesting and relevant to them. The Lecturer in Materials Technology explained that "videos facilitate the assimilation of content, thereby increasing the efficiency of the learning process. In terms of motivation, the fact that after watching a video in class, students send me a video that complements the subject matter is clear evidence of their motivation and involvement".

According to Shephard (2003), students should also be encouraged to learn actively from videos, by "interacting" with them. In this regard, a lecturer stated that: "The video I used worked very well because this course was divided into several techniques and then divided into smaller sections. Because of these features, I created a short video explaining this fragment of information. It was also happy to see students watching this video on their cell phones".

These words motivate the lecturers to make more videos especially on quantitative subjects where students have difficulty understanding certain solutions to these problems. Some mathematical methods lecturers argue that videos reinforces traditional step-by-step based explanations a spreadsheet. The biggest advantage is that students can play the video as often as they think is necessary to understand problem solving. This type of video demonstration works very well with students. Apart from conveying their congratulations, students also asked the lecturer to make more videos, emphasizing that the videos supported the learning process, by providing complementary material. Some of the lecturers observed that in the sessions where they used video, students' doubts lessened. This requires them to create a "material block" for each session, which includes both basic and complementary material, as well as videos related to the topic to be covered. "Continuum mechanics" lecturers conducted a survey of student opinions regarding the use of video on the university's virtual campus.

## REFERENCES

Barford and C. Weston (1997). The use of video as a teaching resource in a new university. *British Journal of Educational Technology*, vol. 28, pp. 40–50.

Fend and W. Sachs (2008). Grounded theory method in management research. *Organizational Research Methods*, vol. 11, pp. 430–455.

Fernandez, P. Simo and J.M. Sallan (2009). Podcasting: A new technological tool to facilitate good practice in higher education. *Computers & Education*, vol. 53, pp. 385–392.

Garrison, W. (2001). Video streaming into the mainstream. *Journal of Audiovisual Media in Medicine*, vol. 24(4), pp. 174–178.

Green, D. Voegeli, M. Harrison, J. Phillips, J. Knowles, M. Weaver, and K. Shephard (2003). Evaluating the use of streaming video to support student learning in a first-year life sciences course for student nurses. *Nurse Education Today*, vol. 23, pp. 255–261.

Joint Information Systems Committee (2002). *Video streaming: A guide for educational development.* Manchester, UK: JISC Click and Go Video Project.

Klass, B. (2003). Streaming media in higher education: Possibilities and pitfalls. *Syllabus* vol. 16(11).

Kozma (1986). Implications of instructional psychology for the design of educational television. *Educational Communication and Technology*, vol. 34(1), pp. 11–19.

Marx and P.J. Frost (1998). Toward optimal use of video in management education: examining the evidence. *Journal of Management Development*, vol. 17, pp. 243–250.

McKinney and K. Page (2009). Podcasts and video streaming: Useful tools to facilitate learning of pathophysiology in undergraduate nurse education? *Nurse Education in Practice*, vol. 9, pp. 372–376.

Michelich, V. (2002). Streaming media to enhance teaching and improve learning. *The Technology Source.* Retrieved from http://ts.mivu.org/default.asp?show=article&id=941

Miles and A.M. Huberman (1994). An Expanded Sourcebook Qualitative Data Analysis. Sage Publications, London.

Ong, J.-Y. Lai and Wang (2004). Factors affecting engineers' acceptance of asynchronous e-learning systems in high-tech companies. *Information & Management*, vol. 41(6), pp. 795–804.

Palmer (2007). An evaluation of streaming digital video resources in on and off-campus engineering management education. *Computers & Education*, vol. 49, pp. 297–308.

Pintrich (1999). The role of motivation in promoting and sustaining self regulated learning. *International Journal of Educational Research*, vol. 31, pp. 459–470.

Rieber (1991). Animation, incidental learning, and continuing motivation. *Journal of Educational Psychology*, vol. 83, pp. 318–328.

Salomon, D. Perkins and T. Globerson (1991). Partners in cognition: extending human intelligence with intelligent technologies. *Educational Researcher*, vol. 20(3), pp. 2–9.

Sellani and W. Harrington (2002). Addressing administrator/faculty conflict in an academic online environment. *Internet and Higher Education*, vol. 5, pp. 131–145.

Shephard (2003). Questioning, promoting and evaluating, the use of streaming video to support student learning. *British Journal of Educational Technology*, vol. 34, pp. 295–308.

Simo, V. Fernandez, I. Algaba, N. Salan, M. Enache and M. Albareda-Sambola (2010). Video stream and teaching channels: quantitative analysis of the use of low-cost educational videos on the web. Procedia Social and Behavioral Sciences, vol. 2, pp. 2937–2941.

Sorensen, D.M. and Baylen (1999). Interaction in interactive television instruction: perception versus reality, in: *Proceedings of the Annual Meeting of the American Educational Research Association*, Montreal, Quebec, Canada.

Stilbore, L., & MacGibbon, P. (2001). *Video/video conferencing in support of distance education*. Retrieve, from http://www.col.org/Knowledge/ks_videoconferencing.htm

Targamadze and R. Petrauskiene (2010). Impact of information technologies on modern learning. *Information Technology and Control*, vol. 39, pp. 169–175.

Valle, R. Cabanach, J. Nunez, J. Gonzalez-Pienda, S. Rodriguez and I. Pineiro (2003). Cognitive, motivational, and volitional dimensions of learning. *Research in Higher Education*, vol. 44, pp. 557–580.

Wang (2003). Assessment of learner satisfaction with asynchronous electronic learning systems. *Information & Management*, vol. 41(1), pp. 75–86.

Zhang, J.L. Zhao, L. Zhou and J. Nunamaker (2004). Can e-learning replace traditional classroom learning— evidence and implication of the evolving e-learning technology. *Communications of the ACM*, vol. 47(5), pp. 75–79.

# An investigation of scientific argumentation skills by using analogical mapping-based on inquiry learning for junior high school

D. Diniya, A. Ilhami, I. Mahartika, N.D. Susilawati & P. Permana
*Universitas Islam Negeri Sultan Syarif Kasim Riau, Indonesia*

N. Hermita
*Universitas Riau, Indonesia*

D. Sulistiowati
*SMP Negeri 13 Bandung, Indonesia*

ABSTRACT: One essential focus of science learning in the 21st century is not only enhancing mastery of science concepts but also improving communication skills. Developing great communication skills is a critical part of contribution to the community. As well, such scientific communication could be demonstrated through argumentative discourse activities and the shift in emphasis on science learning is also related to inquiry learning. In this regard, the current research project was carried out to acquire depth information about the influence on students' scientific argumentation whether delivered through analogical mapping-based on inquiry learning or without analogical mapping-based. Besides using the quasi-experimental method, the present study also employed a pre-test and post-test control group design. The intended participants on the current research project were students of grade VIII in SMPN Bandung, consisted of 68 students, divided into a control experimental class of 34 students for each class. Students in the experimental class received inquiry-based learning with analogies and control class students are received inquiry-based learning without analogies on the selected subject themes such as vibration, waves, and sound. As a matter of fact, the argumentation skills were measured by an essay test consisted of 4 question items. The data analysis technique used was the t-test. The result obtained in this line of research demonstrated that the means differences for student argumentation skills are 0.005. There was a significant difference between mean increases in a selected class taught by using the inquiry model of analogical mapping-based. As suggestions for improvement such as image analogy could be varied with video.

## 1 INTRODUCTION

The shift in emphasis on science learning that characterizes learning in the 21st century is the use of information, computing, technology, and communication (Alpusari et al. 2019; Azriani et al. 2019; Handayani et al. 2019; Hermita et al. 2018; Mahbubah et al. 2020; Malik et al. 2018; Sapriadil et al. 2018; Suhandi et al. 2017, 2018). Communication skills can be demonstrated through argumentation skills (Alexaindre & Rodriguez 2000). The argumentation skills received special attention from many educational researchers (Redmond & Lock 2019; Rupnik n.d.). Most importantly, argumentation is considered necessarily important in education because it is consistent with the purpose of education in general, to encourage students to take reasons for their related problems or issues (Alexaindre & Rodriguez 2000). Gultepe and Kose (2016) similarly take this broad view, noting, modern reform in science education seeks to highlight the context, activities, and scientific conversation. Scientific conversation in the form of argumentation is especially important because it is considered able to improve understanding and changing the understanding

DOI 10.1201/9781003219248-21

of science Scientific argumentation is one of the criteria used to assess students and has been emphasized in the National Standards for science education. Berland and Hammer (2012) also portray that in recent years, scientific arguments have been widely recognized as crucial practices in science education because they encourage students to be actively involved to generate ideas and questions through processes that produce resemblances with practices. McNeill and Pimentel (2010) state this argument as the main mediator for accessing knowledge.

Based on observations in one of the junior high schools in Bandung, it was found that there was argumentation during the learning process in the classroom activity. However, students in certain instances are still difficult in elaborating strong arguments for their claims. In this respect, the teacher has received considerable attention to involving other alternatives, such as analogy. Based on findings in line with this research shows that the ability of students to provide arguments is still low. It was found that the lack of students' argumentative skills can be viewed from how students accomplish the argumentation steps during learning. The difficult step of argumentation for students is constructing a scientific argument in science. Students still have not received attention to scientific evidence while making scientific reasoning. Students have difficulty in collecting and writing scientific facts or evidence that can support claims hence arguments can be said to be theoretically correct (Evagorou & Osborne 2013; Handayani et al. 2015; Heng et al. 2015). Also, a lot of students still use emotional or personal arguments, forming a situation "type of win-win debate" during the argumentation activity (Lin & Hung 2016).

Their difficulties in constructing arguments will guide them to misunderstand the concept of science. In regards to the research of Heng, Surif, and Seng (Heng et al. 2015) noting that if students incorrectly construct arguments it will lead to misconceptions, and therefore innovative ideas in learning are necessary to support argumentation activities and reduce misconceptions. The Ministry of Education and Culture (Kemendikbud 2017) states that science is one of the important foundations in nation-building. Through science learning students are expected to fulfill the ability of learning and innovation skills that include thinking skills and problem-solving skills, creativity and innovation, as well as able to communicate and collaborate. Therefore, science learning should be directed to train communication and collaboration skills for long-term community contribution. Based on the background described, the researcher is concerned to examine further the comparison of scientific argumentation skills of students between the experimental class and the control class through analogical mapping-based on inquiry learning.

## 2 METHOD

An illustration of the improvement inability to master concepts and arguments assisted by the analogical mapping is obtained by using the quasi-experimental approach with the design of pre-test post-test control group design (Table 1).

The population in the current study are all students of class VIII in one of the Bandung Junior High Schools. The selection of samples in this study was taken through a purposive sampling technique, deliberate sample selection. The test instrument used in this study was a test of the ability of scientific argumentation. The test given is in the form of 4 items with each sub-question 4 items.

Table 1. Research design; pre-test post-test control group design.

| Group | Pretest | Treatment | Posttest |
|---|---|---|---|
| *Treatment group* | O | X | O |
| *Control group* | O | C | O |

X→: inquiry-based learning with analogies.
C→: inquiry-based learning without analogies.
O→: students' scientific argumentative skills.

These sub-questions contain claim, data, warrant, and backing as the argumentation indicators based on Toulmin's argumentation. The mastery test of the ability of scientific argumentation is given at the beginning and end of learning.

The validity test used in this study is content validity and empirical validity. For content validity, the instrument judgments were conducted by four competent experts in their respective fields, three expert lecturers, and one science teacher for Junior High School. Judgments are carried out to seek whether the prepared instruments have been able to necessarily measure. Experts were asked to provide responses related to the instrument and provide overall comments on the scope of the instrument content. After the judging process by expert lecturers and teachers in the field of science subject, the matter of the instruments of scientific argumentation skills was tested. Afterward, the empirical validity value will be calculated. To perform the normality test using the Kolmogorov-Smirnov test. If the data is normally distributed, the next step is to do a homogeneity test with Levene's Test. If the data is homogeneous, then the data analysis technique is performed in the form of a two-difference test mean pre-test data using the T-test.

## 3   RESULT AND DISCUSSION

The comparison of the mean value of the pre-test, post-test, and normalized gain between the control class and the experimental class is shown in Table 2.

Based on Table 2, it can be seen that both classes have increased the average scientific argumentation. The control class got an average score of 26.96 in the pre-test, which then increased to 66.42. The amount of increase (gain) generated by the control class was 39.46. Based on this table, it can also be seen that the average value of the experimental class is greater than the control class. The experimental class got an average value for the initial test of 23.71 and the final test of 78.43. The amount of the increase (gain) value of the experimental class was 54.72.

The amount of the increase in value (gain) is shown in Table 2 that the two classes experienced almost the same increase does not reflect the achievement of almost the same abilities as well. Therefore, a high gain value or a low gain value does not necessarily reflect high or low student ability. However, the N-gain value can indicate ability achievement. Therefore, seeing the improvement is not enough to be used as a benchmark so that it can be said that the use of normalized gain values is better than using gain data. The recapitulation average of normalized gain value or N-gain for the two classes can be seen in Table 3.

Based on Table 3, it can be seen that the two classes have increased the ability of scientific argumentation. Increasing the ability of scientific argumentation in the control class is included in the medium category while the experimental class is included in the high category. After calculating the two N-gain mean test in the control class and the experimental class, it was found that both classes experienced an increase in the ability of scientific argumentation between students who took science learning with an inquiry model assisted by analogy mapping and without the assistance of inquiry. However, it is not yet known the difference in the average increase in the ability of scientific argumentation between the two classes, so it is necessary to test the difference in the average increase in the two classes.

Table 2.   Data mean value of pre-test and post-test of scientific argument ability.

| Component | Class | | | | | |
| | Control | | | Experiment | | |
| | Pre-test | Post-test | N-Gain | Pre-test | Post-Test | N-gain |
| --- | --- | --- | --- | --- | --- | --- |
| Average | 26.96 | 66.42 | 0.53 | 23.71 | 78.43 | 0.70 |
| Standard deviation | 8.20 | 16.48 | | 15.57 | 9.83 | |

Table 3. N-gain value (<g>) of scientific argument ability between control class and experiment class students.

Scientific argumentation skill

| Class | N | <g> | Criteria |
|---|---|---|---|
| Control | 34 | 0.53 | Medium |
| Experiment | 34 | 0.70 | High |

Table 4. Results of the N-gain normality test for scientific argument ability in the control class and experiment class.

| Class | N | Shapiro Wilk ($\alpha = 005$) | |
|---|---|---|---|
| | | Sig $\alpha$ | Information |
| Control | 34 | 0.047 | Not normal |
| Experiment | 34 | 0.198 | Normal |

Table 5. Test results of means difference increase on students scientific argumentation.

| Statistic test | Asymp. sig. (2-tailed) | Conclusion |
|---|---|---|
| Mann-Whitney U test | 0.005 | There are differences in the average increase in scientific argumentation skills of the control class and the experimental class |

In Table 4 it can be seen that based on the normality test with the number of subjects 34 students and a confidence level of 0.95 in the control class, it has a significant value of $0.047 < 0.05$. So it can be concluded that the normalized average gain valuable data in the control class is not normally distributed. In the experimental class with several subjects 34 students and a confidence level of 0.95, a significance value of $0.198 > 0.05$ was obtained. The following are the results of the calculation of the Mann-Whitney U test.

Based on Table 5, the acquisition of the Sig. (2-tailed) of 0.005 for the confidence level of 0.95, which means $0.005 < 0.05$. Therefore, H0 is rejected and Ha is accepted. Based on results obtained in this line of research, it is therefore argued that there are significant differences in the increase of scientific argumentation skills between students who have received inquiry based-learning with analogies and students who have received inquiry based-learning without analogies mapping in the selected topics such as vibration, wave, and sound. This means that learning models assisted by analogical mapping can improve students' scientific argumentation skills.

The argumentation indicators are divided into four parts, namely claims, data/evidence, support, and justification. The comparison of N-gain for each argumentation indicator in detail can be seen in Figure 1.

Based on Figure 1, it can be seen that almost every argumentation indicator in the two classes has increased. In the control class, the highest increase was in the support indicator of 61% followed by the claims indicator by 55%, and the data increased by 50%. The indicator that experienced the lowest increase was the justification indicator, which was 49%. In the experimental class, the claim indicator experienced the highest increase, namely 86%, followed by a support indicator of 67%. The data and justification indicators have the same magnitude of the increase, namely 61%.

The findings of this study are in line with the findings made by Emig (2014) that students' argumentative abilities are strongly supported by mastery of concepts possessed by students. In accordance with the results of Samara's research (Samara 2016) that the use of analogies in learning would help students to relate new information to the prior knowledge of the student. The use of

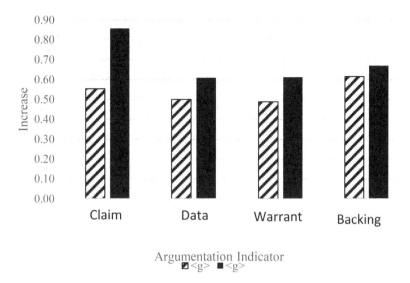

Figure 1. Percentage diagram of the results of increasing the ability of scientific argumentation on each argumentation indicator.

analogies can also help students integrate information with one another. Students who can connect a concept with other concepts through analogy will make the student able to explain the concept well.

In accordance with the results of research by Samara (2011, p. 73) that the use of analogy in learning will help students connect new information to the prior knowledge of these students. The use of analogies can also help students integrate information with one another. Students who are able to relate a concept to another concept through analogy will enable the student to explain the concept well. Each class experienced an increase in argumentation because during early learning, in accordance with inquiry learning, students would be faced with problems that exist in the real world (Avsec & Kocijancic 2014). It is also in line with the statements of several researchers (Duran & Dokme 2016; Kelly 2013; Server & Guven 2014) who state that inquiry-based learning is an approach in which there are activities to ask questions, view information, and find new ideas related to events. This shows that inquiry-based learning requires students to find solutions to these problems through investigative activities and providing scientific reasons and using critical thinking skills when combining scientific knowledge and processes to generate a perception of science (Avsec & Kocijancic 2014; Duran 2016). However, related to inquiry learning assisted by analogy mapping used in learning will greatly assist students in proposing arguments.

Although in the first syntax on inquiry learning students are also given the same issue, the experimental class students who can answer questions discussions with the correct concept in accordance with the theory. If so, of course, the use of analogy is quite effective in developing students' understanding of scientific concepts in accordance with research showing that analogy also helps students remember in the long term against new things learned (Sharma & Rawatee Maharaj 2012). Harrison and Coll (2013, p. 26) state that the use of several analogies will be more effective in building knowledge. In line with the results of the study Rahmawati et al. (2016, p. 109) stated that one of the advantages of analogy is that students can construct the concept very well after gave the analogy through the Student Worksheet (LKS), and discussion group. Thus, of course, when answering discussion questions, the experimental class students can answer them correctly because they have mastered the concept well.

Chui and Lin (2005, p. 4) also investigate how the analogy can improve science learning in the classroom. This is evidenced by the results of his research that the use of analogies can improve students' understanding of concepts. Coupled with the use of analogy mapping which makes it

163

easier for students to find similarities between the parts of teaching aids and hearing aids in humans. The same fact to the research conducted by Fathurohman (2014, pp. 74 & 77) that the use of analogy visualization can also prevent misconceptions. Problems nature of abstract concepts can be addressed using learning model, or the media as a model.

The argument component of Toulmin (1958) was adjusted by McNeill and Krajcik (2011) with the student's ability to understand the meaning of each component, and produced 4 argument components, namely: claim, evidence, reasoning, and rebuttal. A claim is an idea, conclusion, hypothesis, or opinion on an event or phenomenon. Evidence is evidence used to support a claim. The reasoning is the reason given for relating evidence to the claim. The ability of students to determine predictions or solutions to problems is closely related to determining claims on the argumentation indicators. The ability of students to relate claims with facts is one of students' ability to construct arguments that are classified into warrant (justification). The quality of the argument can be determined by adding supporting facts and adding examples of reality. Argumentation is an important ability because in arguing, students compile attitudes to agree or disagree with the opinions of others (Lin & Hung 2016, p. 132). There are other advantages of the inquiry model assisted by analogy mapping group discussions that happen during the investigation will be able to develop communication skills in the form of argumentation skills. Discussion activities were also found to increase students' level of critical thinking, helping students improve their ability to make connections between statements and facts (Avsec dan Kocijancic 2014; Duran 2016, p. 2888; Kelly 2013; Zuiker dan Whitake 2014).

The advantages of inquiry learning models assisted by analogy mapping are that students can find new knowledge independently through investigative activities on problems presented through analogy mapping. Besides, researchers also state that the use of analogies allows for good results (Lin & Hung 2016, p. 132; Samara 2016). However, some things need to be considered in the use of analogies. The thing that must be considered is that students must focus on the concepts taught not by the analogy that will be formed. An analogy is only a medium so students can understand the concepts being taught. Learning through analogy students can overcome misconceptions but teachers need to direct students to master the concept not only focus on the use of analogies.

4 CONCLUSION

As already figured out in the findings above, it is therefore concluded that further efforts should be made for there is a significant difference between the increase of students' scientific argumentation skills taught by the inquiry model of assisted by analogical mapping and students taught by inquiry model without the aid of analogical mapping.

REFERENCES

Alexaindre, J. and Rodriguez, A. B. (2000). Doing the Lesson or Doing Science: Argument in High School Genetics (New York: John Wiley & Sons, Inc).

Alpusari, M., Mulyani, E. A., Putra, Z. H., Widyanthi, A., and Hermita, N. (2019). Identifying Students' Scientific Communication Skills on Vertebrata Organs. Journal of Physics: Conference Series, 1351(1). https://doi.org/10.1088/1742-6596/1351/1/012070

Azriani, N., Islami, N., Hermita, N., Nor, M., Syaodih, E., Handayani, H., …Samsudin, A. (2019). Implementing inquiry learning model to improve primary school students' critical thinking on earth and universe concept. Journal of Physics: Conference Series, 1227(1). https://doi.org/10.1088/1742-6596/1227/1/012033

Berland, L. K. and Hammer, D. (2012). Framing for Scientific Argumentation. Wiley: Journal of Research in Science Teaching, 49, 68–94.

Emig, B. dkk. (2014). Inviting Argument by Analogy: Analogical-Mapping-Based Comparison Activities as a Scaffold for Small-Group Argumentation. Wiley: Science Education Journal, 98, 243–268. DOI 10.1002/sce.21096.

Evagorou, M. and Osborne, J. (2013). Exploring Young Students' Collaborative Argumentation Within a Socioscientific Issue. Journal of Research in Science Teaching, 50, 209–237.

Fraenkel Wallen and Hyun. (2012). How to Design and Evaluate Research in Education (Eight Edition) (New York: McGraw Hill International Edition).

Gultepe, N. and Kose, M. (2016). Which is More Effective: In Groups or as Individuals. (Preprint https://www.researchgate.net/publication/303820799_WHICH_IS_MORE_EFFECTIVE_IN_GROUPS_ OR_AS_INDIVIDUALS pada 5 Desember 2017).

Handayani, H., Sopandi, W., Syaodih, E., Suhandi, A., Maftuh, B., Hermita, N., …Samsudin, A. (2019). Comprehension of in-service primary-science teachers toward 21st century skills: A case study on Purwakarta. Journal of Physics: Conference Series, 1157(4). https://doi.org/10.1088/1742-6596/1157/4/042130

Handayani, P. and Murniati Sardianto, M. S. (2015). Analisis Argumentasi Peserta Didik Kelas X SMA Muhammadiyah 1 Palembang dengan Menggunakan Model Argumentasi Toulmin. E-journal Universitas Srwijaya.

Heng, L. L., Surif, J. and Seng, C. H. (2015). Malaysian Students' Scientific Argumentation: Do groups perform better than individuals? Routledge: International Journal of Science Education, 37, 505–528.

Hermita, N., Suhandi, A., Syaodih, E., Samsudin, A., Marhadi, H., Sapriadil, S., …Wibowo, F. C. (2018). Level conceptual change pre-service elementary teachers on electric current conceptions through visual multimedia supported conceptual change. Journal of Physics: Conference Series, 1013(1). https://doi.org/10.1088/1742-6596/1013/1/012060

Kaya, E., Erduran, S., and Cetin, P. S. (2012). Discourse, Argumentation, and Science Lessons: Match or Mismatch in High School Students' Perceptions and Understanding? Mevlana International Journal of Education (MIJE), 2(3), 1–32.

Kelly, Y. K. (2013). Integrating Direct and Inquiry Based Instruction in The Teaching of Critical Thinking. Springer, DOI: 10.1007/s11251-013-9279-0

Kemendikbud. (2017). Model Silabus Mata Pelajaran Sekolah Menengah Pertama dan Madrasah Tsanawiyah (Jakarta: Kemendikbud).

Lin, Y. R. and Hung, J. F. (2016). The Analysis and Reconciliation of Students' Rebuttals in Argumentation Activities. International Journal of Science Education, 38, 130–155.

Mahbubah, K., Habibulloh, M., Hermita, N., and Samsudin, A. (2020). Measuring Critical Thinking based Multimedia on Buoyant Force Concept: A Preliminary Design. Journal of Physics: Conference Series, 1655(1), 0–6. https://doi.org/10.1088/1742-6596/1655/1/012112

Malik, A., Setiawan, A., Suhandi, A., Permanasari, A., Dirgantara, Y., Yuniarti, H., …Hermita, N. (2018). Enhancing Communication Skills of Pre-service Physics Teacher through HOT Lab Related to Electric Circuit. Journal of Physics: Conference Series, 953(1). https://doi.org/10.1088/1742-6596/953/1/012017

McNeill, K. L. and Pimentel, D. S. (2010). Scientific Discourse in Three Urban Classrooms: The Role of The Teacher in Engaging High School Students in Argumentation. Science Education, 94, 203–229.

Sapriadil, S., Setiawan, A., Suhandi, A., Malik, A., Safitri, D., Lisdiani, S. A. S., and Hermita, N. (2018). Optimizing students' scientific communication skills through higher order thinking virtual laboratory (HOTVL). Journal of Physics: Conference Series, 1013(1). https://doi.org/10.1088/1742-6596/1013/1/012050

Server, D. and Guven, M. (2014). Effect of Inquiry Based Learning Approach on Student Resistance in A Science and Technology Course. Educational Science: Theory and Practice, 1414, 1601–1605. doi: 10.12738/estp.2014.4.1919

Sharma, R. M. (2011). An Examination of Types and Usefulness of Analogies Generated by Upper Primary School Students – A Case Study. Journal of the Science Teachers Association of Nigeria, 46, 8–19.

Shirley, S., Erduran, S. and Osborne, J. (2006). Learning to Teach Argumentation: Research and Development in The Science Classroom. International Journal of Science Education, 28, 235–260.

Suhandi, A., Hermita, N., Samsudin, A., Maftuh, B., and Coştu, B. (2017). Effectiveness of visual multimedia supported conceptual change texts on overcoming students' misconception about boiling concept. Turkish Online Journal of Educational Technology, 2017 (October Special Issue INTE).

Suhandi, A., Muslim, Samsudin, A., Hermita, N., and Supriyatman. (2018). Effectiveness of the use of question-driven levels of inquiry based instruction (QD-LOIBI) assisted visual multimedia supported teaching material on enhancing scientific explanation ability senior high school students. Journal of Physics: Conference Series, 1013(1). https://doi.org/10.1088/1742-6596/1013/1/012026

*Information technology in language education*

*Emerging Trends in Technology for Education in an Uncertain World – Nanto, Rahiem & Khalis Maryati (Eds)*
© 2022 copyright the Author(s), ISBN 978-1-032-11288-6

# The effectiveness of "Kahoot" in English teaching for elementary school students during the pandemic

S. Ratnaningsih, N. Wafiqni, S. Masyithoh & T. Suryaningsih
*Department of Elementary Education, Faculty of Educational Sciences, State Islamic University (UIN) Syarif Hidayatullah Jakarta, Jakarta, Indonesia*

Fahrurrozi
*Department of Elementary Education, Faculty of Educational Sciences, Jakarta State University, Jakarta, Indonesia*

Y. Rahayani
*Centre for Islamic Thought and Education (CITE), University of South Australia, Adelaide, Australia*

ABSTRACT:   The Covid-19 pandemic has evidently spread worldwide, and it has significantly affected the delivery of programs at the educational institutions at all levels. This study aims to determine the effectiveness of the ICT-based Kahoot media in English teaching and learning for elementary school students during the Covid-19 pandemic. The research employs correlational research method by using regression analysis and correlation to analyze and test the hypothesis. The tests are used to measure English learning outcomes by using ICT-based Kahoot media and questionnaires are used to measure learning motivation. This study reveals that media ICT Kahoot could improve students learning motivation and learning outcomes of English in Elementary School in Jakarta. Thus, using ICT Kahoot media in learning English for elementary school improve students' learning achievement.

*Keywords*:   Kahoot, English Teaching for Elementary School Students, Covid-19 Pandemic

## 1   INTRODUCTION

Since the first outbreak in December 2019, the global community was hit by Covid-19 virus which has created significant changes in very aspects of life, including educational institutions (Chandu & Dasari 2020). When the virus was first detected Indonesia, the government established various regulations to slow the progress of transmission from sufferers to healthy population. One of the regulations and safety protocols to address the Covid-19 pandemic is to observe social/physical distancing.

Social/physical distancing is an approach to break the chain of spreading the virus. This approach is reinforced by research conducted in America which shows that social distancing could save more than 1 million lives (Khaitan et al. 2020). In Jakarta, many schools were closed since February until further notice. The extensive number of school closure in Indonesia has forced teachers to adjust their teaching delivery to include the use of technology to introduce online learning.

As one of the subjects that learned in school, English that taught by using online media have to be adapted. Because they are not done face-to-face, English skills must be taught using contextual methods so that they can achieve learning goals. In recent years, English teaching methods by using online media have been researched and found some significant impacts to the students. Some of the online teaching methods using online platform to deliver the material and achieving the learning goals. Kahoot is one game-based learning platform that using ICT especially online media to analyze the knowledge of students and to assess the students (Wang & Tahir 2020). The content that include in Kahoot become popular and inspire many students to join in that platform because it is fun, modern, and contextual (Wang et al. 2016). It is appropriate with the ideal circumstance of students in elementary school that needs playful learning material to make young learners enjoy the lesson.

An online learning in elementary schools shows several obstacles from the perspective of students, teachers and parents (see, for example, Hart et al. 2019). Children tend to feel bored with routines of monotonous tasks with inadequate facilities. It means the basic resources needed to support the learning. Whereas for teachers, online teaching is challenging as they need to adapt to new ways of teaching and how to make a most of it. Moreover, for parents, one of the challenges in moving to online learning arrangements on a wide scale is the variability in the capacity of parents to support their children's learning. In fact, many parent are not be well placed to support their children for variety reasons. New learning mode has added tasks to parents to supervise their children. This also means additional expenses to provide facilities such as internet connection to engage in the new learning mode. These issues have led the teachers to find out some strategies address them in order to achieve the learning goals.

This study aims to determine the effectiveness of the ICT Kahoot media in learning English for elementary school students in the Jakarta during the Covid-19 pandemic. This is an attempt to facilitate successful learning for elementary school students even though the activities are carried out online and from students' own homes.

## 2 LITERATURE REVIEW

A number of studies conducted in the US and Canada pointed out that the success in learning from home depend of the quality of the learners itself (see, for example, Bernard et al. 2004; Bettinger & Loeb 2017; Heppen et al. 2017). Successful online learners tend to have interest or basic skills in technology for making best use of the medium associated with online learning. The students who have independent and self-directed characteristics most likely to succeed. This study will have a look closely to Kahoot as an ICT based media in facilitating students' learning in elementary schools in Jakarta during the Covid-19 pandemic. The use of ICT Kahoot is one of the alternative media to conduct meaningful learning that make students interest to ask and enjoy the learning (Boden et al. 2018).

A literature review by Wang and Tahir specifically discussed about the effect of using Kahoot for learning that analyze 93 studies, which conclude Kahoot! have a positive effect on learning performance, classroom dynamics, students' and teachers' attitudes, and students' anxiety (Wang & Tahir 2020). Anandha et al. (2020) conducted another study related to the implementation of Kahoot as online media for English Vocabulary Teaching to the quadriplegic students The study result that Kahoot is an effective medium in English teaching so that students could memorize English Vocabulary. However, the research has lack of detail explanation in elaborating data and described in qualitative descriptive. Meanwhile, in this study, the result of Kahoot implementation will serve in quantitative data, which is provide more detail explanation on relationship between media ICT Kahoot, students' motivation and outcomes of English lesson in Elementary level.

A pleasant learning atmosphere for students to devote their time and attention fully to students with various strategies and interesting media that can be given to students in class (Plump & LaRosa 2017). Although Kahoot application limit the number of letters, it still give significant effect to learner (Correia & Santos 2017). Therefore, the role of educators as content creators must be able to develop questions and answers to quizzes as clear as possible to enable students accessing the quizzes easily and fun. To sum up, the application of Kahoot as ICT based media in elementary school in Jakarta enhance the students learning. And for those who use this media with high level motivation will provide significant impact on their learning outcomes.

Figure 1.  Kahoot home and features.

## 3  USED TOOLS

The Kahoot game motivates not only for students but also teachers. In order to use Kahoot in the classroom, teachers do not need to acquire specific skills in technology. The features can help teachers to make formative assessments on the development of students' vocabulary mastery abilities (Dellos 2015). Teachers can visit the Kahoot at the address https://kahoot.com, and create account by clicking the "Sign up" button or selecting the Log in button when the account has been successfully created. Figure 1 shows Kahoot home and features.

## 4  RESEARCH METHODS

The combination of two research approaches, which are quantitative and qualitative approach are used (Johns 2015) in this research. In quantitative method, the researchers use simple correlation test X1, X2, and Y, while interviews and participatory observation held in qualitative method.

### 4.1  *Participants*

The participants of this research were 10 teachers and 142 students of elementary school level in Jakarta.

### 4.2  *There are several stages in research method as follows*

*Preparation.* Firstly, the questionnaire are distributed to the teacher to find out the responses in English learning using ICT Kahoot media. To address the effectiveness of the learning, the researcher prepares and distribute teaching materials and learning media for one semester at the beginning of semester.

*Implementations.* The teacher implement English learning process with media ICT Kahoot in eight times meeting, then conducts the tests twice by using Kahoot feature. In this phase, the researchers conduct the observation while the implementation of media ICT Kahoot.

*Data collection and analysis.* The data are collected by using test score, interviews with the participants and observation. Researchers use interview and observation sheets. This method is to determine respondents' experience with Kahoot. Additionally, the researcher uses quantitative analysis to identify the effectiveness of the implementation of Kahoot in the process of English learning to increase students' motivation and learning achievement.

## 5  RESULTS AND DISCUSSION

The perception of respondents in term of media ICT Kahoot in learning English were gained based on the analysis of questionnaire results. The results of questionnaire and interview shows that 99

Table 1. The relationship between media ICT Kahoot, X2 (learning motivation) and Y (learning outcomes).

Correlation

|  |  | X1 | X2 | Y |
|---|---|---|---|---|
| X1 | Pearson Correlation | 1 | .577** | .608** |
|  | Sig. (2-tailed) |  | .000 | .000 |
|  | N | 142 | 142 | 142 |
| X2 | Pearson Correlation | .576** | 1 | .736** |
|  | Sig. (2-tailed) |  | .000 | .000 |
|  | N | 142 | 142 | 142 |
| Y | Pearson Correlation | .608** | 759** | 1 |
|  | Sig. (2-tailed) |  | .000 | .000 |
|  | N | 142 | 142 | 142 |

Correlation is significant at the 0.01 level (2-tailed).

out of 142 respondents (70%) never use media ICT Kahoot in their English learning. Meanwhile, as many as 43 respondents or 30% stated that they had conducted the process of learning English using the ICT Kahoot media with their students online. The results indicates the relationship between variables.

The result for statistical calculations and ANOVA steps are described in detail. Simple correlation technique was used to test first and second hypothesis, while multiple regression techniques was used to test third hypothesis. The results of hypothesis testing in this study explained as follows:

The hypothesis is tested in order to know whether there is a correlation between media ICT Kahoot, learning motivation and learning outcomes of English in Elementary Schools in Jakarta.

The assumptions of the hypothesis are as follow:

Ho: $p = 0.05$
Ha: $p > 0.05$

Ho: There is no positive relationship between media ICT Kahoot, learning motivation and learning outcomes of English at Elementary Schools in Jakarta.

Ha: There is a positive relationship between media ICT Kahoot, learning motivation and learning outcomes of English at Elementary Schools in Jakarta.

The results of the research data will be presented as in Table 1.

Based on Table 1, it can be analyzed that:

The number of r value of ICT Kahoot media with students' learning motivation (X1–X2) is 0.577, which means the correlation between X1 variable and X2 variable. Meanwhile, The number of r value of ICT Kahoot media with English learning outcomes (X1-Y) is 0.608, which means there are correlation between X2 variable and Y variable.

Based on the result of statistical test on the correlation between media ICT Kahoot, learning motivation and learning outcomes of English, it means that Ho is rejected, while Ha is accepted. Thus, the hypothetical conclusion of the research is there is positive relationship between media ICT Kahoot, learning motivation and learning outcomes of English in Elementary School in Jakarta. Based on the result of data analysis, online learning by using ICT Kahoot media increase students' motivation. ICT Kahoot media encourage students to be more active in learning process. Besides, the teacher can also proficient in creating effective and fun learning in delivering the material (Chandu & Dasari 2020; Lime 2018).

Kahoot challenges students to answer questions faster and more accurately. Because each question uses time and there is a score for each correct answer. Therefore, Kahoot can spark student interest and motivation to continue learning (Hartanti 2019). Students will increase the ability to produce creative and innovative thinking (Plump & LaRosa 2017). Based on the results, the use of Media ICT Kahoot in the process of English learning influence students' critical thinking skill and creativity. Besides, students are able to make communication and collaboration among their community.

English learning process by using Media ICT Kahoot boost the students to have good interaction between their learning partners in order to solve the problem that may appear while doing activities. Similar findings from another study reveals that formative assessment that arranged by using online quiz make good interaction between students and teacher to build their knowledge and experiences (Khaitan et al. 2020).

Based on the observation result, the implementation of blended learning by using Media ICT Kahoot improve the ability to socialize, collaborate, and develop sense of responsibility. Theseh skills are needed to face the challenge of global community. The observation shows that collaboration between students are happened while the learning activity whether working in groups, exchanging knowledge or sharing files. The result reveals that most of the students satisfy with media ICT Kahoot platform as their supporting media to learn English. It means that various exercises in online activities that can be accessed by students by using media ICT Kahoot help their learning so that increase their motivation and learning achievement.

## 6  CONCLUSION

To sum up, this study concluded that media ICT Kahoot could improve students learning motivation and learning outcomes of English in Elementary School in Jakarta. In this study, the results of the data analysis above indicate that online learning based on media ICT Kahoot can increase student motivation. Development of Information and Communication Technology (ICT) encourages teachers in the field of English to be able to create innovate learning by emphasizing a competency-oriented approach by using ICT. Furthermore, media ICT Kahoot is one of the innovations in learning that can be applied in ICT learning particularly for English subject to increase student motivation and learning outcomes.

The findings of this study reveals the evidence of the effectiveness of using media ICT Kahoot in the English learning process to increase student motivation through participation in online discussions and assignments as well as to improve their learning achievement. Additionally, with the use of ICT Kahoot media in learning English for elementary school children, learning English becomes a fun lesson. As a result, elementary school children in Jakarta who are learning English online during the Covid-19 pandemic become more enthusiastic. Other indirect impact of using this media is providing a comfortable learning situation both for students and parents which encourage students to have more high enthusiasm in learning English in order to get more higher learning outcomes.

## ACKNOWLEDGMENT

Thank to International Conference of Education in Moslem Society (ICEMS) 2020 FITK UIN Syarif Hidayatullah Jakarta for publication support.

## REFERENCES

Anandha, Anggraheni, D., Yogatama, A. (2020). Online English Vocabulary Teaching Using Kahoot! for Students with Special Needs. Scripta: English Department Journal, 7(15), 35–41.

Bernard, R. M., Abrami, P. C., Lou, Y., Borokhovski, E., Wade, A., Wozney, L., Huang, B. (2004). How Does Distance Education Compare with Classroom Instruction? A MetaAnalysis of the Empirical Literature. Review of Educational Research, 74(3), 379–439. Retrieved from www.jstor.org/stable/3516028

Bettinger, E. P., Loeb, S. (2017). Promises and pitfalls of online education. Brookings Institute, Evidence Speaks Reports, 2(15).

Boden, Gemma, M., Lindsay, H. (2018). Kahoot! Game-based Student Respon System. Compass: Journal of Learning and Teaching, 11(1). Cetin, H. S. (2018). Implementation of the digital assessment tool "kahoot" in elementary school. International Technology and Education Journal, 2(1), 9–20.

Chandu, K., Dasari, M. (2020). Corona virus Covid 19: The Journey around the Globe so Far. International Journal of Advanced Science and Technology, 29(05), 2277–2282.

Correia, M., Santos, R. (2017). Game based learning: the use of Kahoot in teacher education. International Symposium on Computer in Education (SIIE).

Dellos, R. (2015). Kahoot! A digital game resource for learning. International Journal of Instructional Technology and Distance Learning, 12(4), 49–52.

Hart, C. M. D., Berger, D., Jacob, B., Loeb, S., Hill, M. (2019). Online Learning, Offline Outcomes: Online Course Taking and High School Student Performance. AERA Open, 5(1), 2332858419832852. Doi:10.1177/2332858419832852

Hartanti, Dwi. (2019). Meningkatkan Motivasi Belajar Siswa Dengan Media Pembelajaran Interaktif Game Kahoot Berbasis Hypermedia. Prosiding Seminar Nasional: Kebijakan dan Pengembangan Pendidikan di Era Revolusi Industri 4.0. Shapir Hotel, 21 September 2019 Penelitian dan Evaluasi Pendidikan.

Heppen, J. B., Sorensen, N., Allensworth, E., Walters, K., Rickles, J., Taylor, S. S., Michelman, V. (2017). The Struggle to Pass Algebra: Online vs. Face-toFace Credit Recovery for At-Risk Urban Students. Journal of Research on Educational Effectiveness, 10(2), 272–296.

Johns, K. (2015). Engaging and assessing students with technology: A review of Kahoot!. Delta Kappa Gamma Bulletin, 81(4), 89.

Khaitan, S., Mitra, A., Shukla, P., Chakraborty, S. (2020). Statistical Investigation of Novel Corona Virus COVID-19.

Plump, C. M., LaRosa, J. (2017). Using Kahoot! in the Classroom to Create Engagement and Active Learning: A Game-Based Technology Solution for eLearning Novices. Management Teaching Review, 2(2), 151–158. https://doi.org/10.1177/2379298116689783

Wang, A., Tahir, R. (2020). The effect of using Kahoot! for learning – A literature review. Computers & Education, 149. 103818. 10.1016/j.compedu.2020.103818.

Wang, Alf, I., Zhu, M., Sætre, R. (2016). The effect of digitizing and gratifying quizzing in classrooms. European Conference on Games Based Learning. Academic Conferences and Publishing International, 10, 729–736.

*Emerging Trends in Technology for Education in an Uncertain World – Nanto, Rahiem & Khalis Maryati (Eds)*

# Effective and efficient platforms in the pandemic era

Raswan
*Arabic Teaching Program, Faculty of Tarbiya, Islamic State University Syarif Hidayatullah Jakarta, Kota Tangerang Selatan, Banten*

ABSTRACT:   This study aims to find a distance learning application in the fifth semester of Arabic Teaching Program, from the Faculty of Tarbiya, Islamic State University Syarif Hidayatullah Jakarta. It also aims to provide reasons, the most effective method, the most effective assessment model, and suggestions for improvement by students. This study uses a qualitative method using an online questionnaire via google form. The research finding is that the most effective platform is google meet due to the ease of saving data and facilitating understanding, while the most effective method is discussion, the most effective assessment model is multiple choice, and the suggestion is for learning to be carried out more creatively. The conclusion of this study is that the more appropriate the student's needs, the application will be more effective and efficient in implementing learning. Therefore, researchers recommend that lecturers conduct research more often to improve learning in the classroom.

*Keywords*:   blended learning, effective, efficient, pandemic era, platform

## 1   INTRODUCTION

Learning during the pandemic era is challenging. Learning at this time makes teachers, students, and even people know that they have to rack their brains in implementing creativity-based learning. In addition, in order to support the success, effectiveness, and efficiency of learning, adaptation using various communication and information technologies is needed. The latest technology today is a variety of applications that can help implement learning.

Applications have their own advantages and disadvantages. Therefore, it is necessary to have creativity and proficiency in using it so that learning becomes more effective and efficient. If not, the media will become a new problem in learning activities.

Teachers also have to always research and study the implementation of distance learning-based learning (PJJ). PJJ needs to be continuously developed and needs its effectiveness in learning needs to be analyzed. In the context of student-based learning, the effectiveness of various applications must be explored from the student side. Therefore, this paper will answer several questions including the most effective and efficient applications, effective and efficient reasons, the most effective and efficient learning methods, effective and efficient PJ-based learning assessments, proposals for improving PJJ learning, and various obstacles against PJJ-based learning.

In today's era of globalization and technological advances, where there is a movement of human robotization and humanization of robots, we need human teachers, intelligent teachers who are able to create generations with the skills to turn data into information, information into knowledge, and knowledge into wisdom. The expected teacher characteristics are (1) the ability of faith (Thuaimah 2011), (2) being a model human being (Thuaimah 2011), (3) believes in the essence of Allah in which he lives and the essence of human centeredness in it, (4) is unanimous in his belief that life is in a world and in an afterlife, (5) has scientific power(Thuaimah 2011), (6) have cultural insight, (7) have cognitive abilities, (8) have technological abilities (Thuaimah 2011), (9) able to transform information into knowledge and knowledge into wisdom or wisdom because wisdom is the goal of all knowledge (Thuaimah 2011), and (10) teachers have the value of thinking, (11) have a high sense of social responsibility, (12) have mental abilities, (13) have language skills, (14) have professional abilities, (15) have research skills, (16) have session and aesthetic abilities, (17) have democratic abilities, and (18) have family abilities. (Thuaimah 2011), (19) has the ability to keep the gap between the digital and the physical world (Rizwan Matloob Ellahi, Moin Uddin Ali Khan 2019). Number eight indicates that a teacher must be proficient in technology because technology fast-moving, so the teacher must quickly adapt to the latest technological developments, especially those related to the education and learning process.

Using a blended learning model that presents learning all the time because it is able to solve challenges in the 21st century, namely technological, pedagogical, and content knowledge (TPACK) (Sari 2016) is a favorable action. Using STEM-based learning (Rahayu 2017a), multiliterate education movement (Kristiawan 2018a), and strengthening character education (Komara, 2018) are other attributes of effective learning. Using a learning pattern based on remap couple, with three stages of learning, which are reading (reading process), making concept maps (concept mapping), and using cooperative learning models (Zubaidah 2014) should also be investigated. ICT-based learning(Abdullah 2008) is another avenue for research. Using streaming videos and using a learning model with learning cycle 7e: elicit, engage, explore, explain, elaborate, extend, and evaluate (Partini Partini, Budijanto Budijanto 2017) should also be investigated.

The mastery of new literacy is the key in education in the era of the Industrial Revolution 4.0, which ranges from reading, writing and counting to data literacy, technology literacy and human resource literacy or humanism (Ibda 2018). In order for graduates to be competitive in this new era, the curriculum should no longer be based on old literacy (reading, writing, and mathematics) as the basic capital for taking part in society. Data literacy is the ability to read, analyze, and use information (big data) in the digital world. Technological literacy is understanding how machines work, technology applications (coding, artificial intelligence, and engineering principles). Human literacy is communication & design, covering skills to lead and work in teams, agile and mature culture and entrepreneurship through co-extra-curricular thematic studies and apprenticeship learning. Among the solutions are Blended Learning facilitated by SPADA & IdREN: video conferencing, online learning, and resource sharing (Ahmad 2018).

Blended Learning is *"is the combination of instruction from two historically separate models of teaching and learning: traditional face-to-face learning system and distributed learning system. It also emphasizes the central role of computer-based technologies in blended learning (Graham 2006)"* and is a combination of learning between two historically separate teaching and learning models: traditional face-to-face learning systems and distributed learning systems. It also emphasizes the central role of computer-based technology in blended learning. In essence, blended learning is different from several other terms such as distributed learning, e-learning, open and flexible learning, as well as hybrid courses (Graham 2006).

According to Valiathan, blended learning is "used to describe a solution that combines several different delivery methods, such as collaboration software, Web-based courses, EPSS, and knowledge management practices" which is a term used to describe a solution that combines several different delivery methods, such as collaboration software, web-based courses, EPSS, and knowledge management practices. It is also used to describe learning that combines various event-based activities, including face-to-face classrooms, live e-learning, and independent learning (Valiathan 2002)."

According to experts' view, blended learning occurs when "online learning blends with more traditional methods of learning and development (Thorne 2003)" namely combining online learning with more traditional learning and development methods. Thus, blended learning is essentially a learning model that combines traditional learning with e-learning learning. Traditional learning is face-to-face learning. E-learning itself is learning using electronic media with its continuous development without. Starting from just a computer-based learning to mobile-based learning using the internet, either directly or indirectly, online or offline.

Educational applications recommended by UNESCO are (1) Learning management systems such as CenturyTech, ClassDojo, Edmodo, Edraak, EkStep, Google Classroom, Moodle, Nafham, Paper Airplanes, Schoology, Seesaw, and Skooler. (2) video collaboration such as Dingtalk, Lark,

Hangouts Meet, Teams, Skype, WeChat Work, WhatsApp, Zoom. (3) independent access such as ABRA, British Council, Discovery Education, Duolingo, Edraak, Facebook Get Digital, Feed the Monster, Geekie, Khan Academy, KitKit School, LabXchange, Madrasa, Mindspark, Mosoteach, OneCourse, Polyup, Quizlet, Smart History, and YouTube. Online learning can use a partial model for those who are not familiar with complex learning management systems; by using a variety of separate applications. You can also use an integrated system in one particular learning management system such as Edmodo, google classroom, Moodle, bb and so on (Ahsanuddin 2020).

College graduates in 4IRR must have a high intelligence. Students with this ability are able to translate all forms of information quickly. The integrated curriculum is the right curriculum model in facing the challenges of this era, as seen from sources (research unit) consisting of material (subject matter), learning activities (learning activity), and sources (resources), which are abundant (Nurcholiq 2019). *Blended learning* is an ideal type of learning for the 21st century, which is an era of the industrial revolution 4.0. Without blended learning, learning may not be in accordance with developments, needs, and expectations. School age is now a maximum student born in 2001 meaning they are a group of generation Z who prefer the digital world, especially those who are ALFA generation, born in 2010 and after who are now only elementary school age, who need digital-based learning. Likewise, current undergraduate students are generally born in 1997, meaning they are already generation Z. Digital-based learning is a must, although it still needs traditional learning known as blended learning. The problem is that teachers and lecturers who teach have to try their best because if the teacher is generation Y it's a bit heavy, especially Generation X and the Young Boomer generation.

## 2 RESEARCH METHODS

This research is a qualitative research in which the researcher is the main instrument in collecting and interpreting data by using an online questionnaire from Google form. This study aims to analyze and evaluate the fifth semester PBA learning platform of UIN Syarif Hidayatullah Jakarta, which uses a distance learning pattern (PJJ) during the Covid-19 pandemic. The steps that will be taken are developing a research instrument, especially a questionnaire, collecting data, analyzing and interpreting it. The focus of the questions is about the most effective applications, reasons, the most effective research methods, suggestions for improving PJJ learning, and various obstacles in PJJ-based learning.

## 3 RESULTS

This research resulted in five aspects, *first*, regarding the most effective applications in PJJ in the fifth semester student learning of PBA FITK UIN Syarif Hidayatullah Jakarta. The data shows that 47.8% of students answered that the platform that was considered most effective was Google meet, 19.4% of students chose Zoom, 14.9% of students chose Gruf, 13.4% of students chose Google classroom, and the rest chose to use YouTube. The details of platform data that are considered effective in student learning are as follows:

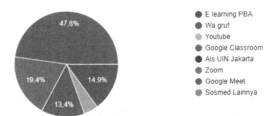

Figure 1.   The most effective applications in PJJ.

Second, the reasons for choosing students to use various platforms that are considered effective is Google Meet, which does not take up a lot of quota, pack, the time is unlimited. Google Meet can be used to meet face to face and can explain explanations from lecturers that it does not use a a lot of quota, and does not need a stable signal. Since Google Meet is more conducive, it can save quota and people do not complain much about the quote because it does not run out. It is easier with the method or flow when the previous semester is using gruf, or you can occasionally use Zoom or Google Meet. Discussions or presentations and the atmosphere of the lecture is livelier, more interactive, and not monotonous and boring, and more economical. Quota versus zoom is simpler, and more economical.

Google Meet can also be used face to face, although it is much different from face to face in class. It can also be used for presentations etc. Similar to the classroom, although i tis not superior to learning in class. Actually, I use zoom more often in the same way. However, because zoom is consumes much quota I personally don't take it. Google Meet it is more effective for discussion because it can facilitate direct question and answer. It also allows for livelier discussion and two-way communication. Since it is more efficient, quotas and speakers are clear. The quota is more efficient because there is interaction between lecturers and students and lecturers can explain the material clearly. Learning becomes more alive and not monotonous. In my opinion, Google Meet is an effective application when used in PJJ because all students will be monitored by the lecturer if all students activate the video. It's more effective, sir, because besides being able to communicate face to face, students' attention will be more focused on Google Meet than on YouTube because it allows students to "just be absent" after that they don't watch learning videos on YouTube. It is easier to understand the material if it is done in person, even though virtually. Signals are more supportive on Google Meet, quota is cheaper than Zoom, and is overall more economical. I tis better to use Google Meet or Zoom because if you don't understand, ask immediately and the lecturer answers immediately. I tis also more affordable. Actually, I still have difficulty in this study from home, but apart from the less quota needed when using Google Meet, learning can also be via audio, so it helps a little in understanding. Because it's easier to discuss and saves more on quota than zooming. It feels like the substitute for learning in class is also good face-to-face, because that is a good solution for now using this application, which is felt both in terms of image and quality. It is more effective when doing questions and answers and explanation of material, besides using data which is also less wasteful. It is more conducive in terms of signal quality but consumes too much internet quota. Because it is economical. unlimited quota and time.

It's easier to access and doesn't require a lot of quota. I tis suitable for conducting discussions. It can be be used with a free account, there is no time limit, materials can be shared during presentations, recordings can be made and the application is well known to students. It doesn't take up a lot of quota, it's easy to attend to students, it's easy to share materials, assignments, etc., and it's also easy to have a discussion. Because this application in my opinion is good and economical in terms of quota. So that it can be used to directly meet students face to face, and more effective, because if you go through group wa, sometimes you don't always respond fast. More effective and efficient and easier communication. Because it is more effective and can be clearer when delivering and presenting material.

Because at that moment we are required to avoid the disturbances in the house. So, like it or not you have to sit in front of your laptop and cellphone to listen, read and discuss about the day's courses. easy to share material, absences, discuss. It is more focused when sharing, and is easier to understand. With Google Classroom, it is easier for students to discuss and receive assignments and collect assignments at predetermined times. Since Google Meet is a 2-way communication tool that makes it easy to convey material and get direct responses from students so it doesn't take too long to discuss too. Does not drain your quota and there must be a signal. Learning is carried out in two directions. I tis more efficient. and reduce the difficulty signal constraints and so on. Because with google meet, there can be interactions between lecturers and students. And it's easier to use.

b) Zoom. Zoom meetings can be recorded and lessons can be recorded as well so it's easy when you want to review but the use of the zoom quota is huge if there are no subsidies. Using Zoom is almost the same as face to face, although a little different. The use of this Zoom absorbs quite a lot of quota and requires a stable signal so that it is a bit difficult for students, but this is the most effective in my opinion, because students can hear what students are presenting directly or from lecturers. It is easier and has complete features. The only drawback is that you must have a premium account. The Zoom application is clearer, besides that the conference application really helps the effectiveness of the online learning process, because it is face-to-face even via video calls. Because there are more options for adjusting learning, such as when recording lessons, Zoom can be audio & video, while Google Meet cannot record videos that are in progress. The reason is that if you use Zoom, you can easily interact with lecturers and other friends through the camera features provided even if you use a cell phone. If you use a similar application like Google Meet, you can't see other friends even if the camera is turned on, when using a Smartphone. However, the drawback is that the zoom drains too much quota and the time is limited to only 40 minutes per meeting.

c) wa gruf, because if someone is not sick / does not enter, they can read the material from the group, and also when using the group WA the signal is rarely cut and does not take up much quota Since it is easier and more affordable in terms of internet access, you can listen to the speakers' explanations via voice notes without any problems even though the signal is not smooth, it docsn't take up too much quota. Because the wa group doesn't drain the quota too much and all students must already have the application and can be fairly active in using the application. It is easy to access the internet.

d) Google Classroom (gcr) does not drain your quota much, is also easy to read, and does not lose files when the account logs out because data can be recorded.

and e) YouTube, because on YouTube videos are stored better, can be viewed repeatedly and can be shared with others. Classroom files are also stored properly, chats or notes will not be deleted, immediately connect the notification in the email so that it is easy to monitor when there is a notification. can be played back. Repeatable is easy to understand.

Third, the most effective learning method according to the students' view is that the majority choose discussion (55, 2%), then active learning (20, 9%), then in number three there are lectures (17, 9%), and assignments (6%). ). And no one chose PBL or problem-based learning.

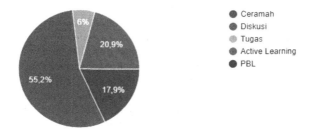

Figure 2.   The most effective learning method.

Fourth, regarding the assessment model that is considered effective in PJJ according to students. The majority of students chose multiple choice questions (29, 9%), followed by essays (25, 4%), then entries (19, 4%), others (14, 9%), the rest chose projects and products.

Fifth, the suggestions for improving PJJ learning that are submitted by students are that they can be more effective. Focused on the task of understanding the books that are read. Can understand how the current conditions are, made easier by learning Google Classroom and their absence there in order not to be given a complicated task. Students and lecturers can communicate fluently. The psychological conditions should be assessed and media that support teaching and learning activities should be used. The holding of discussions meetings via Zoom should be done once every 2 weeks for discussion, etc. and the better protocol is to make a resume and occasionally practice. The lecturer always understands the constraints experienced by students regarding internet connection, giving clear explanations for each subject matter. It can also be more flexible and effective for learning activities.

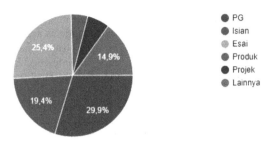

PG
Isian
Esai
Produk
Projek
Lainnya

Figure 3.   The assessment model that is considered effective in PJJ.

There is quota data assistance, because the quota is the main capital in PJJ. In order to keep the spirit, the same as when offline. The task is not many, if possible, avoid making videos because my cellphone is not supportive. I'm easy to understand. This is not a burden for each other. It is also performed on applications that make students and lecturers face to face directly such as Zoom and Google Meet. The learning atmosphere through this application is the closest to the atmosphere of offline lectures in general and not only in Google Classroom, for example. It is also more effective. Students are given sufficient time when there are assignments. It can be understood even though there is no direct interaction. Learning can be understood even more. It can be implemented optimally. It does not make it difficult for either party. Students and teachers need to maintain communication. Multiple tasks are not the right solution. Reaffirm and tighten discipline to ensure presence and activity.

People can opt to use other media for meetings, which saves more quota. It was also suggested that the quota subsidy will be available soon. It runs more effectively, and you can also see the condition of students in this PJJ since students can observe and choose the correct answer. More explanations have been made because of the large number of assignments, which I think is too difficult. Providing appropriate tasks that are not burdensome for students is helpful, learning using the discussion method, and quota assistance to be given quickly because it can be very helpful in the economy in the midst of this pandemic. Learning remains active but assignments should be eliminated. Formative values should be taken from discussions only.

It is more effective than previous online learning, such as activating the camera during learning so that students are monitored as to whether they are really listening or just joining. More conditioned especially regarding the network for those areas who are difficult to network. I propose that in this PJJ use a varied learning system and media at every meeting. The use of PJJ media is effective for all student conditions and relief in giving assignments, considering that not all students are in the same regional conditions. I think for PJJ it is only natural that we understand each other. Assessment focuses more on attendance and assignments, choosing learning methods that involve student activity, giving assignments that do not cost a lot of money, providing learning resources that are easily accessible at any time, understanding if there are signal constraints so that they cannot participate in learning from start to finish.

Maximized again, it does not burden both parties (teacher & student) not to linger and vary in terms of attendance, because it is risky to buy time for lectures, to use the discussion method, so that learning becomes effective and active. It should be accompanied by theory and practice. Can be used according to expectations. To be more conducive and effective, it is better to focus more on discussions and lectures so that what we learn can be understood. You use Zoom or other media more because it can make you feel like you're in a classroom. Regular tasks do not clash with one another. It's okay to use YouTube and papers while reading and repeating. This does not burden the tasks. Not too many tasks and no short deadlines. Active in discussions to minimize obstacles can be used 2 PJJ media, video conferencing such as google meet or discussion in WhatsApp groups or classrooms. More discipline. Can be done directly. All wishes and input were fulfilled. More discussion in learning.

Sixth, various obstacles in PJJ-based learning include quotas and batteries while working. The most important thing is the quota for the internet and a bit of a headache because of many tasks, because many are using the internet because of this pandemic, so the signal is rather difficult and often gets lost. The problem with PJJ and the like is usually in the signal, the quota doesn't not last long if you keep Zooming four times a day. Because they have a minimal signal in the village, the explanation from the teacher or colleagues on Zoom or Google Meet becomes broken sometimes even there is no sound. In addition, also because we as students, apart from wanting to gain knowledge, also want to get grades, so we are scrambling to answer, sometimes forgetting to turn off the mic, because of the dependence on the signal, I myself have a lot of trouble. If the lecturer or speaker displays a show on Zoom and Google Meet, then there even one mic that is on other than the one in charge on that day, will not be able to hear the sound clearly.

Difficult to have discussions with friends and lecturers, difficult to find books, quotas and signals. Personally, the only problem is in the internet connection, which sometimes hinders learning as it progresses. Poor network signals, trying to understand the material in its entirety, and looking for e-book references are other factors. It is difficult to understand, the costs for quotas are of course very large, and there are many more. Quota, signal, quota, signal, sore eyes over time in front of the laptop. Some don't have a laptop and have limited internet access and signal quality. Quotas, gadgets, families who do not believe that we are studying PJJ. Network, quota, looking for book references. (Tangible not in the form of cyberspace). Dizzy looking at laptop / cellphone screens all day, dividing time to help parents. (All wrong) because if you don't get help, it's not good. I am unfamiliar with various virtual resource formats such as e-books. I prefer reading text books. Network, learning motivation that fluctuates. Signals, costs, understanding. Signal difficulty and quota limitations.

It decreases the understanding of the lesson. Difficulty looking for book references, there are but they are limited on the internet and i tis difficult if you want to make a paper because there are no references. Signal because my location is not in the city. Time due to a 2-hour difference which resulted in me sometimes having to choose between praying on time or listening to lectures in full. Or I also have to choose between break time and lecture time. The problem is that the network or signal is sometimes unstable when Zooming in on a meeting or the like, and the quota suddenly runs out. Learning is less effective because sometimes it is hampered by signals and quotas, and understanding of courses is more difficult to understand than face-to-face lectures. Quota, circumstances, and time. Difficulty in discussing because of the signal, the time of each activity, the number of tasks that are difficult to understand, and the very large quota, especially the learning media via cellphones, making it difficult to scare or translate. Quota is running low, and sometimes the signal is erratic because when it rains the signal is very bad. Less quota and girah in learning. Time and network. What is certain is the signal first, then because I am in the eastern part of Indonesia, sometimes I feel hampered by the adjustment of time.

The signal that sometimes likes to go down makes ongoing learning hampered especially if learning is not recorded by the meeting maker. Limited quotas are another problem. An unfriendly network and quota problems that always drain the contents of the wallet. Of course, the availability of quotas is very, very important in learning, therefore if the fulfillment of the quota is hampered, it will greatly hamper learning. Besides that, with a distance like this, sometimes you feel bored, tired and sleepy when learning.

Sometimes the signal. To be honest, the main obstacle is the internet quota, in a day I can use more than 3 GB just for lectures. Quota and cellphone battery. Often there is interference with the signal even when using Wi-Fi. Internet quota that must always be available, difficult internet network when the weather is not good (rain or cloudy and lightning), poor learning accent media (cellphones and laptops that are sometimes slow or hang because of a lot of data and applications). Quotas, of course, have a lot of tasks to do, signals, signals, quotas are very limited as well as the effectiveness of the methods used when PJJ. The main obstacle is the limited quota and signal, which makes learning not run smoothly. It is also difficult to learn online *online* because there are more assignments than offline lectures. Internet quota that requires a lot of usage. The problem with reference books for assignments and writing papers is difficult to find.

Constraints on quotas, references, and discussions with friends are not as effective as during face to face learning in class. There is interference from both within and in the environment, which results in a breakdown of focus while studying. Myself, aka easily bored and lazy. Network that is suddenly lost. The problem is the quota, where I buy the quota by earning my own money. Quota runs out quickly because I use a lot of zoom & google meet applications, when I use video conferencing, sometimes I have trouble getting a stable signal so I often lose connections. Quota. The knowledge gained is not perfect when studying offline. It is more consumptive in using quotas and allows for difficult signals at certain times. Data quota. Signal interference and limited quota.

## 4 DISCUSSION

From the research data that the authors collect, it can answer the first few questions, an affective application in learning is Google Meet with several advantages including requiring a lighter data package, not limited by time, easy use, more describing normal learning, can be discussed, there is a lot of communication and direction. Zoom is considered good because the image is better than Google Meet but it requires a larger quota. Wa gruf was then chosen because it was due to ease of use, required a light quota, and did not require a signal that was too strong. Google Classroom was chosen because it can be done with a minimum quota and the data will be stored neatly. YouTube has the advantage that it can be repeated even though it consumes a large quota.

This research is not much different from the research results, including (a) social media can be an alternative in learning in a pandemic era such as WhatsApp, some use LMS Moodle developed by universities, video conferencing such as zoom meetings and google meet. The delivery of material is mostly done using WhatsApp and other social media. The obstacles that arise are limited internet packages, internet access, and not being used to it; (b) In the context of children's character, the main role that determines online learning is parents. The role of parents as educators, examples, supervisors, motivators and children's heart support. Deviation in children's behavior will be minimized by the main role of parents; and (c) Information technology WhatsApp group, Edmodo, EdLink, Moodle, Google Classroom, Schoology online class. The ones that became favorites were Whatshap group and Google Classroom because of their practicality. The constraints faced are facilities, not having a laptop, difficult signal, wasteful data packages, not getting used to it. The pandemic turned out to provide a positive meaning in digital transformation towards education in the 4.0 era.

Second, the learning methods that are considered effective by students are discussion, active learning, lectures, and assignments, students feel that learning discussions become more meaning-ful. So, in line with that we need an application that supports both oral and written discussions. Inexpensive oral discussion can be with meet, which is expensive, the quota can use zoom, in writing you can use gcr. Lectures can use zoom, meet, YouTube. Tasks can use multiple applications in combination with one another.

Third, the assessment model chosen by students and considered effective and efficient is a) multiple choice with the advantage of being more objective in assessing and the results are known immediately after completion of the assessment activity; and b) The essay is chosen because the essay will train and assess students' abilities in creation and innovation. The same filling as PG is seen as more objective and faster in its assessment. Other student respondents used other types of assessment.

Fourth, the proposed lesson is that creativity is needed in implementing learning so that the results are maximum. The use of blended learning will be more effective and efficient than conventional learning for especially at the student level if it is carried out maximally.

## 5 CONCLUSION

From the various analyzes above, it can be concluded that the more appropriate the student's needs, the more the application will be more effective and efficient in implementing learning. Some data shows that the most effective and efficient application in PJJ is Google Meet, the reason for this is that it is effective and efficient, and is more like normal learning and requires a lighter quota, the most effective and efficient learning method came out in the discussion. The most effective and efficient PJ-based learning assessment is multiple choice questions. The proposals to improve PJJ learning to be more creative and innovative, and various obstacles in PJJ-based learning, including quotas, signals, devices, as well as dense activity interference in the house.

## ACKNOWLEDGMENT

In the publication of this paper the author would like to thank the head of the Arabic language education study program, the dean of the Faculty of Tarbiyah and Teacher Training, and also the students of the Arabic Language Education Study Program who became respondents.

## REFERENCES

Abdullah, D., 2008. Potensi Teknologi informasi Dan Komunikasi Dalam Peningkatan Mutu Pembelajaran Di Kelas, 1.

Ahmad, I., 2018. *Proses pembelajaran digital dalam era revolusi industri 4.0*. Direktur Jenderal Pembelajaran dan Kemahasiswaan. Kemenristek Dikti.

Ahsanuddin, M., 2020. Kompetensi Guru Bahasa Arab untuk Generasi Milenial. *In*: *Kompetensi Guru Bahasa Arab di Era New Normal dan Masyarakat 5.0. UIN Sunan Kalijaga Yogyakarta*.

Graham, C.R., 2006. Blended learning systems. *In*: *The handbook of blended learning: Global perspectives, local designs*.

Ibda, H., 2018. Penguatan Literasi Baru Pada Guru Madrasah Ibtidaiyah Dalam Menjawab Tantangan Era Revolusi Industri 4.0. *JRTIE: Journal of Research and Thought of Islamic Education*, 1 (1).

Komara, E., n.d. 2018. Penguatan Pendidikan Karakter dan Pembelajaran Abad 21. *SIPATAHOENAN 4.1*.

Nurcholiq, M., 2019. Desain Pengembangan Kurikulum Madrasah Aliyah Unggulan Di Era Revolusi Industri 4.0. Hal. 221. *Journal PIWULANG*, 1(2), 208–222.

Partini Partini, Budijanto Budijanto, and S.B., 2017. Penerapan Model Pembelajaran Learning Cycle 7E untuk Meningkatkan Kemampuan Berpikir Kritis Siswa. *Jurnal Pendidikan: Teori, Penelitian, dan Pengembangan*, 2(2), 269.

Rahayu, S., 2017a. Mengoptimalkan aspek literasi dalam pembelajaran kimia abad 21. *In*: *Prosiding Seminar Nasional Kimia Universitas Negeri Yogyakarta*.

Rizwan Matloob Ellahi, Moin Uddin Ali Khan, and A.S., 2019. Redesigning Curriculum in line with Industry 4.0. *In*: *Procedia Computer Science* 151, 699–708.

Sari, M., 2016. Blended Learning, Model Pembelajaran Abad ke-21 di Perguruan Tinggi. *Ta'dib*, 17(2), 134–135.

Thorne, K., 2003. *Blended learning: how to integrate online & traditional learning*. Kogan Page Publishers.

Thuaimah, R.A.T., 2011. *al-Marji Fi> Mana>hij Tali>m al-Lughah al-Arabiyyah li al-Na>thiqi>na bi Lugha>t Ukhra>*.

Valiathan, P., 2002. Blended learning models. *Learning circuits*, 3(8), 50–59.

Zubaidah, S., 2014. Pemberdayaan Keterampilan Penemuan dalam Scientific Approach Melalui Pembelajaran Berbasis Remap Couple. *In*: *Proceeding Biology Education Conference: Biology, Science, Enviromental, and Learning . Vol. 11. No. 1*.1004 .

*Emerging Trends in Technology for Education in an Uncertain World – Nanto, Rahiem & Khalis Maryati (Eds)*

# The correlation between anxiety and students' speaking performance in the EFL classroom

K. Fitri, Z. Anasy, R.S. Dewi, F. Hamid & Fahriany
*Department of English Education, Faculty of Educational Sciences, Universitas Islam Negeri (UIN) Syarif Hidayatullah Jakarta, Tangerang Selatan, Banten, Indonesia*

Khalimi
*Department of Islamic Education, Faculty of Educational Sciences, Universitas Islam Negeri (UIN) Syarif Hidayatullah Jakarta, Tangerang Selatan, Banten, Indonesia*

ABSTRACT: Anxiety has a relationship with speaking performance. It affects students' braveness negatively to speak freely and fluently. This study aimed to know the correlation between anxiety and students' speaking performance at the tenth-grade senior high school's students. The study used a quantitative method with a correlational analysis technique by distributing a set of questionnaires to 31 students which are based on Foreign Language Speaking Anxiety Scale. It was adapted from Cope and Horwitz (1986) and Huang (2004). Moreover, an oral test was carried out based on six aspects; grammar, vocabulary, fluency, pronunciation, comprehension, and performance. The findings revealed that the students gained a higher score of speaking performance if they have a lower anxiety level and vice versa. From the data calculation, it was obtained N. sig $= .000 < 0.05$ and the result of 'r' formula was $-.632$. It indicated that anxiety correlates negatively with students' speaking performance in the EFL classroom.

*Keywords*: anxiety; speaking anxiety; speaking performance

## 1 INTRODUCTION

English language becomes one of foreign language that taught in Indonesia. Nowadays in national curriculum or commonly known as K13 especially for English subject, students need to be able to build up their communication competence both in speaking and writing to gain the literacy goals (Idris 2017). Speaking, however, is not just the oral development of written language but requires the students' competency of a wide range of sub-skills that combined together and built up the competence in the spoken language altogether (McDonough 1993). It can be admitted that speaking is complex activity. Students find it is challenging to produce the language orally and assumed that English is difficult to deal with because it demands the students to think and produce their idea in oral form. "Speaking is the most complex and challenging skill to master" (Li 2003 cited in Zhang 2009).

Additionally, the teaching and learning process of foreign languages in the EFL classroom faces several challenges, particularly when in the speaking class students feel the nervousness for completing or introducing the assignment in the EFL classroom (Nihal 2010). This is supported by the statement from several students of SMA PGRI 56 Ciputat that they have some problems in learning English language especially speaking skills involves insufficient vocabulary, the difficulty in pronunciation, the feeling of nervous, shy, and insecure, and believing that the English language is too difficult. However, most of them revealed they have experienced anxiety when being exposed in front of the class, especially in foreign language. Besides, Ellis (1985) cited in Khasinah (2014,

DOI 10.1201/9781003219248-24

p. 111) stated that several factors influence the second language learning process are anxiety, cognitive factors, motivation and attitude, and age difference, etc. Anxiety is one factor that is worth considering because it can negatively impact the language learning process of the students such as lowering score of performance in standardized test, poor vocabulary acquisition, and reduce word production (Horwitz & Young 1991; MacIntyre & Gardner 1991 cited in Khan, 2010). Anxiety seems has a big impact on students' language learning process. Gardner and his colleagues discovered that anxiety has a significantly destructive outcome on the second language learning progress (Gardner 1985; Gardner et al. 1989, 1991, 1994; Kumaravadivelu 2009). Thus, to examine the close relationship between anxiety and students' speaking performance is the main intention of this study.

## 2 LITERATURE REVIEW

### 2.1 *Speaking and speaking performance*

Burns and Joyce (1997) cited in Nuraini (2016) defined speaking as "the reciprocally active process of building up meaning that involves producing, receiving, and processing information". Chaney cited in Kayi (2006) explained that "speaking is a process of forming and sharing meaning by the usage of written and oral form". Thus, speaking allows the speaker to share the idea and the purpose of speaking which is the vital part of communication. Moreover, speaking is the process of combining the background and linguistic knowledge to produce an oral message (Chastain 1988 cited in Nihal 2010). Brown (1994), speaking is "an interactive process of constructing the meaning that involves producing, receiving, and processing the information", while performance "indicates the production of actual utterances as a result of certain psychological process" (De Kurt and Leerdam cited in Hemerka 2009). From the description above it can be inferred that speaking performance is the application of language knowledge including producing, receiving, and processing the information in actual execution such as story retelling, speech, conversation, role play, oral interview, and the other speaking activities that are conducted in the real execution.

### 2.2 *Factors affecting students' speaking performance*

Many factors can affect students' speaking performance, such as: (1) students' condition factor includes pressure time in planning, the quality of performance, and motivation (Leong 2017), (2) affective factor; motivation, self-confidence, and anxiety (Krashen 1982), (3) feedback during speaking performance (Harmer 1991, p. 104), and (4) topical knowledge; refers to the speaker knowledge of some useful topical information which enable the students to use the vocabulary in respect to the environment in which they live (Mai 2015). This study emphasis the problem on affective factor which is limited to anxiety because it can hinder the information process on the brain and affect students' performance negatively. In a foreign language environment, "anxiety is often associated with speaking ability" (Lucas 1984; Philips 1992; Price 1991 cited in Abrar 2017). In other word, anxiety could hinder them from the productive performance of speaking a second language (Hutabarat 2019).

### 2.3 *Anxiety and students' speaking performance*

Anxiety is defined as "a state of pressure and apprehension as a natural reaction to perceived treat" (Smith 2003, p. 546), means that people will naturally show their anxiety when they are in threatening condition. They may feel rapid breathing or heart rate breathing (Michopoulus 2020). MacIntyre and Gardner (1994) explained foreign language anxiety as "the feeling of pressure related to second language environment, involves speaking, listening, and learning". It can be said that anxiety is affective factors which can be implicitly preventing information process in the brain (Oteir 2019). Alpert and Haber decomposed anxiety into two types, facilitative anxiety, and debilitative anxiety (1960). Facilitative anxiety, or also called "helpful" anxiety, leads to positive results, while debilitative anxiety leads to an impaired result (He 2018).

Moreover, Brown (2000) stated there are two types of anxiety; trait anxiety, and state anxiety, but several researchers have assimilated the situation specific anxiety as an alternative to state anxiety concept. Trait anxiety is inherent, usually long-term stable personality characteristic that has been proven "to impair cognitive function, to disturb memory, to lead to escape from activities, and many others" (MacIntyre & Gardner 1991). The second types of anxiety are state anxiety that refers to transient anxiety caused by a specific temporary situation that will reduce or even fade if the threatening situation disappear (Abrar 2017). The third type of anxiety are situation specific anxiety which limited to a given context such as performing in public, answering the test, speaking in foreign language, or participating in English class.

To divide the construct to researchable issues, the elements of foreign language anxiety had been recognized (Cope & Horwitz 1986) into three: (1) communication apprehension, (2) test anxiety, and (3) fear of negative evaluation. Generally, anxiety affects three functioning systems: cognitive, physical, and behavioral (Carol 2014; Omrod 2005 cited in Debreli 2015). When the students learn to speak English in the classroom, they are demanded to actively communicate with others, such as making a conversation or presenting their opinion in front of others. The anxious students will focus on others' reactions or perceptions about their performance and underestimate the ability in expressing ideas orally. If they cannot cope with anxiety, they will lose control of the idea which will be presented. Leibert and Morris (1967) cited in Woodrow (2006) said that "the reaction of anxiety can be categorized as reflecting worry or emotionality". Worry relates to cognitive response, such as overthinking about the task. This could be harmful to someone due to its' relation with a cognitive capacity which takes a significant role in the language learning process and devoted to the task of speaking a foreign language (Tobias 2010).

## 3 RESEARCH METHOD

### 3.1 *Research setting and participants*

This research took place at SMA PGRI 56 Ciputat for the tenth-grade students in the second semester (academic year 2019/2020). This research used a quantitative method with correlational analysis design to show the percentage and number that used to reveal the correlation between two variables. The population number was 62 students. The study took 31 students for sample both female and male students who learn English as the foreign language with random sampling technique.

### 3.2 *Techniques of collecting data*

Two instruments; the questionnaire and students' spoken test were employed. The questionnaire was applied to discover students' anxiety level, while the spoken test aimed to gain students' score. The questionnaire was adapted from Foreign Language Speaking Anxiety Scale (FLSA) which advanced by Cope and Horwitz (1986) and also from Huang (2004). The result of the questionnaire was analysed by using SPSS program to determine mean, median, modus, and the average of students answer. The second instrument was an oral test which assists six aspects; pronunciation, grammar, vocabulary, fluency, comprehension, and performance. The implementation of speaking assessment was taken from Douglas Brown theory (Arthur 2000). In order to grade their speaking performance, the writer took their voice recorder and assign them a number based on the existing aspects of the assessment. Having collected both of the data, the writer then analysed it by using correlational technique of Pearson Correlation on SPSS 25 program.

## 4 RESULT AND DISCUSSION

### 4.1 *Result*

This study uncovered the negative correlation between anxiety and students' speaking performance, in which an increase in one variable is accompanied by a decrease in the other variable. If students'

Table 1. The correlation between the variables.

**Correlation**

|  |  | Anxiety | Speaking performance |
|---|---|---|---|
| Anxiety | Pearson correlation | 1 | −.632** |
|  | Sig. (2-tailed) |  | .000 |
|  | N | 31 | 31 |
| Speaking performance | Pearson correlation | −.632** |  |
|  | Sig. (2-tailed) | .000 |  |
|  | N | 31 | 31 |

**Correlation is significant at the 0.01 level (2-tailed).

anxiety is higher, their speaking performance will be lower. On the other hand, if students' anxiety is lower, their speaking performance will be higher. Here is the correlation between students' anxiety level and their speaking performance (Table 1).

From the table above it can be seen that the data obtained for sig. $= 0.000 < 0.05$, then the writer analyzed the significance of the variables by using significance test formula:

$$t = r\frac{\sqrt{n-2}}{\sqrt{1-r^2}}$$

$$lt_{count} = -4.398$$

The result is compared by $t_{count}$ in the significance of 5% and 1% and $N = 31$, next step is to find the degree of freedom (DF) with the formula:

$$DF = n - nr$$

$$= 29$$

To analyze the hypothesis, t table should be compared with t count. From DF 29, it is gained $t_{table}$ of $5\% = 2.045$ and $1\% = 2.462$. When $t_{table}$ is compared with $t_{count}$, the writer found that $t_{count}$ is higher than $t_{table}$. $T_{count} = -4.389 > t_{table} - 2.045$ (5%) and $t_{count} = -4.389 > t_{table} - 2.462$ (1%). So, it can be concluded that Ha (alternative hypothesis) is accepted and anxiety correlate negatively with students' speaking performance.

Based on the statistical score of students' anxiety questionnaire, it was obtained mean 118.5161 with the highest score was 140 and the lowest score was 94. From 31 students, there were 14 students got a high level of anxiety, 9 students were in the medium level, and 8 students were in the low level of anxiety. On the basis of evidence, it can be inferred that for the most part of the students has high anxiety level. In addition, from the calculation of students' speaking performance it was obtained mean 50.06 with the highest score was 76 and the lowest score was 32. There were 28 students gain the score below KKM, 3 students were in medium category and there were no students gain the high score category. From the result, it can be inferred that most of the students gain a low score for speaking performance refers to the KKM. When the writer analyzed the correlation between anxiety and students' speaking performance by using SPSS 25, the result was −.632 with N. sig $= .000 < 0.05$. As the consequence, **Ho** is rejected and **Ha** is accepted because there is a significant correlation between two variables.

### 4.2 *Discussion*

Oftentimes, the teachers conducted speaking performance activity to enhance students' ability to communicate. When the students performed speaking in front of the class, many of them took some times to get relax and think about what they are going to say even they stop speaking and got blank. Some of them admitted to have anxiety because they did not accustom to perform in front of public but some others believed their anxiety arose because they did not master speaking. Even so, there are several students who performed well even though they also felt anxious. It means the students get a higher score of speaking performance if they have a lower anxiety level while the students get a lower score of speaking performance if they have a higher anxiety level. As Amini et al. (2019) stated that "anxiety is the main problem of learning process in foreign language especially in oral communication". Moreover, the students who get better speaking performance also felt anxious but not as high as most of them. For them, the researcher concludes that they had a "helpful" anxiety which encourage them to have a positive result. Besides of leading to a negative result, anxiety also can lead to a positive impact.

Furthermore, anxiety cannot be the only one aspect affecting students' speaking performance. The mastery of speaking or their basic knowledge also can be a consideration. It means, speaking itself can caused students' anxiety. It would be necessary for teachers to recognize students' anxiety in the learning process in order to develop a relaxing situation. It is believed it can create fewer anxiety conditions for students. Moreover, the teacher should help them to cope with anxiety and build their self-confidence by doing such an interesting activity in the classroom.

## 5   CONCLUSION AND SUGGESTION

### 5.1   *Conclusion*

Based on the result of data calculation, it can be figured out that anxiety correlates negatively with students' speaking performance. It means the students get a higher score of speaking performance if they have a lower anxiety level and those who got lower score of speaking if they have high anxiety level. The score of students' speaking performance was categorized as low category based on KKM while students' anxiety level was in high category. The correlation between two variables was strong correlation based on the degree guidelines of Product Moment Correlation. It means, there was a significant correlation between anxiety and students' speaking performance in the EFL classroom of the tenth-grade students of SMA PGRI 56 Ciputat.

### 5.2   *Suggestion*

Based on the conclusion above, the writer made some suggestions. First, the teachers should be able to recognize students' anxiety in the learning process in order to develop a relaxing situation and to find the right time and the right way to correct students' errors in order to build their confidence. Second, the students should be able to try to find out what causes their anxiety or analyse the level of anxiety they experience so as to minimize the effects of anxiety by discussing with teachers or peers. Third, to the future researchers, the writer would like to suggest to examine or explore students' anxiety with other factors such as age differences, background knowledge, or school environment to give the meaningful contribution to the language learning process.

## REFERENCES

Abrar, M. (2017). An Investigation into Indonesian EFL University Students' Speaking Anxiety. *JEELS*, 223.
Amini, A. E. (2019). A Correlation Between Students' Anxiety Level and Oral Presentation Performance in EFL Speaking Class. *Journal of English Education and Teaching, Vol. 3, No. 3*, 404.
Arthur, H. (2000). *Testing for Language Teacher Second Edition.* United Kingdom: Cambridge University Press.
Brown, H. D. (2000). *Principles of Language Teaching and Learning Fifth Edition.* New York: Longman.
Brown, H. D. (2004). *Language Assessment Principles and Classroom Practice.* New York: Pearson Education.

Debreli, E. a. (2015). Sources and Levels of Foreign Language Speaking Anxiety of English as a Foreign Language University Students with Regard to Language Proficiency and Gender. *International Journal of English Language Education, Vol. 4, No. 1*, 49–62.

Cope, E. K., Horwitz, H. M. (1986). Foreign Language Classroom Anxiety. *The Modern Language Journal*, 129.

Haber, R. A. (1960). Anxiety in Academic Achievement Situation. *Abnormal and Social Psychology*, 207–215.

Hand, C. (2014). *Living with Anxiety.* USA, Minneapolis, MN: ABDO Publishing.

Harmer, J. (1991). *The Practice of English Language Teaching.* London: Longman.

He, D. (2018). *Foreign Language Learning Anxiety in China.* Singapore: Springer.

Hemerka, V. (2009). Low Speaking Performance in Learners of English, 15.

Hutabarat, A. a. (2019). A Phenomenological Study: Speaking Anxiety Overwhelms English Learners. *Journal of English Language Pedagogy, Literature and Culture Vol. 4, No. 1*, 44–58.

Idris, A. (2017, March 15). *Tiga Agenda Penting Implementasi Kurikulum 2013.* Retrieved from Kompasiana: https://www.kompasiana.com/idrisapandi/58c84e225597733c447dcc57/tiga-agenda-penting-implementasi-kurikulum-2013?page=all

Kayi, H. (2006). Teaching Speaking: Activity to Promote Speaking in a Sccond Languagc. *TESL Journal*, 1.

Khan, Z. (2010). The Effects of Anxiety on Cognitive Processing in English Language Learning. *English Language Teaching, Vol. 3, No. 2*, 199.

Khasinah, S. (2014). Factors Influencing Second Language Acquisition. *Englisia, Vol. 1, No. 2*, 257.

Krashen, D. S. (1982). *Principle and Practice in Second Language Acquisition.* Oxford: Pergamon.

Kumaravadivelu. (2009). *Understanding Language Teaching: From Method to Post method.* New York: Routledge.

Leong, L.-M. a. (2017). An Analysis of Factors Influencing Learners English Speaking Skill. *International Journal of Research in English Education*, 37.

Mai, N. H. (2015). Factors Affecting Students' Speaking Performance At Le Thanh Hien High School. *Asian Journal of Educational Research, Vol. 3, No. 2*, 9.

McDonough, J. S. (1993). *Materials and Methods in ELT.* United Kingdom: Blackwell Publisher.

Michopoulus, V. (2020, 7 17). *Anxiety Physical Symptoms.* Retrieved from Anxiety.org: https://www.anxiety.org/what-is-anxiety

Nuraini, K. (2016). The Barriers of Teaching Speaking English of EFL Learners. *ELLITE, Vol. 1, No. 1*, 7.

Oteir, I. N.-O. (2019). Foreign Language Anxiety: A Systematic Review. *Arab World English Journal, Vol. 10 No. 3*, 309–317.

Smith, P. W. (2003). *Psychology: The Science of Mind and Behavior second edition.* New York: McGraw-Hill.

Tobias, S. (2010). Test Anxiety: Interference, Defective Skills, and Cognitive Capacity. *Educational Psychologist.*

Woodrow, L. (2006). Anxiety and Speaking English as a Second Language. *RELC Journal*, 10.

Zhang, S. (2009). Th Role of Input, Interaction, and Output in the Development of Oral Fluency. *English Language Teaching, Vol. 2, No. 4*, 91.

*Emerging Trends in Technology for Education in an Uncertain World – Nanto, Rahiem & Khalis Maryati (Eds)*
*© 2022 copyright the Author(s), ISBN 978-1-032-11288-6*

# The effect of Reading Questioning Answering (RQA) strategy to improve students' critical reading

F. Fakhrunnisa, R.S. Dewi, Z. Anasy & N. Sunengsih
*Department of English Education, Faculty of Educational Sciences, Universitas Islam Negeri Syarif Hidayatullah Jakarta, Tangerang Selatan, Banten, Indonesia*

Sururin
*Department of Islamic Education, Faculty of Educational Sciences, Universitas Islam Negeri Syarif Hidayatullah Jakarta, Tangerang Selatan, Banten, Indonesia*

Fahrurrozi
*Department of Elementary School Teacher Program, Universitas Negeri Jakarta, Jakarta Timur, DKI Jakarta, Indonesia*

ABSTRACT: The aim of this research was to obtain empirical proof on The Effect of Reading Questioning Answering (RQA) to Improve Students' Critical Reading at eleventh Grade IPA of SMA PGRI 56 Ciputat Academic Year 2019–2020. This research used a quantitative method, and the design used a pre-experimental with types one group pre-test and post-test design. The multiple-choice test, including pre-test and post-test were the instrument of this research. The results using the t-test at $\alpha = 0.05$, df 19 obtained t count $= -4.785$, while $t_{table} = 1.729$. Meanwhile t arithmetic $(-4.785) < t_{table}$ (1.729), therefore Ho $=$ rejected and alternative hypothesis (Ha) $=$ accepted. Post Test had an average value (mean) 59.90 of 20 data, which showed that there was an effect by using RQA strategy at researchers implemented to improve students' critical reading that increased 0.1%. It is suggested to the teachers to build students' critical reading.

*Keywords*: critical reading; RQA strategy; reading comprehension

## 1 INTRODUCTION

Nowadays it's crucial for students to improve their critical reading skills. Students not only need to be an effective learners but need to think critically. In order to achieve this mission, they need the support of the teacher, who are well proficient in critical thinking conceptually and practically especially when it comes to reading lessons. Even though critical thinking in reading has been included a lot of school all around world, but the concept and the aspects are not quite as clear-cut as it is importance.

From this research, the researcher expects that students can evaluate the process in critical reading and not receiving information without a valid source. Whereas critical reading is an important skill in reading, the lack of critical reading in most english classroom and facilitates reading. Students require a variety of critical tools and priorities what especially needed in reading. Many educators already explain that developing critical thinking in reading is useful to make students more creative and innovative, and also "know how to learn and think clearly" (Baker 1989). It's evident with excellent critical reading skills; students can compete with their skills in the global community.

The Indonesian government considers critical thinking to be one of the most important skills to be taught and taught in schools as demonstrated in the 2013 school curriculum and in the 2010 issue of Decree No. 17 on the Indonesian education system and the implementation of this (Mbato

DOI 10.1201/9781003219248-25

2019). However, there is a lack of implementation of critical thinking especially in the classrooms in Indonesia. The main problem with teaching critical reading in Indonesia is the lack of detail of curriculum instruction on what critical reading is, and the unpleasant culture, as well as learning processes within classrooms for students to develop critical ability in reading.

The benefits of RQA strategy will develop student critical reading skills in the process of learning, as reported from previous research. Thalib and Corebima (2017) stated that analytical learning techniques and critical thinking skills could be improved by using RQA strategy. Increasing cognitive ability and critical thinking ability it is influenced by reading (R), generating significant questions (Q) and answering questions (A). This is a critical logical thought form to improve the critical reading process of students.

## 2  LITERATURE REVIEW

### 2.1  *The conceptual definition of critical reading*

Critical reading includes making a reasoned argument that analyses and analyzes what students have read. Critical especially in reading is a style of use thought of every topic, question, substance, meaning that the people increase the consistency of their thought by cleverly making over the assumptions implicit in their thinking and enforcing cognitive expectations on them (Pirozzi & Starks 2012).

Critical reading ensure that the student applies some methods, models, questions and hypotheses that result in increased comprehension. There is more participation, both in skill and comprehension, through critical reading than those in the simple "skimming" of the text. The difference here are if the student skims the text, the basic characteristics and the details are as far as the student is concerned.

As stated in the context of the Day and Park theories (2005), students have been shown to have been useful in understanding reading text. Which also suggests many forms of understanding, as follows:

1) The literary interpretation
2) Interpretive comprehension
3) The reorganization
4) Prognostic comprehension
5) Reflective interpretation
6) Obligated for spesific comprehension

Those are critical reading theory based on an expert and includes some parts. The first, critical reading needs questions to be asked. This means asked a question that have to be answered, asked the right questions, asking questions that are going to the core for that point. Critical reading implies highlighting the fact that, issues need to be addressed. Second, by talking it out, critical reading requires attempting to answer specific questions. Talking the answers to questions is different from answering questions in other ways.

### 2.2  *Critical reading activity*

This kind of activity takes students through a cycle that includes reading a text (headline or review) for assignment or writing a task. Students start with a job assignment or a research query. Then students follow the steps that will help them to learn effectively and think critically (Walker 2011). Students will be presented with the understanding and viewpoint of the author while reading academic content. For example, different writers would have different slants.

Students will also look at what they are read objectively and look for shortcomings, omissions, contradictions, omissions and claims against what they are read. Based on scientific circles, students supposed to consider some different points of view and make their own decisions based on what they are read. Students should consider as a critical reader:

a) What the text tells
b) What is mentioned in the passage
c) Interpretation of the texts

### 2.3  *Developing critical reading in teaching*

Critical thinking includes three processes: analysis, reasoning and assessment, which as follows:

a) Analysis

Analysis step is kind of identify the contents of the claim. When students analyze the text, they try to identify the main idea of the text in specific the primary thoughts, identify the point and the justification, identify inferences or the impacts, and the last is identify if there any persuasion tactics.

b) Reasoning

Reasoning includes all reasoning practice involves making or testing the inferences. This requires inductive reasoning (rational formation) and deductive reasoning (logical argument). Reasoning is often intimately connected to problem-solving and innovation (Geurts 2003). In relation to making inferences that an inference is an academic hypothesis or expectation of something unknown based on the facts and information available (Loenoto 2018). The inference is characterized as understanding deriving from an indirect implication of what is being said. To understanding the reading message, they must be able to read to detect the clues that the researcher gives.

c) Assessment

Winfrey (1999) applies four stages of evaluation based on the assessment principle. In the fourth-level model of Kirkpatrick, each subsequent evaluation level is related to the knowledge given by the lower level. The assessment starts at level one, and then progresses to levels two, three, until four. The data of each previous level serves as a framework for the review of knowledge from the next level (Figure 1).

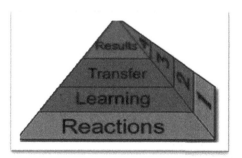

Figure 1.  Four stages of Kirkpatrick theory in assessment curves. Level 1 – reactions, Level 2 – learning, Level 3 – transfer and Level 4 – results.

### 2.4  *Reading, questioning, and answering (RQA) strategy*

RQA strategy is based on the research; students who are given the task of teaching, don't do it as it is told. For all students who had the job of reading the subject matter did not always read it. This resulted in planned learning activities that would be difficult or not carried out to have a low understanding of the subject (Thalib & Corebima 2017).

The researcher explained that RQA learning strategy is a strategy for learning which directs students to read specific topics, for example, outlined in a chapter, a section, a journal article. Students as a whole are expected to read and understand the content of reading and seek to find passages from reading that is significant or very substantial. Then continue by bringing together the answers to the questions in writing and individually. The RQA strategy is formulated on the basis of an approach to constructivism (Darussyamsu 2017).

In short, Reading Questioning Answering (RQA) is a kind of strategy that will enhance critical thinking of students while they are reading comprehension. Because this strategy is used three steps in there, reading (the process to read and understand the text), questioning (the process of synchronization after reading the text and process it in the form of questions and understand questions, based on the meaning absorbed), answering (the last step is answering, in this step, students can answer the questions, when students can answer well, could be inferred students understand well from the interpretation of the message that students has read), from these the researcher can be told that RQA can improve students' thinking abilities.

The learning plan for this RQA consists of three stages: Reading, Questioning, and Answering. Students are given the task of reading each subject matter individually during the reading period. Students are directed in the questioning stage to ask written questions about the essential content about the material that was read (Setiadi 2016). The number of questions, which can vary from 3 to 4 numbers, is tailored to the situation.

## 3 RESEARCH METHOD

### 3.1 *Research setting and participants*

The research is implemented in SMA PGRI 56 Ciputat, located on Jl. Pendidikan No.30, Kec. Ciputat, Kota Tangerang Selatan, Banten 15411. This research is arranged at XI-IPA grade students of SMA PGRI 56 Ciputat on 21 February–6 March 2020 by using pre-experimental one group pre-test and post-test design. The method of this research is quantitative research. This research conducted in pre-experimental research to see how is the effect of RQA strategy to improve students' critical reading at XI-IPA grade students of SMA PGRI 56 Ciputat academic years 2019/2020.

### 3.2 *Techniques of collecting data*

The research design in this is pre-experimental used, with types one group pre- and post-test designs. As stated by Salkind (2010) the pre-experimental designs are systematic observation in a particular situation where the observed criteria are simplified; only a few factors alone are observed so that researchers can overcome the entire process of experimentation. For more details, it can be described as follows:

**The cycle of Pre-experimental design methods:**

In this research, the test items based on the material of the specified national exam reading test (2016–2018). The researcher has modified the test included by:

1. identifying the main idea
2. determining specific information
3. identifying inference

4. making reference
5. understanding vocabulary

## 4 RESULT AND DISCUSSION

There are differences in the effect of reading questioning answered (RQA) strategy to improve students' critical reading. There has been an improvement in the acquisition of values starting from the pre-test before the treatment of students, as well as an increase in learning outcomes based on post-test assessment (Table 1).

The Paired Samples Statistics table shows the informative values for each element in the paired sample.

- Pre-Test has a mean value of 51.40 out of 20 data. The distribution of the data (Std. Deviation) was 6.476, with an error range of 1.448.
- Final Test (Post-test) has an average value (mean) of 59.90 out of 20 info. The data distribution (Std. Deviation) was 8.5897, with an error range of 1.921.

This indicates that the final data check is higher than the initial check. Nevertheless, the range of final test data distribution often increases with higher error levels (Table 2).

From the calculation of the average difference using the t-test at $\alpha = 0.05$, df 19 (in table 4.7 above) obtained t count $= -4.785$, while $t_{table} = 1.729$. Because it uses a two-tailed test, the reception area is $-t_{table}$ arithmetic $\leq t_{table}$. Meanwhile t arithmetic $(-4.785) < t_{table}$ $(1.729)$, therefore **Ho = rejected**. This means that there are a low significant effect of RQA strategy to improve students' critical reading has 0.1%. Here are the results of the acquisition XI-IPA class of test scores, the average student with pre-test score is 5.18, and the average with post-test student score is 5.99. This shows that the RQA strategy implemented by researchers to improve students' critical reading has an increase of 0.1% than before. Even it is just has low effect.

Table 1. Paired sample T-test result.

|        |           | Mean    | N  | Std. deviation | Std. error mean |
|--------|-----------|---------|----|----------------|-----------------|
| Pair 1 | Pre-test  | 51.4000 | 20 | 6.47587        | **1.44805**     |
|        | Post-test | 59.9000 | 20 | 8.58947        | **1.92066**     |

Table 2. Paired samples test table.

|                              | Paired differences | | | | | | | |
|------------------------------|---------|-----------|-----------|----------------------------------------|----------|--------|----|-------------|
|                              |         |           |           | 95% confidence interval of the difference | | | | |
|                              | Mean    | Std. deviation | Std. error mean | Lower | Upper | T | df | Sig. (2-tailed) |
| Pair 1 Pre-test–Post-test    | −8.50000 | 7.94388   | 1.77631   | −12.21785 | −4.78215 | −4.785 | 19 | **.000**    |

# REFERENCES

Ahmada, Adib. 2018. The Effectiveness Of Kwl And Sq3r Techniques In Teaching Reading Comprehension. *Journal of Research in Foreign Language Teaching, 1*, 3–5.

Geurts, B. 2003. Reasoning with Quantifiers. *Cognition international Journal*.

Gilbert & Wiseman, G. Dennis. 2009. *Effective Teaching: Preparation and Implementation*. Charles C Thomas Pub Ltd (1702).

Loenoto, A. Bambang. 2018. *Critical Reading*. UPT. Penerbit dan Percetakan.

Mbato, C. L. 2019. Indonesian EFL Learners' Critical Thinking in Reading. *Jurnal Humaniora*, 92–101.

Salkind, Neil. 2010. *Encyclopedia of Research Design*. SAGE Publications, Inc; 1 edition.

Setiadi, Bambang. 2016. *Language Learning Strategy Questionnaire (LLSQ)*. Graha Ilmu.

Thalib, Murni, Corebima, A. D. & Ghofur, A. 2017. Comparison on Critical Thinking Skill and Cognitive Learning Outcome among Students of X Grade with High and Low Academic Ability through Reading Questioning Answering (RQA) Strategy. *Jurnal Pendidikan Sains, 5*, 26–31.

Walker, Beverley Lloyd. 2011. Authentic leadership for 21st century project delivery. *International Journal of Project Management*, 383–395.

*Emerging Trends in Technology for Education in an Uncertain World – Nanto, Rahiem & Khalis Maryati (Eds)*
*© 2022 copyright the Author(s), ISBN 978-1-032-11288-6*

# Humanism and language pride in learning Indonesian language and literature at school

Nuryani, A. Bahtiar & D. Nurhamidah
*Indonesian Language and Literature Education, Faculty of Tarbiyah and Teacher Training, UIN Syarif Hidayatullah Jakarta*

S. Hudaa
*Management Study Program, Faculty of Economics, Institut Teknologi dan Bisnis Ahmad Dahlan Jakarta*

ABSTRACT:    The essence of education is to humanize humans. For this reason, learning activities must be designed to humanize all parties involved in the learning. The purpose of this study is to describe the learning design that can shape humanism and language pride in Indonesian language learning. The research method and data analysis used descriptive qualitative. The research is literature study with normative studies. Based on the analysis, it can be concluded that learning Indonesian Language and Literature can be designed to instill the values of humanism. With these values of humanism, it is hoped that they will be able to foster a proud attitude towards the Indonesian language. Humanism in Indonesian language learning can be conveyed through cooperative learning activities in the form of interactions that exist between teachers and students. Through these learning activities, it will foster an attitude of pride towards the Indonesian language.

*Keywords*:   humanism, learning Indonesian, language pride, language attitude

## 1   INTRODUCTION

Today the issue of humanism is a very interesting issue to study. Various talks, studies, and articles have been about humanism and have always been the main topic. However, the "crowd" is not followed by practice in everyday life. Likewise in terms of learning, there are still many lessons that go beyond the values of humanism. The essence of humanism is a thought that puts forward human values and makes it a human being who enlivens a sense of humanity (Jamhuri 2018). This is the basis and purpose of implementing an education and learning. Therefore, a learning must take place in accordance with and in line with the values of humanism.

Learning in schools is an interaction that occurs directly with all parties in the school, namely teachers, students, school caretakers, staff, and other parties. Some of these parties interact directly in the learning process and some interact indirectly. Even though the interaction is indirect, it is quite significant in influencing the existing values of humanism. Thus, engagement with all parties must be designed in such a way as to instill character as an interpretation of the values of educational humanism. Especially for parties who interact directly, namely teachers and students, the learning design must reflect the values of humanism more. Based on this, then several questions arise, including how is education that humanizes humans actually applied in learning? How is humanism in learning seen? and how can humanism in learning bring about another attitude of pride? Currently what is happening is learning activities that are carried out without face to face. Longing for school is essentially a longing to do activities at school together (Hudaa et al. 2020). The students missed the involvement with various school parties that had helped shape their character.

In relation to the aforementioned matters, language is an important means so that these human values can be conveyed properly. Learning Indonesian Language and Literature as one of the

DOI 10.1201/9781003219248-26

subjects that must be given in schools for all levels. Considering that this subject is present at all levels of education, the subject of Indonesian Language and Literature (or generally referred to as Indonesian Language) should be the spearhead in the application of humanism in schools. Humanism is expected to be present for all parties involved in learning, namely teachers and students. That way, the values of humanism can be possessed not only by teachers but also by students. Meanwhile, violence against students was also found in several places. One of them is violence committed by teachers who argue for discipline and then violence against students. The incident was found in Mojokerto (bbc.com). This is very far from the values of humanism promoted by our father of education, Ki Hajar Dewantara (Riyanton 2016).

Several studies related to humanism have been carried out by other researchers, among them are (Jamhuri 2018; Mayasari 2017; Riyanton 2016). Based on several studies that have been conducted, there is a *gap* with this research, namely in the element of pride in the Indonesian language. In fact, pride in the Indonesian language is a value of humanism in itself as a sense of love for the Indonesian people. In order to see this *gap*, this research was conducted by developing the concept of pride in the Indonesian language which is represented by the concept of humanism. The essence of man is as a social and cultural being. Therefore, returning to learning that can humanize humans is the right action. As part of society, humans are certainly unique. This uniqueness is the basis for the application of humanism learning. In such a context, education is one of the human endeavors in realizing human characteristics (Mumpuniarti 2010). Roger in Riyanton (2016) suggests six (6) theories of humanism in learning principles. The six principles are (1) humans have a desire to learn naturally, (2) relevance to needs, (3) reducing external threats in learning activities, (4) participatory learning, (5) learning on their own, and (6) always do self-evaluation. These six principles will be used as references in the discussion of humanism in learning.

The Indonesian education figure who aggressively voices the concepts of humanism and multi-culturalism is Malik Fadjar. The former Minister of Education in the Soeharto era was known to be very persistent in instilling the concept of humanism in learning. As stated by the Chairman of PP Muhammadiyah Haedar Nashir that Malik Fadjar is very firm in holding the concepts of humanism and multiculturalism in various aspects, one of which is education. This concept became known as a flexible and broad philosophy of life (Azra 2020). This concept is important to be applied in learning considering that there are many parties involved in these activities. Therefore, it is important to instill a concept of life that is flexible and broad. In addition, Malik Fadjar is known as a figure in humanism education because he is known as a person who aggressively voices concern for anyone regardless of differences in religious, racial or class backgrounds (Hakim 2020). Based on the thoughts and concepts conveyed by Malik Fadjar, education should be the main choice as a means of preventing inhuman acts. Malik Fadjar state a humanist education will be able to human-ize humans. Humanizing humans is essentially an effort to make humans cultured, intelligent and civilized (Hakim 2020). With this nature, education and learning should be carried out with the intent and purpose of being a preventive or preventive measure so that humanity can be upheld. This is in accordance with the understanding of humanism in the Big Indonesian Dictionary (Combs 1978), which is a stream that aims to revive a sense of humanity and aspire to better relationships. Solichin (2019) also states that the humanistic education system approach emphasizes the develop-ment of human dignity who is free to make choices and have courage. Humanism views humans as humans. If viewed as a human being, learning must also be placed as a human being (Tarc 2005).

Regarding language attitudes, Gavin and Mathiot give three characteristics of people's attitudes towards language, namely are fidelity language *(language loyalty),* the pride of the language *(language pride),* and an awareness of the norms of the language *(awareness of the norm)*. Therefore, when discussing the pride of language it cannot be separated from the discussion of language attitudes. Explains that language attitude can be interpreted as a behavior or politeness to react to a linguistic state. Several studies related to language attitude have been carried out by other researchers, among them are Nuryani (2019), Nuryani and Bahtiar (2019) are Mulyaningsih and Itaristanti (2018), Nuryani and Febriana (2017), Solichin (2019), and Suyadi (2013).

The process of implementing learning as above is not something easy. The teacher as the designer of learning activities needs to understand the principles of learning. Iskandar (2009) states that there are six (6) principles of learning, namely the principles of readiness, motivation, attention, persuasion, retention, and transfer of learning. These six principles are needed in learning so that activities can be carried out properly in order to achieve educational goals. In addition to these six principles, learning must also pay attention to the aspects involved in learning. The aspects of learning according to Iskandar (2009) are students, teachers, learning objectives, learning materials, approaches, media, and evaluation. These seven aspects are always present in every learning activity and are related to one another.

In the context of internalizing the values of humanism in learning, one of the subjects that can be used as a benchmark is Indonesian. In addition to being a unifying language, Indonesian also has a function as an advocate for knowledge (Rahardi 2009). Seeing this function, it is appropriate for all parties involved in learning to be able to use Indonesian well and politely. Indonesian, both as the language of instruction and as a subject, still consists of two means, namely spoken and written. Both must be used in communication politely so as to avoid acts of bullying and slander and defamation. Therefore, learning Indonesian must be an example of the use of Indonesian in good communication (Bahtiar et al. 2019).

Indonesian language learning is carried out in schools at all levels. In the curriculum there are basic competencies that are expected in the implementation of Indonesian language learning. In point 2.3 of the basic competencies, it is stated that students have a disciplined attitude and love the country towards the government system and local community services through the use of Indonesian. Meanwhile, in point 2.4, basic competence says having loyalty and pride in the territorial integrity of the Indonesian archipelago through the use of Indonesian (Hindun & dkk 2015). Based on the explanation of these basic competencies, it can be concluded that Indonesian language learning activities in schools must be carried out as an effort to form and develop a sense of loyalty and pride towards the archipelago, which includes Indonesian.

## 2 METHODOLOGY

Researchers used a qualitative descriptive research method. Researchers try to provide guidelines for making Indonesian language learning designs that can foster an attitude of humanism and pride in the Indonesian language. Qualitative research is research in which the researcher is placed as a key instrument (Sugiyono 2012). Researchers do their own observations on learning activities at school. Furthermore, the researcher conducted a literature review of documents related to the theories of humanism and language pride. As stated by Faisal, the use of a qualitative approach aims to describe people's behavior, field events, and certain activities in detail and depth (Faisal 1992). Theory in qualitative research is built on data. Presentation and data analysis were carried out in a narrative manner (Subandi 2011). Therefore, researchers must be able to convey the results of data processing from the theories studied to be presented in a detailed narrative form. Considering that the form of analysis and presentation is narrative, this research is more open than other types of research. In accordance with the open and flexible nature of qualitative research, the types and methods of data collection in qualitative research are also very diverse. This diversity is adjusted to the problem, purpose, and nature of the object under study (Miles & Huberman 2012).

## 3 RESULTS

Discussion will be carried out by presenting the data in the form of a humanism table and a language attitude table. Table 1 is used as a reference for making Indonesian language learning designs. Learning activities and material preparation in Indonesian language learning can include indicators in this table so that the principles of humanism can be instilled. Thus, Indonesian language learning activities are not only a means of transfer of knowledge but also a transfer of humanistic values. This table is compiled based on the theories of humanism and language attitudes. Meanwhile, each indicator is prepared according to current conditions. By using this table as a

Table 1. Theory of humanism and language pride in Indonesian language learning.

| No. | Humanism principles and indicators of language pride |
| --- | --- |
| 1. | The Desire to Learn<br>a. Students make notes that contain things that they feel they don't or have not known about the Indonesian language.<br>b. Teachers provide opportunities for students to find themselves through various sources of things that students must do if they are going to propose Indonesian as an international language. |
| 2. | Relevance to the needs of students<br>a. Practice using Indonesian on social media politely.<br>b. Train students to write about their pride in Indonesian using proper grammar. |
| 3. | Reducing threats<br>a. Providing *rewards* to students who are able to use Indonesian in a day properly and correctly in accordance with the context.<br>b. Give examples of writings in various national media that use Indonesian correctly. |
| 4. | Participatory learning<br>a. Practice speaking Indonesian well and politely throughout the school environment.<br>b. Inviting students to discuss the history of the birth of the Indonesian language and its development. |
| 5. | Learning on his own<br>a. Providing a questionnaire regarding things that are expected related to the development of Indonesian which will become an international language.<br>b. Invite students to make a simulation if Indonesian becomes the international language and they will become Indonesian language ambassadors. |
| 6. | Conduct self-evaluation<br>a. The teacher and students make notes on each of the things or activities that have been carried out so far to advance the Indonesian language.<br>b. teachers and students jointly evaluate the deficiencies of Indonesian when it is proposed as an international language. |

reference, Indonesian language learning can be designed according to current needs and conditions. Learning Indonesian language will be a means of *transfer of knowledge* and *transfer of value*.

## 4 DISCUSSION

There are six theories of humanism related to the principles of learning. This becomes a reference for all parties to be able to plan learning activities to achieve goals. Likewise in Indonesian language learning activities in which there are various materials related to both cognitive, affective, and psychomotor. Therefore, the learning design that is made must consider the various aspects above. In addition, the demands of the curriculum that require students or students to be able to use Indonesian fluently and correctly must also be taken into account.

Indonesia is a country that is known to have many tribes and has an impact on the many regional languages it has. Therefore, all parties should feel grateful because they have one language that functions as a unifying language, namely Indonesian. Related to this, the basic competence also states the pride of the integrity of the Indonesian territory, of course language is an important part of it. With the demands of the curriculum, Indonesian language learning should be designed to foster an attitude of pride in the Indonesian language. Given that language is also used as a means of communicating both orally and in writing, learning Indonesian is also appropriate if it is designed to equip students in communication skills. The ability to communicate is not only related to voicing something, but also the ability to choose diction in the right context.

Based on the table that has been presented above, it can be explained that the theory of humanism can be used as a reference for determining the design of Indonesian language learning, especially in fostering a sense of pride in the Indonesian language. As can be seen in point one (1) which in the principles of humanism it is conveyed that humans naturally have a desire to learn. They are instinctively curious and seek to explore new experiences. Based on these principles, in order to develop a sense of pride in Indonesian, teachers can design learning by referring to two major activities. The two activities, namely students are asked to make notes containing things that they feel they do not or have not known about the Indonesian language and the teacher provides the opportunity for students to search for themselves through various sources of things that must be done by students if they are going to propose Indonesian as a language. International language. By making these notes, it is hoped that a natural desire will emerge which then provides a separate challenge for students to learn and then be able to appreciate the Indonesian language. In point two (2) it is stated that learning will be more meaningful if the things learned are relevant to the needs of students. Therefore, learning can be designed using two major activities. In this activity, students and teachers jointly practice using Indonesian on social media in a polite manner and the teacher trains students to write about their pride in Indonesian using proper grammar. Social media is a media that currently cannot be separated from the world of teenagers. Therefore, it is very relevant when learning polite Indonesian, practice directly on the social media they have. In addition, when they are asked to write things about pride, they will feel that there is so much to be proud of from the Indonesian language.

The next point is about the principle that learning can be improved more by reducing threats. Learning is not carried out to scare people. Therefore, in this principle, neither students nor teachers should threaten each other regardless of their goals. For such learning, the teacher can design activities in the form of giving rewards to students who are able to use Indonesian properly and correctly in a day according to the context. In this activity the treatment given is reversed. Not giving threats of punishment but emphasizing the rewards that will be obtained. In addition, activities that can be carried out to foster pride in the Indonesian language are by providing examples of writings in various national media that use Indonesian correctly. Through this activity students and teachers will get used to seeing the right things so that the correct things will be internalized in students and teachers. The next point is a point regarding participation in learning. If students participate more, the results will be better than one-way learning. Activities can be designed using activities in the form of direct practice in speaking Indonesian well and politely throughout the school environment. These activities are carried out directly and students are required to be active in carrying out communication activities. In addition, it can also be done by inviting students to discuss the history of the birth of the Indonesian language and its development. Through discussion, students will actively participate in voicing their ideas and opinions. Here the role of the teacher is demanded as an active motivator and facilitator so as to stimulate students to "speak out".

Learning on one's own initiative or desire is the next principle of humanism. This principle is related to the internal motivation drive. If students have good internal motivation, they will be more successful than those who do not have internal motivation. Learning activities can be designed by inviting students to fill out a questionnaire about things that are expected related to the development of Indonesian which will become an international language. Based on the questionnaire, the teacher will find out the students' motivation so that it will be easier to invite students to learn. In addition, it can also be done by inviting students to make simulations if Indonesian becomes an international language and they will become Indonesian language ambassadors. based on the simulations they make, they will find the desire to unravel the problems they find. The last principle of humanism is self-evaluation. This activity must involve students and teachers actively. This is important to do because the results of this self-evaluation can be used to improve subsequent learning. What can be done is that the teacher and students make notes on each of the things or activities that have been carried out so far to advance the Indonesian language. Another activity that can be done is for teachers and students to jointly evaluate the deficiencies of Indonesian when it is proposed as an international language.

5   CONCLUSION

Based on the discussion presented in the results and discussion above, it can be concluded that in learning Indonesian in schools it is necessary to make a careful design. The design can refer to the theoretical table and indicators that have been compiled by the researcher. By utilizing these indicators, learning Indonesian will be meaningful learning and can be a means of instilling humanistic values and language pride. This is important because learning Indonesian is the benchmark and spearhead for instilling humanistic values in all parties involved in learning. Indonesian, both in its position as a means of communication and as a subject, needs careful planning by involving all elements. Teachers need to incorporate the principles of humanism in learning Indonesian in order to foster pride in Indonesian as mandated by the curriculum in basic competencies.

## REFERENCES

Azra, A. (2020). *Rekonstruksi dan Modernisasi Pendidikan Islam: Pemikiran dan Kiprah Prof. Dr (HC). A. Malik Fadjar*. UIN Syarif Hidayatullah Jakarta.

Bahtiar, A., Nuryani, & Hudaa, S. (2019). *Khazanah Bahasa: Memaknai Bahasa Indonesia dengan Baik dan Benar* (1st ed.). In Media. http://penerbitinmedia.co.id/search/?q=khazanah bahasa

Combs, A. W. (1978). Humanism, Education, and the Future. *Educational Leadership*.

Faisal, S. (1992). *Format -format Penelitian Sosial*. Rajawali Pers.

Hakim, S. A. (2020). *Pendidikan yang Humanis: Belajar dari Pak Malik*. UIN Syarif Hidayatullah Jakarta.

Hindun, H., & dkk. (2015). *Materi Ajar Guru Kelas MI (GKMI) (Bahasa Indonesia, Matematika, IPA, IPS, dan PKN)*. FITK UIN Syarif Hidayatullah.

Hudaa, S., Bahtiar, A., & Nuryani, N. (2020). Pemanfaatan Teknologi untuk Pengajaran Bahasa Indonesia di Tengah Pandemi Covid-19. *Ranah: Jurnal Kajian Bahasa, 9(2)*. https://doi.org/https://doi.org/10.26499/rnh.v9i2.2361

Iskandar, M. (2009). *Psikologi Pendidikan Sebuah Orientasi Baru*. Ciputat: Gaung Persada Press.

Jamhuri, M. (2018). Humanisme sebagai nilai pendekatan yang efektif dalam pembelajaran dan bersikap, Perspektif multikulturalisme di Universitas Yudharta Pasuruan. *AL MURABBI*.

Mayasari, S. (2017). Filsafat Pendidikan Humanisme dalam Perspektif Pembelajaran Bahasa Inggris Bagi Peserta Didik di Tingkat Sekolah Menengah Atas. *Jurnal Dosen Universitas PGRI*.

Miles, M. B., & Huberman, M. A. (2012). Analisis Data Kualitatif: Buku Sumber Tentang Metode-Metode Baru. In *Universitas Indonesia_UI Press*.

Mulyaningsih, I., & Itaristanti, I. (2018). Pembelajaran Bermuatan HOTS (Higher Order Thinking Skill) di Jurusan Tadris Bahasa Indonesia. *Indonesian Language Education and Literature*. https://doi.org/10.24235/ileal.v4i1.2970

Mumpuniarti, M. (2010). Perspektif Humanis Religius dalam Pendidikan Inklusif. *JPK (Jurnal Pendidikan Khusus)*.

Nuryani. (2019). Sikap Bahasa Remaja Urban terhadap Bahasa Indonesia di Era Milenial (The Language Attitude of Urban Teenagers Towards Indonesian in The Millennial Era). *Kandai, 15*(1), 1. https://doi.org/10.26499/jk.v15i1.1266

Nuryani & Bahtiar, A. (2019). Peran MKWU Bahasa Indonesia sebagai Penguat Identitas dan Nasionalisme Mahasiswa Ptki (Studi Pelaksanaan MKWU Bahasa Indonesia di UIN Syarif Hidayatullah Jakarta). *Jurnal Kembara, 5*(2), 231–244. https://doi.org/https://doi.org/10.22219/KEMBARA.Vol5.No2.

Nuryani, N., & Febriana, H. (2017). Tipe Pembelajaran Bahasa Indonesia di Sekolah Menengah Atas (SMA). *Dialektika: Jurnal Bahasa, Sastra, dan Pendidikan Bahasa Indonesia, 4(1)*

Rahardi, R. K. (2009). *Bahasa Indonesia untuk Perguruan Tinggi* (1st ed.). Erlangga.

Riyanton, M. (2016). Pendidikan humanisme dan implementasinya dalam pembelajaran bahasa indonesia. *Jurnal Ilmiah Lingua Idea*.

Solichin, M. M. (2019). *Pendekatan Humanisme dalam Pembelajaran (Model Penerapannyad di Pondok Pesantren Al-Amin Prenduan Sumenep)*. repository.iainmadura.ac.id.

Subandi, S. (2011). Deskripsi Kualitatif Sebagai Satu Metode Dalam Penelitian Pertunjukan. *Harmonia Journal of Arts Research and Education*.

Sugiyono. (2012). Metode Penelitian Kuantitatif, Kualitatif dan R & D. Bandung:Alfabeta. https://doi.org/10.1017/CBO9781107415324.004

Tarc, A. M. (2005). Education as humanism of the other. *Educational Philosophy and Theory*.

*Emerging Trends in Technology for Education in an Uncertain World – Nanto, Rahiem & Khalis Maryati (Eds)*
© *2022 copyright the Author(s), ISBN 978-1-032-11288-6*

# Affective factors and English learning participation: Student voices

Y.F. Mulyati, D.N. Hidayat & M. Defianty
*Department of English Education, Faculty of Educational Sciences, UIN Syarif Hidayatullah Jakarta, Jakarta, Indonesia*

ABSTRACT: The present study aimed at revealing student participation in English learning. More specifically, this study is aimed to probe the affective factors that hamper students' participation in English language classrooms. To uncover affective factors, the researchers used specific open-ended questionnaires and semi-structured interviews in this study. A semi-structured interview with ten students and two English language lecturers was employed. The findings showed that the most determining factor was the lecturer performance. Further, the study found that the affective factor that hampers students' participation is affected by the individual and relational affective factors. The latter serves to be more dominant than the former. Conclusively, this study suggests that lecturers should always be conscious of how they act in class. The implication of the study suggested necessities in equipping lecturers with sufficient trainings dealing with feedback conducted by related institutions.

*Keywords*: Affective Factors, Language Learning, Students' Participation

## 1 INTRODUCTION

Language learning has reached a broader scope than other vital feeder's fields — for instance, psychology, psycholinguistic, sociolinguistics, neuroscience, and education (Arnold 1999). Among all of the vital feeders field, the education realm is the most developed field for foreign language teaching in recent decades. Language learning might be developed every decade to decade. However, lecturers must remain hungry and never feel satisfied when it comes to gain efficient language learning. To obtain efficient language learning, lecturers should develop interpersonal intelligence that begins with emotional factors. To sum up, the emotional factor is also called "Affective Factors" in the language learning field. "Affective factors" are emotional factors that influence language learning. Arnold (1999) indicates that studying affective elements could contribute to more efficient language teaching. This aims to solve the problems of negative emotions. Negative emotion means that students would instead not be involved in language learning. Furthermore, Arnold (1999) stated that there are two perspectives about the effect on language learning: first, what relates to language learners as individuals. It means that students as individuals. Therefore, all the things that happen are caused by language learners themselves without any interference from others. Second, that focuses on students as participants in socio-cultural situations — this individual connected with other people. The socio-cultural situation means that the student as a student in the classroom is where social interactions and cultural exchanges occur, nearly related to other people. In this situation, everything that happens is due to interference from other people. To sum up, affective factors on language learning are divided into two perspectives; a) individual factors such as anxiety, inhibition, extroversion/introversion, self-esteem, motivation, and learner styles; b) relational factors such as empathy, classroom transactions, and cross-cultural process (Arnold 1999). To obtain efficient language learning, students are also required to participate in the language class. Therefore, lecturers should recognize the affective factor that hampers students' participation in the language class.

DOI 10.1201/9781003219248-27

Many researchers believe that the affective factors that hamper students' participation occur from the individual side, not from the relational side. Zayed and Al-Ghamdi (2019) emphasize that anxiety does not affect students' self-confidence that hampers students' participation. Henter (2014) presented that anxiety and motivation are the affective factors that directly hamper students' participation in language learning. Khaleghi (2016) indicated that self-confidence and anxiety are the essential affective factors influencing reluctance students to participate. Affective factors also influence students' writing. Deb (2018) discovered the correlation between self-efficacy and writing anxiety that directly influences students' writing performance. ESL writing students need to be aware of their affective factors and their feelings.

Furthermore, based on Zhu and Zhou (2012) research, the affective factors at junior high school students are inhibition and low self-esteem in their English learning. Inhibition occurs because students care a lot about their faces and are unwilling to be laughed at by others in the class. Additionally, self-esteem happens because students care much about how parents, teachers, and classmates see them. Furthermore, students will see and judge their image through others' attitudes and responses. Moreover, Nie (2018) stated that to improve the students' oral English proficiency, language teachers should spare no effort to reduce classroom anxiety and create a safe and comfortable classroom environment for learners to learn at ease. Similarly, Prasangani (2015) mentions that affective factors are involved in students' English learning motivation that support students' goals. However, Ni (2012) mentions that the excellent students typically have great motivation, high self-confidence, and a low level of anxiety. Through that, they can receive and take in plenty of language input from their teacher. Some students learn the language with low motivation, little self-confidence, and a high level of anxiety. Required the teachers should give correct guidance on their affective factors. Based on the consideration above, this current study aims to determine the affective factor that hampers students' participation in language learning, focusing on individual factors and a relational factor.

## 2 METHODS

A qualitative case study was conducted at the Department of English Education in one of the state universities in Jakarta, Indonesia. Subjects were chosen using purposive sampling. In purposive sampling, the researchers intentionally pick the individuals to learn and understand the central phenomenon. As discussed earlier, this research aims to find out the students' affective factors while participating in the English language classroom. Based on those considerations, the researcher conducted an open-ended questionnaire distributed to the sixth-semester students of class 6A. Researchers used the questionnaire to find the highest affective factors, along with the general reasons for student participation in language classes. In line with the purpose of the research, Leeuw et al. (2008) mentions that a specific open-ended questionnaire is applied to assess factual information. In this study, the factual information is related to students' participation in the English language classroom, as the researchers explained before. To ensure the questionnaire outcome is accurate, the researcher seeks a more in-depth investigation through an open-ended student's interview.

The researchers used triangulation and data reduction in analyzing the data. This research also used an interactional mechanism with the participant to produce a thick description. The thick description means that the research outcome is described in the specified description. This is suitable for Creswell's (2012) statement that states thick description design is suited to illustrate those phenomena, which will examine to get an in-depth understanding of the process rather than the outcome. In line with the purpose of the research, a qualitative research design is defined by Creswell (2012) as "Qualitative researchers build their patterns, categories, and themes from the bottom up by organizing the data into increasingly more abstract units of information. This inductive process illustrates working back and forth between the themes and the database until the researchers have established a comprehensive set of themes." This inductive process is in accordance with what researchers do in this current research. The researcher finds that after rereading the questionnaire results, the researcher has found a theme that the language researcher wants more deeply. Besides, Ritchie and Lewis (2003) mention that qualitative research aims to present an in-depth understanding of experiences, thoughts, history, social, and significant conditions from the research participants.

## 3 RESULTS

Thirty-one students were included in this study, of which 8 were males and 23 were females. Students mentioned the three most substantial affective factors that encouraged them to participate. Ranked most substantial were inhibition. Motivation ranked second, and self-esteem ranked last.

Inhibition ranked highest in most determining affective factors that hamper students' participation in the English Language classroom. All participants mentioned inhibition in terms of repetition of words as the most substantial factor in determining their participation because of students' claim that they have limited knowledge of vocabulary. The student questionnaire result showed that when students are confused and do not know what to say, they decide to repeat the same words that they say before (Table 1).

Based on the questionnaire, the highest affective factor is inhibition, in terms of lack of vocabulary. However, after further investigation, the researchers interviewed ten students who mentioned inhibition in the previous questionnaire. The interview outcomes showed that 7 out of 10 students

Table 1. Coding and themes for the questionnaire section.

| Raw text/questionnaire text | Themes |
| --- | --- |
| I: When you were speaking in front of an English class, have you ever repeated the same words?<br>R: Yes, I did, because of the limited number of vocabulary words and also because of the spontaneity factor | Inhibition |
| I: In English class, have you studied hard to get high score on exams?<br>R: Yes, very proud and satisfied that my efforts did produce good results | Motivation |
| I: In English class, have you ever felt proud when you succeeded in answering questions from the lecturer?<br>R: Yes, because I can participate in class, because it can show myself that I am capable | Self Esteem |
| I: Have you ever started a conversation with someone you don't know?<br>R: Yes, to ask questions that are urgent or want to invite acquaintances | Extroversion Introversion |
| I: In English class, some lecturers apply class rules and even determine study groups. Do you like lecturers like that?<br>R: Yes, it is more effective in using study time, the more organized the classes | Classroom Transaction |
| I: Have you ever thought about not participating when you are in English class?<br>R: Yes, not in a good mood or maybe not feeling well | Anxiety |
| I: When in English class you saw your classmates speak better English than you, have you ever lost confidence?<br>R: Yes, because I felt insecure when I heard that my friend spoke better English | Empathy |
| I: Do you like the lecturer who uses the lecture method when teaching English classes?<br>R: Yes, I like it. I am an auditory learner. I was enjoying the learning system with listening | Student Learning Style |
| I: When you speak English in a language class, you notice that you have a regional accent. Have you ever used that as a reason why you didn't want to participate in a language class?<br>R: Yes, I felt embarrassed because the accent used was still a regional accent | Cross-Cultural Process |

I = Interviewer.
R = Respondent.

Table 2.  Coding and themes for the interview section.

| Raw text/interview transcript | Code for themes |
|---|---|
| I: This thesis discusses the student participation in the language class based on your answer. It means you don't want to participate in language class because you are afraid/repeating the same words. What is the most significant factor that made you want to participate in the language class? R: In my opinion, the lecturers should provide more opportunities for students to be active in class and not make students down, but must engage them. If a student makes a mistake, do not immediately say wrong and make students feel down. | Lecturer performances |
| I: This thesis discusses the student participation in the language class based on your answer. It means you don't want to participate in language class because you are afraid/repeating the same words. What is the most significant factor that made you want to participate in the language class? R: Participation in the class depends on the motivation of the students. My self-motivation is strong, and even I bad if I don't participate in the language class. In other words, I feel my parents have paid for me to go to college, and I do not act on learning. I thought it is like I dumped my parents' money. | Students motivation |
| I: This thesis discusses the student participation in the language class based on your answer. It means you don't want to participate in language class because you are afraid/repeating the same words. What is the most significant factor that made you want to participate in the language class? R: A supportive friend. When I have a friend, who supports me without commenting or judging me while I speak, I will participate in language classes. | Supportive friend |

I = Interviewer.
R = Respondent.

asserted that inhibition is not the main reason for their hesitation to participate in the English language classroom. The main affective factor is lecturer-performance (Table 2).

The students' questionnaire and interview result prove that inhibition is not the main factor that hampers students' participation in class. However, lecturer-performance is the main factor. Lecturer-performance is one of the classroom transactions aspect called relational affective factors.

## 4  DISCUSSION

The study discovered that the lecturer-performance was the most influential affective factor that hampers students' participation in the English language classroom. This finding strengthens the results of Abdullah et al. (2012) that found instructor traits and skills play an essential role in shaping classroom interaction. In this context, instructors mean lecturers. Traits that have been shown by the teacher, such as supportive, understanding, approachable are necessary. Zhu and Zhou (2012) research that low self-esteem occurs because students care much about how parents, teachers, and classmates see them while participating. Likewise, Henter (2014) said that anxiety that occurs while students' participate in front of the class will make them feel unable to full the requirements of learning a foreign language, and they feel less skilled than their peers or lecturer. Students' biggest fear is being evaluated negatively by their peers while making mistakes in front of the class. Students will see and judge their image through others' attitudes and responses. Mustapha (2010) stated that traits indicate study like being encouraging, understanding, and approachable, not only lecturer nonverbal behaviors that can engage student participation in the English language classroom. Studies carried out by Galishnikova (2014) found that teachers' verbal encouragement helps learners overcome self-doubt. Therefore, teachers' traits and skills are essential in class, especially understanding and approachable skills. However, lectures should pay attention to their verbal and nonverbal behavior too because even nodding and the word "good" can significantly affect students in the class.

While giving students verbal or nonverbal encouragement, the lecturers should have a large scale of authentic or non-authentic material. This finding supports the study done by Hidayat et al. (2020), who found that English teachers are still limited with non-authentic materials, even though thousands of YouTube videos can be used to make English learning and teach more engagement to students. Nevertheless, back again, teachers should lead their students to enrich their vocabulary since YouTube also has marketing purposes, not only the teaching materials.

Lecturers need to make all the students aware of the many materials around them. Students are fully not aware of the knowledge that occur in their environment. Studies carried out by Meerah (2010) found a similar situation. Students think that they only get the environmental learning input mainly from television and newspapers. It can be assumed that they did not know that social media is included in environmental learning input. Lecturers should lead students about social media and environmental knowledge to get better English language learning. However, what if the lecturers themselves are not aware of social media use as experimental knowledge. This is why lecturers should provide training between schools and instances. In lecturers' training, they also learn about using social media in language learning and how to channel it to students. A study carried out by Hidayat (2019) found similar training called program evaluation using Context, Input, Process, and Product (CIPP) to provide a significant contribution to the better value of English teacher education for students'. In addition, the lecturers' evaluation program is also connected with the concept of peer reviews student-teacher by using the evaluation and the evaluated issues. This finding is compatible with researches carried out by Saharov (2012) that stated a complete evaluation of achieving the language learning standards is when teachers and students should always evaluate each other. For instance, lecture asks for their teaching feedback and suggestions to the students'.

From some of the studies above, it is clear why the affective factor that hampers students' participation is the educator's performance. Because educator is the first people who have direct contact with students at school or on campus, based on that reason, lecturer performance is the first thing seen by students in the class. Both verbal and nonverbal. In addition, the way lecturers create an appropriate classroom atmosphere will also significantly affect students. Therefore, lecturers and students should always evaluate each other by giving peer-feedback and suggestions to get meaningful learning and a better teaching method in the future. This study had some limitations. This study is focusing on students' perception, not on lecturer perception. Further research can be carried out by concentrating on lecturer perception considering the same affective aspect that this current study already discussed.

## 5 CONCLUSION

This present study has addressed the most prominent factors between individuals and the relational affective factors that hamper student participation in English language classrooms, specifically in Indonesia. The most prominent factor that hampers students' participation in this study is lecturer-performance. As a result, the educator is expected to held peer-feedback between schools and institutions in Indonesia. On the other hand, this peer-feedback can produce efficient language learning that is connected with emotional intelligence. Based on this result, the relational factor impacts students' participation in the English language classroom than individual factors.

## 6 ACKNOWLEDGMENT

We would like to express our gratitude to International Conference of Education in Moslem Society (ICEMS) 2020 FITK UIN Syarif Hidayatullah Jakarta for publication support.

# REFERENCES

Abdullah, M. Y., N. R. A. Bakar, and M. H. Mahbob. 2012. "Student's Participation in Classroom: What Motivates Them to Speak Up?" *Procedia – Social and Behavioral Sciences* 51:516–22.

Arnold, Jane. 1999. *Affect in Language Learning*. Cambridge University Press.

Creswell, John W. 2012. *Educational Research*. 4th ed. edited by P. A. Smith. 501 Boylston Street, Boston: Pearson Education, Inc.

Deb, Joyshree. 2018. "Affective Factors in Second Language Writing: Is It a Matter of Concern?" *The Morning Watch: Educatonal and Social Analysis* 46(1):1–11.

Galishnikova, Elena M. 2014. "Language Learning Motivation: A Look at the Additional Program." *Procedia – Social and Behavioral Sciences* 152(917):1137–42.

Henter, Ramona. 2014. "Affective Factors Involved in Learning a Foreign Language." *Procedia – Social and Behavioral Sciences* 127:373–78.

Hidayat, D. N. 2019. "The Potential of Context, Input, Process and Product (CIPP) as an Evaluation Model for English Teacher Education Programs in Indonesia." pp. 5–10 in *The 5th International Conference on Education in Muslim Society (ICEMS)*. Vol. 5.

Hidayat, D. N., Y. Septiawan, and A. Sufyan. 2020. "Critical Discourse Analysis and Its Potential for English Language Teaching: A Study on Beauty Advertisement Products in Indonesia." *The Asian ESP Journal Autumn Edition* 16(2):290.

Khaleghi, Abdolnoor. 2016. "Identification of Affective Factors Influencing Students' Low Participation in University EFL Oral Classes: An Iranian Case Study." *International Journal of Humanities and Social Science* 6(7):185–89.

Leeuw, Edith D. de., Joop J. Hox, and Don A. Dillman. 2008. *International Handbook of Survey Methodology*. Taylor & Francis Group/Lawrence Erlbaum Associates.

Meerah, Tamby Subahan Mohd, Lilia Halim, and Thiagarajan Nadeson. 2010. "Environmental Citizenship: What Level of Knowledge, Attitude, Skill and Participation the Students Own?" *Procedia – Social and Behavioral Sciences* 2(2):5715–19.

Mustapha, Siti Maziha, Nik Suryani Nik Abd Rahman, and Melor Md Yunus. 2010. "Factors Influencing Classroom Participation: A Case Study of Malaysian Undergraduate Students." *Procedia – Social and Behavioral Sciences* 9:1079–84.

Ni, Hui. 2012. "The Effects of Affective Factors in SLA and Pedagogical Implications." *Theory and Practice in Language Studies* 2(7):1508–13.

Nie, Yongwei. 2018. "Affective Factors Influencing Oral English Teaching." *DEStech Transactions on Social Science, Education and Human Science* (SSHE):1–7.

Prasangani, K. S. N. 2015. "Global English: A Study of Factors Affect for English Language Learning Motivation in Sri Lankan Undergraduates." *Procedia – Social and Behavioral Sciences* 172:794–800.

Ritchie, Jane, and Jane, Lewis, 2003. *Qualitative Research Practice: A Guide for Social Science Students and Researchers*. SAGE Publication.

Saharov, Natalia. 2012. "Students' Participation in the External Evaluation Process for the Romanian Universities." *Procedia – Social and Behavioral Sciences* 46:5173.

Zayed, Jihan, and Huda, Al-Ghamdi. 2019. "The Relationships among Affective Factors in Learning EFL: A Study of the Saudi Setting." *English Language Teaching* 12(9):105.

Zhu, Biyi, and Yaping Zhou. 2012. "A Study on Students' Affective Factors in Junior High School English Teaching." *English Language Teaching* 5(7):33–41.

*Emerging Trends in Technology for Education in an Uncertain World – Nanto, Rahiem & Khalis Maryati (Eds)*
*© 2022 copyright the Author(s), ISBN 978-1-032-11288-6*

# Lecturer performance and student participation in English learning

D.N. Hidayat, Y.F. Mulyati, M. Defianty, R. Faeruz & N.D. Haryanti
*Department of English Education, Faculty of Educational Sciences, UIN Syarif Hidayatullah Jakarta, Jakarta, Indonesia*

ABSTRACT:   The study sought to investigate lecturer performance impact on student participation and types of language learning fostering student participation. Employing a case study with semi-structured interviews involving students and lecturers, this research focuses on revealing the lecturer performance in relation to student participation in English language classes. The study found positive and negative lecturer performances. Positive lecturer performances, such as lecturer triggering topic, positive lecturer interaction with the students, lecturer giving feedback for student works, and lecturer positive expectations to motivate their students to learn English. Further, this study revealed negative lecturer performances as being monotonous in teaching methods and lack of lecturer engagement in class. To recapitulate, the language learning fostering student participation is an English language classroom that is provided with a positive lecturer performance.

*Keywords*:   English, Lecturer Performance, Participation, Teaching and Learning

## 1   INTRODUCTION

Despite the distinction between assignment and students' participation in language learning, it has been reported that most Indonesian students remain passive in the classroom. A classroom is a place where both students and educators meet in the same place to exchange information in their quest for knowledge. In the classroom, educators present the language learning material effectively to ensure that students understand the learning material. On the other hand, the students are demanded to actively receive, explore, and implement the knowledge gained in the classroom. These complementing engagements between lecturers and students can create language learning that students want but still beneficial for the lecturer and the student side.

A beneficial language learning classroom involved two-way interaction between students and educators (Abdullah et al. 2012b). Beneficial language learning occurred when both educators and students interact and actively participate in a language learning class. Nevertheless, in English language classrooms, we often see that students still do not actively participate or become passive in the classroom, despite using various teaching methods to stimulate students' participation (Abdullah et al. 2012a).

The students' participation leads this current study to investigate why educators' performance impacts students' participation in the language learning classroom. Many other researchers believe that educators' performance is the main factor that hampers students' participation. As Mustapha et al. (2010) concluded, educators' performance includes identifying and paying attention more to passive students' and approaching passive students by calling them by name, engaged in positive nonverbal behaviors such as smiling and nodding. Furthermore, Addis et al. (2017) stated that educators should focus more on the students as individuals and then put individual learning first rather than group work learning. Saville et al. (2011) mention that educators' performance impact on students' participation depends on experienced and inexperienced educators. If the educators are already experienced, it will automatically make the students' participation grow.

Similarly, Tandi Arrang et al. (2016) stated the teachers' experience makes students motivated to learn and think carefully about what they are learning and understanding of the material. On

                                                DOI 10.1201/9781003219248-28

the other hand, Elfindri et al. (2015) mention that lecture-performance depends on the lecturer's graduated university. Budiman and Apriani (2019) mention that lecture-performance is included in lecture role that affects students' communication. In other words, the factor affecting students' communication in terms of participation is the lecturer role. Furthermore, Samian and Noor (2012) stated that educators should be excellent lecturers who can master delivery techniques and establish good relationships with them. However, if educators have inadequate teaching delivery, it will be the main factor for students contributing to lousy performance in class. The study aims to determine why educators' performance impacts students' participation in class and what kind of language learning fosters student participation in class.

## 2 METHODS

A qualitative case study was employed at one Department of English Education in Jakarta, Indonesia. Subjects were chosen using purposive sampling. In purposive sampling, the researcher intentionally picks the individuals to learn and understand the phenomenon's central. This research aims to determine why educators' performance impacts students' participation in class and what kind of language learning fosters student participation in class. Based on those considerations, the researchers conducted a semi-structured interview with ten sixth-semester students and two English language lecturers. In line with this research phenomenon, Ritchie and Lewis (2003) stated that the semi-structured interview allowed the researcher to get a detailed investigation and understanding of someone's thoughts and responses dealing with specific phenomena. This lecturers' interview is held to gain more in-depth information about the teacher teaching method in the class and how students behave while in language class based on lecturer perception.

The researchers employed triangulation between students and lecturer interview. The researchers also used data reduction to make the data analysis easier. This research used an interactional mechanism with the participant to produce a thick description. The thick description means that the research outcome is described in the specified description. This is suitable for Creswell (2012) statement that states thick description design is suited to illustrate those phenomena, which was examined to get an in-depth understanding of the process rather than the outcome. In line with the instrument of the research, a qualitative research design is defined by Creswell (2012) as "By using open-ended interview questions, it could probe further information and elaborate the information". Therefore, the interviews the researchers conducted used an open-ended interview." In addition, Ritchie and Lewis (2003) mention that qualitative research aims to present an in-depth understanding of experiences, thoughts, history, social, and significant conditions from the research participants.

## 3 RESULTS

Ten students were included in this study, of which 4 were males and 6 were females. The student's interview revealed that 7 out of 10 students asserted that lecturer-performance is impacting their reluctance to participate in the English language classroom. To gain the exact reason, the researcher seeks a more in-depth investigation by asking in more detail about why educators' performance impacts students' participation (Table 1).

To gain the exact reason, the researchers sought a more in-depth investigation by asking in more detail about why educators' performance impacts students' participation. The Investigation found out the exact reason why educators' performance impacts students' participation in class was continued with lecturer interviews. The way lecturers create triggering factors that can stimulate students' participation makes lecturer-performance impact student participation (Table 2).

There are two kinds of lecturer performance: positive and negative performance. The positive lecturers' performance in this research means that the lecturers' teaching method improves students' capability in the English language classroom. There are many positive lecturer performances in the

Table 1. Coding and themes for the students' interview.

| Raw text/interview transcript | Themes |
| --- | --- |
| I: This thesis discusses the student participation in the language class based on your answer. It means you don't want to participate in language class because you are afraid/repeating the same words. What is the most significant factor that made you want to participate in the language class?<br>R: In my opinion, the lecturers should provide more opportunities for students to be active in class and not make students down, but must engage them. If a student makes a mistake, do not immediately say wrong and make students feel down. | Lecturer performances |
| I: This thesis discusses the student participation in the language class based on your answer. It means you don't want to participate in language class because you are afraid/repeating the same words. What is the most significant factor that made you want to participate in the language class?<br>R: Participation in the class depends on the motivation of the students. My self-motivation is strong, and even I bad if I don't participate in the language class. In other words, I feel my parents have paid for me to go to college, and I do not act on learning. I thought it is like I dumped my parents' money. | Students, motivation |
| I: This thesis discusses the student participation in the language class based on your answer. It means you don't want to participate in language class because you are afraid/repeating the same words. What is the most significant factor that made you want to participate in the language class?<br>R: A supportive friend. When I have a friend, who supports me without commenting or judging me while I speak, I will participate in language classes. | Supportive friend |

I = Interviewer.
R = Respondent.


Table 2. Coding and themes for the lecturers' interview.

| Raw text/interview transcript | Themes |
| --- | --- |
| I: This thesis result showed that the student participation is caused because of the lecturer's performances. Do you agree with the results of this research?<br>R: Agree because the lecturer is the key, where the relationship between lecturers and students must occur. Lecturers must also create motivation to build self-confidence. Thus, the point is back again to how the lecturer can create an atmosphere so that students want to participate in English classes. | Lecturer performances |
| I: This thesis result showed that the student participation is caused because of the lecturer's performances. Do you agree with the results of this research?<br>R: Agree because the lecturer is the key, where the relationship between lecturers and students must occur. Lecturers must also create motivation to build self-confidence. Thus, the point is back again to how the lecturer can create an atmosphere so that students want to participate in English classes. | |

I = Interviewer.
R = Respondent.

English language classroom. For instance, lecturer triggering topic, Lecturer positive interaction with the student, lecturer giving feedback for student works, and the most important one, educators positive expectations to motivate their students to learn English. Meanwhile, negative lecturer performances in this research are monotonous teaching methods, lack of lecturer engagement in class, and lecturers lack of triggering factors. Based on the consideration above, the researcher concluded that the negative lecturers' performance, such as monotonous teaching methods, where the lecturer used too many monologues, less interaction with students—created students' lack of participation in the English language classroom.

## 4  DISCUSSION

The study discovered that the students did not want to participate in the English language classroom because of the lecturer's performance. Furthermore, there are positive and negative lecturer performances. Positive lecturer performance often encounters in the English language classroom are lecturer interaction with the student, lecturers' feedback for student works, lecturer non-verbal action, and lecturer positive expectations. The statement above is connected with Yavuzer (2000), who mentioned that positive teacher relationships with students could allow the teacher to reinforce student participation.

Similarly, Freeman (2015) mentioned that positive teacher reinforcement would create an effective classroom, as long as the teacher knows their students' needs. Other positive lecturer performances are giving feedback for student works, complimenting and listening to student interest, and a positive lecturer performance. In line with Bitchener and Ferris (2012), lecturer feedback on students' work is an effective way to help the students in mastering specific targeted on structural writing over a short term process. Furthermore, the use of direct written feedback in the students' writing can help them focus on particular topics, for instance, grammar, vocabulary, word order and many more. On the other hand, Frymier (1993, as cited in Keramida 2009) mentioned that the teachers' non-verbal actions such as smiling, having a relaxed stance, various gestures, and facial expressions come first to improve their learning experience. The result of Frymier's (1993) study, in line with Mustapha et al. (2010), indicated that students were more willing to participate when the lecturers called them by name, asked probing questions, and always engaged in positive nonverbal behaviors such as smiling and nodding to acknowledge their answers. In other words, teachers' verbal encouragement helps learners overcome self-doubt. Therefore, educators' traits and skills are essential in class, especially understanding and approachable skills. The lecturers should also pay attention to their verbal and nonverbal behavior because even nodding and the word "good" can significantly affect students in the class.

Furthermore, Yavuzer (2000) defined educators' positive expectations to motivate their students is the most fundamental principle in positive lecturers' performance. In line with this statement, Perry et al. (2006) claimed that teacher expectations might have a more direct and more substantial impact on student motivation. This is a precursor action affecting student achievement. For instance, students keep studying hard, continuing to face their difficulties.

To in-depth this research, the researchers not only discussed the positive and negative lecturer performance that fosters students' participation in the English language classroom. But researchers also observed positive and negative student performance when responding to lecturers in class. Researchers found that positive student performance, such as positive students' thinking skills in the English language class, can increase student abilities and student scores. The statement above is connected with Duckworth et al. (2009) who mentioned the persevering individuals have optimistic thoughts. Students' appropriate behaviors communicated with the lecturer also included positive student performances. Spencer (2015) also mentioned that students' appropriate classroom behavior is increasing because of the teacher's praise. Not only lecturer nonverbal behaviors that can engage students' participation in the English language classroom. The study carried out by Galishnikova (2014) stated that teachers' verbal encouragement helps learners overcome self-doubt. Therefore, lecturers should pay attention to their verbal and nonverbal behavior because even nodding and the word "good" can significantly affect students in the class.

Next, the students' negative performances. Students' negative performance, such as students' limited information about learning material. Students sometimes do not realize that they can find English learning anywhere. Even YouTube ads can be used as learning material. This finding supports the study done by Hidayat et al. (2020), who found that YouTube videos can make English learning and more engagement to students. While using advertisements that automatically played on YouTube, students can practically utilize learning materials from authentic resources such as YouTube advertisements to enrich their vocabulary. Since the word choice in the advertisement from that YouTube will be different from students' daily vocabulary. Findings have shown that students' lack of vocabulary is also the second problem that hampers their English language participation. Students' limitation of knowledge about environmental information makes them unaware of the learning materials is in their hands. Studies carried out by Meerah et al. (2010) found a similar situation. Students think that they get environmental information mainly from television and newspapers. To sum up, that students did not know that social media is included in environmental information.

An essential point of this research is that students cannot blame negative lecturer performance factor affecting their class participation because this student's statement does not match the fact at a related school or university. The reality showed that teachers and lecturers who have been placed in educational institutions had fulfilled the academic qualifications and competencies. As stated in Indonesian Government Regulation No. 14 the Year 2005 about teacher and lecturer "Qualification, Competencies, and Certification." The government is hiring teachers and lecturers in educational institutions with full consideration and academic qualifications and competencies that the teacher and lecture through (Departemen Pendidikan Nasional 2005). In other words, it showed that the teachers and lecturers must fulfill the academic qualifications and competencies first before being able to teach in educational institutions. Based on those considerations, the researcher concluded that students could not demand the lecturers' teaching methods in the class. However, to create English classroom participation, students must also be able to contribute.

The students expect to put much effort into reading the discussion materials before the class started. Students are expected to contribute and participate as much as possible in class. Moreover, the most important one is that students must be ready for what will happen in the course. If there is an incident in the classroom that is not in accordance with the student's desire, then the student must adapt and still try to participate in the English class. This is in line with Brown (2000) mentioned lecture-performances connected with emotional or, in general, its call "ego," where the adolescents ego are flexible and easy to adapt. Based on that reason, students must be able to adapt to every situation in English class because it's one of the students' obligations to study and participate in English without questioning the lecturer's performance. The fundamental thing is that students understand English material and can apply it in their life. In addition, students must adapt to the lecturer's performance and remain enthusiastic about participating in the English Language classroom.

This study had some limitations. This study discusses that the lecturer performances that hamper student participation in the English Language classroom is negative lecturer's performance, which occurs because of the unpreparedness of students while in the English language classroom. Further research can be carried out by focusing on the students' role and the educators' role in classroom participation.

## 5  CONCLUSION AND SUGGESTION

This current study has addressed lecturer's performance is very influencing students' participation at English language classroom. Furthermore, there are positive and negative lecturer performances. The positive lecturers' performance in this research means that the lecturers' teaching method improves students' capability in the English language classroom. For instance, lecturer triggering topic, lecturer positive interaction with the student, lecturer giving feedback for student works, and the most important one, educators positive expectations to motivate their students to learn English.

Meanwhile, this research's negative lecturer performances are monotonous teaching methods, lack of lecturer engagement in class, and lecturers lack of triggering factors. Based on the consideration above, the researcher concluded students do not want to participate if the lecturer shows the negative performance at class, such as monotonous teaching methods, where the lecturer used too many monologues, which created less interaction with students and lecture lack of engagement or triggering factor at English language classroom.

Therefore, students have willingness to participate in the English language classroom if the lecturer has a positive lecturer performance. On the other hand, the students must also take part in classroom participation. Student participation can be created by the lecturer's way of creating a comfortable atmosphere or encouraging quiet students to speak. However, the students expect to put much effort into reading the discussion materials before the class. The students are expected to contribute and participate as much as possible in the English language classroom.

Moreover, the most important one is that students must be ready for what will happen in class. Suppose there will be an incident in the classroom that is not in accordance with the student's hope. In that case, the students must adapt and still try to participate in the English class—one of the students' obligations to study and participate in English without questioning the lecturer's performance. The fundamental thing is that students understand English material and can apply it in their life. In addition, students must adapt to the lecturer's performance and remain enthusiastic about participating in the English Language classroom.

## ACKNOWLEDGMENT

We would like to express our gratitude to International Conference of Education in Moslem Society (ICEMS) 2020 FITK UIN Syarif Hidayatullah Jakarta for publication support.

## REFERENCES

Abdullah, Mohd. Yusof, Noor Rahamah Abu Bakar, and Maizatul Haizan Mahbob. 2012a. "Student's Participation in Classroom: What Motivates Them to Speak Up?" *Procedia – Social and Behavioral Sciences* 51:516–22.

Abdullah, Mohd. Yusof, Noor Rahamah Abu Bakar, and Maizatul Haizan Mahbob. 2012b. "The Dynamics of Student Participation in Classroom: Observation on Level and Forms of Participation." *Procedia – Social and Behavioral Sciences* 59:61–70.

Addis, Yitayal, Kelemua Mengesha, Hilina Ambachew, and Tola Gemeda. 2017. "Enhancing Classroom Participation of Students in Practical Courses: The Case of Environmental Science Students' at Kotebe Metropolitan University." *Journal of Education and Practice* 8(19):28–33.

Bitchener, J. and Ferris, D., R. 2012. *Written Corrective Feedback in Second Language Acquisition and Writing*. New York: Routledge.

Brown, H. Douglas. 2000. "Principles of Language Learning And Teaching." *TESOL Quarterly* 14.

Budiman, Wisnu and Eka Apriani. 2019. "STUDENTS' PERCEPTION OF LECTURERS' ROLE IN ENHANCING EFL LEARNERS' COMMUNICATION ABILITY." *3rd English Language and Literature International Conference (ELLiC)* 3:223–37.

Creswell, John W. 2012. *Educational Research*. 4th ed. edited by P. A. Smith. 501 Boylston Street, Boston: Pearson Education, Inc.

Departemen Pendidikan Nasional. 2005. *Undang-Undang Nomor 14 Tahun 2005 Tentang Guru Dan Dosen*.

Duckworth, Angela Lee, Patrick D. Quinn, and Martin E. P. Seligman. 2009. "Positive Predictors of Teacher Effectiveness." *The Journal of Positive Psychology* 4(6):540–47.

Freeman, Dr. Jennifer. 2015. "An Analysis of the Relationship Between Implementation of School-Wide Positive Behavior Interventions and Supports and High School Dropout Rates." *Project Muse* 290–315.

Galishnikova, Elena M. 2014. "Language Learning Motivation: A Look at the Additional Program." *Procedia – Social and Behavioral Sciences* 152(917):1137–42.

Hidayat, Didin Nuruddin, Yudi Septiawan, and Agus Sufyan. 2020. "Critical Discourse Analysis and Its Potential for English Language Teaching: A Study on Beauty Advertisement Products in Indonesia." *The Asian ESP Journal* 16(2.2):290.

Keramida, Areti. 2009. "Helping Students Overcome Foreign Language Speaking Anxiety in the English Classroom: Theoretical Issues and Practical Recommendations." *Nternational Education Studies Journal* 2(4).

Meerah, Tamby Subahan Mohd, Lilia Halim, and Thiagarajan Nadeson. 2010. "Environmental Citizenship: What Level of Knowledge, Attitude, Skill and Participation the Students Own?" *Procedia – Social and Behavioral Sciences* 2(2):5715–19.

Mustapha, Siti Maziha, Nik Suryani Nik Abd Rahman, and Melor Md Yunus. 2010. "Factors Influencing Classroom Participation: A Case Study of Malaysian Undergraduate Students." *Procedia – Social and Behavioral Sciences* 9:1079–84.

Perry, N. E., Turner, J. C., and Meyer, D. K. 2006. Classrooms as Contexts for Motivating Learning. In P. H. Alexander & P. A. Winne (Eds.), Handbook of Educational Psychology (2nd Ed). Mahwah New Jersey: Lawrence Erlbaum.

Ritchie, Jane, Jane Lewis, Carol McNaughton Nicholls, and Rachel Ormston. 2018. *Qualitative Research Practice: A Guide for Social Science Students and Researchers*. Los Angeles: SAGE.

Samian, Yahya and Norah Md Noor. 2012. "Student's Perception on Good Lecturer Based on Lecturer Performance Assessment." *Procedia – Social and Behavioral Sciences* 56(May):783–90.

Saville, Bryan K., Troy Cox, Sean O'Brien, and Ariana Vanderveldt. 2011. "Interteaching: The Impact of Lectures on Student Performance." *Journal of Applied Behavior Analysis* 44(4):937–41.

Spencer, Joshua P. 2015. "Effect of Positive Behavioral Interventions and Supports on School Wide Discipline in a Title I Intermediate School." *The Online Journal of New Horizons in Education* 5(4):18–27.

Tandi Arrang, Judith Ratu, Arifuddin Hamra, and Baso Jabu. 2016. "The Role of a Lecturer's Performance in Facilitating Problem Solving for Students in Learning Translation." *ELT Worldwide*.

Yavuzer. 2000. *Okul Cagi Cocugu (School Age Child)*. Istanbul: Remzi.

# Author index